INVISIBLE BRIDGE

AN AFRICAN JOURNEY THROUGH CULTURES

Francis Mading Deng

Invisible Bridge

A Note from the Publisher

The publisher wishes to acknowledge and thank Dr Douglas H. Johnson for his invaluable help and support for Africa World Books and its mission of preserving and promoting African cultural and literary traditions and history. Dr Johnson and fellow historians have been instrumental in ensuring that African people remain connected to their past and their identity. Africa World Books is proud to carry on this mission.

© Francis Mading Deng, 2021

ISBN: 978-0-6489291-8-5 (paperback)
ISBN:978-0-6489698-7-7 (hardback)

All rights reserved. No part of this publication may be reproduced, stored in a retrieval system, or transmitted, in any form, or by any means, electronic, mechanical, photocopying, recording or otherwise, without the prior permission of the publishers.
This book is sold subject to the conditions that it shall not, by way of trade or otherwise, be lent, re-sold, hired out or otherwise circulated without the publisher's prior consent in any form of binding or cover other than in which it is published and without a similar condition including the condition being imposed on the subsequent purchaser.
Design and typesetting by Africa World Books.
Cover and graphic design By Dut Atem Yaak.

DEDICATION

This book is dedicated to William Twining, whom I first met as my Law Lecturer in Khartoum University in 1958, and who became a life-long friend. His guidance and pivotal support over the years helped me overcome personal and professional challenges at critical junctures in my journey through cultures. The book was his idea when I was only twenty-five years old and without his persuasion, encouragement and persistence, the project would not have seen the light of day. William made the convincing case that the book was not about me, but about my educational experience at a formative phase in the evolution of our people into the modern world. This is a pioneering saga which, with education among our people now taken for granted, is rapidly disappearing into the ashes of history. I am glad William made me record it for posterity. So, once again, in simple words, thank you William.

LIST OF CONTENTS

	Foreword	9
	Acknowlegements	11
	Introduction	13
Chapter One	BACKGROUND: A Future from the Past	15
Chapter Two	FEUD: Struggle for Power	30
Chapter Three	INHERITANCE: The Sacred Spears	39
Chapter Four	HOME: A Family of Multitudes	49
Chapter Five	SCHOOL: For Father's Love	85
Chapter Six	AWAY: While Women Cried	109
Chapter Seven	FARTHER: Among The Blue Boys	132
Chapter Eight	INTERMEDIATE: A Year of Strife	147
Chapter Nine	SECONDARY: Bridging the Gulf	167
Chapter Ten	TENSIONS: Turmoil Beneath the Calm	196
Chapter Eleven	UNIVERSITY: At the Meeting Point	234
Chapter Twelve	ABROAD: To the Lands Beyond	261
Chapter Thirteen	TRIALS: A Period of Reckoning	315
Chapter Fourteen	SALVATION: In the Land of Refuge	367
Chapter Fifteen	RETURN: Home to Tragedy	398
Chapter Sixteen	DESOLATION: Plight of a People	435
	A Note to the Reader on Dinka Personal Names	467
	About the Author	471

Foreword

It is very strange to write a foreword for a book that began over fifty years ago and even stranger to draw on an earlier draft foreword that was written nearly thirty years ago. This is how it came about. In September 1958 I took up my first ever job, as a Lecturer in Law in the University of Khartoum. I was barely 24 years old and my students told me that I was too young to teach them. Indeed, some were older than me. The only option was to treat them as friends. I was bewildered by this first experience of Sudan and suffered frequent culture shocks. Two students became my local guides: Zaki Mustafa, a Northerner who in time became Dean of Law, Attorney-General and later a partner of Ahmed Zaki Yamani of OPEC fame. The other was Francis Deng, then a promising and charming student, now the Author of this book. In addition to a very distinguished career as a public servant and as a prolific and well-known Author, Francis has remained a close friend ever since.

I left Khartoum in 1961, but we kept in touch and met in London in 1963 when he was undergoing a serious medical, political and academic crisis. We talked for a long time, during which I reminded him how I had been fascinated by his stories of his home life and education. He seemed to me not only to be a brilliant raconteur but also to have a phenomenal memory for detail and for songs. During this conversation I spontaneously blurted out: 'Francis you really ought to write your autobiography.' Both Francis and my wife protested that he was much too young to do that. They had misunderstood me. I was suggesting not a book about Francis himself, but rather about his educational experiences from his mother's

- 9 -

compound, his father's village, a tough primary school which sounded rather like a caricature of an English private preparatory school, on to secondary school in the Arab North, the University of Khartoum, travel in Western Europe, then the University of London, and at the time probably about to go to Yale Law School. I even suggested as a title: 'The Education of Francis Deng'. This book grew out of this impulsive suggestion. I meant no more than that his educational experiences had been so varied and so interesting that he had a duty to record them while they were still fresh in his mind.

In 1965 Francis and I coincided at Yale Law School in New Haven. In addition to becoming marginally involved in his doctoral work, I suggested that we should record some of his memories and songs while they were still fresh. Francis lay on a couch and I worked the tape recorder, feeding him snacks, beer or soft drinks and occasionally prompting him with questions. The tapes were later transcribed and became the initial documentary material for this book. It was fortunate that we did this, as his memories were still fresh and most of his diaries, notes and papers had been destroyed. In addition, while he was a Yale Francis and Godfrey Lienhardt (a mutual friend) edited a collection of Dinka songs which were published (in Dinka and English) by Oxford University Press.

During the next few years Francis completed his doctorate, published a revised version as a book, wrote a great deal else while holding a succession of demanding full-time jobs. However, he did not forget our project {and from time to time wrote another section. By 1983 he had an almost complete manuscript which was probably too long, but nearly ready for publication. However, by then Francis was a public figure in the Sudan and beyond and he eventually decided to withhold publication until he retired. During his 'retirement', which is, of course, a fiction, he has revised and shortened, the original manuscript, which ends sadly with the death of his father.

William Twining
Oxford, August 2020

Acknowledgements

This book has had a very long gestation period, conceived in the 1960s, nurtured and periodically revised and updated over several decades, and eventually delivered in 2020. The principal originator and driver of the project, Professor William Twining, has been duly acknowledged in the dedication. Others who have contributed to the project in a wide variety of ways are too many to mention or count. My immediate family members have always been partners in my writing ventures. I would particularly like to thank my wife, Dorothy, and my longtime friend, Verena Onken von Trott, for their support and encouragement, their wise counsel against publishing while I was still active in public service, and their concurrence that it is now time to publish. Professor Twining always drew a distinction between recording memories while they are still fresh and publishing when the timing is right.

I have decided that the timing to publish is now. I have been very much encouraged in this decision by the enthusiastic response of the respected veteran journalist and literary specialist, Atem Yaak, who continues to promote the culture of his people and country abroad, and by Peter Lual Reech Deng, the founder and publisher of Africa World Books, who has made documenting and promoting the culture and history of his people of South Sudan a professional priority. I would like to thank Douglas Johnson, the renowned scholar of South Sudanese history, for initiating my contact with Africa World Books.

It is my great pleasure to acknowledge all my brothers and sisters, the children of late Deng Majok Kuol Arob, Paramount Chief of the

Ngok Dinka of Abyei, and our parents for the love, affection, unity, and solidarity with which we were raised in a family of multitudes comprising around two hundred mothers and no less than a thousand brothers and sisters. While I am by no means advocating polygamy, I must say that our family, of which I am exceedingly proud, defies the conventional wisdom that polygynous families are doomed to be torn apart by divisions and jealousies. Although differences over succession to chieftainship pose a structural challenge that has at times severely threatened the unity of the family, the conciliatory manner in which these differences have been resolved has vindicated and reaffirmed our family cohesiveness, resilience and solidarity. In many ways, I see this book as a family legacy, which I particularly share with Dr. Zackariah Bol, exactly the same age, though we are not twins. Despite differences in details, we have been partners in most of the experiences recounted in this story. The book is also a tribute to our father and all our mothers, who, in their differing ways, were all very special.

May this legacy, in all its varied lessons, be a source of inspiration to our children and many more generations to come. May it also make some contribution, however modest, to our wider history and culture of South Sudan at a formative phase of our transition and to mutual understanding and cross-cultural exchanges as we travel in our multiple journeys through the diverse cultures of the world.

INTRODUCTION

This book is a story of a journey through cultures. It brings together a wide variety of cross-cultural situations interwoven and integrated into personal experiences. The context into which I was born, a border area between the African South and the Arab North of what was then the Republic of Sudan, now divided into Sudan and South Sudan, provided a unique background that would be the pivot of my life. While my people, the Dinka, are the largest ethnic group, not only in South Sudan, but also in the Old Sudan, my particular group, the Ngok Dinka, occupy an anomalous position as Southerners who, for historical security reasons, were administered in a Northern province. The area, being ideally suited for both agriculture and cattle herding, was, and remains, a seasonal meeting-point between the pastoral tribes of both the North and the South, who converge in search of pastures and water. The area therefore became, and remains, a racial and cultural crossroads and a microcosm of the Afro-Arab Sudan.

In a world in which races, religions and cultures meet, coexist and interact, it is important to understand what each one brings into the process of mutual influence. Since we cannot expect everything from our background to be understood, appreciated and accepted by people with whom we come in contact, this inevitably requires strategic selectivity. It then becomes a question of clarifying for ourselves and others what we consider to be of vital importance, not only to our own sense of identity and dignity, but also to our contribution to the pluralistic context. It is this which justifies the demand for recognition and respect for our identity and culturally oriented behavior from those with whom we relate across the racial and cultural divides. The process need not be consciously calculated or articulated; it is almost inherent and deeply ingrained in our upbringing, although the degree of realisation will differ from one individual to another.

To the extent that this book deals with personal cross-cultural communication, accommodation and influence, it is a story of change and continuity, and the degree to which my background, including events that occurred before I was born, have shaped my attitude and response to new situations. Whether consciously or spontaneously, inside the pluralistic context of my country or abroad, the means by which I remain connected to my background, wherever I have gone and lived, and the dynamic process through which I have related to both ends of the transition, is what I have called the Invisible Bridge.

CHAPTER ONE

BACKGROUND
A FUTURE FROM THE PAST

Chief Arol Kachuol, then an elder in his seventies, one of the people with whom I held extensive conversations about the history of our people, summarised in the following words, the cultural values of lineage continuity and the challenge of social change: "Mading," Chief Arol addressed me in my Dinka name, "the world has been lived in for a long time. It is God who changes the world by giving successive generations their turns. Our forefathers, who have now disappeared, the way their world began, and the way they lived, they managed the affairs of their world. Then God changed things: things continued to change until they reached us; and they will continue to change.

"When God comes to change your world, it will be through you and your wife. You will sleep together and bear a child. When that happens, you should know that God has passed on to your children, from your wife, the things with which you had lived your life.

"Your father, Deng Majok, if he had lived without a child until his death, his would have been the kind of life that continues only as a tale. But if he left behind a big son who can be spoken of, 'This is Mading, son of Deng,' then, even if a person had never met your father, but he hears that you are the son of Deng Majok, in the same way he had heard of your father, he will meet through you your father whom he never met.

"So, the world goes on by the will of God; God, the person who created people and who changes things. You, our children, your fame began when you were chosen to go to school and learn. Here you are, you have gone far. You have left behind the country in which your mother was married. But you were chosen by your father to go and learn the words of other peoples. And in your search for knowledge, things happened.

"For instance, is this girl, your wife, not from America? And you have brought her back to your country. If you bear a child together now, in that child will combine the words of her country and the words of your country."

"Man is one single word with God."

I was about nineteen years old when I experienced a crisis of identity that dramatised to me both the vitality and the fragility of the bonds between fathers and sons in Dinka society and, in particular, my precarious relationship with my father. That year, my father, the paramount chief of the Ngok Dinka, a man whose power was as awesome within his large polygamous family as it was to the tribe, had sent me to the chief of a neighbouring Southern Dinka tribe on a sensitive mission.

One of his junior wives had deserted him; I was to bring her back. Failing that, Father threatened to withdraw the well over a hundred herd of cattle which he had paid for her two years earlier. "Either they send me back my wife, or return my cattle," he had said. In fact, I had drafted a letter for my father to that effect. The mission was to be a follow up.

I knew that Father did not really want a divorce and that he was using the threat to ensure the return of his wife. After Father left for a meeting of chiefs in the North, I decided to undertake the assignment. I asked my half-brother Zachariah Bol, and our cousin Kooch Aguer, to join me on the mission. Our step-mother, supported by her brother, refused to return home. We took advantage of her refusal and opted for divorce, mostly because we needed money for going to school and planned to sell some of the bride wealth cattle that would be repaid on divorce. As we rode on our way back to school, after having sold the cows, we expected to meet Father on the way, returning from his tour of duty. As we approached him, we began to hear reports that he was enraged by what we had done. Since I was the one initially entrusted with the assignment, I felt personally responsible.

I had grown up with considerable doubts about Father's love for me, but that had been delicately balanced by my awareness of his appreciation of me as a promising son. In fact, he had complimented me on the letter I had drafted for him on the matter. "You can always count on my Mading," he had said. What I had done now threatened to jeopardise that delicate balance. It crossed my mind that Father might explode with a devastating insult, as he was prone to do. What if his anger drove him into saying I was not his son?

When I met my father, the reaction I had feared did not occur, but the question had intensified and remained flashing in my mind: Was I really my father's son? In a society where, after a certain age, one acquires an independent identity and status, this might seem as an exercise in futility. But in our Dinka society, where one's status and sense of integrity and dignity are intimately and permanently associated with patrilineal descent, and with the father as the focus of affiliation into the male line, it was a crisis that threatened to shatter the mirror of my life. Despite the ambivalences I felt in my relationship with my father, he had been the pivot of my identity and a model for my aspirations in life. What would my life be if I were to discover that he was in fact not my father?

Because I was back at school, several hundred miles away from home, I could not ask anyone for answers. I would have left the school and returned home if the school authorities had not refused to let me go. Of course, I did not tell them my real problem, even though the intensity of my preoccupation almost wrecked my future. When I did return home during the next vacation, I told my family in general terms that I had not been well.

As my father was away, I spoke to his brother, Uncle Biong, and to my mother. My mother talked a great deal about the importance of my concentrating on my studies. I was then in my final year of secondary school and was preparing for the certificate examination which would give meaning to my many years of schooling. With a foresightedness I still find remarkable for a woman of her traditional background who could not read or write, my mother reminded me of the thin line between success and the loss of all that time.

She also knew that it was not enough to tell a fire to stop burning; something else had to be done. Both she and my uncle concluded that an envious person had probably cast a spell upon me in order to distract me from my studies and make me fail that crucial examination. I would have to undergo the curative ritual of whirling a sacrificial chicken over my head. This would require an expert or my maternal uncle. The Dinka believe that maternal relatives possess the spiritual power to bless or curse their daughter's children, but my maternal kindred were also believed to be endowed with special curative powers.

So, my mother sent word to her only brother, Ngor, to come to administer that rite and to sprinkle me with blessed water, another healing ritual. Maternal uncles are usually close to their nephews, but Ngor and I were unusually close. Whenever I returned from school, he would visit me, and when I left, he would again visit me, and he always administered blessing rites. Hearing that I was unwell, Ngor immediately came.

I told him about my problem, also in general terms. As he and I sat discussing the matter, Ngor told me I was not to worry about anything: "You are a sacred child. You were conceived and born in answer to prayers. And when you nearly died as a child, my father cursed himself to an untimely death so that you might live. Nothing will cross your path."

Ngor then proceeded to explain what he regarded as the sanctity of my life in terms of my parents' marriage and the circumstances of my birth and survival from an early illness. Much of what he said was relevant to the questions that had obsessed me and I was keenly interested in everything he said.

BACKGROUND
A Future from the Past

My mother, Achok Mijok, had been betrothed before puberty to a nephew of Paramount Chief Kuol Arop. He had already paid a large number of cows and was expected to pay a lot more to complete the bride wealth. Then came Deng Majok, Chief Kuol Arop's son, and proposed marriage to her. Although it is customary among the Dinka for men to compete for a bride, Deng Majok's intervention was opposed as improper by relatives on both sides. Among those who opposed it was Chief Kuol Arop himself. Achok's father, Mijok Duor, and Chief Kuol were members of the Koryom (Locusts) warrior age-set. The Dinka name warrior age-sets after animals or creatures that symbolise power.

The age-set system is an institution of military regimentation which every Dinka joins on reaching the age of majority in the mid-teens. Mijok was also Kuol's close friend and one of his prominent and most trusted advisers and court members. Apart from disapproving of Deng taking the girl away from his cousin, Kuol felt that his son's marriage to Mijok's daughter might interfere with their friendship. Achok's family felt it was a matter of pride not to break an early engagement for the son of the chief. Among those opposed was Achok's brother, Ngor. Deng Majok could not be dissuaded. Being a man of strong will and determination, he seemed to have taken it as a challenge.

The situation became increasingly explosive. Rumours had it that Deng Majok was threatening to shoot his competitor. He carried a gun, and guns were then rare among the Dinka. So great was the threat of violence and death over Achok that it turned what should be a girl's pride into misery. For a whole year, she observed the customary avoidances normally associated with mourning. She took off her beads and other ornaments of beautification, and secluded herself from public life, including cattle-camping, dancing, and other social activities. It is not clear whether Achok had really been opposed to the marriage, whether she was secretly in love with Deng Majok, or even whether she started off against him, but was later won over by him.

In any case, Deng managed to persuade her that the best way to circumvent the opposition was to elope. They did. The bride was taken to the bridegroom's father's home in the hope that their demonstrated love for one another would persuade him to consent. Chief Kuol was at first enraged. He wanted the girl returned to her family. Deng was then backed by most of his relatives and Chief Kuol was implored to consent. He eventually gave in, leaving the final decision to the girl's father. Members of their joint Koryom age-set went to Mijok to carry out the dual task of explaining Kuol's position and persuading Mijok to consent to the marriage. Although displeased with Kuol's absence from the scene, Mijok consented and the marriage was concluded.

Mijok's reasons were varied. According to Uncle Ngor, the immediate one was to avoid a blood feud over his daughter. But he also wanted to establish a marriage bond between the two families, both of whom were prominent in the history of leadership in the tribe.

The origins of my paternal line and its place in the leadership of the Dinka are said to begin with Jok from whom the clan derives its name, Pajok. Jok emerged from the Byre of Creation (*Lua Cäk*) with two large "Sacred Spears," one bladed and the other rounded, symbolising his spiritual powers to bless and curse and to reconcile between people. To this day, these spears have remained the insignia of chieftainship among the Ngok Dinka. Otherwise, the power of Pajok's lineage is said to be derived from their clan spirit, *Ri* (Ring), "The Flesh," so called because divine power is believed to be inherent in them. In their descending order, the line includes: Bulabek, Dongbek, Kuoldit, Monydhang, Allor, Biong, Arop, Kuol and Deng Majok, my father. The odds of succession first appeared to be against Deng Majok as his father favoured another son, Deng Abot (also known as Deng Makuei) from another wife. Deng Abot's mother was recognised as the first wife, which favored her son for succession. But the circumstances of their mothers' marriages were somewhat ambiguous, which later made the issue of seniority contestable. Besides, Deng Majok was older in age and considered himself the best qualified for the position. My maternal grandfather could foresee that Deng Majok would win the contest.

My maternal lineage, Dhienagou, had been the chiefs of Bongo

BACKGROUND
A Future from the Past

section. As a result of a blood feud, my great-great grandfather, Maluk, had immigrated into our section, Abior, at the time of my great-grandfather, Chief Arop Biong. He had been very well received and honoured by Arop and the whole of Abior. Successive leaders of the family were reputed to be exceptionally gifted with words, renowned for wisdom, and endowed with curative spiritual powers. From that time on, they became close associates and advisers to the paramount chiefs from Pajok lineage. Mother's father, Mijok, was such adviser to grandfather, Chief Kuol Arop.

Challenged by lack of support from Kuol and realising that the marriages of Deng's younger brothers were an added burden on the young man, Mijok decided to give his daughter to Deng Majok for a nominal bride wealth, clearly antagonising his own clan by rejecting the large herd of the first contender. For the traditional reverse payment, which should be a third of the bride wealth paid from the cattle of the bride's family, Mijok paid Deng Majok far more than was justified by the bride wealth he had paid. My mother was Father's fourth wife.

When a Dinka girl marries after being betrothed before puberty, a sacrifice is made to atone to God and the ancestral spirits because the idea of marriage before puberty, even in the form of engagement, is a degree of ethical violation. This is called *agorot*. The bull that was sacrificed for my mother's *agorot* was of Mading colour pattern, white with sprinkles of brown spots on both sides. Uncle Ngor was to give me more details many years later in a tape-recorded conversation. His account moved me profoundly with the depth of thought and feeling that my grandfather had invested in my being. According to Ngor, my grandfather said to a relative by the name of Dau Malek: "I have given the girl away. Give me the bull, Mading; your bull Mading will not be bartered for a cow-calf. Give him to me to be sacrificed for the spirit, *Agorot*. Give him to me while he is still young, with horns still untouched (according to the custom of training horns to grow into shapes desired by the owner of the bull). That is what I want. That is the bull we should sacrifice for Achok."

He then called a number of elders from his clan to join him in invoking the bull and sacrificing it in the house of Deng Majok.

They went and stood their sacred spears in the ground and prayed as they invoked the bull for sacrifice. My grandfather said, "God, what I have to say is not much. We ask you to give Achok a son whom we shall name Mading after the bull we are about to sacrifice. That is all we ask of you." As Ngor put it, "They prayed and prayed and then sacrificed the bull. Then they left and said, 'It is now up to God to decide whether to accept our prayers or reject our word."

I was born at Maker, the home of my maternal grandparents, several miles from Noong, my father's first home. No one knows the precise date of my birth, but historical coincidences and my mother's recollections suggest that I was born in the autumn of 1938. Despite my grandfather's wishes that I be named Mading after the sacrificial bull, my father's family named me Arop after my father's grandfather. On hearing that, my grandfather, Mijok, was infuriated. He went to my father one early morning. He woke up my father and his half-brother, Deng Abot, and said to them: "All I wanted from the marriage was that Head of Deng Majok that drove away the cattle from my daughter's engagement and imposed his will on me. And I appealed to God for divine justice. If God has responded by giving me my Mading, how could you think of naming him Arop Biong? This Mading of mine, never ever call him by any other name." The brothers apologised to my grandfather and promised to correct the situation. Father later spoke to his family and said, "I do not want to hear the child called Arop anymore. He will be Mading."

I was still an infant when I fell critically ill with a disease which was diagnosed to be hunchback. This threatened deformation if it did not kill. For the Dinka, physical wholesomeness is so highly valued and deformity so dreadful that such a survival would seem only a little short of death. Diviners came, diagnosed and prescribed. Sheep, goats and bulls were sacrificed. Nothing was left undone which was divined and prescribed. But the disease persisted. After an all-night prayer by my grandfather and a crucial sacrifice of a sacred bull that had been donated by one of my maternal uncles and invoked by elders on both sides, including my maternal grandfather himself, the disease miraculously disappeared, leaving no deformity or trace.

BACKGROUND
A Future from the Past

As I was approaching my weaning period, mother went to her farm one day and stayed overnight. I was left under the care of step-mothers and Ajang, my mother's sister's daughter who was my *amuk meth,* "baby-keeper", and a very dear person to me. We all shared my mother's hut. That night, a lion came. Somehow, it managed to rip the door open and peep into the hut, waking us all up. I was not old enough to comprehend the danger. I was therefore not afraid. The women were wise enough not to cry for help to the men in the cattle byre some hundred yards away. They knew that lions often kill in self-defence or attack people who show fear. Inside the hut were spears which some relatives had entrusted to my mother's care. The women rattled them to indicate that they were armed and called themselves male names to fool the lion that they were men.

A slight change in their own names did the trick. Ajäng became Ajääng, Nyanajith became Ajith, and Achol, Chol. This went on for a long time with the lion wandering about in the compound and returning. In the meantime, white ants were dropping their mud-shelters onto the ground. Dinka say that ants feel the presence of a lion and fall. The door being wide open, mosquitoes were infiltrating the hut. But neither the ants nor the mosquitoes seemed to matter. Except for me, all were seated throughout the episode. I remained lying down — seemingly indifferent, but keenly observant. Eventually, a Baggara Arab man came travelling along the main road which was close to my mother's hut. He was singing loudly as nomadic Arabs usually do when travelling at night.

As he approached, we heard a heavy fall. The lion had jumped into the thick bush of trees and crops behind the hut. "*Athor mony jur*", meaning "Bull, man of the Arabs," cried the women in a broken Arabic that was partially Dinka, and indicating their proud identification with cattle. He responded. "Come, there is a lion," continued the broken Arabic.

He came in front of the hut and shouted, "Where?" as he prudently kept his distance from the thicket beyond the cleared compound. Having seen nothing, but obviously pleased with his demonstrated courage, he concluded triumphantly that it must have been a flirtatious man.

As soon as he was gone, the lion returned. The episode continued until close to dawn. Then all of a sudden, a cackle of hyenas, including their cubs, could be heard vibrating with cries as they advanced. That did it. Lions are known to fear hyenas when they are in a pack. As the hyenas neared, the lion disappeared. They took over the compound for the rest of the night.

My mother returned the following day and was told the incident. Without showing any emotion, she said: "No lion would enter my hut, and, if he did, he would not harm anyone; our family and the lions have a pact not to harm each other." Mother then proceeded to tell the story. Her grandfather, Duor, a giant of a man whose physical strength was legendary, even in his lifetime, was sleeping alone in a cattle byre which was a considerable distance from the rest of the village huts. When people came the following morning, they found his bones, flesh, and fat scattered all over. The warriors of Koryom, the age-set of his son, Mijok and Kuol Arop, traced the footprints of the lion into a nearby forest. He was found and killed. Later, the family of Duor underwent a ritual by which they agreed with the lion world not to hurt one another and that whoever tried to harm the other would die from the curse. Since then, members of the lineage have not hunted lions and the lions too are believed to have honored the pact.

It was to take me a long time before I realised the wisdom of the Dinka in reconciling with the hostile elements in their environment, a rite for achieving a sense of harmony and peace through the behaviour of man and what it generates to the animal world in terms of the instincts for reconciliation or confrontation.

I was probably weaned at the age of three years, which was then the length of time the Dinka used to breast-feed their children. A firstborn was supposed to be sent to the maternal kin for weaning to introduce him to the mother's circles since he is the first link between the respective groups. So, I was sent to my maternal relatives. They lived several miles across the river, Nyamora, which lay close to our village. They had huts amidst an enormous agricultural complex, which included their fields. But their main home with the cattle byres was on the periphery of the agricultural complex.

BACKGROUND
A Future from the Past

I found my time among my maternal relatives perhaps the happiest part of my childhood. I was in the center of everything and everyone, and I received as much love as there could be. I remember days when I would sit with my grandfather just playing or conversing, listening to his wisdom and religious intonation as he invoked his clan spirits or responded to the sounds of the totemic animals of his clan. I recall him patting his clan's totemic snake, the puff adder, anointing it with oil, placing butter in front of it to lick, and singing to it, then putting it gently into a container and taking it away from home, assuring it that it was not a rejection but protection from such accidents as cattle trampling over it. We would sit and eat together in a combination of ages which my observation among the Dinka has found to be rare. I was to learn later that my grandfather would ask both my mother and my grandmother to rest and go to sleep while he took care of me at night and sang lullabies to put me to sleep, which is most unusual for a Dinka man.

From my grandmother, Ayak, daughter of Deng Ngor, I received an intensified version of a mother's love, and, among the Dinka, a mother's love is almost unqualified. My grandmother seemed to me the most tender loving person there was. A small incident has stuck in my mind as reflecting this quality. One day, she asked her orphaned granddaughter, Ajang (whose mother had died while she was still a baby, and was raised by grandparents) to do an errand. Ajang had been working hard, and lost her temper; she responded rather angrily to her grandmother. Instantly, my grandmother, in a most apologetic and conciliatory tone, said, "Never mind my child; I am mistaken."

My life among my maternal relatives was not just with adults. With my cousins, Maper and Mareng, I took part in the children activities. I did light work with cattle, sheep and goats and sometimes accompanied older boys to herd in nearby pastures. We also went hunting, collecting fruits or digging the roots of a wild sweet potato-like plant called *aweer*. As usual with Dinka boys, these occasions away from home often involved fighting, sometimes organised, sometimes capriciously provoked, and sometimes just erupting suddenly. But as a daughter's son, and perhaps of the particular circumstances of

Mother's marriage into the paramount chief's family, I was generally respected and protected.

On several occasions, we were attacked by a boy. Twice, he forcefully took all the fruits we had gathered and dared us to fight. At first, we ignored his threats. He was older and he wore sharply barbed bracelets used for fighting. After our second experience with him, we went home and asked for similar bracelets, but were refused as too young to be so dangerously armed. The third experience persuaded our elders to arm us with the bracelets, but our enemy never turned up again. The next time I saw him was at school and it was then that we both discovered that we were cousins, his mother being my father's cousin from an adopted mother. Indeed, we were to become close friends.

My weaning did not cut me off entirely from my paternal relatives, as they occasionally visited me. My mother visited quite frequently. My father also came, but more on his official around-the-tribe tours or some specific public purpose than to visit me. But whenever he came, it was for me always a day for show and anxiety. He sat under a large tree in front of my grandfather's cattle byre. Long before he would arrive, word of his intended visit would precede him and many would come in pursuit of cases or simply to have a glimpse of him or be entertained by litigation. Amidst a large crowd, my dialogue with my father would attract attention and laughter. Questions would pour on me from various elders, and, as usual, they found amusement in my answers, but I was nearly always self-conscious.

In one way or another I was involved with a wide circle of older relatives. From all of them, I learned out of love, not reprimand or punishment. I recall one day wanting to smoke the pipe, which nearly all Dinka — men and women — did. It was obviously too early for me. Rather than prevent me, Uncle Ngor gave me a lit pipe to try. Dinka tobacco is very strong and becomes even stronger when the smoke passes through the pipe-tubes, usually blackened with tar and nicotine. A few puffs and I was dizzy. I never tried it again. Because the Dinka place so much emphasis on continuity through posterity, respect for age is one of their primary values. They also consider the ability to articulate and to persuade to be among the highest of virtues and indicators of intelligence and wisdom. My reputation is that I showed these qualities much earlier than usual. Even today, elders who knew me as a child hear me speak and claim to see similarities in the way I spoke as a child and the way I now speak.

I often found myself in the company of older people, bombarded with questions which I answered only to be followed by admiring laughter. It was as though I was an object of entertainment without embarrassment. I was never made a fool by this performance; quite the contrary, I was always exalted. Things I do not recall saying were later attributed to me. One story has it that I was asked whether I stood a chance of becoming chief, since my mother was only a fourth wife. My alleged answer was that in the world to come it would not be one's mother's seniority, but one's ability, that would determine becoming a chief, of course, much to the pleasure of my maternal relatives. And what was more; they had Father's own experience to go by.

I was with my maternal grandparents when I again fell critically ill. My grandfather, presumably still bearing in mind my earlier illness, was most concerned. One crucial night, as it was raining heavily with violent thunder and lightning, symbols which the Dinka associate with the power of God, he decided to take me outside. My grandmother, Ayak, tried to stop him, but he reacted with rage. As Uncle Ngor later recounted in a tape-recorded interview, he said to my grandmother, "Ayak, did I not marry you with the sacred cows of my clan? How dare you question my ancestral duty? Open the door and let me go out."

He carried me screaming into the rain, and, according to Uncle Ngor prayed, "God, why are you thundering like this? Is it in your heart to take Mading away from me? If you are thundering because you want to take him, then I pray that you take me instead and let him live for me. Take me this very moment as you seem so angry, raining and thundering like this; strike me down. But if you should decide not to take me now, then let me return into the hut and let your fresh water, that has fallen on him, be a blessing so that he can sleep well tonight and wake up tomorrow morning, smiling and playing for me to witness with my own eyes."

"The next morning," said Uncle Ngor, "you woke up miraculously recovered. He held you in his hands and seated you on his lap. And he smiled into your face as he saw you looking so well and smiling."

The following day, he woke up my grandmother and Uncle Ngor in the middle of the night and said to them; "Get up and sit here. Listen to my words very carefully. You witnessed what happened last night. I surrendered myself to save Mading, I will die. And after I am dead, what you hear about the chieftainship will come true. Don't you hear that Deng Majok is trying to take over the chieftainship from his father Kuol Arop? That Head of his which imposed its will on me and made him marry my daughter will make that come true. And should it happen that way, this Mading of mine will one day force his way and find a position in that leadership. Mading will not miss inheriting from the Head of Deng Majok; and he will not miss inheriting from my Head, I, Mijok Duor. From these two Heads, something will emerge in him…That was all I wanted, my dear wife, Ayak, daughter of Deng Ngor. With my Mading, I have been compensated for the loss of cows."

Uncle Ngor continued to recount what his father said to them: "This tribe is ours. Chieftainship is inherent in us. And yet, we have not found the central place in this section called Abior. Now, I have found the centre. I wanted to enter the centre."

A few years later, he announced that he was dying and wanted the rituals of death to be performed. Since he looked well people did not believe him. But he was right; death quickly fell upon him. I was then back at home and in school. As he lay dying, people urged him to have me fetched and taken to him, but he refused. "I do not want Mading to be involved in this," he said. "I have already given him my blessing."

Given the political ambitions behind my mother's marriage and my birth, it is no wonder that I was to grow up being reminded and prepared by my maternal relatives to play a role that would give me a leadership profile in the tribe. Much of the praise I was to receive from them as I grew up was in a sense intended as encouragement and a self-fulfilling prophecy of which I became increasingly aware as a challenging responsibility. In fact, although I played with children, I believe the greatest impact on me was my close association with elders, from which I learned not so much through games as through their words of wisdom. I believe I became aware at a very early age that my life had a meaning and a purpose beyond my personal interest, and that something quite profound and invaluable had been invested in me. The essence of that was leadership and the service of my people.

The Author's father, Chief Deng Majok, Paramount Chief of the Ngok Dinka, with Bishop Baroni of Khartoum.

Photograph of the Author wearing Jallabiya taken in Germany in 1962 at the age of 24.

CHAPTER TWO

FEUD
STRUGGLE FOR POWER

The struggle for power within the leading family which my maternal grandfather predicted my father would win was underway when I was still with my maternal relatives. The climax came with Father's administrative competence in preventing or stopping tribal wars which were then rampant among the Dinka. While I was with my maternal relatives, my mother visited rather frequently. On one of her visits, a tribal war broke out between Abior, our subtribe, and Bongo allied with Mannyuar, the rival subtribe, which produced the deputy paramount chief. The year was around 1942.

I did not know what led to the war. Everything I remember is hearing war drums beating and seeing people everywhere running with shields, spears, helmets and other war equipment, all heading the same way. Women's war cries and men's martial chants filled the air. Together with the women of the area, my mother followed the warriors. Dinka women do not fight but they remain close to the fighting men to boost their motivation and morale, to assist them by collecting the spears and rearming them, and by protecting the wounded.

Dinka war ethics forbid harming women and if a woman shelters an injured warrior, he must be spared any further attack. At the time, I did not know all this and my greatest fear was that my mother and my aunts might get killed. I don't remember whether my grandfather went to war, but the fact that I was not concerned about him indicates that he was away or, in accordance to Dinka war culture, was probably too old to fight. I believe Uncle Ngor, too, did not go as he was too young and still uninitiated as a warrior.

That day, late afternoon, the crowds returned. People were carried on beds (straw or leather stretchers). I did not know whether they were dead or merely wounded. Many others carried their shields and spears in a way sharply contrasting with the manner with which they had gone. According to the Dinka, victims of war should not be mourned. Grief should be internalised into a desire for vengeance and must not be exhausted by external expressions. Many a fight followed as a result of long-standing feuds. But women inevitably cry. That evening, cries came from distant homes, but, although they instinctively saddened me, I was relieved that my mother and my aunts returned safely. People talked about the dead and the wounded. Kuol Tiel, my father's maternal cousin and herdsman, was among those critically wounded. Kuol required a major operation to remove a barbed spear from his chest. The spear had missed the vital organs, but the outcome was by no means certain. Rumors had it that there was little hope for his survival. Although I felt grief because of what I heard and the sadness I saw, Kuol was too remote for me to appreciate then that a close relative was in jeopardy. But Kuol survived and only a deep scar remained on his chest which was later to remind me of those critical days when he was only a remote name to me.

As I was to learn many years later, that tribal war gave my father the opportunity to outwit both his father, Kuol Arop, and his half-brother, Deng Makuei (also known as Deng Abot). As my maternal grandfather, Mijok, had predicted, Father would win the power struggle and become the paramount chief. But the drama is a long story with deep roots in the circumstances under which the mothers of the two sons, Deng Majok and Deng Makuei, were married.

According to the story, Chief Kuol was first betrothed to Nyanaghar, Deng Majok's mother. Kuol's father, Chief Arop, paid betrothal cattle, including sacred cows, towards the bride wealth. But the girl rejected the proposed marriage and eventually eloped with another man. The cattle were returned, but one of Kuol's sacred cows remained to honour the engagement. Kuol went and married another girl, Abiong, Deng Makuei's mother. Having completed the marriage, he received his wife.

In the meantime, Nyanaghar became acutely ill with a disease which diviners diagnosed to be a curse from having refused the chief's marriage proposal. She would die unless they atoned with the chief and reinstated the marriage. With reluctance on the part of Kuol, that was painfully done. Kuol's father completed Nyanaghar's marriage and brought her home after Abiong. For all purposes, Abiong was treated as the first wife.

The tribe then performed a ritual of blessing and prayers for their conception. A bull was invoked and sacrificed. As part of the ritual, Nyanaghar was made to hold the Sacred Rounded Spear, the Dinka male symbol, while Abiong held the Bladed Spear, the female symbol. This implied that they wanted Nyanaghar to have a son for a firstborn and Abiong, a daughter. It further implied that they wanted Nyanaghar to bear the heir to the throne, but there was no attempt to reconcile this with the prior treatment of Abiong as the first wife.

All came to pass. My father was Nyanaghar's first born. Abiong had a daughter, Agorot, followed by Deng Makuei. Kuol Arop became known as Wun-Agorot, Father of Agorot, a deferential way of calling a person by the name of the firstborn of the first wife. As they grew up, Deng Makuei was treated as the son of the first wife. He was allotted the bull colour pattern, Mijok, or Majok, which was due to the senior son. Deng Majok received Marial, the colour pattern due to the second wife's son. Father's pseudonym, "Majok" had nothing to do with his allocated colour pattern, but a perversion of Majö (Majo), "The Doggish", a nickname he received as a child because he owned a dog of which he was unusually fond. The Twic and the Rek Dinka probably thought it was the Ngok dialect for Majok, the firstborn's colour pattern. So, they addressed him as Majok (Majök) and Father quickly took it to his political advantage.

Deng Majok and his mother resented their relegation to second positions when they felt more entitled to the seniority which her first betrothal and his birth as the first son accorded them. Deng Majok's mother continued to be known for tough-mindedness, frequently getting into terrifying fights with her husband and clearly developing in her son a self-assertive character. He in turn soon demonstrated self-assertiveness in promoting his own interests and those of his mother's side of the family against what he saw as the inequities of his father's treatment.

After his mother died, while they were still small children, they were very well taken care of by Deng Makuei's mother on almost equal basis with her own children. But in his relations with his father, Deng Majok became particularly militant as the representative and defender of the interests of his mother's faction. His father saw in him a reflection of his mother's personality and would insult him for that. And worse, his father would liken his conduct to his mother's character in initially rejecting him and eloping with another man. From early childhood, this offended Deng Majok deeply and developed in him a profound sense of grievance, which he nursed and concealed, occasionally exploding in intense confrontation and conflict with his father.

Supported by most loving maternal relatives, who nurtured and encouraged in him aspirations for leadership, and by a number of key individuals among his paternal kin, Deng Majok began to develop and display qualities which distinguished him from early childhood. He was particularly known for intelligence, charm, ability with words, and a striking disposition towards hospitality and generosity. Although initially hot-tempered, physically courageous, and prone to confronting anyone of whatever age to fight for his rights as he saw them, or to defend his honour, dignity and integrity against any insult, he was also said to show great respect for people and to believe in reconciling and restoring peace and harmony, once the differences had been aired out and resolved. So much did he reflect leadership qualities from an early age that people saw in him the makings of an heir to the throne, even though their father preferred his other son, Deng Makuei.

But evidence on his father's attitude is conflicting. My father himself was convinced that his father did not love him. He would later portray his part of the father-son relationships to us, his children, as one of constant attempts to please his father, but with constant rebuffs. He told us that even when a wrong was committed by another son, he would offer the customary appeasement cattle to atone with his father. All in all, he saw himself a son who did the right things, but was still slighted by his father. He had a popular saying, which my mother was later to repeat to me on a number of occasions, that a person loved by God was better off than a person loved by his father. What he meant was that if God approved of one's values and moral conduct, he would reward him in a more significant way than any favour a father might bestow on his son. He is also reported to have said that men can be classified into three categories: a son of man, a son of woman, and a son of God. It is obvious whose son he thought he was.

On the other hand, it is said that my grandfather saw a great deal of administrative and diplomatic competence in my father, which he made use of. This was especially the case in his dealings with the chiefs of other tribes, especially the Arabs, and with the Government. Whenever representatives of the central authorities came for administrative rounds, or my grandfather went on state visits outside the tribe, he always took my father with him. Some people indeed argue that despite his apparent attitude to the contrary, my grandfather loved my father even more than he did Deng Makuei. But that is a viewpoint which is hard to defend. The fact, I think, is that my grandfather was ambivalent towards my father, perhaps because he saw in him early enough that ambition which eventually threatened and usurped my grandfather's own power. That was when the negative side of his ambivalence became more pronounced.

When he was a young man and his great uncle, Bulabek Biong, lay dying, Deng Majok decided to ask him about his status on the issue of succession. Bulabek told him that the issue had been settled long before he was conceived, and that it was indeed his sacred duty to secure succession. "No evil will come your way in front of God and our ancestral spirits; you are the chief." He said that as he held my father's right hand and raised it up symbolising his installation as chief. Morally reinforced and with Achuil Bulabek, the dying man's son, as his witness and supporter, my father began to work for chieftainship. He continued to outshine his half-brother, Deng Makuei, as the obvious leader, not only through his generosity and hospitality, but also by displaying exceptional abilities to resolve disputes between the tribes that converged over the grazing areas of the Ngok Dinka.

Once they were old enough, their father appointed them both as his deputies on equal footing. Deng Majok soon distinguished himself to the tribe and to the central government authorities as the more capable of the two. But that in turn prompted Kuol Arop to gear matters in favour of Deng Makuei. When he chose to send Deng Makuei to the Intertribal Assembly of Southern and Northern Chiefs, discounting the more capable Deng Majok, not only did the tribe fear the consequences, but Deng Majok then realised fully his father's bias or prejudice in favour of Deng Makuei. The outcome of the meeting was that the Ngok "Empire" was broken up; they lost some of their Southern tribes whom the British allowed to break away and join the administration of the Southern provinces, much to the deep sorrow of the Ngok whose elders are said to have lamented the separation with tears.

When he became convinced that he was out of his father's love and his father openly advocated Deng Makuei as the first deputy, Deng Majok disaffiliated himself from their joint court and established his own court. That enraged Chief Kuol Arop, who decreed that anyone attending Deng Majok's court would suffer consequences. But given his generosity and hospitality, together with his wisdom and sense of justice, Deng Majok's court soon became popular with both the Dinka and the Arabs, far beyond the control of Kuol Arop.

Realising that Deng Majok was about to win the contest, Kuol Arop sought to expedite the formal designation of Deng Makuei as the first deputy and heir to the throne. Deng Majok in turn then decided to consolidate his own front with the Ngok Dinka, the neighbouring tribes, and the central government. He entered into a friendship pact with Babo Nimir, the paramount chief of the neighbouring Missiriya Arab tribes, who was highly regarded by the British and was most influential. Both for reasons of their friendship and because of the qualities they saw in Deng Majok, Babo and his people, the Arabs, favoured him as the obvious heir. Babo passed his opinion on to the British, who quickly agreed. But the more their attitude became apparent, the more Kuol Arop panicked, and the more he openly campaigned for Deng Makuei. It was then that Deng Majok worked diligently with Babo Nimir to overthrow the ageing chief and force him into an early retirement.

His opportunity to do so came with their contrasting parts in stopping the 1942 war between Abior and Bongo. Traditionally, a Dinka chief is a divine ruler who must not use force. He should use persuasion. He may ultimately resort to supernatural sanctions by inflicting a curse on an uncooperative or disobedient subject. Divine prerogative is particularly opposed to spilling of blood. A Dinka chief should not even see blood. He is not supposed to go to the battle-field. He is to remain at home praying for victory if the war is with an enemy, or for peace if it is a civil war between segments of his own tribe. He may draw a symbolic line on the ground, then place his sacred spears - the insignia of his office - on the line, appealing to the parties that those who would cross the line and pursue aggression in disobedience to him should suffer defeat. When the war broke out, my grandfather did just that.

In contrast, Deng Majok displayed a remarkable administrative vigour in attempting to stop the fighting, getting onto his horse and galloping to the battlefront before his father and half-brother, even though they were closer to the battle scene, gallantly riding through the battle lines, lashing the combatants with his horse-whip and, although overwhelmed by the fighting, succeeding eventually in breaking it up. All that occurred after he had monitored the situation, sensed the mounting tension in the tribe, and advised his father to do something to prevent the outbreak of hostilities. But his father did not move.

Kuol Arop was summoned to the district headquarters at Nahud in the North and told that he would have to step down for one of his sons. Which one should that be? When he unwittingly exposed himself by mentioning Deng Makuei, the British decided to detain him, while they went to question the tribe to choose between the two sons. Kuol then begged to be allowed to return to his people on the pledge that he would not in any way interfere with the free will of the people. The outcome was the overwhelming choice of Deng Majok as the paramount chief. His father was then asked to retire, retaining only his Sacred Spears, the symbols of Divine Authority. And yet, Kuol's influence throughout the tribe persisted and his retention of the Sacred Spears made him continue to be the chief in the eyes of the Dinka.

Ali Nimir, Brother of Babo Nimir and Deputy Paramount Chief of the Missiriya Arabs.

The Author's uncle Alor-Jok Kuol, by 2021, the only surviving son of grandfather, Chief Kuol Arob, estimated to be over a hundred years old.

Deng Makuei Kuol (Also known as Deng Abot) Deputy Paramount Chief of the Ngok Dinka and half brother of Deng Majok.

The Author's father with Nazir Babo, Nimir of the Missiriya.

INVISIBLE BRIDGE
An African Journey through Cultures

Sheikh Biong Mijak, Chief of Section, Abyor Chiefdom.

Ajuong Deng Tiel, Omda of Anyiel Chiefdom.

Abiem Bagat, Omda of Mannyuar Chiefdom.

Sheikh Mater Ayom, one of sectional chiefs of Alei Chiefdom, with whom Father had a very ambivalent relationship.

Serrer al-Haj Ajbar, Chief of the Missiriya al-Zurug, a close friend and ally of Father.

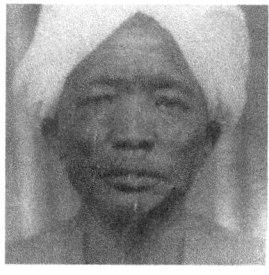

Achuil Bulabek, Omda (Chief) of Abyor Chiefdom and Father's relative, closest friend and political ally, and partner in leadership.

CHAPTER THREE

INHERITANCE
THE SACRED SPEARS

My grandfather, Kuol Arop, did not live long after he had been stripped of power. The following year, Father was decorated with the robe of honour and became a fully-fletched *Nazir Omumi* (Arabic for paramount chief). That was the year my grandfather became ill. There was to be an intertribal assembly in Tongliet village. Father attended in his capacity as the man in charge of the tribe. The Sacred Spears were still in the possession of my grandfather. According to Achuil Bulabek, Father's great cousin and closest ally in the power struggle, "When we went to Tongliet, Deng Majok said to the government that leadership and the Sacred Spears were never separated in Dinka tradition." Jipur Alor, the deputy paramount chief, was consulted by the British authorities on the matter. He supported Father's position.

The British district commissioner decided to meet with more people for further consultations. According to Achuil Bulabek, "There was Jipur and Deng Majok and Deng Abot (Makuei) and Chol Dut and Miyan Arop and myself, Achuil Bulabek. The district commissioner invited comments from those present in the meeting. I spoke and said, 'If it were my judgement, I would say that Kuol Arop should be allowed to keep his Spears until he dies, after which the Spears should then go to Deng Majok. That is the day they will cease to be Kuol's and become Deng's. But if we take the Spears from him now, it will be as if he was dead. It will even hasten his death.'"

The matter was discussed and Achuil's position was endorsed. The district commissioner said, "The case will end in accordance with the opinion of Achuil. I shall leave tomorrow morning, but the assistant district commissioner will remain. And you Achuil will come with me. You will tell Kuol Arop the decision yourself."

Achuil continued his account of the developments: "The next morning, we went into his car and left while the assembly was still in session. The chiefs had met for three days, but there was yet another day to go. We drove until we reached Abyei. When we arrived at Abyei, we found Kuol's condition had become critical. As soon as I got out of the car, I was told of the situation. That evening, Kuol's illness worsened so much that people ran to alert the tribe and gather the cattle for funeral sacrifices and performance of rites. The Deng brothers were still at the assembly in Tongliet. Some people had been sent to them, but our paths had crossed. Word had gone to them, 'Your father is critically ill!'"

On receiving the news, the district commissioner told them that they could take his car once a minor repair had been done. He himself could then be fetched the following day. Deng Makuei, who had been personally approached and informed about his father's position, would not wait for the car. Chol Piok, who was still with my father and Deng Makuei in Tongliet, narrated the developments there: "We were fetched by a horse. Kuol had been ill for some time, but he had begun to improve. And after the people had gone to Tongliet, he suddenly got worse at night. The person who was sent said, 'The chief will not survive the night.' Deng Makuei decided to run all night. But Deng Majok remained. The next morning, he bade farewell to the chiefs and said, 'I must leave. I cannot stay to the end of the Assembly. My father is dying.' Deng went by the commissioner's car and we travelled on horses. At about the time cattle were unpegged to graze, we arrived at Mitrok, the home of Kuol, where he lay dying. Deng Majok also arrived at the same time by car."

According to Achuil Bulabek, "Deng Majok jumped down from the car and entered the hut where his father lay. He approached his father and said, 'Father, are you dying?' And his father said, 'Is it you, Majo?' His voice was no longer audible. He caught Deng Majok's head and placed Deng's ear close to his mouth. What he actually said to Deng, I did not hear. And Deng has never said it to this day. As soon as Deng raised his head, his father passed away; he died."

Before he died, Kuol made known his dying will. In that, he bequeathed to them two sets of shoes symbolic of succession in Dinka tradition. He gave Deng Majok modern shoes which signified his succession to government's power, while he gave Deng Makuei traditional Dinka shoes to symbolise succession to divine traditional authority. He said to Deng Makuei, "This is your path, the path of our ancestral traditions, including the Sacred Spears, and Deng Majö's path is that of the government."

"The grave was then marked", Achuil continued. "The grave was dug and dug and dug. Then Kuol was placed into the grave. You know the Dinka way; as the dead chief is placed in the grave, the new chief must be installed at the same time. No moment is allowed to lapse without a chief. Abior had already agreed on a secret plan unknown to the other tribes. They caught Deng Makuei and installed him. They brushed Deng Majok aside that he was no longer the chief, Deng Makuei was then the chief."

My brothers and I were then in Abyei, having joined the newly established elementary school in the area. We were old enough to understand what was going on, which we followed with intense absorption and fear that violence might erupt between the contesting factions. Achuil Bulabek was a central figure in the developments, being a close relative and the sectional chief (*omda*) of Abior sub-tribe: "When Kuol died in the early morning, the tribe began to assemble. The cattle were then driven to Abyei. I myself went and brought Abior to Abyei. Mitrok was filled with people. The grave was then dug. Even as the grave was being dug, people were conspiring that Deng Makuei should be the heir to chieftainship. But whenever I joined any meeting, people became silent. And when I moved to another gathering, people became silent. That was the plot made by Abior. The whole of Abior had gathered, including women. As the body was lowered into the grave, people stampeded for Deng Makuei. They seized Deng Makuei and ritually acclaimed him the chief.

Achuil Bulabek said "Deng Majok sat at a distance with his brother Arop and myself. Then all the people left to bathe in the River (according to tradition). We bathed separately from the rest of the people. After we had bathed, we proceeded straight to Abyei. The district commissioner had arrived and had set the following day for the discussion about succession. Then I left that evening for my home at Nainai. Of course, according to custom, nobody should milk the cows or cook food or eat during the whole of that day and night. I went to my cattle camp and gave instructions that all the lactating cows should spend the night with their milk - they must not be milked.

"The following morning, I said to the people, 'You may now milk the cows and boil the ghee for offerings on the grave of the chief.' Then I left. Abior had scattered back into their homes. In the morning a group formed and came after me. They caught up with me on the way in that area near Paguot's home. They said, 'Achuil, will you not be forced to accept the way of Abior now that people have decided to bring their case to the Government?' I stopped and stood facing the people who were following behind me. I said, 'You, this entire tribe of Abior, is there anyone among you who is braver than me? They said, 'No! There is no one.' I said, 'Even with spoken words, is there anyone among you, the entire Abior, who is a better speaker than me? And is there anyone among you who is a better speaker than Deng Majok?' They conceded there was none. Then I said, 'Today, Deng will hold one flank and I shall hold the other flank and the commissioner will be in the centre of our battle.' We debated without agreeing. So, we proceeded together to Abyei."

"The senior district commissioner who had come with us had left immediately, but the assistant district commissioner who had remained at the assembly came shortly afterwards. His arrival coincided with Kuol's death. He even attended the burial and then returned to his rest house. The following day, the matter of succession was discussed. When the assembly was convened, Abior all gathered, including women. They filled the shade of the Court Tree and extended as far as the river. The whole of Abior was there."

I vividly recall this moment as the warrior age-sets of Abior boomed with their war songs, creating an atmosphere that was highly charged and explosive, even as the district commissioner conducted the discussions under the Court Tree surrounded by armed police. We were very much afraid that our father's life was in imminent danger.

Achuil Bulabek continued his account of the events: "The district commissioner asked the assembled elders, 'What do you, Abior, say? Who should be the chief?' They said, 'We are opposed to Deng Majok's succession!' He then lined the people up and asked them one by one. When he had questioned some thirty persons, he said, 'That will be enough.' The overwhelming number of Abior wanted Deng Makuei to be the chief. Then he turned to Jipur Alor and said, 'Now that Abior has obviously rejected Deng Majok, what do you say?' Jipur said, 'I am confounded!'

"Then he turned to me. I was sitting all alone; separate from Abior, who were all lined up. He said, 'You are the chief of Abior and therefore their leader. What is your opinion? I held my hands in opposite directions and said, 'You see how far apart my hands are? That is how far apart my position is from the position of Abior. And you yourself, you are like Abior. He said, 'Why do you think I am like Abior?' I said, 'When Kuol died, was he still the chief?' He said, 'No!' I said, 'And who was the chief?' He said, 'Deng Majok was.' I said, 'And did Deng Majok kill a person last night so that the Government has discovered his disqualification for chieftainship? How could this same Deng be honoured with the robe of chieftainship this year and during the same year you come to question people about the same chieftainship? And it was you, the Government, who placed him there in the first place. Is a chief not deposed because he has committed an offence? Chieftainship is contested where a chief dies, leaving the position vacant. Had Kuol died still holding his position as the chief, the matter would then be discussed and the one wanted by the people would then succeed him. But Deng Majok assumed the chieftainship while Kuol was still alive. How can you come now and question us again on the same issue?"

Achuil did not wait for the district commissioner to respond to the series of his obviously rhetorical questions. Instead, he proceeded to explain Deng Majok's qualification for chieftainship in accordance to the Dinka customary rules of succession. "But let me tell you something. You hear it said that Deng Makuei is the eldest son and therefore the rightful heir to their father's position. He is not. Deng Majok is the eldest son. When my father died, Deng Majok sought and obtained his opinion. When he obtained his opinion, my brothers Bol and Miyan were there. Only Biong who is our older brother was absent. Our father took Deng Majok's right hand and raised it up and said, 'chieftainship will not give you even a headache.' So, you better ask Bol and leave aside all these people who have been talking. They know nothing. I am more informed than these elders you were questioning. These Spears came with our original ancestor. They are always handed down to the person who assumes the chieftainship. So, ask Bol, 'Did your father say so or did he not?' My father and Kuol's father are sons of the same father. Arop, the father of Kuol, is the son of Biong and our father, Bulabek, is also the son of Biong.'

"The district commissioner turned to Achuil's brother, Bol, and asked 'Bol, did you hear what Achuil has just said?' Bol remained silent. "Bol, it is you I am asking!" He remained silent. Achuil interjected, 'Sir, he will never deny it. That is why he will not answer. If he answers you and denies it, let him swear on our Sacred Spears." The district commissioner then concluded that Abior were clearly in the wrong and called on Jipur to take punitive action against them. Jipur suggested that Abior be fined 400 cows. The district commissioner wrote that down as the final decision. "Then I got up and said, 'Sir, the cattle you are now demanding for fine will be provided by noble women, whose husbands are dead. People will call on these women and say to each one of them, 'Woman, this is the reason for your membership in this tribe. A challenge has emerged. Contribute cattle to the fine.'"

INHERITANCE
The Sacred Spears

"The district commissioner then asked, 'And what do you suggest we do?' Achuil said, 'Arrest the people responsible and leave the cattle alone. He said, 'And who are the people?' I said, 'There is my brother, Bol, the son of my mother. And there is (Mijak) Mijangdit. These are the people pulling Abior along with them. It is Bol who divides Abior and gives them courage to generate disorder.' I then added other names. People like Biong Mijak and Malwal Chol and his father; they were all arrested to be taken away to jail in the North. Deng Majok then said to me, 'Achuil, I am going to beg you for two or three people. And please do not insist. First, leave Mijangdit out; Mijak is second to our father in seniority. Now that my father is dead, even if Mijak has come to dislike me as he now dislikes me, I cannot extend my hands to touch him. Release him with his son, Biong. Perhaps you can save Biong with a payment of fine in cows. Please, son of my grandfather, release them. Of the four hundred cows mentioned earlier, two hundred will be blood-compensation and two hundred will be fine.' I almost got angry at him, but he pleaded with me. He requested Biong with his father. That was how Deng Majok came into chieftainship and remained in chieftainship."

Once Father's position as the paramount chief had been reaffirmed, the district commissioner declared that the Sacred Spears should be passed on to him. He ordered that the Spears be immediately brought and handed to Father. The elder, Chol Piok, who attended the occasion, recalled: "The commissioner ordered that the Spears be fetched immediately, 'right this moment'. When people tried to be evasive, he called for the police and said, 'If I go with the police to fetch the Spears myself, that village where they are, and even the part of Abyei close to it, will not look good afterwards. I will have it all destroyed with guns.' That was when Deng Majok's uncle, Mahdi Arop, got up and made his famous statement, 'My Roaring Leopard Bull, the country has been captured by foreign powers. Brother Deng Thokloi, son of my Father, we cannot allow the Government to fetch our Sacred Spears. Let us fetch them ourselves and hand them to the Government. We will then see what he will do with them?'

"So, they went and brought the Spears. The Sacred Skin, on which they normally rested, was also brought and laid down in front of the district commissioner and the Spears were placed on it. Then he asked, 'All of you present here, is there anyone who still wants Deng Makuei as the chief?' There was no response. So, he proceeded to call on each person in the group, one by one, and asked him whether he was for Deng Makuei. All of them, including those who had supported Deng Makuei and had been detained, denied in fear. The district commissioner then took the Sacred Spears and placed them in Deng Majok's hands. Deng Majok took them. They were now his and he carried them away to his home."

The district commissioner then had Deng Makuei arrested and banished from Abyei to the district headquarters in the distant town of Nahud. Chol Piok resumed, "Deng Makuei spent both the dry and the rainy seasons there. He spent a whole year. He was detained in the big prison. But he was kept in a separate area from the rest of the prisoners. People were not permitted to see him. Only his single wife that had been taken with him was allowed to stay with him. He was eventually permitted to return after the district commissioner sternly warned him, 'Let me hear not a single word from you about chieftainship any more. Even the position of the deputy chief that you held, you have now lost.' Deng Makuei surrendered. He was returned and seated in his house. He became an ordinary man.

"Two years passed. And when a successor to Deng Makuei as deputy paramount chief was sought, people said it should be Nyok, Deng Makuei's younger brother, who was a teacher in our newly opened elementary school in Abyei. Deng Majok refused. He said, 'Nyok already has his job as a teacher. Let him continue in that position. Let us return Deng Makuei to his position as the deputy.' The district commissioner said, 'but if we put him back into that position, will he not do the same thing he did before?' Deng Majok said, 'No, he will not. Let us at least give him a chance. If we now deny him any position, his heart will break. So, let us place him under me.' That is how Deng Makuei was placed under Deng Majok. It was Deng Majok himself who requested it. The Government was against his being reinstated. They feared that he would start another trouble. That is how it was. Nothing else was said. They never quarrelled about anything else."

INHERITANCE
The Sacred Spears

Uncle Deng Makuei was later to give me his version of the contest for power and the Sacred Spears: "Deng Majok had started the problem during Father's illness. People kept coming to my father to report: 'This is what Deng Majok is saying with Babo Nimir; and this is what Deng is saying with Rahma Nyok (the Arabic interpreter).' That was when my father said to me, 'You, Deng Makuei, as we hear it rumoured, the Sacred Spears might be taken from you by force. If they are taken by force, do not contest the chieftainship in court. If you do, you would be the son of a woman.' That much my father told me; I cannot hide it from you, son of my brother. He said, 'If you should go to court for chieftainship, you would be the son of a woman. Let the Spears go; one day, they will fall by themselves. If our chieftainship is not an ancestral heritage, but a personal achievement of Deng, son of Nyanaghar, leave them to fall on their own.'

"When our father died, we buried him and sacrificed our bulls on his grave. Then we were confronted with the district commissioner, and Jipur and Rahma. We went under the Court Tree. But Deng and I never talked; we did not confront one another in front of the public. Deng had already established his case with the district commissioner.

"When it was announced that Deng Majok was the chief, our people all dispersed, leaving them alone under the tree. So, I got up and went after the people. I said to them, 'You people, come, listen to my words. I am the one to whom you belong. I am your leader. Please, stop! Chieftainship is ours together. It is the authority of our father, the one and only Kuol Arop.' That was when one elder from Mannyuar subtribe, a man of our father's generation, responded to my word and said, 'Oh people, let me tell you, if Deng Makuei has spoken the way he has, I am sure he does not want a lengthy discussion on the issue. Deng knows more than we do. Let the matter come to rest.' That was how the tribe then settled down.

"Then the district commissioner said to me, 'Deng (Makuei), you go and bring the Spears.' That is when I said, 'I will never hold them with this hand of my father. If you want to take them by force, then do so. I will never ask you 'Why?' The district commissioner saddled his horse and rode for the Spears. That is when Mahdi Arop ran and caught up with him in the area which is now the airstrip. Mahdi said to him, 'Go back; I will fetch them myself.' So, it was Mahdi who fetched the Spears from the hut and brought them into court. Your father then got hold of the Spears. I sat there only watching. Is it not over now?

"The issue of the Spears was always discussed, even when your father was alive, but I never said any more about it; I never commented on it again. Even when your father's family sacrifices bulls for the Spears, I never attend the ceremony. I remember my father's words and try to protect myself. I keep my distance for self-protection from my father's word."

My father thus succeeded to both the chieftainship of the government and Divine Authority of the Sacred Spears with a great deal of bitterness from many members of his own clan. But being a great politician and diplomat, he lost no time in winning over most of his enemies. It was indeed strange in the eyes of many that some of those who had been vehemently opposed to him became among his closest courtiers and companions. Those who had also backed him got their rewards, though of course in subtle ways, except for Achuil Bulabek, who became clearly the most favoured. All in all, Father was acknowledged as one of the most impartial chiefs the Dinka had ever known.

Grandfather Kuol Arop was also a great leader of exceeding virtues, acknowledged by both the Ngok and Southern Dinka as one of the greatest leaders in recent history. Although the British reduced his territory under his authority by disaffiliating the Ruweng and the Twic, (one of my father's ambitions was to regain those lost tribes), Kuol's image and influence in those tribes never diminished and remains towering to this day. While he lost government's favour to his son's benefit in later years, the first European travellers and the early British administrators in touch with him have written, and I have heard those living tell me, words of great praise and admiration for my grandfather, Kuol Arop.

CHAPTER FOUR

HOME
A FAMILY OF MULTITUDES

I HAVE OVERSHOT THE STORY OF MY LIFE. THE STRUGGLE FOR POWER within our family started before my mother's marriage, although intensified while I was a child away with my maternal relatives, climaxed after I had returned home and had just entered school in Abyei. As I said earlier, while I was still with my maternal relatives, as part of his around-the-tribe tours, or perhaps for personal reasons, my father visited my grandfather's home on several occasions.

Although I doubt that seeing me figured significantly in his reasons for the visits, whenever he came, it was for me always a day for both joy and anxiety. My father was generally against his children living with their maternal relatives. He made concessions only in favour of firstborns and apparently meant that to be for brief periods. On one occasion, he asked me to go home with him. Instead of responding to him, I turned to my maternal relatives and demanded that whatever my father had come for be granted or else I would leave with him. This technique worked and the conversation shifted to what a clever boy I was. My father understood my preference. With a smile, he allowed me to stay.

I really loved being with my maternal relatives. Leaving was rather difficult. With time, however, my father's objection increased and even when he did not come in person, we received the message through my mother's frequent visits. Father became adamant that I should return home without further delay. I went.

Noong was a beautiful village, far larger than the village of my maternal relatives. Actually, it was a twin village - Noong of Deng Majok, my father, and Noong of Deng Makuei, his half-brother, before their confrontation over power. Each of the villages was on a high piece of land with a large circle of huts and cattle byres surrounded by large thorny trees and those without thorns. My father's village was larger. Between the two villages was a depression in which rain water gathered from nearby lands to form a stream that fed into a large marshy lagoon lying to the west. On the northern side, this lagoon curved and barely touched the river, Nyamora, further west. On the southern side, it fed the river with the inflowing water from the surrounding lands. In between the river and the lagoon was an enclave of higher land which remained dry, except at times of floods.

On the northern side of my father's village was a wide pool, circled with shady trees. East of the village was an extensive stretch of open grassland, dotted with trees standing singly or encircling the smaller pools that broke the monotony of the flat plain. On both the northern and the southern fringes of the panorama, there were clumps of thin thorny trees and shrubs touching on the road which passed our village.

These stretches of land looked dreadfully thirsty during the dry season, except for the few flourishing evergreens. It is then that the plains shimmered with mirages of illusory lakes, and the grass dried and disappeared leaving areas of pavement-like bareness. It is then that flies sheltered where humans resided. The early rains would bring relief and produce a carpet of beautiful virgin green grass with sprinkles of unique crawling creatures like the velvet red *alueeldeeŋ* — the "brown girl of the rain" or *nyankuet-ku-meth*, literally, "the girl with whom we are breeding the child." It is then that birds of all shapes and shades and butterflies of all designs decorated the skies and the grounds.

HOME
A Family of Multitudes

Being surrounded by so many water spots, the sounds of frogs, crickets and birds stood out in the silence of tribal nights and formed lullabies for sleep as well as the morning sounds for waking up.

The early showers of the rainy season would attract us children to run out jumping and chanting excitedly:

Oh yes, our rain is falling,
We shall eat froglets tonight.

And this is despite the fact that we, like all Dinka, did not eat frogs and would have been disgusted at the thought that frogs' legs were a delicacy in some parts of the world and that I would partake of that delicacy in Oxford, England, many years later out of adventurous curiosity. Back in our village at Noong, our rivers and water spots would soon be bubbling with tadpoles and minnows, rapidly growing into frogs and fish, all of which symbolised the new life, which the rainy season promised. That seasonal change would make a big difference between the want of the diminishing crops of last year and the plenty of new crops about to be cultivated. These included sorghum, maize, beans, sesame, groundnuts, pumpkins, okra and tobacco. Nature itself provided fruits, vegetables and other edibles. It was a land of plenty.

Cultivation season would begin with planting, followed by weeding and eventually by harvest, each accompanied with jubilant singing, even as it involved hard labour. Adults would not partake of the new crop until lavish festivities had been made in thanksgiving and offering to God, the deities, and the ancestors. This was a cultural version of what I would witness socially many years later in the American Thanksgiving festivities, said to have originated from the Native Americans. At home, we, the children, would be exempt from the torture of a long wait for Thanksgiving and were permitted to start chewing dura cane and roasting maize as soon as they were sufficiently ripe. Although I have since seen sugar cane and maize available in plenty in various parts of the world, neither of them has ever tasted as delicious to me as they did in my childhood at Noong.

All in all, despite the heat, the flies, the mosquitoes, the wild animals, the snakes, the scorpions, and all other dangerous creatures, Noong was to us the most beautiful place on earth. And indeed, Noong appeared to be the centre of this world, a meeting point of many welcomed guests. Uncle Arop, Father's younger brother, was to express these sentiments in a song:

> *In our clan, we do not cheapen our words*
> *We hold the place we have held*
> *Since man emerged from the Byre of Creation;*
> *Our Noong booms like a marketplace*
> *Anticipated with confidence by travellers.*
> *God has created all kinds of men,*
> *Some he has created to attract guests.*
> *My brother, Deng, the Crested Crane,*
> *Once said: What is given goes around,*
> *And what is eaten is wasted.*

Noong was more than a meeting place; it was a village belonging to a family of multitudes. Let me tell a secret which I was to learn much later. When my father was in his youth, he had relations with a girl who, with the Dinka flexible use of kinship terms, was a daughter of his maternal uncle. I do not know the precise degree of the blood ties, but they surely fell within the prohibited degrees. Among the Dinka, these are very wide and the prohibition is very strict.

My father's wrong was dreadful, but the curse he received was wonderful in his own judgement. The curse was, "Deng, son of my sister, no disease will come your way. Your only disease will be women. It is they who will cause your death." In other words, my father was cursed to love women and to die in their pursuit. He loved them, and, although he died of liver cancer, the Dinka claim that love for women contributed to his death.

As soon as he started marrying, one marriage followed another. Nyanboldit, the Senior Nyanbol, was the first, followed shortly afterwards by Nyanbol Amuor. Almost at the same time, he was involved with Kuei. My mother followed at a time when he was already engaged to Aker Tiel from a prominent Twic family. Nyanbol Deng came next. Then he took Nyanawai from an engagement to another man.

The next, Amel, deserves a special mention because she introduced a modern Sudanese way of life into the family. Her family had migrated into a Northern town, where she was born and raised. She spoke Dinka and was also fluent in Arabic. In addition to her Dinka name, she had an Arab name, Hamdi, although I never knew whether she had converted to Islam. Amel was too short for a Dinka, rather stout, and almost Arab-looking in her brown colour of skin and mannerism. In her form of dress, cooking and housekeeping, she was a "sophisticated" Arabised woman.

Knowing that much influence depended on meeting both Arab and Dinka standards and being himself a model for selective change, Father saw a great deal of merit in Amel. Although she never bore a child, he made her a right-hand woman, furnished her with all necessary modern household equipment: china, cutlery, aluminum cooking pots and utensils, pewter and glassware, silver or aluminum trays and other newly introduced objects, all of which were considered luxury items at that time and in that context.

Above all, Father made Amel an educator for the rest of his family. Within a short time, Amel influenced the family in a way that turned many more into modern homemakers and educators of new ones yet to come. It was generally felt, and Father often acknowledged, that Amel had much to do with his becoming paramount chief. In most ways, Father's younger wives and, to a lesser extent, the older ones, became members of a self-sustaining system in which every newcomer quickly learned the techniques which ultimately went back to Amel: cooking, manner of dress, which included frocks and sari-type *toub* and veil, braiding of the hair and Arab harem-like pattern of behaviour.

The line of newcomers never stopped until my father's death well into his late seventies. When I returned home from weaning around 1942, my father had about fifteen wives. When he died in 1969, he had been married to not less than two hundred wives from nearly all corners of Ngok Dinka land and the neighbouring Malwal, Rek, Ruweng, and Twic Dinka tribes. The Dinka consider it necessary for a chief to have many wives. It is in part a political strategy. My grandfather had between twenty and thirty wives. My father obviously broke the record. The main criticism against him as a leader came from his excessive marriages, and most of the problems he had, private and public, were in one way or another connected with marriages. Many people, from whom he took girls they had intended to marry and to whom they were sometimes already engaged, complained to higher authorities. Political opponents alleged corruption behind his ability to afford so many marriages. His wives, at least the younger ones, wore relatively expensive clothes. And his family was relatively well fed with food for which ingredients had to be bought. There were clearly arguments for whoever wanted to stain my father's name on account of his marriages.

Very costly as these marriages were, polygamy is also an investment of more material value than political support. A man shares in the bride wealth of the female relatives of his wife and in the case of a chief, the circle is wide and the share is gladly and promptly given. Marriages also produce daughters who in turn bring wealth through marriages and the daughters of chiefs are the most expensive. They may not always be the most beautiful, but there is much of that too, since their mothers are carefully selected for reasons which include beauty. Furthermore, the chief does not pay for his marriages alone, for the collection of bride wealth is usually made by a wide circle of relatives and friends. In the case of chiefs, this circle is particularly wide. It is true that many ceased to help as marriages continue, but it is also true that many new sources gladly emerge. So, from the point of view of the Dinka economy, my father's marriages were also lucrative. Father had the greatest number of cattle in the tribe; cattle accrued almost daily.

My father's main fault was that he combined exaggerated polygamy with the abandonment of much of the traditional way of managing a polygynous family from the economic point of view. Traditionally, each woman in a polygynous household had a plot of land to cultivate with the help of the husband or hired labour, and cattle from which they obtained milk and other dairy products. Beyond the initial bride wealth, polygamy did not require much expense. My father, however,

HOME
A Family of Multitudes

deviated from the norm. Only our mothers, the senior wives, cultivated. Otherwise, the younger wives had little or no economic activities, but had many modern needs which implied heavy expenditure. Only much later in his life, when he drifted back into certain aspects of tradition, did he permit younger wives to grow crops with the help of prisoners or hired labour.

The family was divided into three main groups called "Houses" headed by the top three wives: Nyanbol Arop (Nyanboldit), Nyanbol Amuor and Kuëi (Kuën Deng). Aker Tiel assisted Nyanboldit, while my mother assisted Nyanbol Amuor. For reasons of some differences between her and Father, Kuei was without junior wives until Amou was married and made her deputy. That was the time when my father decided to have a branch of the family at Abyei to which he transferred most of his junior wives and appointed the three middle wives, Amel, Nyanawai, and Amou, to represent the seniors in the leadership of the groups. Amel represented Nyanboldit, Nyanawai represented Nyanbol Amuor and Amou represented Kuei.

Among the Dinka, men and women are deferentially referred to by the names of their firstborns, male or female. So, Father was Wun-Adau after Nyanboldit's daughter, Adau, which is why she was also known as Man-Adau. Nyanbol Amuor was Man-Abul after her daughter Abul. Kuei was Man-Arop. My mother was Man-Mading. And Aker Tiel was Man-Bulabek.

The structure and stratification of the family was relative to time and place. Initially, wives like my mother were junior at Noong in relation to the Big Three. But later, with more marriages, and with other villages established, they became among the most senior. Amel, Nyanawai, and Amou became the Head Wives of the three family groupings at Abyei. As another village was established at Nainai, more junior wives were appointed to head the groups there. In due course, even those junior wives became senior in relation to other more junior wives in the even newer villages that Father was to establish. The segmentation process and the relativity of seniority continued with the expansion of the family size and settlements.

Father exercised much of his control over the family through the leading wives. Many conflicts between the wives were investigated and settled by them. These might be extensions of children's quarrels, disagreements over domestic assignments, or minor arguments fanned by deeper sentiments of rivalry and jealousy over the husband and his distribution of family resources. Senior wives wielded considerable authority and commanded great respect. Junior wives addressed them as "Mothers", but gave them greater rituals of respect than Dinka children show their biological mothers.

In certain matters, each wife could go directly to Father, but in most cases, their demands were channeled through their leaders, who also represented Father to them. There was a cardinal rule against jealousy and stringent measures were taken to suppress it, ranging from severe reprimand and physical punishment to Father's abstention from the wife's food and bed.

But loathed as jealousy was among the Dinka, and particularly in our family, it is recognised as an inevitable aspect of polygamy. Success in repressing jealousies is only a matter of degree. In view of the size of our family, this degree was impressively low, but jealousies nonetheless persisted, especially among the leaders of the houses.

It was perhaps the inflated size of everything which first overwhelmed me on my return home. Even the number of wives which was then still small, was out of proportion to anything I had expected. To my Dinka eyes, the village seemed almost as large as quarters in a town, as I later got to know towns. The Dinka generally have dispersed settlements with each individual, his wife, and children occupying their own separate territory around which they rear cattle and cultivate fields. Even in polygynous families, the husband usually keeps his wives well apart. My father's case was quite exceptional, although, in this respect, he was not very different from his own father, Kuol Arop, or his half-brother, Deng Makuei.

My close companions were Bol, the third child and second son of Nyanboldit, and Kuol, the third child and first son of Nyanbol Amuor. There were two older brothers, Chan, the second child and first son of Nyanboldit, and Arop, the first child of Kuei. Arop was in fact the oldest of father's surviving children. This was due to the deaths of the first born of the first two wives and the fact that Arop's mother became pregnant before marriage. For some reason, maybe age difference, my early memories do not bring Chan and Arop into focus. As for Bol and Kuol, we were about the same age. Bol and I were born the same month, and although we eventually ascertained that he was older, for a long time, neither our father nor our mothers could tell us exactly which one of us came first. Kuol was a little younger than us, but that made no difference.

We were known by nicknames which were in fact praise names metaphorically derived from the bull colours supposedly assigned to people on the basis of their seniority in the family, in turn determined by mother's place in the hierarchy or from other social matters, such as associating the name with a senior relative. My praise names included Ngarbeek (from Mangar pattern of white with black spots), Keryou (from the maker pattern of white with black stripes), Athecekou (white plashed on the back with black), Dingweng (white with brown spots), and Mior. Bol's names were Aturjok (dispaying the horse, from the bull name of prominent Twic chief also called Bol), Wun-Awel (from the name of senior relative known as the Father of Awel from his firstborn), and Jong-Aliik (the name of an age-set that must have done something connected with Bol's birth). Kuol was known as Marial (from the colour pattern of white with shades of black), Dor-Jok (the praise name of our grandfather from whom he got the name) and Awet (the crested crane whose colour is Marial).

Bol and Kuol were quite privileged by their mothers' seniority, especially in the number of cattle they owned. As a son of a relatively junior wife, I was in a less privileged position, a sharp contrast to what I had been used to among my maternal relatives. That was my major disappointment. There was no comparison between their cattle and mine. Their mothers owned the sacred cows that had been dedicated to clan spirits. Furthermore, Bol's mother had twins of whom Chan was a survivor and whom Bol, as his name showed, followed.

Twins are accorded a special position in Dinka spiritual values, and cows are consecrated and kept for them. The sacred cows of clan spirits and twins cannot be disposed of, even in marriages. This was a great advantage as our father was marrying all the time, and although cattle came with ease, they left with equal ease. I kept receiving and losing cows while Bol's and Kuol's herds remained more or less constant. The two cattle byres were known by the names of the top two wives and therefore more associated with their sons. Kuei's cattle byre was built later when my father decided to allocate some junior wives to her.

As part of the solidarity of the larger family, Uncle Arop asked for me to help take care of his livestock, as his first son, Deng, was still too young. I went to Uncle Arop's house. This suited me because my mother had an agricultural field near Uncle Arop's compound and she often went there anyway.

My memories of this period are mixed, both good and bad. Uncle Arop and his wives treated me well. His son, Deng, and I engaged in many outdoor activities collecting wild fruits, digging for the sweet potato plant called *awer*, trapping guinea fowls and hunting small game, but not infrequently, fighting. Although Deng Arop was too young to be my match, I felt a sense of being the outsider. I don't know how long I stayed there, but I began to miss home and was delighted to be back at Noong.

Home was now a place of my own choosing and I took little time to integrate into the family. One obvious way was to live up to the values of family solidarity and loyalty to my father. This was not really a change since those values had been inculcated in me among my maternal relations. It was now evident to me that I enjoyed among my paternal relatives general appreciation similar to that I had enjoyed among my maternal relatives.

I was particularly fond of attending Father's court under the tree, some distance outside the main compound, and interacting with the court members and other attendants. Although Father was not explicit about his attitude, it was obvious that he took pride in my performance and in the lavish praise I received. People in my father's court would send me to fetch fire for lighting pipes, water to drink, or on any one of many errands. My father's court always sat some distance away from the women's quarters where these things were: I would run. Even my father came to rely on me heavily as a messenger between his court and home. There came a time when my mother was so concerned about the danger of my being bewitched that she told me to stop my displays at court.

HOME
A Family of Multitudes

But I had already reached the point where I felt that, according to Dinka values, a mother's advice was not to be taken seriously to avoid being perceived as *mɛnh e tik* "son of a woman" in the man's world of the Dinka. My mother knew that on the whole my formula was correct. She loved me and believed in me so much that she was not going to let mother's control block my way. At the same time, she knew that I loved her so much that whatever I did externally against her was not a qualification to my love, but an assertion of how best I thought our common goal could be achieved. I think this was the most important understanding between my mother and me.

There was something quite unique about my mother which is impossible to describe. Although she was over six feet tall, in the context of the Dinka, she did not strike me as particularly tall; I saw her as average. By Dinka standards of colour, she was also average, more on the darker side, but less so than some. She was slender, but not lean. Her facial features were sharp and expressive, with high cheek-bones and a smallish nose. Contrasting with her strikingly black gums, she had distinctively white teeth. In accordance with Dinka custom, her lower six-canines and incisors- front teeth were removed not long after losing her milk teeth as was the custom in those days. A gap separated her upper front teeth in the center, giving her what the Dinka call *weer*, their idea of a perfect set.

Like all Dinka women, including the first generation of Father's wives, my mother wore leather skirts around her waist, hanging down well below her knees, and sometimes almost touching the ground. The skirts were made of goat or sheep hides, treated in various ways, and oiled to be soft and dark in colour, trimmed with shells or beads along the edges. Sometimes, she wrapped a sheet of cloth around her waist in place of the leather skirt. While she was informally at home, she went without covering the rest of her body, but in front of strangers or when travelling, she hung a sheet of cloth across her shoulders, covering her body down to the legs.

Initially, she left her head in the traditional Dinka way, either shaven bare or with the hair treated in various styles. But very early in my childhood, my mother adopted the Northern style of braiding the hair and allowing it to grow as long as possible, which at most brought it hanging just below her head, touching the shoulders. Within these modest limits, my mother was very meticulous about her appearance, and was always well groomed. The mere sight of her gave me a great sense of pride, joy and security. But as I got to know my mother, it was not the physical aspect that I grew to admire so much as her character, wisdom, discretion, courtesy, generosity and charm. She had great success with people: intelligent, prudent and well spoken, she won admiration from all circles. Her persuasiveness also made her a peace-maker in the family. I grew up hearing a great deal of praise for her, not only among elders, but also from my brothers and sisters, relatives and other associates of my generation.

Perhaps the most beautiful words I ever heard about my mother came from my father much later in my life. And they were the most beautiful because they came from him. I was then in the university. The two of us sat in a man-to-man candid discussion of our father-son relationship that I had initiated. When I think back now, I am amazed that I was so daring. To reassure me of his approval of me, my father surprised me by bringing my mother into the picture. He said that among the Dinka, a father's attitude towards his child is in significant part related to his view of the child's mother. He spoke in lavish praise of my mother and concluded with the words, "She is like a first wife to me. When I am away and Achok is present at home with Nyanboldit, I do not worry: I trust that she will keep things under control. Even if Nyanboldit is away and Achok is present, I feel I have a first wife present." This was most unlike my father, for he was not one to be so lavish in his praise.

As for me, I could never praise my mother sufficiently. Whenever I was away at school, especially after reaching adulthood, I would feel regretful that I never revealed my feelings for, and to, her. I feared she might have doubts. Some of my European female friends who got to know of her through me would urge me to let my mother know how much I loved her. But it was not the Dinka way to express such feelings, except perhaps in songs. Besides, I was sure that she knew exactly how much I loved her and I knew how much she loved me. We did not need to say it in words. Even when we disagreed, our mutual love was never in doubt.

HOME
A Family of Multitudes

One area in which my mother and I differed concerned our small share of cattle compared with my giant labour in cattle husbandry. By and large, cattle care was performed according to Houses. Although Kuol and I worked together, I did most of the work, being a little older. And there was a great deal to be done. We would see to it that we took the animals out of the cattle byre in the morning and cleaned the byre. We would spread the cow dung to dry into fuel from which we made fires to smoke away the flies and mosquitos. We would take part in joint-herding of sheep, goats and calves. Herding the cows was for older boys and men. We would go thirsty and hungry away from home for most of the day. In the late afternoon, when the herds returned, we would tether the goats, the sheep and the calves — sometimes the cows too, although that was for older people. Only then would we have time to rest. If it was during the rainy season, we would help take the cattle into the byre after some hours in the open courtyard, where we tethered them for the evening. At first, we continued to sleep in our mothers' huts, but later we slept in the cattle byre with the herds.

Bol had more responsibility since his group had more cattle. I would also help him. I often found myself doing work which was not strictly within my domain. To my mother, I was doing too much. And for what - just a few cows which my father would sooner or later give away in marriage? I recall her warning me, "If you are not careful, you may end up being the slave of Deng Majok's family." I would reproach my mother with the argument that they were all my father's cattle and therefore ours together. I would never succumb to any advice that seemed divisive, especially from my mother.

Whatever polygynous "jealousy" meant; I was determined not to reflect it. I also hoped it would not be shown to me. Generally, it was not. My father's wives took me as their own son and I felt worthy of their approval. Dinka culture teaches one to conceal love and affection for one's own mother, but demonstrate them to step-mothers as a means of reinforcing family unity and solidarity. Although one calls one's mother by her name, one must address one's father's wife as "Tiŋwäär", a polite "Wife of my father."

I showed my father's wives great respect and did for them services which I did not do for my own mother. Because of my dedication to the family and its solidarity, there was not much they could hold against me. My mother, who complained about my excessive labour for the family, was the very one who conditioned me this way. If there was something, I could do for her, but for which a step-mother also needed my help, she would urge me to do it for the step-mother. When I was old enough to help in cultivation, she would ask me to assist in the fields of step-mothers instead of hers. She told me to give the first money I ever earned to my father and be content with whatever he would then give me back. She taught me to offer gifts to my step-mothers before I could think of her. It was typical of my mother to say, "Forget about me." She always denied herself where she thought it would promote my interest.

My mother also criticised me for respecting my father to the point of being timid. She thought that I did not complain sufficiently for the meagreness of our cattle wealth and the freedom with which my father disposed of our cows into his marriages. She once criticised me by way of comparison: "If my father, Mijok, ever treated me that way, he would certainly know how I felt about it." The point was effectively communicated and I was touched. Dinka culture encourages a child, especially a son, to assert his rights, even at the risk of getting into conflict with his father. Indeed, sons are admired for their courage to face their fathers on their rights, or whenever they see them in the wrong. And here was my mother, a woman, claiming that she would have done more in a similar situation.

I pondered over Mother's point, but dismissed it with the justification that she must have been exceptionally close to her father. I was not. Besides, my father was a chief and his relations with his children obviously differed from those of other men with their children. The more I thought about my mother's point, the more I convinced myself that my situation was different and my approach quite appropriate.

I was simply scared of my father. He had one of the tongues capable of discharging the most piercing words I had ever heard and this was common knowledge at home and in the tribe. He would not hesitate to insult anyone in front of the crowds that constantly surrounded him. And whatever he said amused those crowds. Although some might be sympathetic to a victim of his insults, there were bound to be *adol beny thok*, "laughers-at-the-mouth-of-the-chief" in his assembly. His insults were bad enough without the ridicule they aroused.

As a chief, my father had to be a man of peace, resorting only to the sanctions of state power. As a family leader, he used the horrific punishment of beating his wives. Although beating wives among the Dinka was not common, it was also acknowledged to exist, but Father was conspicuously excessive. The wife with whom he fought almost regularly was Nyanbol Deng, the third in seniority in the House of Nyanboldit, the First Wife. Nyanbol Deng was a tough-minded woman who would not succumb easily to Father's dictates. At a time when wives would generally submit to Father's will, she would fight back verbally and thereby provoke Father even more. Nyanbol Deng had only two children, a son, Miyar and a daughter, Nyangei, both of whom acquired their mother's tough-mindedness, which also alienated them from Father.

Father's style of punishing women was unique in the procedure he followed, which was akin to judicial. Apart from a few sudden outbreaks, my father followed a prescribed procedure in beating his wives. He would convene a one-man court to try a wife or a number of wives, who had allegedly committed a wrong. He would sentence anyone found guilty to a number of lashes, which he himself executed with a whip. For beating children, he did not use a whip, but his bare hands, canes or thin fresh twigs of trees. These are the normal ways Dinka children are beaten as a disciplinary measure. I don't distinctly remember being beaten by him and my mother was later to assure me that I never gave my father cause to beat me. Bol also did not recall ever being beaten by Father.

Another sanction my father used against his wives, and one which though rare occurs among the Dinka, and, for some reason, had a higher profile in our family, was abstention from a wife's food, whether brought from her relatives, acquired by her own efforts, or prepared by her from what he himself provided. This implied avoidance of conjugal relations and therefore deprived a wife of the fundamental objective of a Dinka marriage — children. The Dinka consider it the severest punishment against a woman; it therefore calls for speedy settlement. The procedure of the settlement is usually for the woman to inform her relatives. As the man is generally assumed to be in the right, her relatives apologise to him, offer him a cow or more, according to the gravity of the conflict, as a token of appeasement. Assuming he is reconciled, a ritual is performed during a feast to end the abstention.

My father's most important power of control was the force of his personality, which was reinforced by his physical appearance. He was about six feet three inches tall, slim but not unduly thin. Like an Arab sultan, he wore long robes and a turban. Only once did I see him in western clothes: a dark suit, a shirt, a tie, and a hat. His face was rather long and his features were sharp. On his upper lip was a scar said to be the result of a fight with a lion in defence of his younger brother, Arop. Rather than disfigure his face, it added character to it, almost looking like nature's final touch. The face itself was stern and determined, but by no means cruel. His intelligence glowed and the power of his eyes penetrated. He was very particular about his appearance, and it was total in its impact. I have still to meet a man who left no question whatsoever about his superiority, even among his administrative superiors, as my father did.

My father's wives feared and respected him. He was not just a husband; he was the paramount chief and they referred to him as *Bëny* - Chief. Occasionally, the senior wives called him by his name. Junior wives would run into hiding whenever he was heard to approach. They would never eat in his presence. When they talked to him, they always covered their faces or looked away. They never looked straight into his face.

My feelings and thoughts about my father consolidated themselves with time and they continued to be obsessive to me until his death. The more I knew him, the more I feared him, admired him and adored him. I felt insecure about how much he loved me and that itself imposed a confusing qualification on my love for him. Whether I loved him more than I feared him or feared him more than I loved him is something I still ponder. He seemed to me so far beyond any human being that he was hardly human to be judged by normal standards.

What made me accept the formality between us was my early realisation that love and affection for the father in Dinka society were largely objective. One loved one's father if one lived up to the ideals of the family. By meeting that challenge, one could count on the objective love of a wide circle of relatives and associates. I was confident that, excepting doubts about my father, I was loved by a wide circle of my father's relatives and admired by the many strangers I encountered at home.

Although I had doubts about the mutuality of feeling between my father and me, I observed him keenly and took him as the model of what I should be in the future. At night and even during the day, I would be awake with closed eyes and fantasise. I would fancy myself in my father's place as the chief, a man of great wisdom, power and importance. I think it was in part my wanting to be like my father that I enjoyed my reputation for showing hospitality. Noong was a most hospitable place and my father was unmatched in his hospitality and generosity, a factor which all agreed had influenced his succession to chieftainship. Although I was not conscious of it at the time, I must have been trying to live up to Father's values in this respect.

I always came across individuals in my father's court for whom I played host. Whether they were distant relatives or people I knew or who knew me, I would come to my mother insisting that she should provide food. When my father sent me to ask the women to prepare food for particular guests, I might accept a negative response from anyone, but never from my mother. When my father was away, I felt obligated to take his place as the host and would sometimes slaughter a lamb or a goat for guests despite my meagre resources.

One season, we had a constant chain of Southern Dinka who had been expelled from the North by the Arabs, following a tribal fight between their respective tribes. My father was away from Noong. A group came with an old man who was suffering from an ailment in addition to the strains of the long journey on foot; they stopped in our village for some days, during which they were my guests, until the old man recovered. When it was time for them to leave, the old man blessed me and prayed to God to ensure my succession to my father, taking my hospitality as the major qualification. I recall him saying, "Son, I do not know the seniority of your mother, but from the way I have watched you do things, God will make you the chief."

I was not conscious of the fact that there were other boys with whom to share hospitality and whose mothers were senior to my mother. My mother sometimes complained about my exaggeration of hospitality, arguing that I was far too extravagant when there were others to share the responsibility. But she never let me down. It is considered a mark of distinction for a woman always to have some food to serve even during the leanest of seasons. My mother always had something hidden somewhere; she would also succumb to my pressure and bring it out.

She came to expect that I expected to be given when I asked. She also came to accept that I took it as a matter of a man's dignity not to succumb to his mother. Her hesitation to obey might make me raise my voice with determination. Sometimes, I persuaded her with affectionate words. She always gave in eventually, even though she might quietly complain to me later. But even when my mother complained about my exaggerations, she herself showed the kind of hospitality I expected from her. When neither my father nor I was around and people passed by, I would never feel that I should have been present if she were there. And indeed, I always got raving reports on how she had treated visitors.

Although my mother remained in close partnership with Nyanbol Amuor, she was virtually established as a senior wife from the early days of my childhood. This was partly why I considered myself an equal to Bol and Kuol and resented my subordination to them, but the seniority of their mothers also made me rationalise and tolerate our differences.

The three of us became very close. In a way, I had a special bond with each of them. I was in Kuol's mother's group and in that sense, closer to him. At the same time, Bol and I were particularly close, perhaps because we were more of the same age, Kuol being a little younger, and later because we continued to be together throughout our education up the ladder.

One way to show our solidarity as children was to eat together, sharing whatever one's mother gave her son. We also herded together, played together and fought together in defence of one another. Depending on the nature of the game, we were joined by our sisters and brothers, and we played as one big family in which factionalism was repressed and suppressed.

I have no way of knowing whether the games we played were similar to the games all Dinka children played. On the whole, I believe they were. One game which could not have been so elaborate among ordinary Dinka children was that of acting the roles of our father and other prominent personalities in the Ngok political and judicial hierarchy. Such notables as Deng Makuei, (our uncle and deputy paramount chief), Achuil Bulabek, (our great uncle and the chief of our subtribe), Chan Dau (a sub-chief), Malai Kat (a sectional chief) and Matet Ayom, a notable court member, were prominent in our games. But these are only a few of the many notables who frequented our father's court. In their long robes and turbans, riding their beautiful Arabian horses, masters of their land, they provided symbols of pride and dignity to their posterity, a picture we would see sadly diminished in later life.

Apart from games, another form of entertainment was telling stories which were told after we had gone to bed and lay down ready to fall asleep. These are known as *köör,* lion stories, because interaction with the lion-world was the central theme. The first person who would volunteer or be requested to tell a story would usually insist on knowing who would tell a story after her or him. With Ajang, half-sisters, and Father's junior wives, there was always a good supply of storytellers. One after another would tell stories and as the storytelling progressed, people would begin to fall asleep one by one.

The storyteller would start to ask from time to time, "Are you awake?" As long as there were people still awake, storytelling continued. These stories largely dealt with themes of Dinka values and social relationships. Some of them seemed to reflect the kind of problems our family was so determined to repress or suppress.

Lions would turn humans and humans transform into lions, the determining factor being the degree of violation of the basic norms of the Dinka moral code. One story told of a son who killed his mother when she went wild, becoming a lioness, wanting to eat his half-brother and injuring him in the process. Co-wife jealousies were a major preoccupation for us, an evil to be suppressed or punished, and so was it in the stories; and so was the need for the solidarity of the polygynous family and the clan.

Stories were not the only bedtime entertainment I enjoyed at Noong. It used to move me greatly to hear a woman try to put her crying baby to sleep by singing at the peak of her voice in the middle of the night, rattling a gourd known as *lëi,* containing grain or beans in accompaniment. The baby would be crying frantically as though the singing was an aggravation. No one would ever complain about being kept awake by this singing. As for me, I simply loved it.

I was, and continue to be, interested in Dinka songs, especially those composed or sung by women. There was always something unique about those night concerts: the singing, the rattling, the screaming, the entire combination. The child would eventually collapse with exhaustion; the mother would carry on either to ensure a deep sleep for the child, to complete a song, or simply because she would be carried away by her own voice or by the song. I would lie there wishing that she would not stop, almost as if the song were for me and I resisted the objective of my being put to sleep.

There was always some plaintive and rather sad quality in women's songs and in their voices, especially in the stillness of the night, that I found spellbinding. It was as though I felt a deep bond with them and shared the discreet grievances they nursed against the inequities of the system, for which their songs were in some way or other lamentations from the depths of their souls. I recall a woman at Noong forcefully separated from the man she loved and with whom she had eloped, imprisoned for eloping, bound legs and hands, beaten and tortured into marrying a man she did not love and might have hated. When all strength and hope had left her, she surrendered amidst the screams and shrieks of agony: "I have accepted him; take me to him this very night."

HOME
A Family of Multitudes

Like all Dinka children, we liked going to the cattle camp. We usually arrived in the evening. I still see quite vividly the scene of one of our arrivals at a cattle camp. As we approached, it was impossible to miss the aura in the atmosphere of the cattle camp from a distance. The first signal that the camp was in sight was a beacon of cow dung fires reaching into the sky and spotlighting the location of the camp. As we drew nearer, the singing of the men, the dancing of the children, the bellows of the herds, the jiggling of the bells on the necks of the oxen, the jokes and the laughter, all indicated the profound difference between the jubilant air of the cattle camp and the subdued atmosphere of the village. As we entered the camp, dogs heightened their barks; the first children to see us arrive shouted, "Bringing flies into the camp?" which was echoed throughout the camp. All this was in sharp contrast with the arrival of visitors from the camp in the villages, who were viewed as guests with a sense of superiority and dignity, healthy-looking and proud.

The camp itself was a sizeable settlement, about a mile in diameter, broken up into several "cattle hearths" or *gol*, which represented the cattle wealth of a family unit. That unit was in turn broken up into sections, each one having two sitting areas, one for men, located in the center of the herds, and the other for women, located on the edge of the cattle-camp and screened in on the outside by a thorned fence.

Life at the camp was one of self-conscious sensuous flirtation between men and women, boys and girls, all in their native dress - naked - and freely exposed to each other's scrutiny. Men and women sat separated from one another and yet very much involved with one another. Men would be engaged in a loud jocular conversation, consciously or sub-consciously geared towards winning the attention of the girls. The girls would be in their screened-in camping site, conversing, seemingly indifferent to the men, gossiping and laughing with their own air of self-possessiveness, but very self-conscious of the men, and in many ways intimidated by them.

The village sounds of women singing in the night to put their children to sleep were replaced by the singing of young men over their oxen intentionally aimed at keeping people, especially girls, awake to listen. Several men might sing at the same time, but far enough from one another for their voices not to conflict. The girls were the targeted audience and the ultimate judges of a singer's ability, although anyone else was in a way involved and could have an influence in shaping public opinion in appraising the singer's talent. A singer attracted to a particular girl might stop his ox near her spot until she "released" him with either a symbolic gift or something deeper like a "friendship" that might end in marriage. Even if she was not herself the object of his immediate interest, an admiring girl might also offer a gift of "release."

I loved listening to ox songs, especially at night. In much the same way as I loved the songs in the village. I found the cattle camp to be an environment in which the rhythm of the daytime calmed down with the night, but never totally disappeared and sometimes cultivated greater depths, as the noise level ebbed and eventually diminished, leaving the attention of the interested few to be focused on the songs of the night.

One occasion at the cattle camp stands out in my mind as quite eventful. The evening following our arrival, a dance was called, which was exclusively for boys. We went at the appropriate time to find bullies of varying ages. At first, it was a friendly meeting and other than the unusual absence of girls, quite ordinary. Then came a call for silence and a boy, who was unquestionably the leader, spoke: "Fellows, we have newcomers among us and we have to determine their age-set."

Age sets among the adults are determined on, and by, initiation into adulthood. The test is really the ability to endure the dreadful pain of the deep marks cut across the forehead. With boys, age-sets are determined by physical courage, strength and bravery. It is best to be courageous and strong enough to defeat your opponent in whatever manner of fight you are placed, but it is good enough to be brave and not cry or surrender. To be physically weak is bad, but to be a coward is worse.

The procedure was for a newcomer to select from among those present anyone whom he felt he should be in the same age-set with and through whom he would enter the set by fighting and faring well as an equal. We wanted to join the age-set of our peers, boys who were roughly our age. Bol and Kuol refrained from choosing. That was interpreted as cowardice. My turn came. I chose someone I thought I could handle well, a one-eyed fellow whom I was to learn was among the toughest and had indeed lost his eye in a fight. Such fights among the Dinka were strictly regulated.

We first wrestled and he threw me down. Usually, the fighters were allowed to struggle in one position; the one thrown being tortured or reversing the position and climbing on top. I did. Then we struggled some more and were eventually put back on our feet for a second round of wrestling. This went on for a number of rounds. I was thrown more than I threw, but the difference was marginal. Then came the second stage when we were given slender twigs with which to lash at one another. I liked this form of fighting. I could stand physical pain more than I could tackle. Given his fighting skill, he did not seem good at this form and I made up for the points lost in wrestling. Having more or less reached a stalemate, we were stopped and I was awarded membership of the age-set. Bol and Kuol were then allowed to join through me. This did not relieve us of further fights.

Fighting was a common occurrence in Dinka life. Just as we played Dinka field hockey, ran, high-jumped or played a variety of other competitive sports, we engaged in fighting, both as a sport and as a means of resolving conflict. On the collective level, fighting as a sport was between groups. Using long thin sharpened shafts as spears, we would dart ourselves to imitate a real battle. Serious injuries resulted from these mock fights. On the personal level, fights were provoked in endless ways by the boys themselves or by their elders. Anything from "This boy has insulted your mother" or "That boy says he scorns your fighting skill," to allegations of territorial or property violations were sure to result in spontaneous blows or regulated fights.

One late afternoon, as we were playing hockey on the periphery of the camp, one of the young men from our part of the camp came to announce to me that a boy by the name of Nyuat Kuol Mariau had defiantly taken Kuol's bull from our herds. This was supposed to be a challenge to us. But I don't think Kuol was told. The idea was to test and foster our sense of solidarity as brothers. In such situations, a Dinka boy would think twice. To ask investigating questions would be branded as cowardice. One simply fought, whatever the real facts about the wrongs or the rights involved. It was the principles that mattered and not the merits of a particular provocation. I learned later that Nyuat was a cousin, a member of our lineage, Pajok, I believe meeting at our great, great grandfather, Biong Alor. But in this staged fight, he was a relative outsider and aggressor. He was a little older than me, but that only made the challenge greater. I jumped the fence into the camp and raced for Nyuat's section. I was not a keen fighter, but I strongly resented disrespect and disdain, and would fight in defense of honour.

The expected behaviour was simply to insult the opponent's father, mother, sister or any other relative. Some spectators had followed me; others were already waiting with Nyuat. I pronounced the formula and gave Nyuat, already in expectation, the first blow. We exchanged a few blows and were then made to wrestle. No one was thrown. So, we were given long well-prepared branches made available for the purpose for the next phase-lashing. That was my preferred form of fighting. Suddenly, Nyuat threw his whip away, embraced me in a way that made beating difficult, and before I realised it, bit me on the jaw. We were then severed; he had broken the rules and I was the victor.

But before long, I realised that my jaw was bleeding. The sight and the amount of blood frightened me. Although I made no sounds of crying, tears streamed from my eyes. I was mocked for crying. The wound got infected and the jaw swelled. I became so sick that I was taken home, where the wound was opened to remove the pus. It took a while before it healed and my jaw still bears the scar. But what I remember the most about the incident is my father saying to me, "I hear that you cried". Although he did not straightforwardly criticise me, I felt humiliated.

While my account of our childhood has so far focused on our family circle, Noong had many other residents. Apart from my father's court, which was attended by all sorts of people, nobles and commoners alike, there were retainers and servants (some of whom were relatives), not to mention the prisoners who were then kept in our home, as there was yet no prison in the tribe.

One of the permanent residents was an Arab, by the name of Osman, pronounced by the Baggara more classically as Othman and by the Dinka more improperly as Attiman. It was he who slaughtered in our house according to Muslim rites. My father never ate anything not slaughtered accordingly. As he once explained, his purpose was not to pretend to be a Muslim, but to avoid his guests worrying about the food served in his house, and the Muslims were the only ones who had conditions to be met. Since Osman slaughtered chickens most of the time, he acquired the nickname, *Jɔŋ-Ajiith*, or "Chickens' Disease."

An Arab called Shoke also lived at Noong with his family. He was a blacksmith. His son, Mohammed, was our age-mate and playmate. Mohammed was skilled with his hands. He was very good at making bird-traps with hairs from a horse tail. He also made slingshots for stoning birds. We included Mohammed in our outdoor activities, except those which were typically Dinka, and for which he did not have much interest anyway, even though he spoke excellent Dinka.

Apart from these Arabs, there were Arab petty traders who came seasonally to sell their millet (*awuɔu*) when the Dinka ran short of their own staple crops. There was then hardly a market in Abyei, except for two or three shops owned by Arabs and a Greek. These nomadic traders brought goods to the people in their villages riding bulls, horses, and camels. They therefore played a vital economic role, but one for which the Dinka also paid heavily. During famines, bulls and cows were exchanged for small sacks of millet, while the millet value of goats and sheep was measured in small cups. Nonetheless, the demand was so great and the Dinka so rich with livestock that the problem was always shortage of Arab grain, salt, or whatever products they had to sell. As children, we used to chant: "There are the camels," or "There are the horses" in a way that recalled the terrifying days of slavery, when the Arabs would come on camels or horses and seize children or even adults, never to be seen again. But we also looked forward to their millet, *awuɔu,* which we craved. We used to chant,

"Oh, when will the Arabs come with their *awuɔu,* so that I enjoy a hot meal, digging into it with a gourd spoon or a shell?"

Apart from these traders and other Baggara Arab nomads, contacts with the outside world were minimal. Cars rarely came and, and when they did, the occasion was sensational. Usually, they were lorries whose engine noise could be heard a long distance away. We, the children, would all shout "*Thurumbil aba*" or "car is coming" and would race to see it pass by, as dust rose from the sandy beaten track and the smell of petrol and the rubber on the heated tires fumed the air. On very few occasions, "the children of lorries"- saloon cars - came with the visits of such important personalities as the British district commissioner and even more rarely, the governor. That was very exciting.

We saw a white man only on those rare occasions when the British administrators came on their official rounds. And when they did, they provided us with an odd specimen for curious observation. Once, we saw the district commissioner sitting under the tree in our father's court. When we saw him laugh, then pick up fruit of *thäu,* (*lalob* in Arabic and *Balanites aegyptiaca* to the scientific world) fruit and eat it, we were amazed and amused that he could laugh and eat "just like a Dinka." To us, he was so different that he was outside our scheme of reference. Issues of superiority and inferiority did not really arise, except to the extent that we used the Dinka and their ways as the standard of what was natural, normal and dignified in being a human being. And as I think back, how small was our world and how narrow our conception of humanity and dignity.

HOME
A Family of Multitudes

The Author with his wife, Dorothy, and their four sons. Sitting between his parents is Dennis Biong, and standing behind them, from left to right, are Donald Deng, David Kuol, and Daniel Jok.

The Author's sister Nyanluak, with my niece Aluel, and his other sister Ayan.

INVISIBLE BRIDGE
An African Journey through Cultures

Author's son, Daniel Jok, with his cousins, and Siamma, the wife of the Author's half brother, Gen. Pieng Deng, in the center.

The Author's uncle, Ngor Mijok, Mother's brother, with his daughter Awut and members of his family.

HOME
A Family of Multitudes

The Author's third son, David, with his grandmother and cousins.

Nyanthon, daughter of the Author's sister, Aluong.

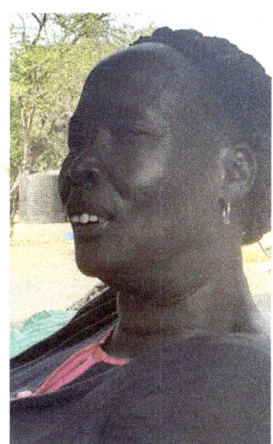

The Author's sister, Aluong.

INVISIBLE BRIDGE
An African Journey through Cultures

The Author's niece, Nyanwut Loth, Ayan's daughter.

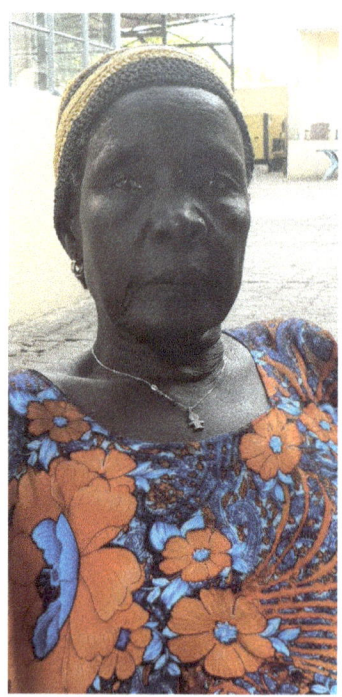

Nganluak, Author's sister.

The Author's sister, Ayan.

HOME
A Family of Multitudes

Angeer Ajing, daughter of the Author's sister, Nyanluak.

The Author's youngest sister, Aluong.

The Author's uncle Ngor Mijok with his daughter Awut.

The Author's niece, Nyanwut Loth, daughter of his sister, Ayan.

The Author's parents-in-law, Lawrence Augustus Ludwig and Catherine Teter Ludwig.

The Author's mother, Achok Mijok.

The Author's son, David, with his bride, Elizabeth, aunt Nyandeeng Nyok, and cousins.

The Author's four sons, from left to right, in their order of age seniority, Donald Deng, Daniel Jok, David Kuol, and Dennis Biong, at the wedding of David Kuol.

Kaya, daughter of Daniel Jok, the Author's second son.

Donald Deng newly wed bride, Jeita Phillips, at their marriage in Boston, on July 4, 2015.

Author's mother, Achok Mijok, with his mother-in-law, Catherine Ludwig.

Dr. Zachariah Bol Deng and his wife, Santina.

Author's wife Dorothy with their grandchildren.

The Author with his family and his wife's extended family.

Author's son, David Kuol, with his newly wed bride, Elizabeth Ashamu, at their wedding, on October 6, 2012, in Charlottesville, USA.

Author's son, Daniel Jok, with his newly wed bride, Atong Ajak Demach, at their wedding in Nairobi, Kenya, on December 20, 2017.

THE NEW YORK TIMES, SUNDAY, FEBRUARY 20, 1972

Dr. Deng Weds Dorothy Ann Ludwig

Miss Dorothy Ann Ludwig, a Ph.D. degree candidate at Teachers College, Columbia University, and Dr. Francis Mading Deng, a post-doctoral research fellow in the law and modernization program at Yale University, were married yesterday afternoon in the Church Center for the United Nations. The Rev. Melvin Hawthorne performed the Protestant ceremony, assisted by the Rev. Robert Bauers, director of the center's Lutheran Community Services.

Sudanese and East Indian delicacies were served with champagne to 150 guests at a reception at the center.

Dr. Deng, who is on leave as an officer of the Division of Human Rights at the United Nations Secretariat, and his bride met at the United Nations, where she was recording conversation in various world languages for the Cantometric Project of Columbia University. The bride is doing her doctoral research under the supervision of Margaret Mead, adjunct professor of anthropology at Columbia University.

Dr. Deng, who also is a lecturer in law at Columbia University, is a son of the late Deng Majok, paramount chief of the Ngok Dinka, the largest tribal group in the Sudan, numbering over two million people. His mother, Mrs. Majok, lives in Abyei, the Sudan.

Mrs. Deng is a daughter of Mr. and Mrs. Lawrence A. Ludwig of Miraleste, Calif. Mr. Ludwig, a senior executive in the project administration of Mobil Research and Development Corporation in Los Angeles, formerly served overseas with Mobil in Iran, Australia and England.

Mrs. William Teter was matron of honor. Other attendants were Mrs. Robert A. Ludwig and Mrs. Richard D. Ludwig, the bride's sisters-in-law, and 4-year-old Donna Ludwig, the bride's niece, who was flower girl.

Alan D. Cullison, professor at the University of Connecticut Law School and a Yale roommate of the bridegroom's, was best man. The ushers were Dr. Roy Skwang Lee, also an officer of the Human Rights Division, and Bona Malwal Ring, a former member of Parliament in the Sudan.

The bridegroom's brother, Dr. Zackariah Bol Deng of London, and a cousin, Miss Akur Mathiang, a student in London, attended the ceremony.

Mrs. Deng's gown, made in 1902, was decorated with 42 hand-crocheted buttons and many yards of soutache. It

wife of the Secretary of War under President Woodrow Wilson.

The bride attended Oberlin College and was graduated from the University of California at Berkeley, where she received a B.A. degree in Slavic languages and literature in 1961 and from Teachers College, where she received an M.A. degree in teaching English as a second language. She was a Peace Corps volunteer in Kandahar, Afghanistan, and later trained Peace Corps groups for teaching English in South America and Africa.

Dr. Deng was graduated with honors with an LL.B. degree from Khartoum University, where he was appointed to the faculty of law. He holds an LL.M. and JS.D. degrees in law from Yale University. He also attended King's College of London University.

The bridegroom is author

Mr. and Mrs. Francis M. Deng, who were married yesterday. Bride is former Miss Dorothy A. Ludwig.

The New York Times article of the Author's wedding to Dorothy Anne Ludwig.

The Author and his bride, Dorothy Anne.

CHAPTER FIVE

SCHOOL
FOR FATHER'S LOVE

One afternoon, as we played on the periphery of Noong, our father returned from a visit to Abyei town. He had only recently taken over the leadership of the tribe from his father, who was forced to retire, although he was still very influential. Father was beginning to establish a home in Abyei, being the administrative centre of the tribe. A short time after his arrival from Abyei, he summoned us under his Court Tree. We were two: Kuol and myself. Bol had gone with his mother to Abyei, where his older brother, Chan, was under treatment in the dispensary after he had been very badly burned in the cattle camp during an epileptic convulsion, his first in what would become a lifelong affliction.

With a demonstration of paternal love and affection that was rare for him, Father held us close to him, stroked our heads, called us by our praise-names, and then asked, "Which of you loves his father?" We both said we did. "Which of you loves his father so much that he would do anything for him?" We did, or so we said. "Enough to leave his mother and go away for his father?" The answer continued to be affirmative. We thought it was all part of the usual test of paternal loyalty. The point eventually came; he wanted us to go to school at Abyei. We had little time to make ourselves ready for departure. Our mothers were informed. They hurriedly prepared some food for us to eat.

A short time afterwards, we were summoned again; the donkeys were ready and it was time to go. I was not aware at the time of my mother's opposition to my leaving; but my sister Ayan told me many years later that Achok confronted Deng Majok on the issue. "My only son, Mading, how can he be taken away? If he should go to school, I will leave this home. What would I do without him?"

Father of course prevailed. According to Ayan, he reasoned, "The fact that Mading is a single son will escape your mind, you, Achok, and leave me aside since I am the one who is sending him to school. His being a single son is insignificant. Education will turn him into three sons for me." Although the twelve miles between Noong and Abyei can now be walked in two and half hours, in those days it seemed very long, I guess because we were very young; I could not have been more than five years old.

I don't know about Kuol; as for me, I thought a great deal as we rode those donkeys; and my thoughts remain vivid: There I was, going to school where one obtained knowledge, wisdom and power. I thought it was going to be an instantaneous event and not a long, evolutionary process. I was so eager to succeed. But what if I failed? My father had so strongly associated love for him with going to school. What if I let him down? That frightening thought was recurrent in my mind until we arrived at Abyei. Father had not yet built a home at Abyei, but Abbo, a Sudanese "Arab" of Nigerian origin, had provided accommodation for him and his family. Father had a few junior wives with him at Abyei and, as I have said, Nyanboldit was there taking care of Chan.

Bol's mother was strongly opposed to his going to school, feeling perhaps that, with Chan's epilepsy, Bol remained the heir and education might take him away from the traditional culture that guaranteed his leadership. Her opposition continued for a very long time, and as far as I could judge, she never changed her mind. She only acknowledged the value of education when Bol and I took the body of our father, who had died in Cairo, from Khartoum to Abyei by plane during the rainy season, when that was unprecedented and was seen as a virtual miracle. Anyway, Bol stayed in school.

A day after our arrival at Abyei, we went to the shop to buy clothes. Traditionally, Dinka children and men went naked. It was because clothes were a novelty that school children soon became known as: "The children wearing clothes," or "the age-set in white." Our clothes consisted of long, Arabian-type garments, *araagi* and underwear, *thurual*. Bol and I got the same colors - white with black stripes. We also wore the brown Egyptian caps with tassels hanging down from the top.

Then we went to school. Classes were held in temporary shelters made of dura stalks. The two masters could not have been better chosen for cultivating virgin minds. They were educated in both the South and the North, and although they did not go high up the educational ladder, they spoke English and Arabic fluently and had an air of sophistication which distinguished them markedly from anyone else in the area.

This was particularly true of the headmaster, Lino Wuor Abyei. He was a relative of our father from his mother's side. Wuor was medium in height, slim in figure, and quite brown for a Dinka, with fine, but stern features and was always very well dressed. Most conscious of himself, Lino Wuor spoke and bore himself in a quiet, gentle, dignified, self-conscious manner, careful about every word he uttered and every gesture he made and its impact on his surroundings. Bol was later to say that during the early days of our conversion to Christianity, he always had a feeling that Lino Wuor was the embodiment of Jesus Christ, the son of God.

The assistant headmaster was Luis Nyok Kuol, our uncle, the brother of Deng Makuei. It will be recalled that he had been proposed to replace him as deputy to my father, but father chose to let him remain in his position as a teacher and insisted on reinstating Deng Makuei as his second-in-command. Nyok was impressive in a way very different from Wuor. Unlike Wuor, he had undergone initiation into a warrior age-set. Their age-set of Abior subtribe was *Cuor,* the

Eagle. Uncle Nyok was also an excellent singer of the traditional ox-songs. His traditional songs were famous, at least in his subtribe.

Nyok was tall, perhaps six feet five inches. Although he, too, was well dressed and neat, he was never as meticulous as Wuor. He spoke and behaved freely, and was prone to hearty laughter. Although he was stern, his face often bore a wide smile, which revealed his white separated teeth, *weer*, the Dinka ideal of a perfect set. Nyok was obviously conscious of his family standing and had a deep sense of preeminence, so much so that I think he resented the fact that he was not himself the headmaster. Both Nyok and Wuor were equally feared and revered, but Nyok was reputed for his hot temper and quick resort to corporeal punishment.

Despite my excitement and apprehension about school, I do not recall the very first lesson we had, but I now know that the school opened on January 1, 1943. One day, a few days after the school had started, a tall slim boy walked in, completely naked, decorated with patterns of white and red ashes plastered with oil on his skin. He seemed quite unconcerned that he was the only "tradition-looking" Dinka in the class and that he should have been clothed. The class roared with laughter, as Nyok sneered jokingly at the new boy.

It took some careful looking and reflecting, but I soon recognised the boy to be the one with whom I had fought during my stay with my maternal relations. I got to know that his name was Ayong Monyyom. I still didn't know our relationship until later: his mother, Ayok, was an adoptive cousin of my father. Another day, there walked into the classroom another tall boy wrapped up in a heavy large size winter coat which we later learned belonged to his father who was the chief of Achueng subtribe. We had not known him before, but we soon got to know that he was Deng Aguer, the eldest son of our father's sister, Awor. Deng and Ayong were to become close companions, and Bol and I also became quite close to both of them.

It soon became apparent to me that learning was a more gradual process than I had anticipated. But I enjoyed the classes. Somehow, I transferred into the classroom some of the same characteristics for which I had been known and appreciated by the elders – the power of articulation, rationality and wit. I drew the attention of my teachers and won their compliments in much the same way I had won the elders in my father's court.

One morning, Father walked into the classroom. A seat was placed in front of the class for him. That day seemed to be the day of reckoning which I had thought about on my way to school. I was now to succeed for my father to see or else fail and fail him. Though inwardly nervous, my hand went up frequently and I scored my points. My inner focus was on my father; the teacher and the blackboard were only external means.

When my father eventually got up to go, I was delighted that there had not been a single failure or embarrassment and that there had been many points in my favour. There was however one problem - my father never smiled or made any gesture of satisfaction or pleasure. Was it indifference or perhaps disapproval of the way I had appeared to be showing-off? I hoped he did not think I had merely been showing off; I consoled myself by thinking that his attitude perhaps revealed the usual polite modesty of a Dinka parent. Deep within him, I thought, he had to be proud of me.

I thought back to my maternal grandfather and wondered whether he too would be proud of how I was performing in the class. That same evening, as we sat outside in the open air, I overheard a solemn conversation from the women sitting some distance away. I had a feeling something very significant for me had gone wrong somewhere. And rightly so, for in a while, one of the step-mothers approached me to say that my grandfather Mijok, mother's father, had died. I cannot describe what I felt at the time, not because I don't remember it, for I do remember it very vividly, but rather because it was unbelievable, in fact not clear to me what his death meant. I cried quietly. My cry was not that of a child. Tears poured from my eyes and I sobbed. But I was much more deeply injured than cries or words could express. That I was among relatives did not alleviate the loneliness I felt as my weaning period came and passed, flashing memories of a wonderful past.

It was only about two years later that my grandmother followed my grandfather. She had been ill for some time, but had almost recovered when she suddenly died. I recall that day too very well.

When the news came, I was repairing ropes for tethering our animals and was in a jovial mood, singing as I worked. Then, suddenly, I heard the voice of my mother wailing loudly in a way that left no doubt in my mind that someone very close to us had died. Without asking, I assumed it must be my grandmother and I started to cry at the peak of my voice as I went towards my mother's hut.

I was now more aware of things than I had been when my grandfather had died. It was as though the world had come to an end. Seeing my mother throwing herself down as she cried left no hope in me. As my sisters heard us cry, they too cried and our part of the village became a madhouse. Later, when we calmed down, but were still clouded with grief, people came to visit my mother, supposedly to console her. They spoke of what a great lady my grandmother had been, but, to my utter surprise, especially now that I think back, they speculated on the misery my mother was bound to experience because of her mother's death. "But what can you do? You just have to face the facts and the reality of the tragedy." Hearing them talk gave me a deep sense of doom for my mother and for us, her children.

Until we went to school, I associated the idea of grandparents with my mother's parents only. My father's mother died when my father was barely a teenager. My father's father, Chief Kuol Arop, was too far from where I was born and raised. I got to know him about the time I lost my mother's father. I remember when he first came into our class in quite the same manner Father had come. His son, Nyok, was taking the class. Chief Kuol asked whose sons the various pupils were. Some were distant relatives whom he could not be expected to know. But when his questioning reached us, Nyok laughed in criticism, "But Father," he said, "these are your grandchildren!"

My memories about my father's father are rather vague, but I recall how I used to frequent his court and how he would seat me next to him on his bed or hold me standing between his legs as he sat on his chair or bed, affectionately rubbing my head. Even though I now know that he had opposed my father's marriage to my mother, Grandfather Kuol Arop was very affectionate towards me. The image I had formed of him based on what I had heard from early childhood was that of the ideal chief.

The years that followed were eventful and very formative in the educational revolution of the Ngok. Wuor and Nyok proved to be more than professional teachers – they were sons of the land, with the interest of their people ingrained in their hearts. Our literacy began with the vernacular for which the books of Father Arthur Nebel, an Austrian priest from Verona Fathers, and a missionary, were the sources.

When we got to learning English more seriously, we were expected to practise speaking it as well. Two medals called "marks" were circulated to be passed on to anyone who spoke Dinka. Each day, the medals started with the prefect on duty and circulated until late afternoon at the rollcall. The person possessing one then, other than the prefect initially holding it, was lashed. Since our area was then under the Southern educational system and fell within the Catholic sphere of influence, according to British colonial allocation to Missionary Societies, we were taught Catholicism. Our teachers were themselves Catholics.

So seriously was religion taken that anyone who did not memorise his catechism correctly was prevented from going home for lunch and left hungry in the classroom to memorise for the following day's test. I recall a day when I alone returned home to find an unexpected feast. A Rek Dinka section had come with gifts of food items and cattle to express their gratitude to Father for granting them grazing rights in Ngok territory. Father honoured them with a feast. When I arrived, there was much singing and dancing. As I entered his assembly, my father's only remark was: "Is it you alone they have sent back to me?" I did not know whether to be proud or ashamed. I have never forgotten the strange combination of pride and loneliness I felt on that festive occasion.

Even though we were only catechumens, religion meant very much to us. Part of this was a carryover from tradition, for the Dinka are an intensely religious people. In addition, missionaries in Dinkaland quickly discovered the best way to tap the feelings of the Dinka – singing – to vitalise their religious indoctrination.

Praying and singing under the leadership of Wuor and Nyok was an experience of absolution in which we felt a deep sense of guidance, salvation and even worldly security. Occasional visits by priests added more to an environment already saturated with spiritualism and ritualism.

Our religiosity in those days can be illustrated by the way in which we spent one retreat. We had been told that retreat was a solemn occasion on which we were to fast, withdraw from social life and remain in isolation, reading stories from the Bible (which Father Nebel had translated into Dinka) and reflecting on God and the teachings of the Church. Eager to demonstrate our commitment to the principles enunciated, we exaggerated every aspect of it.

The day before the fasting, we told our mothers that we were not to eat the following day until sunset, that our hut was to be out of bounds, and that we were to be left undisturbed. My mother cooked for us at about four o'clock that morning. We ate our fill, went to school for prayers and returned to meditate. Now, when I look back to those days, we might have been also influenced by the Muslim fasting of Ramadan, in which one eats and drinks before dawn and fasts for the rest of the day. Using the hut of one of our junior step-mothers, Tiet Aguar, where mats lay spread on the floor, we read the Bible and other religious books or otherwise lay silent in meditation. No one spoke to anyone; laughing was out of the question. At about midday, Bol's mother, Nyanboldit, came and tried to persuade us against the idea. Although she amused us into controlled giggles, she failed and left.

After a while, she returned and announced that she could no longer tolerate our idiocy and was going to see the headmaster. She went and came back to say that the headmaster had denied having anything to do with our behaviour and that he did not approve of what we were doing. Naturally, we took what she said as an attempt to persuade us. Except for the temptation to laugh, we dismissed it. Eventually Nyanboldit gave up with an amusing curse. Shortly afterwards, Kuol cried out: "For what are we killing ourselves?" And he left the room laughing and provoking us into laughter. As he was getting out, Kuol saw Ayan, my sister, with a plate of food. Calling her by affectionate terms, he won himself a share of her food, and then returned to disturb us.

SCHOOL
For Father's Love

The retreat almost turned into a joke and the more we repressed laughter, the more we felt like laughing. But we kept the faith until dusk, when we strolled to the river to bathe. There, we met the headmaster, Lino Wuor, having his late afternoon walk. When he confirmed what Nyanboldit had said, our day's achievement seemed worthless, but still felt a sense of gratification at the endurance.

It would be several years before we would be baptised as Christians. We were then about ten years old. Our father's consent was required by law. We chose to talk to him one moonlit evening. He was sitting outside in the open air of his section of our enclosure conversing informally with junior chiefs and tribal elders. There was much laughter until we broke in with our request and told him we wanted "to have our heads sprinkled with God's water." That was the Dinka terminology for baptism. Smiling and holding us affectionately, but in a way which clearly belittled the subject, Father asked why we wanted to be baptised. We told him what we had been told: unless a person was baptised to be a Christian, he or she could not enter heaven; he or she must burn in hell.

Although our father had had sufficient contact with our educational content and especially with our teachers to know what we were talking about, both he and his companions took the whole thing as a joke and teased us with more questions. We gave answers they paradoxically considered "superstitious," and at best thought amusing. Father's last question was: "Assuming that the word of the Missionaries is correct and that only the Christians will go to the Home of God and the non-Christians will go to the Home of fire, will you children be happy in the Home of God while the rest of your family burns in the Home of fire?" We answered by telling them what we had been told, that after death and "on the day of the Big Court," everyone would stand on his or her own as an individual, and would not recognise, far less care about, his relatives. Looking at it from the Dinka belief system in which death does not sever family ties, it is extraordinary how ignorant of our culture and insensitive we were.

Seeing that we had frivolous answers for every sensible question, Father ceased to smile, and after a brief silence during which the women in the female section could be heard, said wittily: "Nothing is altogether bad; at least you will save my cattle from too many marriages." But our conversion was primarily opposed by many relatives precisely because they could not see how a son of a chief could marry only one wife.

We were baptised at Mayen Abun, a station run by Catholic missionaries in the area of the Twic Dinka to the south of us, one of the leading Catholic missionary centres in the South. The occasion was Christmas and the mission was lively with Christian rituals and competitive celebrations between affiliate missions in the area. The eve of our baptism, Bol and I prayed a great deal. That night, while we were sleeping, Bol called Ayong, our older cousin, almost in a murmur: "Ayong, a snake has wrapped itself around my neck". Ayong jumped up, telling Bol not to move. He went to the hut of Chief Lang Juuk of Twic tribe, who was a very religious man and was still awake, praying and reading the Bible with a lit kerosene lamp. They came with the lamp, carefully extending to see the snake. Instead, they saw a rosary on Bol's neck. As I think back, now that I am aware of Freudian psychology, I wonder what the symbolism of Bol's experience means in the context of our conversion and the conflict of religious cultural values it entailed.

The following morning, we were baptised; I became Francis and Bol Frederick, until he later changed to Zachariah. I vividly recall how holy and confident of salvation we felt on that occasion. It was part of our religious conversion to disrespect totems of traditional religions and not to eat the meat of any animal slaughtered in sacrifice to them. In particular, we were to kill snakes, as they symbolised evil in Christian mythology. But to the Dinka, depending on the snake, they often represent the spirits of the clan and are considered "relatives," who must not be harmed, just as they are also expected not to harm their clansmen capriciously. The Dinka, of course, dread snakes and the Ngok term for "snake" is *kërac*, "the bad thing," so that the religious significance of snakes may be a way of pacifying them.

Bol and I once killed a snake with beautiful black, red and white colour stripes. As its name Dengdit suggests, it was a totem of our clan. We killed it in our father's sleeping hut and that made our offence even worse, as it was considered to have been on a sacred mission. Killing it was spiritually dangerous to the family. So serious was our wrong that we were beaten by Nyanboldit. The snake was buried ceremonially and ceremonies of atonement were carried out.

Our education also emphasised physical training and a military-like drilling and discipline. We drilled every morning and late afternoon and fancied ourselves as soldiers. In the school songs, which were composed for us, we were presented as a traditional age-set of warriors with pens for spears and as a modern regiment of soldiers with pens for guns.

The emphasis on military discipline was particularly spearheaded by Nyok, who, though not a soldier, had been initiated as a member of a warrior age-set and had lived the life of military regimentation and training. Nyok was our physical educationalist. To go out of step or harmony in a march or to be awkward in a drill invited prompt punishment. One was either lashed or made to hold a heavy weight with outstretched arms for a length of time.

The Governor General of Sudan once came on a visit to Ngokland. An intertribal fair attended by chiefs and administrators from the neighbouring provinces of the North and the South was being held at a place called Leu, some fifteen miles from Abyei. It was to include sports, dances, and a school show. We had an intensive preparation for the occasion. Older boys walked to go to Leu, but we, the small children, went in a lorry. That was our first experience with motor car transportation. With trees swiftly dashing by and the world turning around, it was a sensational trip.

The meeting place was equally impressive. The residences that had been built for the occasion turned the place into a temporary town bigger than Abyei. The important day came. When it was all over, we thought all had gone well, but our teachers, and especially Nyok, had a different opinion. The drill and the group singing had been disharmonious and in their opinion our show had failed. They did not say much at the time, but when we were back at school; Nyok surprised us with a very serious punishment. We were all lashed and for a long time to come, any other punishment was crowned with "And of the Leu," one bitter lash in memory of the Leu fiasco.

Ironically, it was at Leu that I allegedly got "bewitched" for my good public performance. A few days before, I had met a group of British administrators walking with my father, the headmaster and scores of chiefs and elders, and had answered in English such elementary questions as "How are you?", "What is your name?", "Where are you going?" To the Dinka, to have spoken with the English in their own language demonstrated an impressive knowledge of English. I was highly complimented. Then at the Leu show, I was the youngest of the boys who were selected to step forward from the school lines in front of the assembled guests to recite brief welcoming phrases, which we had memorised. Based on height, and as I was the shortest, I also led the drill and that was misinterpreted by the Dinka as a sign of my excellence.

On my return, I had a severe stomach trouble. The medical attention I received from the dispensary did not help. My father had accompanied his guests to the North. Uncle Biong and my mother decided to employ a witchdoctor. At first, I would have nothing to do with such pagan ways. But the elders persisted and as I was desperate, I was prevailed upon. The witchdoctor was a famous magician called Madut Agorjok. Very short for a Dinka, crooked in build, lumps protruding all over his body, his face frightfully distorted, his teeth disorderly and red-stained, Madut seemed deformed in every way, and, judging from his looks, a perfect magician.

Now that I think of it, Madut's case is one of the best illustrations of how the Dinka sometimes turn a defect into an asset, a compensation for misfortune, a sort of social security for the disabled. It is well known among the Dinka, for instance, that a person who has suffered a deformity as a result of disease is believed to be spiritually capable of curing such a disease. A person whose cattle have been wiped out by an epidemic disease may also become recognised as a preventer or a curer of such a disease. There are many similar illustrations. Since the services such a person renders are paid for, a victim of disease is compensated. I don't know what Madut had suffered from, but it showed.

Calm and confident, Madut stayed for a day, sipping beer and eating well, seemingly unconcerned about the vital issue of my health. His divination had revealed that I had been bewitched by envious eyes, probably at the Leu show. A black snake had been cast into my stomach and was eating it away. He could transfer the snake magically into a black lamb. The lamb was brought. At the crucial time, I lay down in a circle of on lookers. Madut anointed my lower belly with oil. The lamb was held across my belly by sturdy hands. Its struggle was neutralised and its mouth was tightly closed to block pitiful cries. Madut pressed his magical eyes onto my belly, then massaged it as though to squeeze something from my stomach into the lamb. The lamb began to quiver without much resistance. In a short while, blood flowed from its mouth and nostrils. It was dead. The snakes had supposedly entered the lamb and killed it.

Madut said I would continue to ache for a day or so, but would soon recover. He was right. The following day, I showed signs of recovery and in two days, I was on my feet fully recovered.

In those days, education was despised by the Dinka. To go to school was seen as a defection to a foreign culture which reduced a Dinka into the defiled life of the Arabs or "foreigners" in towns. My father was especially blamed for sending all his sons to school, leaving none to take care of the cattle. He would lecture on the hidden treasures of education that would eventually accrue, but his words mostly fell on deaf ears.

Because of this attitude towards education, Wuor and Nyok included in the school programme activities designed to interest the public in the value of education. Chiefs, elders, and the general public were invited to watch shows in which we displayed the evils of ignorance and the virtues of enlightenment. A child would be depicted dangerously ill; parents would anxiously call on a witch-doctor's cure and fail; an educated person would come passing by and suggest that the child be taken for modern medical care; he would explain that witchdoctors were ineffective and deceitful; after some resistance, he would prevail upon the desperate relatives to "try and see"; the child would be cured and education would triumph.

Sometimes, the whole school or the senior classes would tour the tribe presenting educational programmes. We marched in military formations singing songs about the value of education, thanking the government for opening the school in our area, praising our parents for sending us to school, and thanking our teachers for persevering to teach us and open our minds.

These are some of the lines of the songs we sang:

Watch us, our age-set of education,
Watch us our age-set of education
Watch us our age-set of education.

These lines were repeated three times with varying vocal tones and then many times over.

Most mothers, even more than fathers, were known to resist education. They were also addressed in our campaign school songs:

Our mothers all cry:
"Our children have all been taken away
There is no child left in the land."
We do not blame you oh mothers
There is nothing you know, nothing;
The word is creeping on throughout the world,
It is coming to us crossing all lands;
In Khartoum, a child is born
And goes to school.
Am I to compensate you with a white cow?
What about the White One in the market (paper)
And my pen?

Even before the fruits of education accrued or were visible, they were predicted and exalted:

Education is good,
Education is good,
Brothers in learning,
Let us go early in the morning;

SCHOOL
For Father's Love

Education is good.
Our teachers, open our minds
Open our minds,
Our minds hard like rocks,
Our minds dense like the earth
Brighten them with light.
And thanks to the Government,
Thanks to the Government.

The value of education was seen in the context of the challenging hardships confronting both the children and the teachers:

Even though we suffer,
We shall endure,
And find the value of education in the future.
Those children who run away,
They lack prudent hearts,
They do not even bid farewell to their teachers.
I will not run away
I am a man;
I am the gentleman of the future.
Teach us well
You, our teachers;
Even if you suffer,
Hold your hearts tight;
Do not despair,
We are your brothers.

And indeed, there was a great deal of hardship for both pupils and teachers. Seats in the class rooms were made of mud. The droppings of the goitered stork, dheel, were used as chalk. Charcoal provided the pencils. Hardships of various kinds were intolerable for most of the children. Some were too young to be separated from their parents, especially mothers. They wanted to escape back home. But the teachers were determined to keep them in school. We once escaped to go back to our village at Noong. Lino Wor ran after us and caught up with us at Nainai. We were allowed just enough time to eat corn on the cob and return with him.

Our teachers worked very closely with the chiefs, elders and the communities. Wherever we went in the campaigns around the Tribe, bulls and lambs were slaughtered and plenty of food prepared in hospitality. We sang to explain the value of education to our people and call upon them to send their children to school:

Father and mother,
You have raised me;
Together, you have raised me;
I love you both.
Now that God has saved you for me
See the pleasure of a child;
See the pleasure of your child.
You, our fathers,
We greet you all,
Please accept our greetings with all your hearts.
Our own hearts are filled with joy,
Now that we have seen you.
God, the Creator who created all people,
We pray to you
Protect our fathers,
Our brothers and our sisters,
Our chiefs who are holding our land,
Our court members,
Our communities,
And our teachers.
Thank you, Creator,
If you have saved us to this day,
Then open our minds to learn.

Unity and solidarity were strongly advocated and jealousy condemned. And our area was negatively compared with other areas that had long embraced education, leaving us behind. Chiefs were praised for supporting education. And teachers were implored to endure the

SCHOOL
For Father's Love

demanding task of helping us to catch up with other areas:

> *Our Chiefs, welcome in good health,*
> *All our Chiefs …*
> *Come, so that we express to you our happiness;*
> *We love you all,*
> *Our senior Chiefs;*
> *What you have done is pleasing to our hearts.*
> *We greet you all:*
> *Our Heads of Clans,*
> *Chiefs of all our sections,*
> *And the Omdas (Chiefs of the sub-tribes).*
> *Brothers, let us all love one another,*
> *You, brothers in learning,*
> *Let us all love one another.*
> *Let us abandon jealousy between us,*
> *And love one another.*
> *And you, brothers,*
> *Let us devote ourselves to education.*
> *The whole world has gone far ahead,*
> *Will we be able to catch up with them?*
> *Can we really catch up with them?*
> *Let us pray to God our Father,*
> *And teach us well, you, our teachers.*

There was strict military type discipline in learning and projecting a dignified mannerism. And indeed, drills combined the traditional age-set warrior culture with that of modern soldiering:

> *The display of the Age-set of Wor,*
> *Is presented on the plains with guns;*
> *The rhythm of the drill is loud,*
> *It is the display of gentlemen.*

Work on self-help projects for constructing and maintaining school facilities was part of the educational agenda. It should be noted that the children varied considerably in age from those of us who were as young as five years old and those who were much older, some teenagers. There were therefore children old enough for physical construction work:

> *We grabbed our spears,*
> *And boomed with war songs;*
> *We sang our war songs and stampeded,*
> *Our warriors age-set performed the ritual of war and stampeded;*
> *Nothing subdues our determined group.*
> *We lined up the poles and stones,*
> *And drew our plans on the ground.*
> *We pulled the shrubs for the fence,*
> *And marked the plans;*
> *We are building our home,*
> *We are building our home,*
> *The home of the children of learning,*
> *The home to which words flow.*
> *Our Age-set does not fear the heat of the sun.*
> *Brother who is left behind,*
> *When you come, do not delay,*
> *Our Age-set is marching on;*
> *Look around, look around,*
> *Look behind, you are late.*
> *You are late.*

Many years later, in my interaction with our legendary teacher, Lino Wor, I saw in him great joy in seeing the fruits of his pioneering contribution to the education of his people. I was particularly delighted to receive a letter from him when I was working on the biography of my father, The Man Called Deng Majok, in which he recounted the challenges they confronted in pioneering education in the area, the pivotal support they received from Chief Deng Majok, and the great satisfaction he felt in seeing his students rise to high levels of education and public service at home and abroad.

SCHOOL
For Father's Love

Writing and reading were a total mystery to our people. When we began to show off what we had learned from school, we were closely tested and scrutinized. A school boy would be taken far away while another one was asked to write a name in the sand. The one taken away was brought back to read what was written. When he read it correctly, onlookers would all burst in hilarious bewildered laughter: "This is Jok", they would cry out, indicating that it was a miracle, a divine manifestation.

The miracle of writing and reading was seen as a facilitation of justice within and between tribes in the communication between chiefs:

> *Writing is an ancient legacy,*
> *It is the heritage of the children of Adam,*
> *That is known to our Age-set who write.*
> *A child who is lost*
> *Cannot be sought;*
> *And a cow captured*
> *Cannot be sought;*
> *Searching for them will need us:*
> *"One in White who writes for the Chief,*
> *Write the letter."*
> *The letter I will write,*
> *Cannot be read by the person carrying it,*
> *It will be seen by someone who can read,*
> *Not by your priests;*
> *I have no regard for your priests.*
> *The One in White knows the words of knowledge,*

Wherever we went, chiefs and notables would give us a warm reception, slaughter hospitality beasts, have the nourishing native beer brewed and watch our show. Usually, chiefs and elders, even the common men, were so impressed that they surrendered their children for recruitment. Every one of us was implored to labour individually and collectively during our vacations to recruit for the school. By 1945, when Father took full charge of the tribe as the paramount chief, he demanded that chiefs at all levels of the hierarchy "levy" boys for the school from their own children and the children of their people. Subtle measures were used to induce people to surrender their children for recruitment or once recruited to prevent parents from withdrawing them.

The school became well provided with students and the attitude of the Dinka began to change as they saw the feedback of education. Foremost was the miracle of writing and reading. At home, the crowds that were always around our father constantly put us to the test and could not believe what they saw. Some of them would lead one of us far away making sure that he did not even turn as he walked away. Those who remained would be asked to write down names of people totally strange to us. The person led away would be brought back and, as soon as he read the names correctly, all would burst into laughter of amazement. "This is Jok, divine power," they would say, and think of other ways to test the skill they seemed to associate with the magical powers of the spirits.

As the enrolment increased, boarding houses were built for the students, but we and our close relatives remained in our house. Our home was Arab-like in its inner structure. We had moved into our father's new home which was quite a complex setup. A brick and corrugated iron building with a number of huts formed the female part of the enclosure. There was only one door into this part and it opened into the children's section. We shared our section with the horses, but there was a lot of space. The children's section was separated from the section where our father held his "house court" or otherwise met chiefs, elders, and the general public. The main gate was in the children's section close to the door linking the children's section with Father's section.

The law was that we were to keep out of the female section. The rule against keeping out of Father's section was less strict. A policeman stood at the main gate to keep the public out of the whole enclosure. Only special dignitaries or people my father had expressly authorised were allowed in, although even that always meant a crowd. The gate was locked from the inside, but the guarding policeman slept near to see to it that unauthorised people did not get in at night.

SCHOOL
For Father's Love

Once, we were sleeping in the open air not far away from the gate where the policeman was. A knock at the gate woke me up along with the policeman. I heard him ask in a voice heavy with sleep, "Who is there?" I could only faintly hear the response. Apparently, the policeman, too, could not hear well. Cursing, he asked again, and the voice outside merely asked for the gate to be opened. That infuriated the policeman even more. He shouted curses and uttered words that conveyed something like "Who the hell do you think you are?" He opened the gate more out of angry curiosity than a willingness to let the man in. There stood Father holding the reins of his horse, surrendering the horse to the speechless policeman, and walking into the enclosure as though nothing odd had just happened. That was my first and only time to see my father wearing a full European suit and a hat. He had been on one of his courtship visits.

Something about my father intimidated me beyond description. He seemed critical of everything I did. I remember once I complained about not receiving new clothes because I had kept mine in good condition while Kuol or Bol or both (I do not remember) received new ones because of having worn out their old clothes. Should they gain for being careless and I lose for being careful? I argued. Father reprimanded me, accusing me of jealousy. I felt humiliated. Whenever I served tea, it was as though his eyes were fixed on my hands. If I filled a cup too much, or somehow my hand shook and spilled the tea, abuses would immediately come from him. If I hesitated as to which of the many worthy guests deserved a cup, he asked whether I was blind. If I served in the wrong order of seniority, he might ask me to give the next cup to a certain person with a tone that criticised my last judgement. And if I delayed for a split second from refilling an empty cup, he wondered where my mind was.

When he sat in court under a tree, I would walk away from the court feeling his eyes and for that matter the rest of the court fixed on me. I would walk or run very self-consciously. Father had a way of calling one to his chair and whispering orders into one's ears. Sometimes he spoke in Arabic to have some privacy as most Dinka did not know Arabic. If one did not catch his words well, there was always the question, at least for me, whether one could dare ask him to repeat his words.

On one occasion, I was so self-conscious that on my way to the women's quarters, I forgot what he had asked me to do. I don't remember what I did, but I had to think of the most likely errand. Of course, could not dare go back to ascertain what he had sent me for. Even my performance at school by which I had hoped to win recognition did not seem to satisfy my father. Once, I overheard a conversation between him and the headmaster, Lino Wuor. The headmaster was praising me for my performance at school. My father's response was: "But he is so short." With the ground shifted to my height rather than my learning ability, the headmaster graciously argued that I would pull myself up. I am now six feet, and once mistaken by a nurse as six foot two, either of which is not tall by Dinka standards, but not short either.

I was in my last year at Abyei when my mother nearly died. She was at the end of her pregnancy with her fifth child. Illness accelerated her labour and caused complications in her delivery. News of her critical condition came to Abyei in rapid succession. I wanted to go, but was refused by the school authorities on the ground that my absence might harm me in the final examinations and that my presence would anyway not be of much help to her. One evening, I overheard a woman who had just come from Noong report that it was almost hopeless and that if she survived the night, it would be a mysterious work of God. That night, I never slept. I knelt in prayer, or otherwise lay awake, begging God to save my mother's life. I could not conceive of this world without her. I promised God that if my mother lived, I would be devoted to Him in gratitude. Then I heard Him respond in words which rang in my head: "Have faith, your mother will live." And although I never ceased to be anxious all night, I felt that I had been granted a clemency and that my mother would not die.

The next morning, my eyes heavy with sleeplessness, I went to beg the school authorities again to let me go to my mother, but was once more refused. I came back to our house to find news that my mother had miraculously survived the night of my prayers. She was still in a serious condition, but the worst had been averted. I had no doubt that my prayers had saved my mother, and for once in my life, I felt that I had done my mother a favour; I also knew that even more than it was for her, it was for me. Two days later, without asking for permission, I got onto the lorry of some Arabs who were going to hunt near our village. I was hardly listening to the driver trying to get me down, when Uncle Luis Nyok, the assistant headmaster, came and saw me. Rather than persist on his refusal, he asked the driver to let me go, but made me promise to return by the same lorry the same day.

When I got to my mother's hut, she had delivered, but the baby had died. Because of the combination of her sickness with the rituals of mourning her baby, she lay in an ashy skin on the ground. Her dusty body matched her surroundings. A fire was burning by her side, and my cousin, Ajang, was with her. When my mother sat up and I had a better view of her, I saw her reduced to skin and bones in that short period. I would have cried had I not known that it had nearly been worse.

The baby would have been my first full brother, all the rest being girls. I saw the little grave near the hut and Ajang and others had a lot to say about the most beautiful baby he had been. I felt a dim sense of loss which I did not allow to sink into my consciousness. Simply grateful that my mother was alive, I buried my brothers' death and did not reflect on it. When my mother spoke to me, her voice was full of the love I knew she felt for me. She told me that I should have attended to my studies and that death had passed.

Although I had undertaken to return, I knew that would depend on the condition I would find my mother in. But my mother herself urged me to return and work for my forthcoming examination. I never told my mother about my prayers, although I continued to be convinced that they saved her life. For a long time afterwards, whenever I did not pray or when I sinned, I felt a deep sense of guilt and betrayal in front of God and renewed my pledge of gratitude for my mother's life. It was not until much later in my adolescence that I realsed I was carrying out an impossible undertaking.

Despite all the challenges which confronted our teachers and supportive tribal leaders, Abyei Elementary School was a solid foundation for education in the Ngok Dinka area. And it would over the years produce a flow of pupils who would play important roles in the history, not only of the Ngok Dinka, but indeed of the Sudan. Many years later, in my interaction with our legendary headmaster, Lino Wuor Abyei, I saw in him great joy in seeing the fruits of his pioneering contribution to the education of his people. I was particularly delighted to receive a letter from him when I was working on the biography of my father, *The Man Called Deng Majok,* in which he recounted the challenges they confronted in pioneering education in the area, the pivotal support they received from Chief Deng Majok, whom he referred to as "my brother," and the great satisfaction he felt in seeing his students rise to high levels of education and public service at home and abroad.

Ayong Mayom, the Author's cousin and schoolmate at Abyei Elementary School.

The Author's uncle Luis Nyok Kuol, Assistant Headmaster of Abyei Elementary School, sibling brother of Deng Makuei (Abot), Deputy Paramount Chief..

Lino Wuor Abyei, First Headmaster, Abyei Elementary School.

CHAPTER SIX

AWAY
WHILE WOMEN CRIED

Although we did well in the examination, and I shared the first position with Kuaja Deng Kuei, the oldest boy in the class, only four older students, including our cousins, Ayong Monyyom, Atem Malai and Deng Aguer, were promoted to Kwajok Missionary School, the first and best known missionary educational institution among the Dinka of Bahr el Ghazal Province in the South. We were said to be too young and would have to wait another year.

Shortly after the senior pupils were gone, Mr Ramshaw, the British Senior Inspector of Education for the Southern Provinces, came to Abyei on an inspection tour. Although the Ngok Dinka were in a Northern province, they fell under the Southern educational system. My father was away at Tongliet attending an intertribal assembly of chiefs and administrators when Mr Ramshaw came to our school. Although we were not given the details of what went on, it was obvious that he was surprised to see us left behind. The instructions that reached us that day in school were that Chan, Bol and myself were to leave with Mr Ramshaw that same day. Kuol was to stay behind.

We were told that we did not have enough time to go home. As we did not have possessions other than the clothes we wore, going home was not really necessary. Some boys ran to tell the women we were being taken away. They rushed back to say that the women were in tears and that we must go to bid them goodbye. It was against the law of the house for them to come to school. We asked the authorities, but were refused. The boys rushed back and returned with food. We ate and left. We were not going straight to school. The Inspector had to get our father's permission first. So, we went to Tongliet, driving on the beaten track which tribes repaired every dry season, still barely a road. Tongliet was a crowded "town" of temporary shelters for the large gathering of neighbouring tribes and administrative representatives of the provincial and central governments.

Our father was at first reluctant about sending us to the South, but Mr Ramshaw convinced him that by having some of his children educated in the South and some in the North, my father would strengthen his position on both grounds. Educating all in one part would be like putting all his eggs in one basket.

That was our first major departure from home, from our father, and from our mothers and step-mothers. As we bade them farewell, the junior wives who had come with our father also cried. Mr Ramshaw left for Wau, the capital of Bahr el Ghazal Province before we left Tongliet. Our journey on the other hand ended in Kwajok, where our cousins had gone with the senior boys.

Kwajok was a booming Catholic missionary centre, the largest in Dinkaland. I recall vividly the modern buildings, the lush gardens of mangoes, pawpaws, bananas, guavas, oranges, lemon trees and other tropical plants, with flowers lining the lanes and paths. The impressive sight of the church, and the priests and nuns in their long, spotless white robes, all made Kwajok look like something of a paradise.

The school children were more modestly clothed in shorts or aprons without shirts, but adorned with rosary beads, the cross and other religious medals hanging from their necks. The ritual of prayers recited in the church, at meal time, or while walking the paths in the late afternoon, was a characteristic feature of the place. In the classroom, it was obvious that our Abyei schooling had prepared us well for the next step up the educational ladder.

We had stayed only a few days in Kwajok when one day Mr Ramshaw suddenly appeared in the classroom and announced that there had been a mistake. The three of us, Chan, Bol and myself, and one of the first arrivals, Atem Malai, a son of a subchief, were to go to Tonj Primary School. We were asked to be ready to leave immediately with Mr Ramshaw, first for Wau and then to Tonj.

We were overwhelmed by Wau: the size, the red rocky soil, the strange people, all in all, a totally foreign and intimidating place. In Mr Ramshaw's house, Bol and I shared a room with a non-Dinka servant from the group of tribes the Dinka called Nyamnyam, partly because they are believed to be cannibals. We had seen a few of them in Abyei and had feared them even there. In Wau, we saw them in large numbers, some with filed teeth. We never slept that night. Whenever the servant turned or moved and his bed creaked, we felt that the moment of reckoning had come; he was about to jump on us and break our necks. The morning brought great relief: we were on our way to Tonj.

After Wau - a provincial capital - Tonj was quite small. But the school was very impressive beyond anything we had seen before. The layout was extensive. The main compound comprised a large horseshoe of four spread out "villages," each with four dormitories. Each dormitory boarded eight to ten pupils. Two extension villages were later added on either side of the horseshoe. On the opposite side of the villages stood the school - an enormous building on which focused the entire combination. In the centre was a widespread empty space. Parts of this comprised the assembly grounds. Parts were cleared for cultivation. And the rest remained virgin land. Outside the main compound lay the houses of the teachers and other employees. The football field also lay outside the main school compound.

Tonj Primary School was the first government school to be opened among the Bahr el Ghazal Dinka in 1944. Abyei preceded it by one year, but in quality, Tonj was "special." It was meant to prepare sons of chiefs and government officials for future leadership in the modern Sudan. An informal song the boys used to sing at Tonj comprised the words:

*Tonj Schoolboys,
Sons of Chiefs
You will be the Kings of the Sudan.*

To prepare them for this role, the school had to be excellent in scholarship, military-like in discipline, and a bridge between the old system that gave legitimacy to their status and the new world in which they were to lead. The headmaster, Eric Daniels, was, we heard and never doubted, a former military officer and a war veteran. Mr Daniels was a huge man whose shirts were constantly soaked with sweat. In line with his reputed career, he was a man for utmost discipline and respect for order, but was by no means unkind. He could shift from a gentle smile to fury, each one suiting him according to the circumstances. His Sudanese colleagues and subordinates were of a somewhat similar nature. The assistant headmaster, Alfred Kotjak, was a Dinka of average height, medium size, and a powerful character. He was one of the first Southerners to achieve that level of education in Uganda. The sight of Kotjak or the sound of his distinctive whistling, invoked in pupils' fear, respect and submission. He was nicknamed "The Hawk." Tonj was an institution in which toughness was an important yardstick for measuring importance.

It was because Tonj was meant to be a bridge between tradition and modernisation that the dormitories were grouped into "villages." Being a Dinka school and the Dinka being lovers of, and dependents on, cattle, each pupil was expected to bring at least a cow from his family and the school kept a big herd for milk. In view of the distance involved, we were excused. It was the law of the school that pupils should go naked, except the pupils in senior classes, from fourth to sixth year, who could wear clothes or go naked as they pleased. The administration was organised on lines comparable to tribal administration. The head of the administrative hierarchy was the Big Chief, *Bënydït*, the equivalent of paramount chief. Each village had a chief, *bëny*, who was assisted by the chiefs of the dormitories - something like the chiefs and subchiefs of subtribes and sections. The chiefs were students from the upper classes.

A position akin to that of a deputy paramount chief rotated weekly among the village chiefs. The chief on duty was answerable to the permanent paramount chief, who was answerable to the teacher on duty. Of course, Mr Daniels headed the whole hierarchy. These were the principal elements of the power structure, but there were many other collateral and subsidiary elements in the complex. For instance, the chiefs of the dormitories had assistants who were only known within the village and with a power limited to the particular dormitory. There were also "policemen" whose significance was relative to the level of their operation.

There was a lot to be learned in the classroom at Tonj. Although it was felt that Atem Malai could proceed to Class V, we were considered still too young and were placed in Class IV, where we were still the youngest, about nine years old. Chan, alas, did not stay long. He had a bad epileptic convulsion one night and the headmaster decided to send him back home.

As one might expect, there was as much beating in the class as there was excitement in teaching and learning. Kotjak would begin his arithmetic classes at the door by asking questions which had to be answered in a split second or passed on. Failure to provide the correct answers invited a look of disapproval from Kotjak and might end up with a number of lashes on the hands and perhaps on the buttocks. Sometimes, it took the form of a game where people stood in grading line, changing positions according to their scores.

Neither of the teachers was really an exception to the rule of physical correction for learning. Luckily, neither Bol nor I experienced beating in the class. In sharp contrast, a boy by the name of Gum Maluach was constantly lashed. Gum, a son of a police officer, was ironically quite bright, judging from anything but performance in the class. And even there, he was very witty in his ignorance. His responses to the habitual beating were almost theatrical. Gum either enjoyed the attention, or was willing to pay the price, or the threat of punishment simply erased his mind whenever he was asked. He rarely gave a correct answer to any question. It was as though Alfred

Kotjak enjoyed exercising his right arm on Gum; in any case, they both entertained the class in a sadistic way.

The real drama of Tonj life was outside the class. A glance at a few features of daily activities, expectation, and apprehensions will illustrate the extent to which Tonj was as much a military training center as it was a primary school. A typical day began at about six, when the drums beat. The first drum beat announced that it was time to get up and be ready for the rollcall. About half an hour later, the drums beat again and everyone had to run to the assembly ground in the centre of the school complex. Again, we were allowed a few minutes to reach it. During these minutes, the air was filled with cries of "hurry up" from everywhere. Most boys hardly knew the English combination of "hurry" and "up" and simply pronounced it as "*arriyɔ́p*" (arriyop) a new word, I thought. The head chiefs, the prefect on duty, and his subordinates, would all have arrived before everyone and would themselves be shouting orders at people to "run," "hurry," and the like.

The teacher on duty would also have arrived, but he was not bound to be there that early, as long as he came during the rollcall. About five to ten minutes after the final beating of the drums, the prefects on duty lined themselves up in all directions, ready to stop the late arrivals. They had a number of choices: lash them on the spot, jot their names down for later punishment of the same or another kind, leave them if they had good excuses, which was rare, or perhaps just warn them and forgive them — even rarer.

Then the rollcall began. As everyone stood alert to hear the orders, the prefect on duty, standing erect and motionless at a military "attention," gave the "Markers, fall in" order. The prefects of the dormitories fell in. After some "rests," "attentions," "about turns, "quick marches" and other orders, they stood "at ease" scattered according to a special order waiting to be joined by their men. Then the "school, fall in" order was given and every pupil joined the line of his dormitory forming to the left of their prefect.

Then the prefect on duty shouted at the peak of his voice a long order, the words of which I never understood. All I could hear were such words as "guards" and "correct." Then followed an impressive few steps forward march of all the dormitory prefects, a left turn, and a few more steps, another left turn and a few more steps, another left turn and a stop facing their men — all done with perfect rhythm of the loud military-like stamping of feet on the ground. The slightest disharmony and the "As you were" order was given. Actually, there were usually many "As you weres" and other repetitions, just to make the whole thing more elaborate and more impressive.

When no "As you were" brought the prefects back into their lines, they each shouted something like "arridain steady" which I never understood, but probably meant "ready" and "steady." Then they each gave other orders to their men and the whole atmosphere was filled with mutually independent shouts, echoes, answers, and counts of "One, two, three, four" and on as each pupil announced his number in the order of standing. With the many repetitions there were, the place soon turned into a mad house, then slowly returned to normal, until there was dead silence.

The prefect on duty then gave orders which were responded to by the prefects one by one reporting on their men's attendance. Standing at an "Attention," a prefect might say "All present and correct," if it were so, or give such details as "Six present, one in the dispensary, one absent," or whatever the facts happened to be. The prefect took down appropriate notes. When all was completed, he made a military march to the head prefect, stopped, saluted and then gave his report. Sometimes, he reported directly to the master on duty or else the head prefect reported to the master following the same military procedure.

The prefect on duty then got feedback orders of the morning's work assignments. He would normally know well in advance what was to be done so that the feedback orders were only additions or some matters of detail. After walking around informally assigning the prefects and their boys to various functions and leaving them time to make their own reassignments, he returned to his command position and after a few "rests" and "attentions" gave the dispersal order.

For a period of about two hours the pupils would engage in intensive menial work. This included digging the ditches for drainage; cutting down trees; digging out their roots and levelling down ant hills to prepare playing grounds; drawing water from deep wells; sweeping the school compound; cutting the grass with sickles; ploughing the fields for cultivation; or any one of the many different assignments, according to the season and the particular circumstances.

Whatever the work, prefects and other leaders stood nearby supervising and policing. The stop and stretch which was a necessity, in view of the incessant stooping and back-cracking physical strain of the labour, would be noticed with displeasure; to stop for a little more than to stretch would mean having one's name jotted down for later punishment, getting caned in the back by a surprise visitor, or even getting sentenced to lashes, which were executed on the spot. To be safe, one worked non-stop, and if one needed some relief, one had to look carefully in all directions before sneaking into it. One could get leave to answer a call of nature, but then time was marked.

Naturally, the nature of the job determined how harsh menial work was. Those who worked in the houses of the teachers were lucky. So were those who went to water the calves and otherwise take care of the cows. And there were even better ones, like taking food to Mr Daniel's babysitter, who, apparently, did not share in their food at home.

During the cultivation period, certain times or days were allowed for the pupils to work in their own fields. Two pupils owned a field jointly on which they grew mostly groundnuts (peanuts) which the school bought from them with cash. My partner was Maleng Juuk from the ruling Lang Juuk family of the Twic Dinka, a very kind, gentle and dignified man who was considerably older than me and treated me well. Groundnuts formed an important ingredient of the school diet. In addition to cash motivation, pupils competed in their production just for the sake of competition. Supervision was lacking when work was in private fields. In the public sector, so to speak, one eagerly awaited the beautiful sounds of the drums which announced the end of the working hours. Then people washed and had breakfast, often of roast peanuts, but sometimes the traditional porridge with milk.

Drums beat again at about nine and we ran to school. Depending on the weather, the school would assemble under a tree or in the huge assembly hall in the main building. This was not a military parade, but a meeting in which one stood or sat anywhere one pleased. The masters stood in front of the assembly. The assembly always began with prayers and although about half of the pupils were Catholics, the "official religion" of the school appeared to have been Protestant. And so were the prayers and hymns. Usually, they were led by Alfred Kotjak and included singing of some Dinka hymns.

Singing was what most of us enjoyed in those prayers. Alfred Kotjak spent a great deal of his private time teaching us the hymns and training a special choir, many of whom were Catholics, including Bol and me. We usually had our lessons in the evenings at Alfred Kotjak's residence. It was this specially trained group which made the hymn singing an enjoyable part of the morning prayers. Despite the emphasis on prayers, religion was not taught at Tonj and to that extent, it was neutral along confessional lines.

After the prayers, we sat and Mr Daniels or anyone of the other masters made whatever announcements they wanted to make. Kotjak was the interpreter. Then classes began and continued until about two o'clock in the afternoon, when it was time to go to the villages for lunch. Students ate by dormitories, with several sharing a dish, using hands or spoons depending on the food. Rank or how much one was favoured by the prefects also counted in who shared with whom. The prefects got such special privileges as more milk and a smaller sharing group. Eating with them was therefore a privilege which only a few got.

No sooner would people eat than they were called to the village assembly. Minor internal affairs were discussed in a hurry, and all were put to the village work, which usually entailed clearing and sweeping the compound. Only occasionally was lunch followed with a brief rest, which was soon interrupted by the four o'clock announcement by drum beat for a general assembly of the same nature as that of the morning.

The main objective of that assembly was the afternoon work, which continued until six. That was the time for the main parade of the day and all the details of rollcall were strictly followed. The master on duty might miss the morning and afternoon rollcall for their main objective was to send boys to work, but he would hardly ever miss the evening rollcall.

When it ended, the boys went to the villages for dinner, usually followed by one internal meeting or another — if not of the whole village, at least of the dormitories. Strictness and show of authority were equally reflected on all levels of meetings from the overall school assembly to the meetings of dormitories. Work, whether on the overall school level or inside the various dormitories, was equally demanding and strenuous.

By about eight, the drums would beat for the small boys to go to bed. Nine was the deadline for all, and prefects went around making sure that the hurricane lamps, the only source of light, were out and everyone was quietly in bed. Anyone talking was identified and his name written down for later punishment.

Saturday was a very special day. That was the day of the inspection in which villages competed for personal and environmental cleanliness. A great deal of the week went into the cleaning of the dormitories and the compounds. And, of course, personal cleanliness was regularly observed. All this became most intense on Friday into Saturday. People hardly slept on Friday night. On Saturday they would wake up very early for the final hour. Blankets were washed and dried. The floors of the dormitories were washed; the walls and the open ceilings were cleared of the most inconspicuous spiderwebs that had evaded the eye during the week; the compound was swept so much that the slightest fragment of grass became disturbing litter. Personal clothes were thoroughly washed, dried and ironed to the point where the fibre weaving hardly showed.

But since at inspection time all the pupils had to be naked, a great deal of work went into one's own body. The large pools near the well in each village were filled with water and the children plunged into them to bathe. They washed with soap, rubbing each other's back until the skin nearly peeled off. But to leave a dry cracking gray skin would not have been "clean" and yet to use oil would be considered "dirty." Many would rub on soap in the end, but that too had to be so light as not to show when the rubbing test was made on the skin by the inspectors. The ears, the nose, the hair, the nails, the teeth, everything was carefully cleaned because everything was to be carefully inspected.

Then came the big hour starting around nine. The inspecting team, which included all the masters with Mr Daniels at the head, started the march from the school headquarters. It was a matter of grave concern where they started and I don't remember if any principle was applied to the choice. Once the starting point was known, the rest followed according to the geographical order of the villages and the dormitories. As they approached a village, pupils stood in rows in front of their dormitories, while the village prefect met the inspectors and escorted them around. Each dormitory prefect, when approached, gave the "rest" and "attention" orders and prepared his group for the drama.

One by one, the inspectors went around the pupils inspecting everyone with the utmost meticulousness. Using fingers and handkerchiefs, they rubbed the skin to see what came off; they looked into the ears, the noses, and the eyes for anything that might have escaped what they knew had been a thorough cleaning. They opened mouths and exposed the teeth. They did everything.

Then they went inside the dormitories. How really tidy were the beddings made? How well washed were the cement floors? Was there perhaps some insignificant insect at the corners of the walls or in between the large naked wooden complex supporting the ceiling? They asked themselves all questions and sought answers. All this time they took notes. With the slow pace which the strictness of their inspection required, the whole process took quite a while.

When each dormitory or each village ended, the pupils went into introspection, evaluating how so and so had stood, who was responsible for this or that, which probably subtracted marks. There were claims and counterclaims of responsibility, and, of course, anxiety as to what the final results might be. They then put on their best and cleanest clothes, if they had any, and waited for the general assembly to follow the inspection. When all the villages were done, the inspectors met for consideration and judgement. Then the drums beat for the general assembly, where the results were to be announced.

But instead of rushing onto the scene, each village, lined up by dormitories, came marching orderly and singing marching songs to boost their expectations. The result soon divided the mood into one of excited pleasure and proud marching and singing on the one hand, and disappointed gloomy march back for further internal squabbles on the other hand. The winners would receive a silver cup and had a special meal for a feast. But above all, they had the privilege to march everywhere, including into town, singing. This is one of the songs they would sing:

Dirty pigs, look at us,
Clean boys, march along,
Clean boys, march along,
Hurrah, hurrah,
March along,
March along.

Given the frequent beating or the threat of it, the regular back aching labour, and the unceasing intimidation, it is not surprising that a great number of Tonj boys wet their beds. In fact, this was one of the major problems at Tonj. Of course, children were punished — usually beaten — for it, and the more they were beaten the more they wetted their beddings. It was a most embarrassing, though unavoidable consequence of life in Tonj, and yet nobody realised this point; if they did, I never heard it expressed.

Sports were also important at Tonj, and two days a week were set aside for some pupils to play in alternation for the work. That was compulsory, and since it was instead of work it had to be taken seriously. The games were football (soccer) and hockey. There were also competitions between the villages, but to the best of my memory, not as consequential as the Saturday cleanliness contests. Matches against the town were more exciting, and when the school won, drew a demonstration similar to that of the winning villages in the cleanliness contest.

Save for the evening rollcall or any ideas a village prefect might have, Saturdays were free after the inspection. Sometimes, boys were permitted to dance and the hours before going to bed were relaxed. By dancing, I mean Dinka traditional dance. Girls — daughters or sisters of school workers — were allowed to join and that gave the dances special attraction. Although the main dances were Rek and Twic, other Dinka too could represent their own dances. The Ngok dance was the most unusual of all – so different that it was exotic. As years went by, the number of Ngok boys increased and so did the quality of our show. Everyone begged us to perform and even though we were neither skilled in singing nor in dancing, we took pride in responding.

Saturday evenings had another distinctive feature. It was then that the "supreme court" met to hear appeals and other important cases; civil and criminal alike. Village prefects were permanent members of the court and the rest of the memberships rotated between dormitory prefects. I am not sure whether the presidency of the court rotated with duty among the village prefects or whether it was permanently vested in the head prefect. As the court was open, any number of spectators was permitted attendance. A number of policemen maintained order. The procedure was just like in any other Dinka court and the offenders were sentenced to hard labour or to lashes.

The only relaxing day was Sunday, which most boys spent bathing in the Jur River, where there was a steep cliff on the bank for diving. On Monday morning, an extraordinary meeting was held inside the assembly hall in which important matters were discussed and those who had been sentenced on Saturday by the court were lashed. Mr Daniels usually administered the lashes, but Mr Kotjak sometimes took his place. The convict went before the assembly, pulled down his shorts, if he wore any, and lay to receive the punishment. A long whip was used and a great force was applied. Sometimes buttocks bled; whip marks always showed in swollen lines that sometimes opened into wounds which left scars.

I got a beating once because of a fight I had with a boy called Akot Kuach who was much older than me, and was one class senior to me. He was also a dormitory prefect. I provoked the fight quite unwittingly by remarking about Akot's shorts that if dirt showed on khaki, as it did on his pair, it must be really dirty. Somehow, I thought I was making a joking statement of fact, and perhaps an indirect advice, but obviously a very unwise bad joke or advice; it never occurred to me that I was insulting him, especially because we were neither friends nor close acquaintances. Akot hit me without discussing my remark. We fought, if such power imbalance could be called a fight. He could have beaten me badly if we had not been stopped by the intervention of prefects. We were taken to court. Akot was sentenced to six lashes and I to five. At his initiative we surprisingly became best friends.

A strange kind of friendship existed among Tonj boys. It might be between agemates or between people of different ages, and in either case it was highly formalised with respect symbols. Friends, even of the same age, were shy in front of one another, and despite being in the same school, they communicated mostly through letters. Gifts were also exchanged.

Akot and I were less formal than was the norm. In many ways, he was like an older brother to me. But I also had experience with the formal side of friendship at Tonj. Through a curious coincidence, I picked up a piece of paper on the ground to find that it was a letter in which my name appeared. The temptation to read it was irresistible. It was from Benjamin Ajongo Unguec, a son of a leading Jur chief, and the brightest of his class, the most senior class. Ajongo was also prominent because he had an excellent voice and was the solo in the school hymn-singing, despite his being a Catholic. His letter was addressed to his best friend, who was a year my junior, asking his permission or consent to Ajongo's plan to offer me his friendship. The letter spoke of how he, Ajongo, had observed me closely, what he thought of me, and his hope that his friend would have no objection to the proposed friendship.

I had not had any idea of the intended friendship proposal. Quite the contrary, I had just had a confrontation with Ajongo and his younger brother, Unguel, and if anything, I thought he would be bitter. I had bought excellent leather shoes from Unguel for a very small amount and Ajongo objected to the sale after it had been concluded. He asked me to return the shoes and I naturally refused. They took me to the village court, alleging that the sale was too unfair to be binding. They lost, appealed, and lost again. They gave up only because they had no recourse left.

I had then transferred from Ajongo's dormitory on account of the conflict. So, the talk of friendship really baffled me. I have no idea what Ajongo's friend said in reply, but I reckon it was positive, because I got a letter offering reconciliation and friendship. I accepted. To be a friend to one did not necessarily imply being close to the friend's friends. On the contrary, jealousies were expected. Hence Ajongo's letter to his friend.

I don't know what the unconscious or the subconscious motives of such friendships were, but I know that they were totally devoid of homosexual tendencies. Homosexuality did not exist at Tonj - just as it did not exist in Dinka society. Indeed, the roots of such friendship could be attributed to a form of contractual friendship known among the traditional Dinka, whereby gifts of cattle are exchanged and while friends assist one another in the payment and share in the distribution of bride wealth as relatives, maintain certain standards of respect which are ordinarily associated with actual or potential in-law relationships.

My dormitory prefect after Ajongo was Salvatore Mawien Ariik and even after I had reconciled with Ajongo and became friends, I remained in my new dormitory. Mawien and I were friends to the extent possible with one's prefect. I had a favoured position with him and I saw to it that I deserved it. Among the other dormitory prefects, Mawien had a more powerful position, as he was the assistant to the village prefect, Wada Manyiel. Wada, too, was well-disposed towards me. All in all, my position in the village was favourable.

Bol and I also had a favourable position with the teachers. I remember one afternoon, meeting the headmaster and his wife strolling with the district commissioner and his wife, also British. Mr Daniels called me and introduced me to his companions, said some complimentary words about me, and then concluded with a teasing warning that I should not let his words get to my head, in other words spoil me. I felt proud and encouraged, rather than spoiled.

The admiration of our teachers gained for us the jealousy and dislike of some of the leading prefects who were our classmates. Not that the older students were not bright; on the contrary, some of them took top positions. However, some of the youngest in the class were also in the lead and some of the older ones who were prefects dragged far behind. We were among - if not - the youngest, and were also well up on the list in our class performance.

Our uncle, Bona Bulabek Kuol, who was younger than us, came from Abyei and joined us in Class V, where he soon excelled. Wherever he went, Bona was always top of the class; he was an acknowledged genius. There is, at least for the Dinka, an explanation for Bulabek's genius. When our grandfather, Chief Kuol Arop, was in his death-bed declaring his final will, he is said to have called for his baby son, Bulabek, to be brought to him. Putting a pencil in his hand, he said, "Son, this is what I bequeath to you. It will be your life." With such a bequest from such a divine leader, no Dinka doubted that Bulabek was destined to excel in education.

But his mother aided the magic. She brought Bulabek up to be interested in school, and when, during the early school days, he disliked learning and would run away, his mother is reported to have lured him back to school and encouraged his performance with such incentives as brewing him the native beer, which Bulabek, like all Dinka children, drank and loved. Ironically, Bulabek later became a teetotaller, and in fact throughout the time I knew him, I never saw him drink. As a young child, however, he won his mother's favour by consistently being the top. Almost throughout his life, he was top. In our class, he was also the youngest.

Alfred Kotjak made no secret of the shame he thought older boys, with notable exceptions (people like Isaiah Kulang Mabor and Joseph Lok Aguek were among the top students) should feel in the defeat by the younger boys. He would shoot some questions at the older boys; they would fail to answer; he would then make some disparaging remarks about them; and then, turn to Bulabek, saying, "Tell your older brothers the answer." Bulabek never failed him.

The conflict between the best-youngest and the worst-oldest became particularly striking in our final year when our senior classmates assumed the top leadership of the student body. It was worse when we also asserted ourselves as seniors. To give one example, beds were brought to the school for the first time. Before that, pupils all slept on the floor. Since the beds were not sufficient for all, they were supposed to be issued to the senior classes. Being in the top class, we were in the category that was considered to be among those entitled. Yet, the beds were issued to older boys in the lower classes and we were left out. I seized the opportunity in an English lesson taught by the headmaster and complained to him. Mr Daniels immediately asked the head prefect, Ngor Ajuot, why we had not received beds. Ngor explained the shortage of supply and the priority he gave to the prefects in lower classes. Mr Daniels told Ngor that we should be given beds.

Ngor knew the limits of discussion with Mr Daniels. With a "Yes, sir," he swallowed his pride, sank back into his seat, and nursed the already existing resentment which my complaint had just aggravated. That evening, in the public rollcall, Ngor, in a language unmistakably aimed at us, though without mentioning our names, threatened that those who thought they could bypass him and get their way through other channels must beware of the dangers of their schemes; that he, "By the foot of my father, Ajuot," (a swearing common among the Twic Dinka and which Ngor frequently used), would face the consequences; they were bound to be the losers.

Ngor was serious and he soon made the attempt to punish us. His opportunity came with some English magazines which Mr Daniels had given to Class VI to circulate among them. They got lost and somehow, Bol and I were the last to whom they could be traced. We were taken to court and Ngor was the president. Acting as though the prosecutor, he pointed out the seriousness of our offense as the magazines belonged to the headmaster. The court's function was not so much to determine guilt as it was to pass a sentence.

Most of the members began giving sentences: some said ten lashes, others six, and yet others five. One member called Agoth Giir, son of a prominent Rek Dinka chief, Giir Thiik (otherwise known as Giir Kiro), spoke after many of his colleagues. He argued that it was premature to sentence us on the available evidence, without knowing from Mr Daniels what significance he attached to the magazines and what he himself thought of our offense. That would determine whether we were to be punished for depriving the class of the periodicals or for the loss we had caused Mr Daniels, or for both.

To most members, Agoth was complicating a very simple matter. He was outvoted and we were sentenced to five lashes each.

Sentences went to Mr Daniels early Monday before the execution time. Mr Daniels quashed the decision on the grounds that since the magazines were for us, the loss was ours. Since the magazines were not for us alone, but for the whole class, I always thought there was more to our exoneration than was stated. Obviously, we were in Mr Daniel's good book. Nonetheless, the court's main contention was that we had lost the headmaster's magazines and therefore had committed a serious offence. Had they based their argument on our having deprived our fellow classmates, Mr Daniels' reaction might have been different. As the Dinka saying goes: "Trickery returns against its originator". In Dinka folktales, the cleverness of the Fox eventually turns against the Fox. Ngor lost.

Towards the end of our final year, Tonj was supposed to send two boy scouts and their scout leader to Uganda for an international scout's camp during the long vacation. Bol and I were nominated by the school and our names were sent to Uganda. Towards the end of the year, Mr Daniels called us to say that he had been told that they could only send one person with the scout leader. One of us would have to remain. Bol had joined the scouts before me and knew more about it than I did. So, I volunteered my withdrawal.

Bol left immediately after the examinations for the scout camping. That was our first time since early childhood to be separated, even for a short time, and although the separation did not last long, it was to disturb people at home a great deal. I recall Bol's mother saying disbelievingly, "Mading, if Bol is dead, why don't you tell us the truth?"

The examination results were announced after Bol was gone. All three of us - Bulabek, Bol and I - were among the top six in a class of sixty and were admitted to Rumbek Junior Secondary School. Despite its tough discipline, hard labour, and generally repressive atmosphere, there was no question about the rigour and qualitative excellence of education at Tonj. Even the physical and psychological strains of the extreme discipline had mixed potentials; they could destroy some, weaken others, and develop in others the qualities of endurance and resilience, not to mention a bias for a more humane treatment of other people. For us, Tonj was also a major first step in the extension of our horizons to the wider world of the Dinka and the South. In fact, one of the emotional strains of Tonj was the isolation from home and our people. Naturally, we did not return to Ngokland during the short vacations and for the whole academic year, we remained in school. Tonj was in Dinka territory, but no Ngok Dinka was to be seen anywhere in sight.

Indeed, a very important aspect of our schooling at Tonj was that we were not only isolated from our tribal context, but were in another context in which there were many children whose fathers were prominent chiefs. And although we felt that there was no match for our father as a chief, the situation did not flatter us specifically as sons of a chief. Nearly all the children were sons of chiefs. And although their elders probably knew the leadership role our family had played in the history of the Dinka as a whole, those boys were obviously not aware of that role, except perhaps vaguely. Unlike us, they were close enough to be provided with cattle by their families. And, of course, cattle were a symbol of status among the Dinka. Admittedly, our not having cows in school was on account of distance, but those details were mostly unknown to the other children and might be seen as only excuses; the fact was that we did not possess cows, and for the Dinka, that could be significant.

As compared to our brothers who were close to home and Father, and whom he so lavishly provided to the point where they were conscious of their higher status as sons of the paramount chief, the situation at Tonj had a humbling effect on us. It reinforced our own tendency to be self-reliant, largely independent of our father's image as paramount chief, but propelled by the objective of proving ourselves through education, not least to our father, our family, and our tribe. Another aspect was that within the Southern context, we became more conscious of our Northern connection, so much so that when Northern teachers were later transferred to Tonj to start the teaching of Arabic, we felt some affinity with them. The fact that one of them was from Kordofan, our province, gave the affinity an element of nostalgia.

I recall a visit by the first minister for Education, Abdel Rahman Ali Taha, with the new teachers from the North. One of them, Sheikh Idris, was to supersede Kotjak as the assistant headmaster. Somehow, I was introduced as one of the boys from Kordofan. We had a few minutes' conversation in which the minister asked me why some boys were naked. It is unlikely that they had not investigated earlier. Anyway, I explained to him that it was part of the school policy. With a nationalistic oversimplification, we agreed that it was part of the colonialist plot to keep the South backward in order to impede the progress towards independence. Before he left, Minister Abdel Rahman Ali Taha gave orders that all pupils be clothed with a uniform to be provided by the government.

There was more to our feeling of isolation than mere lack of contact with home. Although our people loathed and detested many Arab ways, they had come to regard Arab civilisation, especially as represented by the urban Arab from further North, as one from which they could benefit. Both our family and the tribe at large had adopted and adapted to Arab culture quite considerably, though also preserving what they saw as the essence and the best in their own culture and way of life and remaining unassimilated and distinctly Dinka. So, we also missed home from the cultural point of view.

Vacations back home were always a well-earned relief from the hardships of schooling at Tonj. Indeed, I have never enjoyed the idea of vacation as much as I did at Tonj. The journey home was not easy. Lorries took us as far as Gogrial, at best Wunrok. We would then cover the rest of the distance, on foot.

In many places, our way was so flooded that we walked for miles without a dry spot. Wild animals were a constant threat. Quite often, people advised us not to enter a particular forest because a lion, a buffalo, a rhino, or some other ferocious beasts were known to attack people from a particular danger spot. Sometimes, we found newly dropped dung or the urine of a beast still steaming. We sometimes saw them. This was quite apart from snakes, mosquitoes, and other dangerous or disturbing creatures.

The first Ngok villages always brought a sense of relief. We were met with hospitality wherever we stopped. Animals were slaughtered and food prepared in plenty. We sometimes deviated slightly to visit the relatives of some boys who were on the way, but as a rule, we first all went to our homes at Abyei and Noong and then dispersed, or accompanied our colleagues to their various homes. We always received warm welcome and lavish hospitality wherever we went.

Our first return home was most dramatic. At Abyei, we arrived in the evening. The women – Father's wives, our sisters and other relatives – tossed us about from hand to hand, and from lips to lips until we were simply worn out. Some cried with joy while others hushed them into silence that crying was a bad omen. As we got into the female enclosure in the evening, lamps and torches were brought to see how the year away had changed us. The older women at Noong were even more uninhibited in demonstrating their welcoming affection. But our own mothers coated everything with a cold reception in line with the usual symbols of restrained mother-child affection which represented either appropriate modesty or a way of deflecting evil eyes.

Our vacation time was mostly spent where our father was at Abyei, although we occasionally visited our mothers at Noong and stayed with them for some time. Wherever we were, we more or less drifted back into our previous life style, but with an enhanced status. Our time mostly passed on games of cards, especially "Whist," keeping the records of taxation for our father, and writing his personal and official correspondence. When we were home, my father's clerk, an Arabised Southerner from Bahr el Ghazal by the name of Fodul, had very little to do beyond the official registry of court cases.

It was during our first vacation back home that we went by a lorry through the hundred and thirty miles of beaten track that links Abyei with the Arab town of Muglad. With the beating from the entangled thorny trees through which the lorry went, searching for passable areas, the shaking of the lorry due to the roughness of the road, and the frequent stopping and getting down to push the lorry when the it got stuck in the sand, the journey was as tiring as it was exciting. When we arrived, our first observations of a Northern town were overwhelming: people in white robes, shops crowded with consumer items, topless Baggara Arab girls with brown, erect and shining breasts, urban women veiled in refined fabric, and youthful rogues displaying their sensuality to draw the attention of females. All in all, Muglad seemed a place for excitement. Little did I know that this was only a faint picture of Northern culture and that in the deep North, the Baggara were reputed as uninhibited, un-Islamic, and more "African" than most Sudanese "Arabs."

The Baggara themselves did not doubt their Arabism. With some of them as black as the Dinka and occasionally blacker, most of them trace their ancestry to Arabia, speak an Arabic dialect that is as distorted as it has remained classical, and consider their neighbours and maternal uncles, the Dinka, as *abiid*, slaves, merely because their Arab ancestors had raided them for slaves. It never occurred to them, as indeed it doesn't to most Northern Sudanese, that the Dinka and other Southerners are the remnants of a raided field, the descendants of still free men and women, while they, the Northerners, are, for the most part, the products of captured or otherwise assimilated African men and women. Many, if not most of them, are descended from slaves, at least on one parental side, but passing as Arabs, thanks to the liberal and fluid concept of Arabism. The more threatening that reality, the greater the myths of distortion; the Baggara had to make greater underdogs of their Southern neighbours to feel proud as passing overlords.

As we were walking the narrow, sandy and trashy streets of Muglad, we came across a group of small children who made us realise that this racial complex was more than skin deep. With their worn-out garments, they were as dirty as their muddy surroundings. As we passed near them, one with an imbecilic smile on his face said something we thought was "*thayibiin*," a local greeting which means, "Are you in good health?" We responded accordingly. To our surprise and dismay, our cousin Kooch Aguer, Deng Aguer's brother, who was among our relatives in Muglad Elementary School, walked towards the boy and slapped him on the face. The boy cried pitifully while Kooch returned to explain that he had insulted us as *abiid,* Arabic for "slaves." We all laughed in angry humour and lost sympathy for the boy, even though he was of course only a mirror of his society.

While Women Cried

Although we no longer looked after cattle and hardly ever visited the cattle-camp, we spent a brief part of our last vacation from Tonj in the cattle camp in 1951, but more as outside insiders than as participants in our Dinka culture. The cattle camp was in the extensive open grassland called the *toch*, quite a long way from Abyei. We travelled on horseback and our luggage was carried by donkeys. We took flour, tea, sugar, and beddings, all of which was amusingly odd in the eyes of the Dinka to whom the pleasure of camp life went hand in hand with its rustic hardship and endurance. But we had become accepted as cultural renegades. We fussed about many things which confirmed our departure from our indigenous culture. We insisted on our milk being filtered and boiled instead of drinking it warm and fresh from the cow's udder, which amused our people who considered fresh milk healthy and proper.

We had been in the cattle camp for weeks when we began to run out of our supplies. Since menstruating women do not drink cows' milk or eat dairy food, our sisters had been sharing our flour with the menstruating girls in the cattle camp. Our tea, too, was broadly shared. The camp was also to move further away from home. But life in the camp had become too exciting to give up for reasons of mere shortage of flour or tea, and we knew our school dates left us a few more days. We pondered whether to go home or to move with the camp. Then an unexpected message came from our father that we should return promptly to join him on his planned tour to the South on our way back to school. We of course had to heed our father's call. We bade the camp farewell and headed home.

CHAPTER SEVEN

FARTHER
AMONG THE BLUE BOYS

WHEN WE REACHED HOME, WE FOUND OUR FATHER PREPARING TO LEAVE for the South. And as he had suggested, we were to go with him. That year, the Government had given the Ngok Dinka the option of disaffiliating themselves from Kordofan and joining either of the neighbouring Southern provinces: Bahr el Ghazal or Upper Nile. Father was disinclined to the idea, but would think it over. To facilitate his decision, he was invited to tour the South to familiarise himself with the conditions in the region. He was accompanied by a number of his subordinate chiefs.

The excitement of promotion to a higher school combined with the glamour of going with our father on the trip was an unusual treat. We went to Aweil, Gogrial, and Wau, the headquarters of Bahr el Ghazal Province, which we had first seen on our way to Tonj in 1948. At Wau, we were accommodated in the Province Rest House, a modern building which appeared luxurious to us. Wherever we went, Father and his delegation were very well received. In Wau itself, Father was warmly welcomed by the governor, Richard Owen, who had been our district commissioner in Western Kordofan, and who encouraged the Ngok Dinka rejoining their kith and kin in the South. From Wau, we proceeded to Tonj and put up in the government resthouse.

Father's programme at Tonj included a visit to our primary school and the newly established teachers training school. Eric Daniels, the headmaster, and the assistant headmaster, Sheikh Idris, were to meet him and his team and take them around. For some reason, Father and company were delayed in the district headquarters. We accompanied them when they went to the school. As we approached his office, Mr Daniels stepped out to meet us. At first, I thought it was a gesture of warm welcome, but the look on his face and his disorderly hair told me that he was in an angry mood. With an English intonation, he greeted my father in Dinka, and then asked me to tell him that they were very late, that he had been waiting for nearly an hour, and that he had another engagement. He had to leave; Sheikh Idris would take care of them.

Without waiting for an explanation, he was gone. My father could not have been more negatively impressed, but he concealed it; he apologised to Sheikh Idris and explained their delay. Sheikh Idris, a smiling dignified gentleman, in turn apologised for the headmaster's conduct. After taking the delegation around, he invited them for tea in his house where the other Arabic teacher joined the group. Between the Arab teachers and the visiting Ngok leaders was a mutual identification as "Northerners", which put them apart from the Southern environment into which the visit was meant to attract them.

The next morning, Bol and I returned to the school and found Mr Daniels quite receptive and responsive. He even asked us to convey his apologies to our father and hoped they would be in Tonj long enough for him to see them again. Sheikh Idris must have said something to the headmaster about his earlier conduct.

But Father was ready to move on. Early the following day, the lorry was loaded and we moved to the district commissioner's office, ready to proceed on our way to Rumbek. To our surprise, Father changed his plans; he would go back to Wau and from there return home. He never quite explained what the matter was. I later got to learn that he felt that he had been away from his area for far too long and that it was a season of migration into his area by cattle herders from both the North and the South, with security challenges. But we ourselves had little doubt that the trip had failed. Father's predisposition against leaving Kordofan was strengthened rather than weakened by the tour.

Shortly after our father was gone, we left for Rumbek. In our eyes, Rumbek was a complex of new, modern and beautiful buildings. It was an amalgamation of two schools, for us, flatteringly termed junior and senior secondary school, instead of intermediate and secondary, which were the terms then in use throughout the country. At Atar in Upper Nile Province, where the school had been founded, boys at the junior level had worn a blue uniform, which had distinguished them from the unrestricted senior students. Atar senior boys had taken advantage of this and had condescendingly referred to the junior boys as "Blue Boys." This term was applied by the senior secondary school students to the junior secondary (intermediate) school students at Rumbek.

Although "Blue Boys" had a derogatory origin and was used as such in Rumbek, it lost its significance. To me, the label came to connote junior, but privileged boys of noble birth, although I never shared that interpretation with anyone. In view of the Tonj Primary School requirements of chiefly background, this understanding was natural. But there was more to it, for we were treated in Rumbek as almost the equals of the senior students. Residence was segregated in that two blocks belonged to the seniors and the other two to the juniors. But there were no differences in their construction and no discrimination in the provision of services.

Some of the most senior members of the staff were housemasters for the junior blocks, while their juniors were sometimes housemasters for the senior blocks. Classes were naturally segregated, but the same staff taught both. In one subject - Arabic - the junior and the senior schools were amalgamated and divided into "sets." There were seven sets, from special set at the top to set six at the bottom.

A student in fourth year senior secondary, who had not learned Arabic earlier, found himself with boys from the first year junior secondary. Bulabek and I were in the special set; I thought Bol was with us, but he later corrected me that he was not. He must then have been in set one.

Except for the morning assembly, which was conducted with a military-like discipline, Rumbek was totally different from Tonj. There were classes in the morning and preparation in the evenings; otherwise, the students were free. Although there were prefects — from head prefect to prefects of the blocks and the dormitories — their function was largely that of oversight, guidance and coordinating between the authorities and the students. Their authority was far from oppressive.

With all the ease and peace that Rumbek offered, instead of the strains and tensions of Tonj, it was not difficult to assimilate quickly into the Rumbek atmosphere. I found the classes quite exciting and as a cause or a consequence of that, I liked nearly all my teachers. My main delight was English, which was taught by Mrs Williams, the wife of the headmaster, a distinguished character in her own right. Mrs Williams was a chain smoker and she coughed a great deal. Although a bit overweight, she seemed healthy and vigorous in whatever she did. She walked as though she raced with time. Thorough in teaching and in discipline, she sometimes seemed more powerful than her husband. In the classroom, she made the subject extremely interesting, at least to me

But Mrs Williams was as feared as her classes were entertaining. Her discipline was sometimes capricious. I remember an occasion in the class when she was talking to a student who had not done his homework. She told him that it had to be done by a certain time and the boy answered, "Alright." To our stunning surprise, Mrs Williams screamed at him with anger: "Don't you ever say 'alright' to me, you silly boy!" Since that time, I don't think I have ever said "alright" to my seniors, or, for that matter, to anybody.

Feared as she was, I had nothing but pleasure from Mrs Williams' classes and she had an obvious liking for me. I think I am right in saying that I was invariably the best of my class in English. Once, Mrs Williams escorted into the class a young, tall and handsome teacher called Mr Vanstone. It was clear that she liked the man. After introducing Mr Vanstone to the class, she turned to me and said, "Francis, I can rely on you to be of help to Mr Vanstone," then she asked me to prepare a plan of the class with the names of the students in their sitting order to guide Mr Vanstone. As I was not the class monitor who should normally perform such functions, I thought it was a confirmation of her positive attitude towards me.

Mr Williams, the headmaster, was a tallish man on the heavier side, who had a peculiar, but distinguished, way of walking with hands folded and head sharply tilted to the left. He had a rather violent face and flashing eyes when he was angry. When he smiled or laughed, which he often did, his face appeared to be masked with a chronic apprehension that seemed as frightened as it was frightening. But this was more in appearance, for in reality Mr Williams was a kind and gentle person, at least as I saw him.

As far as I was concerned, Mr Williams seemed to share the mutual affection between his wife and me. Perhaps his attitude was influenced by her, but he sometimes took his wife's classes and was for a brief time our regular English teacher. So, we also had independent contact. One day, during our first year, while we were having an English lesson with his wife, a messenger came in and handed her a note. Then she told me that I was wanted in the headmaster's office. My heart beat with a sudden apprehension: something terrible must have happened, presumably bad news from home. But why was Bol not coming with me? Then I thought there might be a telegram about my mother. Was she dead? All these thoughts crossed my mind in less than a minute, for the headmaster's office was very close to our classroom. When I got into his office, there was a Dinka man – presumably a labourer - standing in front of Mr Williams. Within seconds, I knew I was needed to interpret. I did it with concealed excitement. In a school in which the Dinka were the majority up to the fourth year secondary and most of them from areas which spoke the dialect of that labourer or dialects closer to it than that of the Ngok Dinka from where Mr Williams knew I came - certainly, this was a great compliment.

The following year, Mr Williams, who was a keen football player, often asked me to join the games of first year students, which he refereed, so that I would interpret to the students who were mostly Dinka. This made my role very sensitive to the feelings of the students. Although Mr Williams did not seem to notice anything, I could see protest in their faces. This was clearly the case with Ambrose Riiny Thiik, with whom I later developed a warm lifelong friendship. I believe Ambrose discreetly voiced his objection. The students were of course right to be offended by having me translate to them, for they knew English as much as I did, since it was the medium of instruction. Perhaps Mr Williams simply wanted to make sure that his instructions were well understood. For me, it was flattering, but precarious.

While all three of us - Bulabek, Bol and I - were performing well in the class, Bulabek excelled and was indeed the star of the school. Soon after we joined Rumbek, we were given a surprise test, which resulted in the immediate promotion of three boys to the second year. Bulabek was one of them. Within the same year, second year students were examined to see whether some of them could be promoted to sit for entrance exam into the senior secondary level. Of the three who had been promoted, Bulabek was chosen. He sat and passed, but was not permitted to proceed to the secondary level. Had he been, he would have completed the intermediate school, which was normally four years, in only one year - a near miracle.

Although among the youngest, we had close contacts even with some of the oldest students on the senior secondary level without imposing ourselves. Of course, all senior students, especially of the upper classes, enjoyed a high prestige in the school and in every way, we felt their seniority even when they were friendly and informal with us. Some smiled and greeted us whenever we met, but otherwise displayed an importance which put them above and beyond.

But despite our age and our juniority, Bol and I seemed better versed in Sudanese politics than most students, including our seniors. It was not really surprising, since we were closer to the North, the origin and centre of Sudanese political consciousness against British colonialism. In those days, Egypt and the North were very active in winning the South over against the British. A group of Black, non-Arab Northerners, who traced their ethnicity to the South, were travelling in the South. They came to Rumbek with many Northern political leaders to bridge the gulf. That added much glamour to the political atmosphere in the school.

The July 23, 1952 Egyptian revolution staged by the military officers who styled themselves Free Officers, initially led by General Mohammed Neguib, whose mother was Sudanese, from whom Gamal Abdel Nasser later took over in 1954, was an inspiration for our political awakening. I recall reading a magazine, with a large photograph of Neguib on the cover. The title of the article was, "How I seized power". I still remember this passage from the article: "Naturally, we hoped to win the day, but it was also possible that we would find ourselves in prison, or in front of a firing squad. My wife was well aware of this, but she was not afraid. On the contrary, she kept urging me, 'Mohammed, it is time to do something for the country; and God will be your aide'"

Being more politically conscious did not mean that we knew much. Indeed, we hardly knew anything, except our opposition to colonialism and commitment to the demand for independence, with the support of Egypt. Some Southern colleagues would warn against the possible danger of Arab domination stepping into the place of the British. But we argued that the British were too advanced and more powerful, with more developed tools of control for us to defeat, once they entrenched themselves in the South. Should the North achieve its independence, the South would then be without the help of Egypt and the North. If the South chose to remain in a united Sudan, the Arabs of the North were less powerful than the British. Once we were rid of British colonialism, we could handle the Northerners, if they should attempt to exploit the situation to our detriment. There was not an afternoon or a free day spent without a heated discussion in which Bol and I featured quite prominently.

Together with political consciousness was a rise in student movement against the conditions in the school. The immediate issue was the quality of the food and social conditions in general. But judging from the sympathy the students got from the Northern teachers, the crisis had political undertones. The explosion came when the students decided to go on strike. As we were then in the first year, our class was excused as too young to face the possible repercussions. Bol and I were among those who actively tried to involve our class, but we were prevailed upon by the senior students not to join the strike.

At first, the strike was peaceful, but tensions soon developed which culminated in students blocking Mr Williams' office, preventing him from going home. One Dinka student went as far as assaulting him and ripping his pocket as he said, "Does this money come out of your pocket?"

As all this was going on, Mr Stevens, the assistant headmaster, sent for the police to protect the headmaster. But the police made it clear that they were not going to beat their sons. They, however, reasoned with the students and persuaded them away from the headmaster's office. The school was closed.

That strike made Mr Williams quite unpopular, especially to the senior students. To us, and especially to me, he remained a kind and gentle person. His apparent harshness seemed quite harmless. For instance, he used to walk around the school during the preparation in the evening, inspecting the classes to make sure the students were working. I recall him one evening turning towards our class and shouting: "Quiet there, you horrible children." But the tone and the inconsequential manner with which he said it made it more amusing than disciplinary.

Once, Bol told me that he was walking near the Williams' garden when he heard him shout: "Frederick, children walking in front of my house get hurt; go around." Again, there was no offence, but tease in his voice and manner.

What really brought some of us younger students close to Mr Williams was football. As a result of his commitment to intensive training, Rumbek was well known for its football team. Some of the students on both the senior and the junior levels were wonderful to watch in the field. Isaac Eli, for instance, could have been an international star. His speed, his resilience to any foul play, his subtle but swift styles, the force of his kicks, and not least, his ever-smiling face, made him the delight of any audience. The shots of James Hakim went like bullets. I can't recall whether it was Isaac or James whose shot broke Mr Williams' arm, as he tried to obstruct the ball with folded fists, while playing as goal keeper. People like Martin Omer and Angelo Kenyi came later, but were almost equally striking.

Football was such a popular entertainment that even when Joseph Kabulu's leg rattled loud in a match, his brutal fracture did not seem to have any scarring effects on me, as I aspired to becoming like our senior sport heroes. I fancied myself in my daydreams as a football star who did wonders to the delight of large audiences. I never thought I would ever give football up at all, let alone as early as I eventually did.

Mr Williams championed our aspiration. He took a keen interest in selecting prospective good footballers, trained them, and eventually formed his own team, which he named "The Nimbles." We were nearly all among the youngest in the school and were all Dinka with one exception, Ireneo Dimo, a Dinkanised Jur-Chol, who became our captain. I recall a somewhat humorous incident with Dimo. We had a bit of a quarrelling encounter at a game which left us somewhat distant socially. Then I must have done something at a game that made Dimo approach me in a friendly manner. I responded somewhat mischievously by saying that I thought we were no longer friends. Dimo responded in broken Dinka with a hilarious comment I still often cite: "Mading, *na cak kɔc adɔl, ke lec kek a yuom*", which translates, "Mading, even when people smile, teeth are only bones." Mr Williams gave us his attention, training and affection, which won us envious enemies from both the junior and the senior circles.

Perhaps the highlight of our football days at Rumbek was the tour around the South with both Mr and Mrs Williams, playing with school and town teams wherever we went. Unfortunately, we went with the big name of Rumbek Secondary School, at that time the highest educational institution in the South, while we were among the youngest of what was in effect an intermediate school. We were therefore met with teams of older boys, who were also good players. In some places, it did not matter - we won. But in many, indeed most, the combination of age and good sportsmanship worked against us and we lost. Mr and Mrs Williams always impressed upon us that sportsmanship required someone aspiring to win, but losing gracefully, and with dignity.

Mr and Mrs Williams did not stay long. They were leaving Sudan and he was taking up an appointment in Nigeria as the principal of a college. His wife was to continue teaching in Rumbek until the end of the academic year. Mr Williams's successor, Mr Creighton, came before he left. For some time, they were often together as Mr Williams acquainted Mr Creighton with the place and gradually handed the school over to him.

Mr Williams introduced Bol and me to Mr Creighton. Although I did not hear any complimentary words, I had no doubt that we had been well recommended. When Mr Williams left, the road he was to take was lined up by the students. Many seemed indifferent and some even happy to see him go. I was deeply saddened. A few secret tears dropped from my eyes as I saw him go. I hid my face from the students and took refuge in isolation.

I corresponded with Mr Williams and later also with his wife. Their letters were rich with deep and sincere sentiments and affection. They expressed the conviction that we would meet again in England, as they were sure I would go up for higher studies. It is one of my saddest failures that I was later not able to meet them in England. Worse, I learned that at the time of my writing in the late 1960s, Mr Williams had died.

That year, we then left for home through the river route to Kosti, then to El Obeid by train and on to Abyei by lorries. In the steamer, a significant incident took place. As I said earlier, political consciousness in the South was rapidly rising. There was a strong resentment of British colonialism, which was generally reflected against the Europeans. In the steamer, we met some European tourists with whom we, and particularly I, had heated discussions. One of them said that one of the things he disliked about Africa was that children like me (I was then 14) should be so intensely politically-minded. I took that as part of the plot to keep us ignorant of the political processes and pointed out the important role we had to play as the educated sons of our people.

The next morning an unfortunate thing happened – one of the women tourists taking photographs at the station was stoned on the head. We, of course, hated the photographs of our naked people being taken. In those days, that meant that the Europeans were planning to show the world how backward and still not ready for independence we were. They could take the scenery all they wanted, for we thought our country was the most beautiful in the world – that was why the Europeans wanted it. But taking photographs of naked people or their "primitive" environment was provocative. But, of course, we did not want the woman stoned and were sincerely sorry about that.

No one knew who had stoned the woman other than "Rumbek boys." At the time of the incident, Bol and I were in fact inside our cabin. Rumours began to circulate around that the matter had been reported to the authorities at Malakal and that we would be questioned on arrival. As soon as the steamer stopped at Malakal, the police came aboard and all Rumbek boys and students from other schools too were taken to the district commissioner's office. We waited under a tree for a long time during which the *mamur* (a rank lower than the district commissioner), a Northern Sudanese, chatted with us and gave us his moral support.

Then came the British district commissioner, arrogant and confident. When he began to address us as Rumbek boys, one student said he was from Mundri and not Rumbek; he was let go. Several others said the same and were let go. Then it dawned on the district commissioner that the question was not whether a student was from Rumbek, but whether he had taken part in the assault. The unlucky ones were stopped from leaving.

He then asked why we had been so hostile to the tourists in general and so violent to the woman in particular. Several of us tried to speak at once and with apparent impatience he silenced us and asked for only one to speak at a time. Somehow, he was told that we objected to the photograph of naked people being taken. His next question was, "Where in the law is it said that photographs of naked people should not be taken?" Again, several of us tried to respond at once and he screamed "Silence!" He asked for only one to answer.

He repeated the question. I spoke, saying that what was important was not whether it was written into the law or not, but whether it was offensive to our pride and dignity and therefore provocative. He totally disregarded my argument, which many of us shared and said, "Answer my question?" He repeated the question about the law preventing naked people from being photographed. He refused to listen to any answers as irrelevant and insisted that we answer his question, which he kept repeating to the letter. Even if there was a law prohibiting such photography, he knew we did not know.

Having won his obvious point, he went on to preach to us about the bad international image we were creating by being hostile to tourists. He compared us uncharitably with the Northerners and argued that we were enhancing the already existing prejudice against the South as primitive and savage, as compared to the North, which he presented as more civilised and respectful to foreign visitors. He concluded that we would have to pay for our misconduct. The punishment would be determined later. Since we, from Abyei, were proceeding beyond Malakal, we told him that we had not much time, as the steamer had already hooted twice and was about to leave. He asked us where we were when the woman was stoned and when we said we were in our cabin, he allowed us to leave.

By the time we reached the boat, word followed that all the rest without exception were lashed, almost immediately after we were gone. Our school teachers from the North, who were on the boat, met and decided to send a message to Khartoum reporting and protesting the punishment. The telegram was in fact sent, but I don't know what ever became of it.

At home, I continued to be devoted to my father's service, doing clerical work. By then, writing had become well established in our area and was no longer a miracle. The issue was now whether one could write and read well. We were in a sense above the test, whether the writing or the reading was in Dinka or English. But one incident showed me that the test had to be passed on both ends, the sender's and the recipient's. A letter I had written in English and which had been taken to a Nuer chief (whose clerk apparently did not know English), was returned with the advice from the chief's clerk telling my father to look for a better clerk, as the one who had written the letter could not write. My father laughed scornfully of the other chief's clerk, adding to the amusement of his court: "Anyone who accuses my Mading of not knowing how to write must have something wrong with his ability to read!" Needless to say, I was elated by my father's confidence.

But my father also continued to be a cause of anxiety for me. I knew he thought highly of my abilities, but I did not feel his love. On the contrary, I saw a kind of disapproval that I could not explain. One day, while the family was spending a drought season in a temporary structure on the River Kiir, I came running into his sitting room, looking for someone or something. The room was dark and I did not realise that my father was there in serious marriage negotiations with very distinguished relatives of the girl in question, Amou, from Ruweng tribe, who would become one of his wives he valued most. As I stood in the centre of the room looking around and trying to clear my vision, I heard my father's terrifying voice, "What are you doing there standing like a *darwish*?" The word, which meant "dervish", had the connotation of a fool. Of course, I stepped out of the room, deeply hurt and humiliated. Interestingly enough, the brother of Amou, whose marriage Father was negotiating, and who had presumably been in that meeting, became one of my cherished relatives-law, and Amou herself, one my most adored step-mothers.

Sometimes, the indication I got as to why my Father was behaving that way towards me was even more confusing than lack of explanation. For instance, Deng Aguer and I once accompanied Chan to the river, where he often liked to fish against the advice of everyone. Water and fire are known by the Dinka to be particularly alluring to epileptics. Fits drive them into fire or water and thus expose them to grave dangers. But Chan was very obstinate about what he wanted to do and all others could do was to follow and protect him, if need should arise. That was what Deng Aguer and I did.

On that particular fishing occasion, Chan had a bad fit which nearly drowned him. As he would become exceptionally strong under a convulsion, Deng and I had difficulty getting him out of the water. When we did eventually succeed, he took a much longer time to recover than usual. When my father heard of the incident and the fact that I had been there, his remark, which Miyar, who also had the Muslim name of Mekki, Nyanbol Deng's son, later told me, was: "Why does no one counsel Mading? Is his name to be found in everything?" For someone who was not interested in fishing, but had gone only to help, I thought it was grossly unfair, and I was deeply hurt.

Another blow came with a report again from Miyar who said he had overheard Father say to Bol, "Don't let yourself be led astray by Mading." I did not know whether my father did not want Bol to be influenced or overshadowed by me, but whichever it was, I felt discriminated against and unloved.

Many years later, I would learn from an elder who had asked my grandfather, Kuol Arop, why he hated his son, Deng Majok, who had done nothing wrong against him. Grandfather's answer was that he did not hate Deng Majok; he was afraid that he would outwit his brother, Deng Abot, who was not as articulate and outspoken as Deng Majok. My brothers always made me take the lead to speak on our joint behalf whenever we confronted our father, which probably gave me the profile of being their ringleader. I was later to ask Bol why they always put me in that position, and his simple answer was "Because you spoke well." I wondered whether my father was seeing me the same way his own father had seen him.

The fact that these reports came from Miyar might have made them unreliable because even then Miyar had developed an adverse attitude towards Father, and the feeling between them seemed to be mutual. The manner in which Father had treated, and was still treating, his mother was offensive to him, but their mutual adversity had achieved a momentum of its own. Miyar had also developed a tough-mindedness, which though reminiscent of his mother's, could no longer be blamed on her. But all this, rather than a reason for not believing Miyar's reports about my father's critical attitude towards me, only explained why he reported it to me.

I never discussed my grievances with anyone - not even with my mother. In her turn, my mother never complained against my father's attitude to her or to me, but she continued to blame me for being too timid to assert my rights over cattle. On this I felt that as long as my father was paying for my education, he was basically fulfilling his obligations as a father. In this respect, my father was fair. Despite Bol's mother's seniority, he treated us equally on financial matters.

From the day I entered school in Abyei, I had decided almost consciously that education was going to be the key to improving my situation in the family and to eventually acquiring status in the wider world of the Dinka. My mother knew this, for whenever we came to go to school, she talked to me movingly about working hard in school. On several occasions, my mother also cited my father's words that a child loved by God was far better off than a child loved by his father. Whether it was because my mother considered me blessed by his father or because of my own moral conduct, I knew that she felt God approved of me and that I could count on God's love, even if I found something lacking in Father's love.

CHAPTER EIGHT

INTERMEDIATE
A YEAR OF STRIFE

After two years at Rumbek, our junior secondary school was moved to Tonj, where an intermediate school had just been built. Since intermediate schools normally had four years, our class was to be broken up into two, the top fifteen were to jump the third year to found the fourth year and the third year was to increase with some of the boys from the first year. Our final examination was therefore of special significance. The results did not show the exact order, but we were among the fifteen who jumped to the fourth class.

Tonj in our childish judgement seemed rich and glamorous, a modern complex of glass windows and doors. The headmaster, Fahmi Suleiman, was a Northern Sudanese of mixed Sudanese (I believe Southern) and foreign (I believe Egyptian) extraction which, in his colour, features and character, seemed more obvious than describable. Fahmi was a Protestant and, in many respects, culturally Europeanised. He was married to a slender, delicate, white Christian woman who looked European. Fahmi had been a teacher and the scoutmaster at Rumbek, but although hearsay had it that he would be the headmaster at Tonj, he was less prominent than he was a potential dynamite.

As the headmaster, Fahmi came forth in full force. He was an enthusiastic teacher, a physical educationalist, a moralist, and a man of demanding discipline, which he concealed with a misleadingly charming smile. Fahmi formulated his own authentic administration, which maintained high standards, but appeared too repressive. Fahmi often dressed in shorts, high stockings, and short-sleeved shirts which, by Sudanese standards, was informal, but on Fahmi, was more European-like than informal. He was always neat and well-trimmed. Although outwardly pleasant, with a deceptive childlike smile often accompanying his speech, Fahmi was a stern awe-inducing man, whose eyes glowed and radiated a quality of physical, psychological and intellectual strength. Boys feared him tremendously.

An interesting supplement to Fahmi was Sharafeldin, his assistant headmaster. Sharafeldin was from Kordofan Province and was quite dark, a characteristic he bragged about and used to back his proud claim that his grandmother was a Dinka. He was clean, but untidy, and he often dressed informally in shorts, stockings and half-buttoned shirts, with a shabby hair that he frequently forgot to comb. He used snuff in his mouth, stuffing and holding it under his lower teeth. This made his smiles reveal only his upper teeth, but evidence of the snuff nevertheless remained bulging. As he spoke, his bloodshot eyes shone and protruded according to the point he made or depending on whether he was provoked into anger or laughter.

Sharafeldin was a philosopher who enjoyed exchanging ideas with his students. Religion was a topic he liked, and his theme was that the Dinka had been misled by the Christian missionaries into abandoning their noble traditional religion and adopting a foreign religion, which was in no way superior to theirs. He often cited the story of Deng, whom he called the Dinka Prophet, and the miracles he was said to have performed from the moment he was born.

He would liken these to the miracles of Jesus Christ who, according to the Quran, like Deng, explained the mystery of his conception to his mother, while still a newborn baby. Despite his sociability with the students, Sharafeldin was able to detach himself enough not only to be official, but also to be tough and rough. His combination of informality and friendliness with formality and sternness made the students mistrust him as dangerous in disguise. But I liked him and I thought him genuine. And I thought he also had a positive attitude towards me.

With the combination of Fahmi and Sharafeldin, Tonj as an institution was a place which emphasised meticulousness in whatever was being done. Work was introduced and the playing grounds were cleared by the students. Games were made compulsory. Food was economical, basic, coarse and not so tasty, but supposedly nutritious. Access into town on weekends was deemed to expose the students to alcohol and sexual temptation and was therefore forbidden. A system of surprise rollcalls was instituted to check students' movements over the weekends. This was the first area of confrontation and conflict between the administration and the students.

One crucial weekend, the bell rang and the rollcall showed that many boys were out of the premises. Bol was among them. I had myself been out, visiting some friends in the teachers training school, but had just returned before the rollcall. No one knew where the absentees were, but they were not necessarily all in town. Some, including Bol, had gone for a walk into the woods where, in addition to the beauty of nature, there were all sorts of wild fruits. All of them were to be lashed. They refused to accept the punishment. Fahmi gave them a deadline within which they were to accept or be dismissed.

During the crisis, the minister for Education came for a visit and noticed boys in the dormitories, while the school was formally assembled. When he inquired in front of the assembly, Fahmi explained, and the minister seemed to approve of Fahmi's decision. Once the specified period expired, they were declared dismissed. The matter seemed much more serious than we had thought. Something had to be done.

Bol and I were close friends with Eric Deng Mawiir, a son of a leading Twic Dinka chief, Mawiir Rian (also known as Monywiir). Deng and I at first tried to involve the student body into supporting the punished students. Our ground was that they had done nothing wrong by simply walking into the woods and that the rule had been unduly strict. But the rest of the students refused to be involved. We had to think of a different approach. I thought reconciliation between the headmaster and the students, if initiated by a neutral body, was the best face-saving device for both sides. There were two views to reconcile: Fahmi had declared the students dismissed and the students had refused to be lashed. Deng and I went to Fahmi's house and implored him to give the students another chance to remain in the school, if they accepted their punishment. Fahmi said he was impressed with our concern for the education of our fellow students; he would accept that by giving them another chance.

We knew that our main task would be to convince the students to accept the punishment. We also knew that many of them would be too proud to accept. All the same, we approached them and argued that accepting the punishment was nothing compared to the price of losing their education which, we said, would not only be a personal loss, but a loss to the country; they owed it to themselves and to the country to concede and proceed with their education.

The strength of our argument did not convince them to accept lashing, but it made them agree to accept a different form of punishment. As that seemed a significant concession, we rushed back to the headmaster to try to convince him to alter the form of punishment into something like cutting the grass in the school compound. He agreed after a long discussion. It was clear to us that he was not compromising from a weak position, but in appreciation of our efforts and because of his interest in their own education. Two students, Thomas Dhol, and Ajang Chan Nyal, refused to accept any punishment. After abusing the headmaster in front of an assembled student body, they handed over their school belongings and left triumphant losers.

That problem solved, it was as though unity and harmony had been achieved in the school. But a different issue was soon to cause another explosion. The food which was served the students, though nutritious, was coarse and insufficient. Fahmi was aware of the problem and used to go hunting for meat, although it was never quite clear whether it was the sport or the students' need which motivated him. Bol and I, though not prefects, played a role in influencing the students about the dreadfulness of our food, compared to that available in schools in the North.

We were particularly close to two young teachers, Abu Bakr Osman and Abdullahi, both of whom had newly graduated from Hantoub Secondary School and had been colleagues of our brother, Ahmed (Arop). They supported the comparisons we made between our situation and the situation in the North and agreed that if our food was introduced to a Northern school, the students would no doubt go on strike. I would reconnect with Abu Bahr Osman many years later, first as ambassadors and then as members of Nimeiri's cabinet, with him as Minister for Cabinet Affairs, and I as Minister of State for Foreign Affairs.

Since the prefects were from our class and were good acquaintances and friends, the grievances were echoed in important student circles. The final outcome was a meeting of the prefects which led to a general meeting of the student body to discuss the conditions of food. It was agreed that we should go on a hunger strike for a day. We did. Classes were not to be affected.

During the assembly, Fahmi tried to explain the difficulties that were caused by being a new, ill-equipped school. He said that there were provisions that had not yet arrived and that he was trying to keep the school open with minimum provisions. All that was fine and persuasive. But he made one gross mistake: he insulted the Dinka, and most of the students were Dinka. "The trouble with you Dinka," he said, "is that you never think of tomorrow. You consume all your produce during the season of plenty only to be forced into hunger shortly afterwards." As he spoke, students started to leave the assembly and retire to their dormitories. Although no decision was made to boycott the classes, a spontaneous strike took place and the problem suddenly took a wider, more difficult dimension. Some students went to the classes, but the overwhelming majority did not. Bol and I joined the strike. The headmaster closed the school. Within a short time, lorries were brought to take the students away.

As we prepared to leave for Abyei through Wau and Gogrial, Fahmi called Bol and me into his office and told us that it was his responsibility to see to it that we arrived home safely; that as it was a rainy season, he could not be sure we would find mechanical transportation home through Wau; that the only way he could authorise was by steamer through Shambe to Kosti; that we were therefore to wait within the school premises for a few days, when we could then leave to catch the boat from Shambe. To no avail, we argued that we could easily go home through Wau, even if that meant walking, and that if we were faced with difficulties, we could stay with our friends. We also argued that if we had to wait for the boat, we should be permitted to stay with friends outside the school. But Fahmi argued that he was obligated to guarantee our safety, until it was time to catch the boat. We therefore had to stay in the school. We remained very disappointed that our friends and colleagues were gone, but sure that it was only a matter of time and we could go home the surest, though longer, way through Northern Sudan.

Two days after all the strikers were gone, Fahmi called us into his office and told us that the school was to be opened in two weeks; that if we were to go as far as home, we would not be back for long; that since we were in our final year, such a delay would be detrimental to our chances for higher education. He had therefore retained us in order to save us from losing our future. Bol became enraged and started talking very rudely, even insultingly: "This is cheating. We wanted to go with our friends. You should not have lied to us…" Abusive words flowed from Bol. Fahmi's only remark was, "Frederick, this is not the way to speak to your headmaster." I felt that a different approach was called for. It was obvious that the man had acted in our favour. Our only problem was how to maintain solidarity with our friends and colleagues while benefitting from the consideration he had made for us. "There is no need to quarrel," I said to them, as though I was their elder, "It is a question of how we solve the problems raised by the situation."

Bol was too angry even to reason, but Fahmi and I managed to agree and Bol eventually acquiesced that we remain in the school as strikers; we were not obligated to attend classes, but we had to attend meals, a very convenient rule! Now that I think of it, Fahmi was so much kinder to us than we realised. It was a great pleasure to receive our friends and colleagues back to school, unfortunately, some of our closest friends were never to return: they were dismissed as the ringleaders of the strike. Among them were people like Joseph Lok Aguek and Isaiah Kulang Mabor, who were among the best in the class and were sure to go high up the educational ladder.

By this time, we were so close to the final examination that the cause was submerged in the excitement with future chances. We did try to do something to back our gone friends, but our efforts fell on academically ambitious but politically dead hearts. The fact that we had lost our friends and leaders made us feel guilt and hostility. I remember how we once appeared so uncontrollable for Sharafeldin, the assistant headmaster, who taught mathematics, that he took a whole pile of papers, threw them on the table in front of him, and with a typical Northern accent, said: "Here are your syllabi; you can study by yourselves for one month, for two months, for three months, or a year", and he left the classroom in a rage.

So much was Bol affected by the situation that he became a rebel within the system. Once, he and Sharafeldin had an argument in the class. Sharafeldin said: "You either become attentive or leave the class." Bol left the class, which naturally infuriated Sharafeldin even more. Sharafeldin left the class almost immediately to report Bol to the headmaster. Bol was summoned and questioned. His defence was that he had heard Sharafeldin to be saying "Leave the class!" He was warned, but forgiven.

Shortly afterwards, Sharafeldin called me and solemnly talked to me about Bol, urging me to "please talk to your brother." He told me that they knew Bol to have been one of the ringleaders, that they had considered dismissing him, but that both for my sake and in consideration for Bol's future, they had decided to give him a chance. He said all the teachers were sure we both had a bright future, which he thought Bol was placing in jeopardy. Since his objective was more explanatory than punitive, I did not feel the need to tell Bol, as that would only have provoked him to be even more confrontational with the authorities.

Bol and I were soon to have another blow. A letter arrived from cousin Lino Ayong Monyyom that our father had been stabbed four times in the chest in an attempted assassination, that he had been taken to Nahud hospital (several hundred miles from Abyei) and that his condition remained critical. Ayong gave scanty facts about the failed assassination. For a man to try to kill our father was completely beyond imagination, let alone expectation.

Our thoughts concentrated and wandered. By the time we received the letter, our father was probably dead; and what kind of a home, tribe or even world would it be without him. It was impossible to envision anything, but disaster, chaos and uncorrectable deprivation. We went to the headmaster and asked to be allowed to leave immediately. His advice was that we would only harm our future without helping the situation. In any case, nothing was clear and for all he knew, we might be worrying for nothing. He suggested that he would send a telegram to the administrative authorities of Kordofan enquiring about our father's condition in particular and the whole family and tribal situation in general. We waited in anguish for the return cable which confirmed that the assassination attempt had indeed occurred, but assured us that our father had recovered speedily and was now well, back at home and in control.

With all these problems jammed into one year, Tonj might sound as an academically barren school, but that would be a wrong impression. Rumbek had laid a solid foundation for scholarship and both the staff and the students at Tonj were keen on their academic work when they were otherwise not distracted by strikes or politics. It was part of my work style that I stopped studying a few days before the examination and apart from revising with colleagues, rested.

The examination came and went. The anxieties passed, but the waiting period came with even worse anxieties. We waited and waited for so long that we nearly forgot we were waiting and our anxieties almost disappeared. One afternoon, as we were playing football, Fahmi came riding his sports bicycle and whistling. In no time, word was echoed throughout the school that the results had just been cabled from Rumbek and Fahmi was going to read them to the students in his house. All, including students from other classes, stampeded to Fahmi's house, filled the verandah, and stood outside, peeping in or resting their ears on the wire screen to listen. Fahmi had given the impression that the results were awful and that he was deeply disappointed. Hearts were beating fast, while Fahmi played with nerves.

Then Fahmi read the list. Bol was top, I was second. The names of those who had been accepted in Rumbek were read. Those who had passed, but were not accepted followed. Only one name remained unread – it was that of our dear friend, Eric Deng Mawiir. It was impossible to believe. Eric Deng was by no means stupid; in our view, he was quite intelligent and, in any case, we were such close friends that it seemed wrong for such a wide gulf to exist between us. We walked away so miserable that it was hard to believe we were on top of the list. As people came excitedly to congratulate us, they found it necessary instead to console us. Even Eric Deng himself contributed words of encouragement.

Fahmi's disappointment was not unjustified, for although Tonj was the best in the total percentages of those who passed and those accepted in Rumbek, the top three positions went to other schools. Bol was fourth and I fifth in the whole South. Other schools intervened again. The next person from Tonj was seventeenth. Fahmi had expected Tonj to be top in every sense. That was the evidence of the harm which the instabilities of the year had done to the school.

Father was not happy about our being educated in the South. He would make that clear every single year we were at home on vacation. He would also mention our brother Ahmed Arop and our cousin Hassan Arop, who, apart from Lino Wuor and Luis Nyok, the headmaster and his assistant, were the first to be educated in the North. Father cited them as examples of the superior education the Northern system had to offer. Once, he said to us, "My sons, I fear you will later complain that I have treated you unfairly for educating you in the South." He wanted to transfer us to the North.

He once made that suggestion in front of Wuor, the headmaster of Abyei Elementary School. Wuor argued that it would be better to leave us in the South where education was much cheaper. At the time, the maximum school fees in both the intermediate and the secondary schools in the South were only three pounds, while in the North they were fifteen and thirty pounds respectively. My father's reply to Wuor was, "If you find expensive and cheap clothes in a shop, are not the expensive ones likely to be of better quality than the cheap ones? And if you can afford the expensive ones, are you not better off?" The argument that education was cheap in the South to make it attractive for the reluctant Southerners, or that it was subsidised without diminishing its quality because of the relative poverty of the South, did not impress Father.

By the time we were in intermediate school, Ahmed Arop Deng, who had become employed in the local government, advocated the same view as Father. So much was the comparison belittling to our education that Bol and I felt deeply affected. I remember getting onto a horse as we were leaving for the South and Father, who was seeing us off, smiled and said, "Is that the way you ride horses in the South?" Being himself an excellent rider, his critical comment was based on his expertise and was painfully belittling.

We had become quite convinced that as long as we received our education in the South, we could not fully please our father. But to transfer to the North would be to put ourselves at a disadvantage, since Arabic and not English was the medium of instruction below the secondary level. We therefore decided to finish the intermediate level in the South and then request transfer to a Northern Secondary School. So, just before leaving Rumbek after our second year, we mentioned to Mr Creighton, the new headmaster, that if we passed the entrance exam, we wanted to go to Khor Taqqat Secondary School in the North, instead of joining Rumbek Secondary School. Mr Creighton himself had taught at Hantoub Secondary School in the North, where our brother, Ahmed, had gone. At the time, he seemed sympathetic and promised to help, once we had passed. We assured our father that we would not continue in the South beyond the intermediate level, if transfer could be arranged.

Now that we had passed, we decided to pass through Rumbek to raise the matter with Mr Creighton and then to proceed by steamer from Shambe to Kosti. From Kosti we would proceed by train to El Obeid, where we were to take a lorry transport home. At Rumbek, we went through the classes to recall old memories. It was good to see our names on the notice board, next to one another, out of all the Southern students. That in itself gave us such prominence that we found most people knew of the Deng Brothers. Bulabek, our young uncle, was there and our cousin, Justin Deng, had also joined Rumbek the year before.

When we got to Rumbek, Mr Creighton was away, but we later met with him on the road to Shambe. He got out of his car and congratulated us warmly in a way that told us he was delighted to have us return to Rumbek. It was not easy to remind him of our wish to go to the North and his undertaking to help. Mr Creighton's remark to the latter was "I did not promise that, did I?" Creighton tried to persuade us against going to the North with such arguments as, "You are different from them; they are Arabs and you are Dinka; they are Muslims and you are Christians; how can you be happy among them? Besides, your relatives are in Rumbek, Bona [Bulabek] and Justin [Deng] would miss you." Our arguments did not include the pressure at home. We laid stress on the distance and the bad means of transportation to the South, as opposed to the better means to the North. They knew that we never went home, except on long vacations. Our reasons were therefore quite justified. But Mr Creighton was not convinced and made it clear that he had no intention to help us transfer to the North; so, we left disappointed and discouraged.

The night we arrived at El Obeid; we were wonderfully surprised to learn that our father had just arrived. It was too late to see him that night. Early the next morning, we went to the rest house, where he was accommodated. It was our first time to see him since his injury in the attempted assassination. Feelings were high on both sides. Instead of the usual Arab greeting which we had always followed, when a child stands passively in contact with the elder, who touches him on the shoulders, Father surprisingly approached us with a warm embrace before shaking hands. After tea, father ordered coffee for us. This was quite a promotion, for although he himself always had coffee after tea, we, as children had been limited to tea and never drank coffee.

We told Father about our success in the entrance examination, our interest in transferring to Khor Taqqat Secondary school, instead of Rumbek, and our failure to arrange it. Father thought of a way which had not occurred to us; he would go to the governor to seek his help. After breakfast, we went to the provincial headquarters. Mr Michael Tibbs, the last British district commissioner for our district, was there. Father went from office to office with Mr Tibbs and finally, we were called into the office of the deputy governor, who asked us a few questions, such as why we wanted to transfer and how well we had done in school. A cable was sent to Rumbek to verify our results. The response promptly came back, confirming how well we had done in the entrance examination. We were told that the matter would be considered and we would be informed in due course. We then returned home together with our father and awaited the result.

The result came after quite a long suspense. We heard it on the radio. A letter came later which began rather amusingly with the phrase, "There are many Dengs, but this case concerns Francis Mading and Zachariah Bol Deng." Justin Deng had also applied for a transfer, but was refused on the ground that there was no place in the second year.

Owing to differences in the timetables for the Southern and the Northern schools, that year gave us the longest vacation of our life - nearly six months. Most of that time was spent at Noong, even though we frequently visited Abyei. Our visits to Abyei were often motivated by the need to acquire provisions and of course to obtain the money from our father for purchasing the supplies. Since commercial lorries from Muglad to Abyei passed by Noong nearly every day, we had no difficulty hitchhiking, although calling it that is to reduce the dignified way in which it was done. We sat under our father's Court Tree at Noong, which was virtually on the edge of the road. At first, we would ask a driver to stop by making the appropriate gestures. But we eventually made a number of friends among the drivers and they would in any case stop. Whether we asked them or they stopped by themselves, we invited them to have tea and a short rest before proceeding.

Once, we decided we were going to have a party at Noong to which we would invite our friends, the drivers, and some people from Abyei. We got most of what we needed for the party. The day before it was to be, we were at Abyei getting more things. The women at Noong had already started the preparations. We wanted to come back to Noong to be followed by our guests the next day, and had to hitchhike. The lorries left late afternoon when the day was cooling.

Determined that we had to get to Noong that evening, we searched for places in the lorries that were leaving for Muglad, but could not find front seats in any. So, we decided to take back seats. The lorries were so highly stacked with cotton sacks that they had to be increased in size by poles. Bol found a seat in a lorry whose driver was so drunk that people at first tried to stop him from driving, but as he was adamant, he was allowed to drive. Bol, with a friend called Zachariah Atem Piyin and the assistant drivers, sat on the deck of the front seats. A relative called Minyiel Deng Tiel, a nephew of Kuol Tiel who was injured in the 1942 tribal war, sat on top of the sacks. I took the lorry immediately following them and sat on the deck of the front seat with the turnboys.

The two lorries drove close to each other. From the time their lorry started, it was on two side wheels and was going at a high speed. Even before ours started, Miyar drew our attention to that and we drove after it apprehending danger. About a mile from Abyei lay a bridge that had deep pits alongside it from which mud had been dug to build the bridge. We saw the driver ahead of us leave the main road and head towards the side-pits. We could not believe what we saw. It was almost a fantasy. We saw the assistant drivers climb down despite the speed at which the lorry was running. Before we fully comprehended what was happening, the lorry had plunged into a ditch and overturned.

We stopped quite close and got down. As we ran towards the fallen lorry, we saw Atem Piyin limping towards us crying, "Zachariah! Oh Zachariah!" I passed him running towards the lorry. At that point, I ceased to be conscious of what was happening except vaguely. I was the first to reach the lorry and I moved about frantically, anxious to see Bol. Even when I saw the driver sitting on the sacks and seemingly unperturbed, I was hardly aware of the fact that he had caused the accident and I went on searching for Bol.

Then I saw him lying under the sacks, head swollen even in that short time, and his thigh almost flat under one of the supportive poles. I don't know whether I thought he was dead or barely alive. I was about fourteen, old enough not to be expected to cry by Dinka standards. But I cried so hysterically that all I remember is being held by people and put into a car in which Bol was taken to Abyei dispensary. Although I had been a boy scout, it never occurred to me to perform first aid. Bol's badly fractured leg was carelessly dragged into the car. When the accident occurred, my father was still in court. I saw him being held by people near the dispensary. He was being dragged as though he was totally paralysed. I was myself being held, but unlike my father, I was crying out loud.

Everywhere, women and men were crying and it was impossible to tell just what their relationship to us was. The whole of Abyei was in an uproar. Bol received his first aid in the dispensary. It was there that he told our father that he wanted to be buried straight, instead of coiled into a round grave, according to Dinka burial. As he was carried to our house in a bed, I saw his right arm waving and I thought he was saying goodbye to the crowd. That evening, a car was sent to cover the rough unbeaten tracks of Dinkaland to trail the Dinka bone expert- Rou Minyiel. It took the whole night to find Rou.

Another Dinka expert was brought for the skull. By that time, Bol's head was so swollen that when he moved his head, blood roared streaming from side to side. The Dinka skull expert suggested that the floating blood be let out. He would then see whether the skull needed an operation to close the cracks. But the medical assistance refused and said that any operation by the skull expert would be a criminal offence and that if Bol died, the expert would be charged with murder.

No one seemed to be aware of the other victims of the accident. Minyiel had been found unconscious and had not yet recovered. He was given up as dead. Atem had only received minor injuries and was out of anybody's concern. One relative, Deng Tiel, the brother of Kuol Tiel, Minyiel's uncle, said a prayer in which he offered Minyiel's life as a sacrifice for Bol's life. "We give you Minyiel," he prayed to God and the ancestral spirits. "But please save Bol." I was pleased to later hear my mother openly criticise Deng's prayer on human and moral grounds. My father himself invoked and prayed for Bol's life, one of the few times I saw him sincerely plead with his traditional divinities and ancestral spirits. But there was also modernity in what he prayed for. He said that if modern education had a virtue to offer the Dinka, "they", presumedly Bol and I, represented that virtue. It was a pragmatic plea, but Father's emotional agony was obvious.

Bol's mother on the other hand saw modern education as the root cause of her son's fate. She neither cried nor ceased to talk and most of what she said was in defence of her original position against Bol going to school. To her, the accident was a logical consequence of education; it would not have happened to Bol had he remained in the cattle camp, far from motor cars. It was obvious that much of what she said displeased our father. But it was not a time to argue back. The medical assistant was concerned about the encroachment on Bol. He suggested that people be sent away with the exception of one or two to take care of him. My mother and Nyanbol Amuor together with Bol's own mother were taking care of Bol.

When everybody, including Father, had eventually gone to bed, Uncle Biong decided that he would take full responsibility and ask the skull expert to do what he thought appropriate. After some reluctance on the expert's side, naturally fearing criminal consequences, he was persuaded to operate. He opened Bol's head and emptied it of the floating blood. The swelling went down to naught. After examining the crack in the skull, he declared that there was no fracture to worry about. He did what little adjustment had to be done to the skull. The following morning, the medical assistant was surprised and impressed that the swelling had disappeared. He was told of the operation only after he had expressed happiness at Bol's condition.

The bone specialist, Rou, came in the morning. Rou was renowned throughout Dinkaland and his profession had become a family enterprise. It was believed that as long as the bone marrow was not broken, Rou could adjust any fracture whatsoever. His skill was believed to be religiously ordained and inheritable. He himself was old enough to retire, but he was still the most experienced.

The calmness with which he approached Bol confirmed his expertise. After briefly examining him, he concluded that, though a serious fracture, Bol would be cured. What was important was that the marrow was not broken. Rou used pieces of sticks and leather to tie Bol's thigh and also gave it a hot bath. But his treatment was interrupted by the coming of the district commissioner, Mr Michael Tibbs, who told Father that he should not leave his son in the care of a native expert. He should send him to a modern hospital, and he, the district commissioner himself, would take him.

For a combination of reasons, Father was persuaded. For one thing, he did not want to appear "primitive", even though he confessed that he had never seen a Dinka dying or becoming lame once he had come under the care of Rou. For another thing, there was no reason for him to doubt that modern surgeons might do a better job. He agreed to send Bol with Mr Tibbs to Nahud Hospital, the nearest health facility to Abyei, yet several hundred miles away. Nahud used to be our district headquarters when we were under Western Kordofan District. But since the establishment of the Missiriya District, Rigil el Fulah, known simply as Fulah, had become the headquarters. Fulah was closer, but as yet, had no hospital. The road to both Nahud and Fulah was opened only in the dry season, and even then, it was simply a beaten track.

Father decided that my mother should go with Bol's mother to take care of him. I learned from my mother later that Father decided on Bol's request. My mother was very anxious about leaving her children, especially her youngest, but she of course went. For both Bol's mother and my mother, that was their first trip to such a distant land and to a town. Since there was no room in the car, I was to follow later in a lorry. Bol was to tell me later that my father spoke with him before they left, imploring him never to accept amputation, if the doctors should suggest it. He said he would prefer for Bol to die than to be one-legged.

As they journeyed to Nahud, Bol nearly died. That he survived was almost a miracle. I came shortly after. At first, I put up with our mothers in the house of Sheikh Abdel Majid whose Dinka name was Ajith. Ajith had been Father's retainer and then brother-in-law. Father then appointed him leader of the Ngok immigrants in Nahud and in that capacity he sat on the magistrates' bench as the expert on Dinka law. He became a prominent personality and had a comfortable house. As soon as the hospital authorities could permit – and that took some string-pulling, I slept in the hospital on the floor next to Bol. As his leg was plastered and tied to a large frame, Bol could not move and with the help of the nurses, I assisted him in everything. As he did not like the hospital food, his meals were prepared by my mother.

Ever since the accident, Bol's mother never ceased to complain against our father. Bol's having been sent to school in the first place continued to be an object of her attack. Another one was Father's remaining behind and sending me, a child, with the women instead of coming to at least ensure adequate care for Bol and then return. She was particularly bitter about Father's negotiating a marriage while Bol was at the brink of death a day or two after the accident. Two months passed and no word came from Father. By now, Nyanboldit had become bitter beyond endurance. She hardly ever slept. She would sit and talk to herself out loud for most of the night. But that was so from the very start. Before I was allowed to sleep in the hospital, we all slept in the open air in Abdel Majid's house.

Nyanboldit also voiced a great deal of appreciation to my mother and myself, even when she spoke out loud to herself. But instead of simply expressing appreciation, she often spoke of the role she had played to secure my recovery from an infant illness that nearly killed me. According to her, she was a force behind the sacrifices that were made. I particularly recall the words she said she used as she urged my father to act whenever diviners suggested new sacrifices: "Deng, a son born should not be abandoned when God has revealed what must be done!" Needless to say, her talks made me feel ambivalent. While I of course appreciated her appreciation for what my mother and I were doing for Bol, she was implying, and I think she even expressed the thought, that my having lived had proved to be of benefit to her, because of my contribution to Bol's care.

Bol had also become very bitter against Father. His bitterness found its expression in intense anxiety about his condition. Much of the pain and the discomfort he felt could not be explained by the doctors, and Bol became known as a difficult patient. He would cry in seeming agony and the more he did, the more our apprehensions rose, and the more Nyanboldit complained. Only my mother maintained a mature attitude and she would preach to Bol about fighting with the will to recover. As Bol was virtually on a hunger strike, my mother would urge him to eat and to look at life instead of surrendering to death. My mother would also preach to Nyanboldit, and occasionally also to me, about the importance of encouraging Bol, rather than inducing in him self-pity and apprehension of death, which only helped make his condition worse.

One day, we had all been sitting with Bol and he seemed calm. Suddenly, he started to complain, then he began to tremble, and before we could get a nurse, he was in a convulsion and making his dying declaration. It only consisted of "I am dying; please take good care of Chan." Chan of course was his epileptic older brother. Both Nyanboldit and I were crying hysterically. Our cries dominated that part of the hospital. My mother held Bol as she pleaded with us to at least behave in a way that would make the hospital authorities permit us to remain with Bol instead of him being taken or we being asked to leave. The nurses said the doctor – the only one in the hospital – had gone home. The medical assistants and nurses did not, of course, understand what the matter was with Bol. I ran out of the hospital crying to fetch the doctor. When I described to him what was happening, he smiled and told me not to worry – he would be alright. He and I returned to the hospital. He gave Bol an injection and in a matter of minutes, things were back to normal.

Father came suddenly, and as he always did, acted in a way that modified, if not remedied, what had appeared as neglect. That soothed much of the bitterness that was in Nyanboldit and Bol. Of course, he was very surprised that Bol was still not recovered. As he was constantly blamed for not having allowed the Dinka bone expert to treat Bol, he felt guilty in a sense. Now that he had given modern surgeons a chance, he thought it was only logical that the Dinka expert should get a turn. So, he decided that he would get Bol out of the hospital and take him back home. With Bol still in such a serious condition, it was most unlikely that the doctor would allow his discharge. Quite apart from professional ethics, the doctor would be risking criminal prosecution. But that sort of obstacle never really stood in Father's way. He knew which strings to pull and he pulled them from the district commissioner to the resident magistrate. The medical officer gave his permission. Within days, Bol was taken out of the hospital. Only a most unusual exception would permit a person who could only be moved by a stretcher and was laid in mattresses arranged in the car to be taken hundreds of miles away from a modern surgeon and hospital facilities to a traditional practitioner.

As soon as we arrived in Noong, Rou was summoned. He held no grievance about Bol's being sent to a hospital. On the contrary, he had said that since his objective was to cure Bol, he could only be glad if it could be better done in the hospital. He came with his eldest son, Monyluak, who was virtually taking over the profession from his ageing father.

It was popularly believed that they refractured and reset the bones, but I later understood from Bol that this was not the case. Whatever they did, they went through their usual stages, using leather and pieces of wood to keep the bones in position, bathing the wound in hot water day and night, using physical therapy and exercising the leg frequently. Within two weeks, they could make Bol get up and be supported to move gently inside the cattle byre. Then he was left to support himself with the walls of the byre as he moved. Finally, he was given a stick to move more freely around the village.

After a month, Bol still carried the stick, but was sufficiently recovered for us to leave for the school. It had been open for a month and we were too late to wait for Bol to recover fully. Father was to go with us as far as Muglad. He would then attend the Missiriya Rural Council meeting at Fulah. It was the rainy season, and so we had to travel by horses, bulls and donkeys. Many walked. My father also had cattle to be sold in the North. Together with his chiefs and councillors, policemen, retainers and cowboys, it was an enormous company. The journey took more than five days because we had to go very slowly, as Bol was still a patient, and the cattle were grazing as we went.

Despite the constraints of Bol's condition and the slow move of the cattle, it was an enjoyable trip. The presence of our father with his large entourage almost made it a home. We even carried a large tent, which was erected when need arose - that is when it threatened to rain. Because of the cattle, we camped early - that is late afternoon. That would give the herders time to collect firewood and make large fires so vital for the protection from wild animals of which there were many. As people sat in the evening and chatted, there was an intimacy and an informality which was lacking at home and which therefore made the trip even more pleasurable and a rare treat for us.

One evening, after chatting for some time, we retired for the night. The sky was so clear that everyone slept where they pleased in the open air. Suddenly, the clouds began to form. It thundered. Rain seemed imminent. Attempts to stop it by prayers failed to clear the clouds. So, the tent was erected and we moved in with our father. Father slept in a cot. The rest of us spread our sleeping bags on the ground and fell asleep. The rain took us by surprise. We did not know it was falling until we felt completely soaked with our bags and blankets. Water flowed in under the tent. We got up and sat, cold and miserable for the rest of the night.

One night, the sky was so clear and the moon shining so brightly that it was decided we should travel at night. All went well except that as the horses rode well ahead of us, we kept hearing lions roar, and our father's rifle firing and echoing in the woods. We thought they were in confrontation with lions, but we later learned that Father was shooting in the air to frighten the animals and clear the way for us and the cattle as we followed behind. Anyway, we eventually arrived at Muglad, from where Bol and I proceeded to El Obeid in a lorry. We were full of thoughts and apprehensions as to what things would be like in a school where all, but the two of us, were Northerners and, we thought, all Muslims and Arabs.

CHAPTER NINE

SECONDARY
Bridging the Gulf

We spent a few days in El Obeid where we acquired an impressive assortment of clothes, Western and Arab, including, for the first time, the traditional Northern garment, the *jallabiya*. Then we went to Khor Taqqat in a rented truck, a distance of seven miles which seemed much longer. The countryside was not much different from what we had seen, especially in entering El Obeid, a shrub land spotted with low bushes of varying thickness, some thorny and others with broad, shady leaves. Sand dunes undulated between the bushes, and although pressed down to its lowest in the centre of the dirt road, obstinately bulged on both sides and at the centre of the road and between the more depressed two lanes of the car tracks, forcing lorries to maintain a delicate steering in high gear, sending the sounds of their roaring engines a considerable distance ahead.

But there was something special about that same landscape as we drove to Khor Taqqat, something beautiful, composed and serene, a natural work of art in which the skyline blended delicately with the low-lying growth below, down to the base of the underlying sand beneath. The road, stark, sandy and difficult, was concealed by the bushes, unravelled and revealed only in short stretches as the lorry meandered teasingly between the shrubs. This whole scene was particularly picturesque in the later afternoons as the long rays of the setting sun reached deep, sensuously violating the privacy of the virgin land.

On our arrival, and in order to encourage our integration, we were assigned to separate dormitories, Bol to Ali Dinar and I to Abu Sinn. Each of the dormitories was a rectangular structure with two main wings lined up with large rooms, each accommodating about ten students. Although we were not conscious of the significance of the naming of dormitories and classrooms at the time, it was clearly a symbol of the division between North and South Sudan on racial, ethnic and cultural grounds. Dormitories were named after prominent chiefs of Northern Sudanese tribes. There was not a single Southern Sudanese tribal chief among them. Classrooms were named after famous Arab scholars and literary authors. There was not a single African among them.

There we were, in Khor Taqqat, a totally novel setting, among people whom Mr Creighton, the headmaster of Rumbek Secondary School, had previously warned us were racially, culturally and by faith too different from us to be schoolmates.

It was not that we had not known Arabs or Northerners before; we had seen them in Abyei, and indeed had grown up seeing them at home, and had been playmates with two or three of them. We had also visited Muglad and travelled through Northern towns while studying in the South. But there was something different and more intimidating about Khor Taqqat. It symbolised a higher model of what was best or more developed and sophisticated about the Northern identity and civilisation. These were the educated sons of the Arab North, some of them from very distinguished backgrounds, all of them sure of their racial and cultural superiority over the African South. They were of varied colours and features, some virtually white and European-looking, others as black as we were and in their features typical of black African ancestry, but they all seemed in perfect unity with their identity as Northerners, Arabs and Muslims.

SECONDARY
Bridging the Gulf

As Muslims and Arabs, they sharply contrasted with our sense of racial, cultural and religious identity. Whatever their real wealth or poverty, they all seemed to convey the appearance of affluence, refinement and sophistication. To plunge in, claim equality, and compete for excellence was a most unnerving challenge, about which we were quite self-conscious, but prepared. It was as though my earliest apprehensions when I had first joined Abyei Elementary School were repeating themselves: How would we perform? Would we succeed and make a positive impression or would we fail? But how could we afford to fail and disappoint the expectations of our father and the relatives back home? We saw the task as monumental, but we were determined to do our best at meeting the challenge. Perhaps even more important than our class performance, or at least equally important, was how we looked, how we dressed, how we carried ourselves, and all in all, the competing dignity we projected among the students and in the general Khor Taqqat atmosphere.

But, if one is struck by how different we felt and how much we strove to fit ourselves into Khor Taqqat and to be equal, one must also give enormous credit to the warmth, the friendliness, and the wealth of humanity with which our Northern colleagues received us. We quickly found ourselves fully accepted and respected by our roommates and also in the wider context of our dormitories. We were obviously popular, although there was an element of curiosity in our popularity. Our poor Arabic and our unfamiliar aura drew attention and occasionally provocative teasing. My negative reaction to such teasing was aggravated by the language deficiency and by cultural and racial sensitivity. One day, Meimoun, perhaps the most extroverted, friendly and yet rowdy of all my roommates, said something in Arabic which I did not understand, but which aroused a roaring laughter from the others. I was not amused. I thought he had insulted me, probably with a racial slur. My anger signalled danger and the matter was killed by a sudden, almost artificial silence. We rarely spotted insults, but when we did, our response was sharp, provoking in turn a quick apologetic response. Our sensitivity in this respect was symptomatic of a deep ambivalence and insecurity.

Despite unquestionable pride in our Dinka racial and cultural identity, and although the Dinka considered themselves superior to the Arabs in so many ways, a complex set of circumstances had nurtured in us the feeling that Arab ways were more advanced than our Dinka ways and that becoming civilised for the Dinka implied becoming somewhat Arabised. This was precisely why our father had insisted so much on our coming to the North. Just as we were being supposedly "civilised", we were becoming equally insecure and emotive about our racial and cultural background. But in the Northern context, the issue of racial and cultural identity was more confusing than that. A "black" Northerner could be playfully called "*Abid*" (slave), without provocation, an excelling black Northern sportsman would be cheered and hailed with a tone of paradoxical insult-and-praise as "*el abid, el abid*", (the slave, the slave), without risk of provocation. But not us! If one made the mistake of joking with us in a racial slur, one soon discovered that our sense of humour was acutely different and didn't extend to such value-loaded, and ambivalent words.

Our continuing struggle implied a precarious balance between the acceptance of Arabisation as the integrating national framework, and consciousness of Dinka identity as a background of which we were still very proud. This was illustrated by an embarrassing experience I had one morning of a working day in Khor Taqqat. We had just left the morning classes and gone to the dining room for breakfast when I spilt milk on myself and had to rush to the dormitory to change, making me the first to leave the dining room. On entering the dormitory, I was told by one of the janitors that I had an uncle waiting for me. I could not imagine who the uncle could be. Curious and apprehensive, I followed the janitor to meet my supposed uncle.

As we entered the corridor linking the bathrooms with the dormitory, we were met by an emaciated Dinka, of typical ethnic height, unshaven, almost toothless; his few remaining teeth were heavily stained. He wore a dirty, sweaty, sticky, *jibba*, a variant of *jallibiya*, that looked as though it belonged to the dump, certainly not to the Khor Taqqat environment. I saw him and felt incoherent with shock. Sensing no time for reflection, I found myself greeting him in physical automation, but with an inner rejection, indeed revulsion.

"Arop", he said, mistaking me for Ahmed, Father's eldest son, "don't you recognise me?" I corrected his error more to dismiss him than to be factual that my name was not Arop. But that did not sufficiently make the point. "Oh, don't you remember seeing me in your father's court? You may not know me, but I am well known to your father and to your brother, Arop. I heard in El Obeid that a son of Deng Majok was in this school. So, I said I should come and seek your help. I am without clothes." He was right, but so disrupted was my fragile world of identity and equality that I hardly listened. I was preoccupied with how to be rid of him before the students emerged.

"This place is out of bounds," I said with a tone of certainty. "You had better leave before people come." I spoke in a matter-of-fact manner that left no room for doubt. Convinced or not, he left without further discussion. As soon as he was gone, the tension that had driven me into the rejecting him unfolded and my sentiments were totally reversed. I went into a guilty panic. How could I have rejected one of my own? How could I have been reduced into pretending I did not belong to a people among whom some were unclothed, destitute, and physically unattractive?

Filled with a deep sense of shame and self-reproach, I decided to follow him, going from janitor to janitor, from one passerby to another, asking hysterically whether they had seen a person of the description I offered. In my arms were a jallabiya and a set of underwear. But he was gone and could not be traced. I returned, defeated and humiliated to myself, doomed to nurse my shame and guilt in total secrecy until I eventually gathered the courage, ten years later in London, to tell my brother Bol, as we reminisced about our childhood.

Academically, we felt equal, perhaps even more advanced, except in Arabic and Arabic-oriented subjects like Islam and the history of the Arabs, which was taught in standard Arabic. Most subjects appeared to be revisions of what we had learned at the intermediate level. This was both reassuring and dangerous, for despite our coming to school rather late because of Bol's accident, we felt ahead of our class and saw no need for hard work. It is difficult to tell which of our teachers was instrumental in our academic survival at Khor Taqqat. Their attitude was generally sympathetic and supportive. Heading the hierarchy was the headmaster, who, as an institution and a person, seemed far more removed from the students than had been the case in Rumbek or Tonj.

When we first got to Khor Taqqat, the headmaster was Abdel Haleem Ali Taha, the brother of the first Sudanese minister for Education, Abdel Rahman Ali Taha, whom I had encountered first at Tonj Primary School and later at Tonj Intermediate School. Abdel Haleem was a serious-looking man, paradoxically solemn and well-disposed. He rarely laughed, but compensated with broad, teeth-revealing smiles that were rather frequent but often seemed mistimed, and contrived; his smiles nearly always vanished with the same suddenness with which they had appeared. Because he was so remote and hardly accessible, except during the morning assembly, he still appeared distant even when his dignified humour aroused roaring laughter from the students.

When Abdel Haleem was transferred and I believe promoted to the level of permanent undersecretary in the Ministry of Education, he was replaced by Bushra Abdel Rahman, taller and larger in build, equally solemn and removed, meticulous about his dress and appearance, but more susceptible to gossip, and criticism. Students nicknamed him "Kamfoush", which I never understood, and never asked about, and "Abul-Gazaz", the Bottle Man, which I suppose I understood. Bushra Abdel Rahman and I would meet eight years later in London, when he was the cultural attaché and I was a post-graduate student.

The assistant headmaster, Khalid Musa, a light-skinned man of considerable physical and authoritative weight, reacted to my name rather negatively, but jokingly. First, he wondered, light-heartedly of course, why I would want to be a Christian; did I not believe in democracy and did I not realise that Islam was the religion of the majority in the Sudan? When that made no visible impact, he referred to his several daughters, whose beauty had captured the attention of the school: "You know I have daughters. If your brother Ahmed came and asked me for one of them, I would give her to him because he is a Muslim; but if you asked me for one, I would refuse because you are a Christian. On the other hand, if you became a Muslim, I would happily give her to you." All this aside, Khalid Musa decided that Francis was too foreign a name; my new name was to be Faris – "Knight", and from that time on, I was Faris as far as Khalid Musa was concerned. Secretly, I rather liked his choice of the name because it implied being a warrior, which, in my Dinka warrior culture was a compliment.

Khalid Musa was replaced by El Tayeb Shibeika, a tall lean gentleman who was deliberately outgoing and friendly with the students. When military training was introduced in our third year in the wake of the deteriorating Halaib incident with Egypt, Shibeika participated in the training with the students, subjecting himself to being ordered by non-commissioned officers who did not distinguish between the students and their assistant headmaster, sometimes with hilarious exchanges between the trainers and their senior trainee. At one point, Shibeika tried to identify himself and the Nuba trainer made it clear that he did not care who he was. As far as he was concerned, he was training to be a soldier.

One very illustrative incident about the anomalies of Shibeika's relations with the students occurred in our last year. It concerned our English teacher. A young Northern Sudanese Khartoum University graduate by the name Jaafar was assigned to be our English teacher. Until then, our teacher had been Mr Jones. Our class, which had the reputation of being insolent and difficult, requested that they be given an Englishman for a teacher. The department insisted on the Sudanese teacher. When that teacher came into the class, the students confronted him. They argued that passing the English language was critical to getting the Cambridge School Certificate, that he was not as qualified as an Englishman for whom English was the mother tongue. They urged the teacher to excuse himself from teaching us and be replaced by an Englishman. For some reason, Bol and I were away when this happened. We came into the picture with later developments.

Ustaz Jaafar went and reported to the head of the department, Mr Taller, what had transpired between him and the students. One day, after Bol and I were back in the class, El Tayeb Shibeika was teaching us a subject I do not recall, when Mr Taller walked into the class, as he was fuming with anger. He told the class that he had heard what had happened, that it was not for them to decide who should teach them, that the teacher would remain their teacher, and that anyone who did not want him was free not to attend his classes, but anyone failing the mid-term English examination would be dismissed from school. He exited the class without taking questions or comments.

El Tayeb Shibeika then displayed the informal friendly attitude he liked to use with the students. "What happened? Please talk to me quite frankly as your older brother, not assistant headmaster. I hate all these formalities about status. Just see me as your older brother." Someone decided to tell him what was going on, the significance of English for the school certificate and the importance of having the best qualified teacher. Shibeika responded very sympathetically. "You are absolutely right. Mr Taller himself should be the one to reach you." His understanding seemed so contrived and exaggerated that one student, Ali Sheikhun, a Communist, who was well known for being outspoken, said, "Sir, this is between us and the teacher. You have nothing to do with it. I suggest we do not discuss this matter any further." Shibeika responded in the same spirit, "I wanted to help, but if that is the way you want it, then let us leave the matter."

The next time Ustaz Jaafar came in, he spoke in a manner that I found pitiful and indeed painful. He said that he was sorry he was being imposed on the class, that he had considered resigning, but decided that he had to earn a living, and must therefore do what he had been assigned to do. I felt very bad for him and decided to raise my hand and speak. I said the issue was no longer what we thought of him as our teacher, but that in light of what had happened, whether he felt comfortable and genuinely interested in teaching the class. His answer was sincere. He said that as long as he had accepted the responsibility, he would do his best to do his duty.

I can't clearly recall for how long he taught us. I do recall, however, that I enjoyed his classes and thought of him as a good teacher. Our classmates had based their position on the prejudiced assumption that as a Sudanese, he could not be as good as an English person teaching mother tongue in teaching the language. I later learned that he left teaching and joined the foreign service. We later reconnected as colleagues, fellow ambassadors, and good friends. But we never talked about the painful experience at Khor Taggat. I do not even know whether he remembered that I was one of the students in that class.

Our science teacher, was an Egyptian, whose name I do not remember. Like Khalid Musa, the first assistant headmaster, he also thought that Francis was too foreign a name and decided to call me Ramses, the well-known name of a long line of ancient Egyptian pharaohs. To this day, Bol teasingly calls me Ramses. Our Arabic teacher, Satti, from the Shaigiyya tribe, judging from the marks on his cheeks, arranged for us to be given remedial classes by Khalifa, one of the brighter students, but that only made it possible for us to barely pass. Geography was taught by Mr Crawford who made Physical Geography and travelling around the world by sea, land and air to the capitals of major countries around the world quite exciting.

History, one of my best subjects, was taught by a member of a Shaigiyya tribe who seemed to relish the heroic, if predatory accomplishments of a man he proudly called his close relative, none other than Zubeir Rahma, the notorious slave trader. But his enthusiasm and mastery of the subject made his classes entertaining and enjoyable. Civics, though taught in Arabic, was also enjoyable, and when we were allowed to answer examination questions in English, I got a high mark. Mathematics was taught by an eccentric and humorous Englishman who was a master of his subject, but seemed to be under the influence of alcohol. Art was taught by Idris al-Banna, who gave the subject a pleasant appeal through his combination of art and fun. He would later join politics and rise to become a member of the Supreme Council of State, a shared multiparty institution that represented collective Head of State.

English, by far my most enjoyable subject in which I always had the top position, was taught by Mr Jones, a lean pleasant man, whose gentle and respectful mannerism added to the attraction of the subject. I remember sharing the bus to El Obeid with another English teacher whose name I believe was Gray. In our conversation, he asked me whether I was a Southern Sudanese. I answered "Not quite" and explained that I was from Abyei which was administratively in the North. Mr Gray surprised me by saying, "You speak very good English. Few people in Khor Taggat would say 'Not quite'".

Apart from the conflict over the assignment of a Sudanese to teach us English, my recollection was that we were for the most part taught by Mr Jones. I remember his advising me to aim at Distinction One in English at the Cambridge School Certificate Examination. We also discussed what I hoped to study at the university, which was law, and for which knowledge of English was a requirement.

Interestingly enough, Bol and I had different interests in the subjects. He was interested in the sciences and did so well that he was nicknamed "Doctor". I was interested and good at the arts subjects, especially History and languages, and was known to head the class in English. Since one's position in the results of the exams was determined by performance in all the subjects combined, we always fell behind most of our classmates, however, well we did in the subjects taught in English. We later requested to be given the special Arabic for the South in the Cambridge School Certificate Examination. The approval came while we were in the third year, ensuring our success in the examination, but unfortunately stifling our progress in Arabic.

Although we were naturally far behind our colleagues in Arabic, we were improving fast, especially in the spoken version. My outgoing social attitude was a definite advantage. I soon won the praise of my peers and teachers for my Arabic and even the headmaster, Abdel Haleem Ali Taha, praised me to my father when he visited the school during our first year.

That visit was in many ways a source of great pride and assurance to us. Unlike the South, where Mr Daniels had been very rude to Father for being late, Father was very well received in Khor Taqqat. The headmaster not only gave him a tour of the school, including our dormitories, to see how we lived, but also honoured him with a lunch party at his house.

SECONDARY
Bridging the Gulf

In his characteristic manner, Father donated a substantial sum of money to the school "just for tea". As we progressed, we became increasingly more relaxed with our colleagues, except outside the school environment on such trips or tours as were conducted to nearby areas or towns. Such occasions plunged us into the more conventional Northern circles whose ways and manners were less familiar to us than those of our schoolmates. As we were rather conspicuous because of our Southern identity, we tended to be the centre of attention, out of both curiosity and courtesy.

Our geography tour took us to the Gezira, the green belt of the Sudan that produced, among other crops, "white gold", cotton, the backbone of the country's economy. We went by train to Kosti, then proceeded on lorries visiting towns, villages, and the plantations. The relatively high standard of living which greeted us everywhere was as impressive as it was intimidating.

At Khor Taqqat, Bol and I tried to remedy our sense of social and cultural discomfort in a variety of ways. The most popular was to take walks in the surrounding areas in the coolness of the late afternoons. Those were wonderful moments when we would forget all about Khor Taqqat, reminisce about our childhood days, and otherwise deliberate over Father's excessive marriages and contemplate the grim future that awaited our family, should anything unexpected go wrong or in the inevitable process of ageing and eventual death. Deeply disturbing as the subject matter was, those moments of walking reflections were a great joy to Bol and me, as we lightened our shared burdens by joking and laughing a great deal, including about otherwise depressing subjects.

The cultural context of Khor Taqqat added a complication to the problem of Father's too many marriages because, according to the precepts of Islam, whose cultural values we were fashioning ourselves after, four wives was the legitimate maximum. Finding it embarrassing to reveal the true number of our father's wives, we pretended that he had only four wives. It did not occur to us then that the number of wives our father had could be a symbol of something which those Arabs admired and respected, despite religious disapproval. Indeed, Arab chiefs also married many wives, the only exception being that their system prevented the presence of more than four wives together at one time. Through divorces they engaged in multiple marriages, while maintaining four as a constant number. To us, as Dinka, for whom divorce was highly undesirable and very rare, the stigma of divorce was reflected on the children. I do not recall a single case of Father divorcing a wife, although some left on their own volition.

An area which facilitated and aided our social integration, though in itself volatile, was that of politics. As I said earlier, Northerners, even students, were more politically-minded, better informed, and more active than their Southern counterparts. For some reason, perhaps because it was a meeting ground of students from all over the country, Khor Taqqat's students tended to be more radical than most other schools in the North, which were closer to the centre. During the early years of its establishment, well over a hundred students had been dismissed en masse because of political action. The school developed a flair for politics and became something of a prototype in the radical movement of students throughout the country. Whether by chance or by design, Khor Taqqat brought together students from the extreme North, the West, the East, and through us, the South, not to mention the central regions. It was truly a melting pot and a microcosm of Sudan.

Within the Southern context, despite our age, Bol and I had been very active in politics and were leaders, even among our seniors. But at Khor Taqqat, in addition to our Northern colleagues being politically more aware and better informed, we had the added language disadvantage. Among Northern, Arabic oriented students, oratorical skill in public speaking in Arabic, the revered language of the holy book of Islam, The Quran, was an essential requirement for leadership. We were therefore reduced to the ranks of the silent audience, in our case, absorbing only a fraction of the eloquent speeches, and otherwise cheering with the rest in support of those whose political principles we shared.

As anywhere else in Northern schools, there were three main political factions in Khor Taqqat: the Muslim Brothers were a radical religious rightist group; the Democrats were members of the leftist Democratic Front, which was master-minded and led by the

Communists; and the third faction, the Independents, were supposed to be what the word meant, even though they sometimes floated between the two main factions. Naturally, we couldn't be Muslim Brothers, as we were Christians. And as the national political scene was then dominated by the Southern problem, we also could not be as indifferent and apathetic as the Independents were presumed to be. So, we became Democrats.

Although we never joined the Communist Party, we were assigned "Comrades," with whom to study the ideology and application of Communism. We read works on Capitalism, Dialectic Materialism, and many books and booklets by, and on, Marx, Engels, Lenin and Stalin. An Arabic song which was popular in our student circles, ran something like:

Stalin never died,
The Great Stalin,
No, No, he never died.
He only moved from the Kremlin,
To live in our hearts,
The hearts of the struggling masses.

The Democrats and even the Communists appealed to us then, not only because they represented the more reasonable alternative open to us, but also because they were the only Northerners who held any sympathy for the Southern Cause. Indeed, only the Communist Party of the Sudan, then known as the Anti-Imperialist Front, had any political programme for the South, promising local autonomy, and a socialist platform of equality for all the Sudanese.

Meanwhile, the situation in the South had deteriorated. Steps towards independence were well underway. A Sudanisation Committee had been formed and had just published its results, which were a shocking disappointment to the South. Accounts about impending Northern domination began to spread. In August 1955, a few months before the Declaration of Independence on January 1, 1956, a company of Southern troops in Torit, Equatoria Province, mutinied, igniting an uprising that was to result in the brutal killing of several hundred Northerners, as well as Southerners, in the South. A civil war erupted that was to last seventeen years before it was peacefully resolved by the Addis Ababa Agreement of 1972.

Looking back now, I feel impressed by the peaceful way in which the students at Khor Taqqat discussed the highly charged problem of the South, even during the period of the tragic bloodbath. While news of the butchering of Northerners, including women and children, continued to engage Radio Omdurman, punctuated by the sad mourning music and the chanting of from the Quran, students displayed no animosity whatsoever towards us. Even though some of the students had lost close relatives, at no time at all did we see an attitude of anger or hostility, far less vengeance, displayed towards us.

Although our limited command of Arabic forced us to refrain from making public political speeches, I often found myself in heated discussions with the Muslim Brothers in small discussion circles, usually in English. Our ability with English was in itself something our Communist friends wanted to exploit, especially because it put the Muslim Brothers at a disadvantage.

Even religion was a subject of these heated discussions, with Communists and us taking one side against the Muslim Brothers. But the Communists, being themselves the products of the Northern Muslim community, were more restrained in religious discussions and careful to avoid offending the Muslim Brothers on religious grounds. While Bol's leg problem restricted his involvement in sports, one of the factors which facilitated my social integration in the dormitory was my interest in games and sports. I played football, basketball, volleyball and table-tennis; I ran, high-jumped, long-jumped, pole-jumped, threw the javelin, weight-lifted and threw the discus. But while my earlier daydreams in the South had made me a star in the world of sports, my position and self-image at in Khor Taqqat was one of a more modest competition for the dormitory.

In line with my interest in sports was my enthusiasm for military training in the cadet corps. At one time during the Algerian war of liberation, students had demonstrated, demanding, rather figuratively, to be given arms to join the Algerian struggle. Fate had it that the Egyptians moved into a strip of Sudanese territory known as Halaib. Within no time, the Sudanese nation, North and South alike, had buried their internal differences and mobilised against Egypt. For a brief period, it looked as though we were inexorably headed for war. Gamal Abdel Nasser later denied the whole thing and to many Sudanese it was as though the prime minister, Abdalla Khalil of the anti-Egyptian Umma Party, was simply trying to divert attention from his domestic difficulties. The matter died down, but a compulsory military training was instituted for students in the last two years of secondary school. This involved intense drilling, target shooting, and camping. The training was conducted by privates and non-commissioned officers, mostly from the Nuba Mountains and the West, under the supervision of commissioned officers.

On the part of many students, the seriousness of the training and the toughness with which it was conducted made the task arduous with no conceivable relevance to their future application. The earlier call for arms was soon replaced by complaints against the training. Some took it as a humorous and frivolous pastime exercise. But for me, although I now look back and wonder what invoked in me that desire for military discipline, I took the training seriously and loved it. The way I walked in the drill, carried out my responsibilities in the camp, or performed in the target shooting contest, I totally absorbed myself in the task and worked to excel as a good soldier.

Apart from the intensive academic work, our walks, sports and later, military training, there was really nothing much to do at Khor Taqqat. There was no physical labor of any kind; our rooms were cleaned and clothes laundered. Food was relatively good and varied, even though students made a habit of complaining against stews and potatoes, lentils and white beans known in Sudan as *fasulia*, preferring the special dish of Egyptian fuul beans. All in all, it was a life of relative luxury. Weekends were the only occasions for visiting El Obeid, some seven miles away, and even then, only for the day. However, with the permission of the house master, one could stay for the night.

We occasionally visited relatives, Deng Alak and Peter Michar Alor, who were then undergoing technical veterinary training in El Obeid. Once, we spent the night with them and had such a good time that we hardly slept at all. We all slept in one large room, but remained awake most of the night, reminiscing about home, playing the game of Dinka tongue-twisters, and otherwise testing our Dinka linguistic ability. The more difficult it was to pronounce such sentences as *"Tin diït thik tït"* "A huge mahogany larger than all mahoganies", or *"Rou acï löl Rual riöp",* "The hippopotamus has messed the Rual pool", or *"Abël eban, abël cen abël gäny abël dänga",* "All fools, among whom there was not a single fool to alert the other fools", the more we roared with hysterical laughter, and the more we appreciated the hidden qualities of our language and culture. It was like home all over again, and better, because it was a remedy for home-sickness in a culturally alien environment. It is extraordinary how much joy such small things can give. But the joy we felt that night had a far deeper meaning than the mere fun of the game or the pleasure of the company.

As I have tried to explain, at Khor Taqqat we were in a totally unfamiliar context in which the pressures of adjustment were considerable. Even while we appeared serene and in harmony with that setting, it was a situation of internalised tensions and strains. To be back in a familiar relaxed atmosphere with old acquaintances and in our own social and cultural milieu, where we did not have to live up to any alien standards and expectations was simply fabulous.

While there were initially hardly any Dinka in El Obeid, except for people like Deng Alak and Peter Michar Alor, later years witnessed an increase in the circles of the Dinka. Some held respectable positions in such areas as the army and the police, others depended on handouts from their labouring tribesmen. Our contacts with the people we knew among them were very limited and quite occasional, but they provided useful opportunities for maintaining links with our people, and of course with memories of home, even when the conditions under which they lived were unbelievably depressed, dirty, smelly, and by all standards, slummy in the worst order, sharply contrasting with the dignified conditions of traditional lifestyle.

Throughout our years at Khor Taqqat, we spent all our vacations at home. Although Khor Taqqat was more physically comfortable and culturally sophisticated, home brought well-earned relief from the stresses of schooling and adjustment to a culturally alien environment. It also provided the opportunity of renewing our companionship with relatives and old friends. Although we did not realise it at the time, this kept us rooted in our traditional values and institutions and reinforced our sense of identity and our ability to withstand the onslaught of radical and concentrated change. It was also at home that we felt most appreciated for our education, which was viewed as an investment in the interest not only of ourselves and our own family, but also of our people.

The journey home usually took several days of high gear driving in sandy dunes, in which the lorries frequently got stuck. In the back of the lorry would be a heap of passengers, mostly Dinka and Arab tribesmen, sitting on steel boxes, fuel barrels, sacks of grain or anything that might chance to be on the lorry. Whenever the lorry got stuck, the passengers had to disembark to lighten the weight and to aid the engine with a push.

During our first journey home, we witnessed a tragic incident. We were driving from El Obeid to Kadugli on our way to Muglad en route to Abyei. On the way, our lorry developed problems and had to stop frequently. With us was a trader who was in a hurry and was getting restless about the delay. As other lorries came, stopped, enquired, and proceeded, the trader decided at one point that he should get onto another lorry. Generally, moving out of a lorry with a problem and leaving co-passengers behind is frowned upon and considered not only in bad taste, but an invitation to misfortune. In this particular case, it seems that the driver appreciated the situation of the trader. So, when we heard the sound of a lorry coming behind, we stopped and gestured the other lorry to stop, which it did. The transfer was duly negotiated and the trader moved to the front seat of the other lorry.

That lorry then started and began to roll on as we watched. The assistant driver, in the standard practice of assistant drivers, stood until the lorry had moved. He ran alongside the lorry until the acceleration had reached the desired point. Then he leaped, first getting hold of a pole, and then trying to place his feet and climb. Suddenly, and within fifty to a hundred metres from where we stood, he slipped, first appearing to have fallen alongside the dirt road, but then throwing himself back under the lorry in time for the hind tire of the left side to roll over his chest. He did not move again. He was dead.

Meanwhile, the confident driver continued to roll on completely unaware of what had happened. Even the passengers on the lorry did not seem initially aware. It was not until we jumped down and started running in their direction and waving at them that the back passengers began to knock on the roof of the front seat to alert the driver. We found the body in a puddle of blood which seemed to have saturated the sand and overflowed. At our age of about sixteen, sheltered from the sight of death, that was our first time to come face to face with death; it was a dreadful experience.

Although we knew the dead man was a Muslim, we automatically found ourselves making the Christian sign of the cross. Bol turned back as he made the sign and walked away. I went after him and said we should be with the people or else it would seem as though we were segregating ourselves on the very sensitive matter of death, which Muslims consider an occasion for demonstrating solidarity. So, we came back and witnessed the wrapping of the body in a sack. The lorry then headed for the nearest police station. That day, I could not eat or sleep and indeed for days to follow, that scene of death haunted me with nightmares.

In Muglad, we were usually accommodated in the house of Nimir Horgas, the son of an Arab *omda* and the head accountant of the council. Occasionally, we also put up with Sheikh Mekki Ali Julla, the uncle of Babo Nimir, the paramount chief of the Missiriya Arabs. Mekki was the sheikh in charge of the market. Other people with whom we stayed occasionally were Mahmoud and Ibrahim Ali Julla, Mekki's half-brothers and also uncles to Babo and his brother, Ali. Both Mahmoud and Ibrahim were the full brothers of Shemelle, who was the medical assistant in Abyei and a close friend of the family. Wherever we put up, we nearly always went for a meal or tea in the house of either Babo or his deputy brother, Ali, whether in a collective meal-time gathering of the extended circle or by special invitation. I mention all these people to show that in a way, although our being Christians made us different, we were increasingly becoming culturally integrated into friendly Arab-Muslim circles.

This also shows the extent to which we and our family were on the South-North cultural convergence. I remember a conversation with Chief Babo Nimir the year we joined Khor Taqqat. It was in the office of Michael Tibbs, the British district commissioner, who had been instrumental in our transfer to Khor Taqqat. It was Babo's first time to get to know us. He was told that we were the sons of Chief Deng Majok. That made him feel close to us, but surprised that he hadn't known or heard of us before. After a while, he asked for our names again. He took Zachariah as a Muslim name. Then he turned to me and said, "My son, what are you doing with that foreign name? Don't you see all your brothers have Arab names?" Mr Tibbs intervened and explained to him that I was a Christian. Babo was puzzled even more. How did a son of Deng Majok become a Christian? Mr Tibbs went beyond to explain that Bol too was a Christian and that Zachariah was not a name exclusive to the Muslims. Although the matter was dropped, Babo was not persuaded.

Babo's concern about our religious status in itself indicated our entrance into the Northern circle. At home, the situation was far more complex than that. We had been educated in the South and were known to be Christians. Our brothers, who had started their education in the North, were Muslims. The illiterate members of the family had remained traditional in their religious beliefs. The result was such an amalgam that despite external forces to tear us asunder, there was an organic whole which kept us together. Christianity and Islam grew differentiating roots in us; and so did Western and Arab elements we picked up from the South and Arab influence from the North. But at home, they blended and built invisible bridges over the gulfs inherent in these various streams of acculturation.

We never quarrelled over religion even though we sometimes discussed it and argued vigorously. Our father used it as a tool of influence. He himself was never formally converted to Islam, but he was culturally Arabised and he observed certain Islamic rites. For instance, he ate only the meat of animals slaughtered in the Muslim tradition. He had a *fakki* (a Muslim holy man) at home, who wrote verses from the Quran in ink on his wooden tablet and washed them into water for our father to drink. That was supposed to bring protection and success. We also had a Dinka priest in the house with functions very similar to those of the fakki. The Dinka would sing his hymns in the middle of the night and the Muslim would chant his verses from the Quran towards the early hours of the morning. I distinctly recall waking up to the voice of each and in addition to enjoying them both musically, feeling a deep sense of spiritualism.

Almost all of us, Christians and Muslims alike, started very religiously in our new faiths, but in due course, the excitement of conversion receded. Ahmed was a Muslim Brother; Bol and I were members of the Legion of Mary; and the rest were devout Muslims or Christians. As our father celebrated both Muslim and Christian feasts, we all united in their enjoyment. Sometimes, we even shared in the pain of Muslim fasting, Ramadan, although that was more social than it was spiritual solidarity.

As we were now becoming of age and with the then highly valued secondary school education, we were increasingly accepted by Father and others as qualified to participate in the discussions of more serious family or tribal matters, and to give our opinion on the issues involved. However, we nevertheless maintained a delicate, sensitive balance between being with our father, yet not intruding in the affairs of the elders, and giving ourselves the freedom of our own circle. The large one-room rectangular building in which our father held his morning and daytime court sessions at home was both our sleeping and our living room.

Father would rise and join us for his morning tea at about 6:30 in the morning. We would already have woken up, brushed our teeth, washed our faces, made our beds and were ready to receive him and his audience. One by one, the audience would begin to assemble. Some of the chiefs and elders, who were close and frequent companions of our father, would turn up before his arrival. Only rarely did Father find us alone. In any case, whatever time he chose to emerge, waves of his approaching presence would be felt even before he appeared. The room would be filled in literally no time. Always well-dressed in spotlessly clean jallabiyas, a skilfully wound turban, and a powerful fragrance of Arab perfumes, his approach, certainly his presence, was unmistakable. His seat was always predetermined and kept vacant. In front of him would be a table. The rest of his visitors would sit on the more modest canvas chairs and on our beds, arranged for the purpose.

If our father got in before our presence was overshadowed by the courtiers and elders, we would exchange morning greetings and perhaps enter into some lighthearted conversation, yet all with restraint and considerable formality. For us, every word had to be considered and balanced before being uttered. While the mere fact of talking to our father was a rare privilege, which we longed for and appreciated when granted, the experience was always tense and unnerving. If he happened to laugh or smile at a point, the person making the point had reason to feel exalted, even exhilarated. Father was very close and yet very far! Even then, it appeared incredible; now it is indescribable.

Tea would soon follow his arrival. There was always a special cup for him, quite distinct amidst other china cups. Morning tea was always served with milk, while after-meal or daytime tea was without milk and was served in transparent glasses in which the red color was part of the enjoyment. Generally, the servant exercised his discretion on the priority of serving tea to those present, but Father would sometimes gear things in such a way that the more deserving did not get overlooked. Tea in Sudan, especially in the West, was a special treat and at that time a symbol of status and privilege. A lot more was therefore at stake in the ritual than simply taking tea.

Along with chiefs and elders in these morning tea sessions would also be eager litigants. Strictly speaking, that was not the time for pleading cases, but the Dinka would never miss any opportunity for introducing a claim. In any case, they had a passion for being in the company of Father, if only to gaze at him and listen. In the circumstances, there had to be a limit on who should get in, but although we occasionally and politely complained about the room being too crowded, the anti-social task of actually preventing people from entering the room was the domain of the policemen, who sometimes had to use physical force to prevent entry.

Prevented from entry, litigants and court attendants would gather outside our room, waiting in two's and three's for the opportunity to say something to Father or simply to be in his company when he emerged to proceed for his day's work in the open court under the famous Court Tree, also known as Chuen Ayak, the Tamarind Tree of Ayak. Father would get up without warning anyone, step outside, and indicate where he was going only by heading in that direction. Usually, it was towards the court tree through the market place, where he might decide to stop in this or that shop. He would drop in the shop of Ali Beshir, the head merchant, or Abdullahi Dugal, Ali's competitor, or Merida, a politician-trader.

A young Dinka by the name of Ayii Akol from Aweil was Ali Beshir's shop assistant. He became a close friend of the family. Ayii became a Muslim and adopted the name of Abdel Bagi Ayii. He would eventually return to Aweil where he succeeded his brother who was killed during the first Anya Nya war and became a tribal chief. Many years later he became the leader of a rebel militia that would enter the power struggle in the independent South Sudan and his son Hussein Abdel Bagi would become one of five Vice Presidents of the Republic.

Going back to our early days in Abyei, although our father was the unquestioned lord of the land to those Arabs, he was also in frequent need of their readily available cash. Within an hour of visiting any of those shops, he would spend nearly his entire salary on clothes or other commodities for his family. While his salary was much higher than his Southern counterparts, and at par with those of his Northern colleagues, it meant nothing in comparison to the needs of his vast family. So, it was no surprise that he generally spent far beyond his salary and was often allowed by those Arab traders to receive goods on credit to be paid for in cattle or after the sale of cattle. In cattle wealth, his resources were considerable, for, as I said earlier, his marriages were investments that paid considerable returns.

Returning to the programme of his typical day, whether directly or with stopovers, Father would eventually arrive in court to find the space around the tree literally full of attendants, a large horseshoe of chiefs and elders seated on chairs facing a far larger audience of litigants, self-styled assembly members, and countless spectators. His chair, as always, would be in the centre, conspicuously unmistakable.

The arduous and time-consuming court work would then begin with one case following another, until late afternoon. Father's court, like all tribal courts in Sudan, was empowered by national legislation to try both criminal and civil cases. Criminal cases were mostly a flexible application of the penal code, adapted to tribal conditions and customs. Civil cases concerned mostly personal matters relating to cattle claims from kinship obligations, rights and duties. Father would sit either as the president of the court of first instance to try cases of a certain gravity or as an appellate authority to hear appeals from the courts presided over by his subordinate chiefs.

In all of these cases, the court would listen to the claims, court members would question the litigants, call on the witnesses, and debate the evidence with minimum involvement by Father. Only if he felt that the trend of investigation was missing the point would he intervene to redirect the discussion. Otherwise he would appear to be thinking of other things and sometimes might even close his eyes, lean back on his chair, and look asleep in the middle of a serious case. Eventually, and at the crucial point, he would open his eyes, sit upright, and make his remarks. Whether someone might have been talking then or not, the turn was his and it would suddenly prompt dead silence. He was a most articulate and well-reasoned person; whose words drew attention from everyone. When he ended, his judgement was not only final, but always seemed to strike a note of consensus, so that even those who had entertained other views would be heard to say, "That's it; that is the true and final word." To the Dinka, his word was not only the law, but the "truth" and ultimate wisdom. When I later interviewed people, Dinka, Arabs, administrators, relatives and strangers alike, on the life of my father, I was struck by the fact that they all stressed this point, literally without exception, and with a surprising unanimity of opinion. Granted, they were saying it to his son, but there was something genuine and sincere about the way they said it. Only one man, Deng Makuei, his half-brother, with whom he had competed for leadership, once made a sardonic comment to me, pleased that I was collecting information on Dinka customary law in his court, instead of depending on what he half-jokingly described as "the lies your father says in his court and calls Dinka law". We both laughed.

The day's work done, almost nonstop, except for a brief moment for breakfast at work or back home, my father would return in the late afternoon, followed by a large crowd of people for whom the working day had not been sufficient. Some would be people who still hoped to state their cases to him personally, even though the formal trial might follow later. Others would be people who felt they belonged to his off-duty intimate circle of friends and associates. Others might simply want to be there and continue to watch. Yet others had a variety of personal matters, from requests for assistance, to offers of information on the political situation or on a beautiful girl he might be interested in marrying and whom he might indeed have commissioned individuals to pursue on his behalf. In any case, a considerable fraction of the huge court would accompany the chief home.

For his usually very late lunch, trays of the native Arab *kisra*, a paper-thin bread, with saucy stews and other dishes, would be placed in front of his large circle of elders and attendants, and would then be distributed by the servants, using their discretion or under Father's direction. Father would remove the cover from one tray or platter to another and determine, sometimes by gesturing, what was to go to which guests. He himself would eat with his closest associates, although he was a very small eater, and rarely complained of hunger. He would then retire for his afternoon siesta and re-emerge around 6:00 in the evening to hold his evening sessions. Those were strictly speaking not working occasions, but informal conversations with chiefs, elders, and desired companions. In fact, they nearly always involved anxious complainants and appellants. We would be part or out of the show, depending on how crowded and businesslike the sitting was. If it was too businesslike, we might choose to observe, but not participate. Even when we participated, the situation was always so constrained and formal that it was virtually impossible to expect the gratification of a family-type father-sons informal conversation.

SECONDARY
Bridging the Gulf

In those evening sessions, and indeed on most occasions outside the court, Father's seat would be encircled by people standing in front of him, stooping or kneeling by the side of his chair, yet others standing behind his seat, waiting for their turn, all trying to draw his attention and make a point. Some would be making personal claims, others would be messengers from wives requesting money or something, yet others would have been sent by relatives or strangers asking for some form of assistance. In many cases, he responded by listening, distributing money left and right, and otherwise giving varied instructions on the issues involved. But quite often, too, he would listen without responding, as though he was not hearing a thing. The persons standing, stooping or kneeling, would remain in that position until they would give up and retire. They might report the disappointing fact or distort the truth in any way they deemed appropriate, to mitigate the injury to the sender. Then there would be evening tea, followed by dinner. Both the tea and the dinner would be served in the usual manner by the retainer-policeman. Father would then go on a late walk "to the forest", with a retainer carrying a container of water for cleaning in "the Arab sanitary manner." Coming from his late-night walk, he would go straight to bed, unless he had further night appointments with "dates", to which he was escorted by an agent or a few selected and trusted men.

Because Father was such a small eater, the wives always kept certain delicacies to be served to him when he went to bed. He would take a bite in appreciation of the wives' concern and otherwise redirect the food back to the special guests or to us children, whom he feared might have been overlooked by the wives in their eagerness to please only him.

While Father was in bed for his afternoon siesta or for the night, it was obvious that he had very little rest. His wives lined up in the hope of being with him or talking to him about their personal affairs. Bed relations were left for the senior wives to organise and regulate. The main objective was to facilitate access for those wives who were in their prime period of fertility. The overriding goal was to have children. Information about the condition of the wives would be channelled up the hierarchy, until it reached him. He would then call the wives one by one, simply saying, "Let so and so come." But despite the priority given to those in fertility, it was generally recognised that his personal desires also came high, if not first, in the order of importance.

Despite all the conjugal pressures of the day and night, Father never appeared overwhelmed or even tired. He might yawn from time to time with uninhibited sounds, or might doze off in public, without apologies, but he nearly always looked fresh, alert and in control.

Our day was independent of Father's day, but in some respects, they were parallel. While Father was in court, we would spend the day under the tree on the stream behind our home or under the even larger tree on the river farther away, playing cards, and otherwise passing the time in relative relaxation, until it was virtually time for our father to be back home.

Despite the leisure, my memory is that I worked hard for my father. Although he had an excellent and experienced clerk by the standards of the time, he continued to rely on me for clerical services and particularly for drafting letters he considered to be of particular importance, whether on official or personal matters. Once, he asked me to write a letter to the chief of another Dinka tribe seeking his help in arranging his marriage to a girl from that chief's tribe. After drafting the letter, I read it back to him as he sat with his emissaries, who were to deliver the letter and negotiate on his behalf. When I finished reading, my father and his associates reacted with satisfaction at the way I had presented the arguments. Father then remarked, "You can always count on my Mading!" I was elated.

On several occasions, when litigation in his court involved Arabs, he would ask me to interpret, despite the presence of a professional court interpreter. Complimentary comments would flow on my Arabic, which of course flattered me and I am sure also pleased my father. An Arab once complimented me to my father in a manner that unwittingly revealed their chauvinism. "Nazir", he addressed my father by his Arabic title of chief, "your son has become an Arab". I am sure Father and I appreciated the compliment and overlooked racial condescension. One time, Father took me with him to an Arab gathering where he was to mediate between Babo Nimir, the paramount chief of the Missiriya Arabs, and his opponents, and asked me to be the interpreter.

All this was not simply a performance of duties, but also an education for me. Far from spoiling me, Father's recognition and appreciation of my services, supplemented by the compliments I received from his companions, merely encouraged and challenged me in the direction I had chosen for my self-realisation - education - as an avenue to leadership. And although this was an area in which one might assume that our interests would converge with those of our father, it also posed a potential threat to Father's role as the patriarch and the leader of the tribe, whose word was final.

It was perhaps Father's understanding that our education was making us overstep our bounds that he reacted adversely to our counselling him on the issue of his marriages. We had talked to him while in Tonj Primary School and he had indeed been agreeably responsive. He had even intimated to us that his government superiors always praised him as a leader and pointed out his marriages as their only area of reservation. He said he would moderate his habit. But as nothing had changed, Bol, Kuol and I decided to give it another trial during the last vacation of our second school period. As usual, we had to make an appointment. This time, we decided to have a tea-party and to invite family elders and a selected number of tribal leaders. The party was very formally seated at a long cloth-covered table. Father sat at one end; the other elders were spread around the table; and we sat in between. As was the pattern, my brothers asked me to introduce our case. In my opening statement, I spoke emphasising the changing values of our times, the importance of securing a more modern and higher standard of living for the family, and the political, social, and material strains Father's continuous marriages were exerting on the welfare of the family. We urged him to invest his wealth in shops, commercial lorries, and better housing, rather than in acquiring more wives. The arguments were known; at least they were not new, only strengthened by repetition, our age, and our enhanced level of education.

As I spoke, Father displayed a suspiciously calm, but solemn mood. I could read his nonverbal language as one of unease. When I finished, he did not comment on my words; he simply wondered whether the others had anything to say. Kuol spoke, essentially supporting my theme. Father, still well controlled and composed, but visibly on edge, turned to Bol and said, "I have heard what Mading had to say, and I have also heard Kuol's words; let me hear your words." Bol had the advantage of being the last speaker, for by now it was quite obvious that Father was offended. Bol retracted a little from what we had said: "Father, it is not that we want you to stop marrying; it is just that we think it would be better if you would space the marriages to allow longer intervals, so that instead of marrying every season, you let some time lapse before your next marriage."

When Father eventually spoke, he was more retaliatory than he had ever been on the subject. During our first discussion, he had conceded that we were right, that the same opinion had been expressed to him by government leaders, British and Sudanese alike, that he had a few engagements and that once he had procured those wives, he would stop. This time, the story was different; sons had no right to talk to their father about such matters. We were entitled to make claims that we had a right to as children, to have our education provided for, to request our father to buy us commercial lorries as a business, to open stores for trade, or to have our maintenance secured, but not to ask our father to stop marrying. Had he stopped marrying as early as some people wanted, some of us would not be there to discuss the issue of marriage. I could not help, but think that since my mother was the most junior of the mothers of those who spoke, Father must have had me in mind. He concluded by saying that Bol's line of argument was more acceptable, that he should space his marriages more. In the future, he was not going to entertain any further discussion of the matter. That was that.

To our surprise, all the elders present, who had always supported our line, and had indeed impressed upon us that it was primarily our obligation as sons to discourage our father from perpetual marriages, now appeared so intimidated by Father's response that their attitude was to persuade us to drop the matter. We of course did.

SECONDARY
Bridging the Gulf

Kuol and I were later to mock Bol in a light-hearted manner about his last-minute compromise. Kuol was to declare that in the future, far from criticising Father on the issue of seemingly never-ending marriage, he would indeed win his approval by encouraging him to continue his marriages.

The Author and his brother, Zachariah Bol, sitting in the middle, wearing Jallabiyas, the only South Sudanese at Khor Taqqat Secondary School in Northern Sudan.

Dr. Zachariah Bol Deng, Author's brother and classmate in school.

Author's young Uncle Bona Bulabek.

The Author

CHAPTER TEN

TENSIONS
TURMOIL BENEATH THE CALM

Surrounded as we were by young women, whom custom or fate had labelled as our stepmothers, one would expect temptations to be unavoidable. But as I think back, whatever might be said about how we felt or thought about our father's junior wives, the surprising thing was how well we controlled ourselves. At least for our age group of Bol, Kuol and myself, nothing ever happened to create conflict between Father and us, his three sons.

Nevertheless, we were conscious of Father's junior wives as young women and their presence had an impact on the way we carried ourselves and behaved. Nor were we entirely outside Father's watchful eyes and jealous guard over his wives. From our childhood days in Abyei Elementary School, our quarters with Father's wives were separate and access across the dividing lines was regulated and limited. Contact became increasingly more guarded as we grew up.

While in secondary school, during one of the occasions when we spent part of our vacations at Noong, we went to Abyei to seek reinforcements in financial form from Father. We noticed that he was unusually reserved. Several times, we tried to draw his attention, but he continued to ignore us. Then, he suddenly got up and walked towards the market. We went after him. When we reached the shop of Ali Beshir, the head merchant, he went into the verandah, where he was received and seated. As Ali ordered coffee, our father told his accompanying policeman that he did not want anybody to disturb us, as he had asked us, Bol and me, to join him and sit. It sounded quite serious, but it was impossible to read his mind. Then he began to speak, giving us the history of his relations with his father and step-mothers. He said that the only hut of a step-mother that he ever entered was that of Abiong, the mother of Deng Makuei. He recalled the words of a great uncle to him: "Son, we have a curse in this clan against anyone who goes with another man's wife. Do not even smile with the wife of another man!"

It was obvious that something had gone seriously wrong. According to Father, two of his wives, who were with us at Noong, had been overheard talking. One was said to have said: "If only I could be inherited by Mading!" When I heard my name, I felt an internal disintegration; my mind and senses seemed suddenly numbed. This was more serious than anything I had expected. The next thing he said was ironically more consoling, for Bol and I were placed in the same boat, and I knew that the chances of our being believed as innocent were better if we were accused together. According to Father, another wife had said in response to the wishes of the first, "And Bol, if only I could be inherited by him."

Then followed a moment of silence. One of us had to talk. I took onto myself the burden of responding first, since I was in any case the first accused. I told Father that I had no words to express my surprise and shock at the fact that this could have happened. I said we could only rely on his faith in us and hoped that he did not think we were in any way associated with whatever wishes any of those wives might have expressed. Bol spoke in the same vain.

Father showed a degree of restlessness as we threw the suspicions away. He virtually interrupted us to say that he would investigate the situation and if it were established that the women had indeed said what they had been reported to have said, he would expect us to beat them ourselves, or else he would take us as supporting them. He went on to say that the matter was of utmost confidentiality and that it should be confined to himself and us; under no circumstances should it go beyond. Then, almost as though he had overstated his case and needed to compensate us for doing so, he granted us all our wishes. We left for Noong that evening, not sharing our secret with anyone, not even with Kuol.

One evening a few days later, as we sat around our fireplace chit-chatting, I overheard the women talk some fifty yards from us. Shortly after that, Kuol's mother, Nyanbol Amuor, came and informed us of the news from Abyei. The whole story, as our father had told it to us, was brought by a woman who had just returned from Abyei, none other than the one who had been alleged to have wished for me. According to the version she had heard in Abyei, there was said to be a third woman within hearing distance outside the hut, where the two wives were alleged to have made their wishes. It was she who overheard the conversation and reported to Father. Kuol, to whom all this was news, wondered how we could possibly have heard our father's report without insisting on knowing his source of information and why that source had not first informed us. According to him, our first quarrel should be with the woman who had sidestepped us, which implied that we were implicated in a plot. She should be the first for us to punish. Since there was no way of knowing who had really talked to Father, except through our father himself, Kuol thought we should insist on Father exposing his source before we could take any steps against the accused wives. Kuol seemed so right in what he said that our submissive reaction to our father seemed embarrassing.

What was even more perplexing was Father telling us to keep the matter a secret and then proceeding to reveal the affair. According to the account the woman brought, she went to ask our father for some jewelry. After ignoring her for some time, Father asked sarcastically, "Do you want the jewelry to attract your son?" The woman had responded with "What do you mean, chief?" Father then rebuked her, "Get out of my sight; I don't want to see you. The sight of you nauseates my heart!"

TENSIONS
Turmoil Beneath the Calm

Father had already talked to other wives in Abyei, for when the woman left his room, she heard the story circulating among the wives. We felt betrayed and decided to leave the next morning to confront our father. We quickly secured the appointment with him. Although we did not consider it prudent to blame him for betraying the secret, we impressed upon him our indignation for being kept in the dark about his source and requested that he had to reveal her identity. As was typical of Father, he turned the tables around, displaying a restlessness about our attitude. He said he was waiting for the district commissioner to leave before bringing the matter up for further discussion in the family. He went on to say that he might draw the conclusion from our attitude that there was a degree of discomfort on account of some guilt. Father was always good at making the innocent feel guilty so that he himself would feel innocent. We went back to Noong with no new insight into the crisis.

The whole affair seemed to disappear quietly. We never heard of the matter from Father again. It was typical of Father, when he was convinced by an argument, not to expressly concede, but to eventually act or not act in accordance with the advisory opinion. As for the women, I later learned that they were among those who dropped out, leaving no children, no traces, and probably not even a scandal beyond that event.

Although our group of brothers, Bol, Kuol and myself, stayed among Father's wives without scandals, there were to be scandals in our family, not only involving wives, but also sons. Perhaps the first and the most dramatic case of a son committing adultery with Father's wives was that of Ahmed Arop, Father's eldest son. But the source of tension and conflict between Father and Ahmed went much deeper, perhaps back to the relations between Ahmed's mother and Father, which were said to have been prickly.

Apparently, Ahmed grew up not only with the complex of having had formal marriage procedures had been completed, but also, at least in the reported view of his maternal relatives, that of his Father's mistreatment of his mother. None of this was obvious to us as we grew up. For us, Ahmed was an older brother of whom we were proud. And so was our father, we thought. Ahmed was the first member of the Deng Majok family to acquire higher education. With the special concern the British had about the post-colonial position of the Dinka in the context of Arab domination, and Father's own influence among both the British and Arab authorities, they quickly groomed Ahmed, who was then a clerk in the district headquarters, into becoming a local government executive officer. That was then a position of high central government power that was seen as senior to the chief's authority. Within a short time, Ahmed established his image as a force to be reckoned with in political power, social prestige, and even charisma. His rising position was primarily seen as a limitation on his father's. To make things worse, they were neighbours.

It was rightly or wrongly discussed that Ahmed's self-assertiveness in competition with his father was the result of pressures from his maternal relatives, who reminded him of the past in relations between his father and mother, and disposed him towards using that golden opportunity to avenge the indignity his mother had suffered in the hands of his father. But Father was an old hand in power politics. Just as he had successfully coached the promotion of his son among both the British and the Sudanese officials, especially as his appointment to that senior executive position was unpopular among the Arabs, he was capable of arousing sentiments against Ahmed. Indeed, the Arabs were quick to seize the opportunity of the deteriorating relations between Father and son. Arab administrators began to intensify their efforts at convincing our father that Ahmed was not in his long-term interest and that the promise for the future lay more in Bol and me.

I believe it was at this point that Father talked to me about one of us running for the forthcoming national parliamentary elections. He asked me which of us, Bol and me, was older. When I said he should be the one to tell us and not me to inform him, he said he thought I was older and that he wanted me to run for parliament. Although I was of course flattered, the suggestion was absurd. I was then still in high school and certainly not of age to run. What is noteworthy is that his consideration did not include Ahmed, a clear indication of how things then stood between them. When I told Father that I was underage to be a member of parliament, he said that could be arranged. We never discussed how he could do that.

TENSIONS
Turmoil Beneath the Calm

While we were back in the final year at school, word reached us that Chol Jipur, one of Father's two deputy paramount chiefs, had raised a case of corruption and misappropriation of public funds against our father and Ahmed. When the confrontation materialised and the central government authorities came to investigate the case, Chol Jipur, like those before him, failed dreadfully and was arrested and deported for falsely accusing his superior. But the opposition did not fail altogether, for while Father was fully exonerated, the prima facie case against Ahmed was found to justify his suspension, pending further enquiry and eventual trial. There is little doubt that those who held the case against Ahmed to be at least worth further investigation also realised that he was no longer in father's good books and that Father would at worse be ambivalent about his son's fate.

But things were to get worse for Ahmed, for while he was awaiting further investigation and trial, two of our father's wives confessed that he had committed adultery with them and had made them pregnant. According to the news reaching us in school, the effect of those events was shattering relations between Father and Ahmed and understandably so, considering the degree of our Father's jealousy over his wives.

Ahmed's fortunes were suddenly on a downhill slide. Now in extreme conflict with his father, having committed an offence the Dinka consider not only morally depraved but spiritually contaminating, accused of a crime and threatened with imprisonment, dismissal, and disgrace, Ahmed soon became a haunted man, a social outcast, a rebel without a cause, and a deteriorating loner, who began to drink heavily.

Although we had heard in school about the gravity of the conflict between our father and Ahmed, and could imagine our father's reaction, it was not until we returned home and witnessed the situation ourselves that we fully realised the impact on our father. Shortly after our return, there arrived a delegation of medical students from Khartoum University accompanied by their Scottish professor on an academic tour. As part of our entertainment for them, together with our father, we took the delegation to the ferry on the River Kiir at Akech-nhial, quite close to Ahmed's isolation home across the river. Since a number of the students had been Ahmed's colleagues at Hantoub Secondary School, and had indeed been friends, they requested to see him. We agreed to take them and Ahmed was duly informed. Father was with us in accompanying the delegation. When the group arrived at Akech-nhial, Ahmed came from across the River to meet them. He greeted the guests, but did not approach Father for greeting. Meeting him for the first time since our return from school, we greeted Ahmed with embrace. Our father was watching, apparently enraged by the warmth of our greeting.

That same afternoon, when we were back in Abyei, Father called a meeting of all his wives and sons in his bedroom. Present also was his sister, Aunt Awor, Deng Aguer's mother. Our father spoke about the moral principles that had been handed down by our ancestors as guidelines on the question of social, let alone sexual, relations with married women and in particular, stepmothers. He spoke again of his own attitude as a young man growing up among his father's wives, and the extent to which he had avoided even their huts.

Turning to what Ahmed had done, he said it had first crossed his mind to take the gun and shoot him, forgetting the chieftainship, and ready to face trial for murder. He said he decided against that, but did not tell on what grounds. However, he said the least he could do was to cut off Ahmed from the family, never again to be regarded as his son. He said he had been shocked to see us greet Ahmed with such enthusiasm and warmth as to embrace him. He said we would have to make a choice between Ahmed and Father. Those who chose to be with Ahmed had to leave the family and join him. Those who were on Father's side were not to have anything to do with Ahmed and were to immediately break all ties with him. He said he was going to convene a general assembly of the family at Noong and carry out the rituals of Ahmed's severance from the family.

Father spoke in such a bitter and categorical way that it was unthinkable for anyone to contradict him. It was even difficult to find adequate words of support for him. So, with me taking the floor first, followed by Bol and Kuol, we spoke simply to reassure Father of our agreement with the moral values he had expounded, to express our indignation at what Ahmed had done, and our sympathy for

Father's feelings on the matter. We said nothing directly connected with the issue of ritualised severance of Ahmed, but, unfortunately, by omission, we implicitly appeared to be in agreement with Father.

Aunt Awor was obviously didn't like our passive stance on the issue of severance of blood ties. She went to her brothers, Uncles Biong and Arop, and received unequivocal support against the idea. They in turn chose to talk to us, instead of to our father directly. In a serious business-like meeting, they told us that sons were the most appropriate persons to confront their father on such a matter as what was at issue between Ahmed and our father; that there was no way Ahmed could be disaffiliated. However much he was denied by the family, he would remain the blood and social member of the family and his image anywhere would remain part of the family. They said it was our responsibility to persuade our father to abandon his plan to banish Ahmed from the family. Indeed, they expressed strong disappointment at our implied support for Father's position and urged us to undo that by immediately initiating a talk with him on the matter. They were undoubtedly persuasive in their arguments.

Before we could approach Father, a letter came from Ahmed addressed to Father, and sent to me to read to him. I knew this was bound to be an unpleasant assignment, but one I had to perform. After going through the letter, I waited for Father and approached him as he emerged from the female enclosure where he slept, and was going to his morning teatime meetings in our room. I told Father that I had a letter for him from Ahmed. I hoped he would patiently listen to the letter before going into the public meeting place. Very impatiently, Father asked what the letter was about. I told him it was about the quarrel between him and Ahmed. He said, "And what is he saying about it?" I tried to summarise the letter, but there was no way of politely rephrasing the substance and tone of the letter which was an angry reaction to what Father had said in his meeting with the family. How Ahmed knew, I do not know. Essentially, he said he had heard of Father's meeting with the family and his intentions to eject him from the family. Ahmed wrote of how saddened he was that his father had not only disowned himself from him, but would go to the extent of cutting him off from his family. He wrote, and I reported faithfully to my father, that only God would be the judge. With that point, Father's patience was exhausted; he said, "Stop there; God will be our judge." He would not listen to any further translation of the letter, which, in any case, had nothing more of substance to add.

Having decided to talk to Father on the issue of Ahmed, we sought an appointment as we had always done on such occasions. Father granted the audience. As always, the brothers designated me to open the discussion. I spoke reaffirming our stand behind the values Father had espoused in our earlier meeting with him and our sympathy with the reason behind his decision to expel Ahmed from the family. But, reiterating the argument of Aunt Awor and Uncles Biong and Arop, we told Father that there was no way we could strip Ahmed of his family identity and that wherever he went, he would still be Deng Majok's son. What was more, I said, introducing a highly sensitive aspect, Ahmed had been his father's top aide and partner in tribal power. I noted that there had been, and still were, many critics who made serious accusations against him, including allegations of corruption. If Ahmed were to be cast out, humiliated and forced to take the side of Father's enemies and expose the secrets of father-son power collaboration, might that not be damaging to Father? I argued that people might then conclude that since Ahmed had been working very closely with his father and probably shared the secrets of their work, he must know the facts about the allegations against his father. And however false the allegations and what Ahmed might confess against his father, there would be a tendency to believe him as someone who ought to know the truth. Such embarrassment, I concluded, should be avoided in order not to give our enemies a weapon to use.

The strength of the argument seemed to antagonise our father even more. As usual, he wanted to hear from Bol and Kuol. They concurred with what I had said. After having listened to all of us, confirming our joint line of argument, Father spoke with deep disappointment. He said angrily that he had never realised that he had a bunch of cowards for sons. If we had all become intimidated by Ahmed, then he would stand on his own and proceed with his plans for severing Ahmed from his family. "Let him do what he wants to do, I do not care; if you are afraid of him, I am not." That was his concluding remark. Of course, we argued beyond our normal limits of courage, but he was clearly not to be persuaded otherwise. Our meeting ended with no position changed, but certainly with a full exchange of views. On our part, I felt satisfied that we had adequately performed our duty as his senior sons.

No family council was ever held as planned by our father, and, knowing that he was never one to recognise being in the wrong, or to admit that he had been persuaded otherwise, we watched with interest the passage of time without action on his part and convinced ourselves that our message had registered and that Ahmed would not be disaffiliated after all. In fact, our father's attitude improved considerably with time, and although he never forgave Ahmed publicly, he did nothing to disavow him publicly either.

When Ahmed's trial eventually came, Father did nothing to defend or protect him, but he was less than openly negative towards him. Yet, everyone knew that Ahmed did not have his father's backing and support. He faced the case as a loner and in the realistic world of law and politics, there could be no way of divorcing the finding of guilt from the loss of his father's sympathy and support. This was particularly apparent when he was sentenced to a prison term that I believe could have been replaced by financial settlement, which Father could have made, had he chosen to do so.

As it was, Ahmed went to jail in far-off Nahud, suffered a greater emotional ordeal on account of his father's disregard for his fate, lost a dedicated wife who died while with him in Nahud, trying to provide him with some care and consolation, and ultimately survived to the extent that he did only because of his resilience and strength of character, ironically, at least in part, inherited from his father.

The year of conflict between Ahmed and Father was the year of our final vacation at home from Khor Taqqat. We were then graduating from our third year and about to enter our final year. As the third year exams had been interrupted by a strike, we were expected to study during our vacation. This necessitated finding an alternative to the normal living conditions of our family, which were utterly prohibitive to any studies. We succeeded in taking over an abandoned brick wall and corrugated iron roof house that had belonged to the medical assistant. For the first time in our lives, Bol and I lived in a house with two separate rooms, each of us occupying his own room with a door in between.

That year, Mekki Miyar, the son of Nyanbol Deng, the sixth wife in seniority, was to play what in retrospect was a heroic act which provoked our father, not least because of undermining the authority of his father. We were invited to attend a meeting of the school selection board which was chaired by our father and which was to admit first year pupils. The headmaster was a Northern Sudanese and as a part of the Arabisation and Islamisation policies that the government had embarked upon in the South, Abyei school system had been changed from the vernacular-English-Christian Southern system to the Arab-Islamic system of the North. Theoretically, while Islam was favoured by the authorities, the parents of the children were expected to make their choice of religion for their children.

Of course, it was generally assumed that the competition was between Islam and Christianity, as traditional Dinka religion was not accorded any recognition as a religion. The new headmaster, who directed the proceedings, went beyond the usual limits of official prejudice for Islam. He informed the committee that the policy of the government was to promote Islam and that there was therefore no room for the parents of the children to choose Christianity for the children from families following African traditional beliefs and practices, who must be assumed to have become Muslims by joining the school. We were all surprised and of course offended by this discriminatory attitude, but since he claimed to have received orders from the Ministry of Education to that effect, we could not hold him responsible.

Among the crowds who blocked the windows to peek and listen was Mekki Miyar, who had received his elementary and part of his intermediate education in the North, had been converted to Islam, and had acquired the Muslim name of Mekki. Like his mother, Nyanbol Deng, who frequently got into confrontation with Father, Mekki was a stubborn boy who, throughout his childhood, had never given into intimidation or the use of force.

TENSIONS
Turmoil Beneath the Calm

One late afternoon, we returned from hunting to find our father and the headmaster sitting outside our house, waiting for us. From the look on Father's face, something quite serious had gone wrong. He handed me a letter to read, asking whether we knew anything about the matter concerned. I anxiously read the letter and passed it on to Bol. It was from Mekki, addressed to the headmaster. Mekki wrote of how surprised he had been by what the headmaster had said at the admission committee meeting, and asked him where in the laws of the Sudan it was provided that all pupils in government schools had to be Muslims.

It was a simple, logical, political letter which was why it was all the more disturbing to the headmaster. As he put it, before he saw the name, he had thought the letter was from a Christian missionary and could not believe it had been written by one of what he described as "our sons." We told Father that Mekki had not at all talked to us about the matter. Mekki was fetched and as soon as he came, Father exploded in extreme anger, bordering on physical assault. Mekki did not withdraw, but indeed continued to defend his position and to condemn the headmaster's action. Our father became enraged. He wanted to call the police and order them to arrest Mekki and take him to jail. The headmaster intervened and urged our father not to take such drastic action. We too tried to convince Mekki that however right he was on the issue, it was wrong for him to address himself to the headmaster, by passing not only his father, but also his senior brothers. We urged him to apologise. But Mekki completely refused to apologise or admit any wrong-doing. We were all helpless, for Mekki would not compromise and there was no way Father would let him get away with such insubordination.

Before getting up to leave, Father said to Mekki, "I want you to leave Abyei and be out of my tribe by tomorrow." The next morning, Mekki took a lorry going to Wau, where he got employed. After being transferred to the North, he returned to Wau where he died in 1965 in the Northern massacre of an elite group of Southern Sudanese government officials during a wedding party. Until his death, Mekki visited home on vacations, but otherwise maintained absolute independence from Father and even made financial arrangements for his mother.

One of the most bizarre incidents in our relationship with Father was participating in his glamorous marriage to Apiny in Twicland and then, only two years later, overstretched our mandate by divorcing her on Father's behalf. It was during our first vacation from Khor Taqqat that we accompanied Father on his marriage expedition to the Twic area of Chief Awich Ayuel. We went in an impressive entourage which included our father himself, several of his leading associates, and a number of wives. At least one hundred cows and some twenty oxen and bulls, all carefully selected, were driven by a group of young men.

Apparently, the negotiations were expected to be difficult. My father was being rejected on the grounds that there had in the past been a blood feud between the clans. But that was understood to be an excuse. The real reason was to make the girl difficult to procure and therefore to raise her value in cattle and enhance the social character of the celebration. As was to be apparent later, the girl herself and her brother were more genuinely opposed, presumably because of Father's large number of wives, but the clan and the tribe were to prove more amenable to persuasion through wealth and social status. Indeed, Father was known for his readiness to face any challenge of rejection with a determination that knew no limits to his ostentatious ways of persuasion.

The afternoon of our arrival in the village of the girl was one of the most dramatic expressions of Father's ostentatiousness and social pride. As we emerged from the woods that concealed the open area in which the village was located, riders raced their horses into the stretches of open space, encircled by the wide spreading settlements of the girl's village. As they raced, all dressed in white jallabiyas, their turbans flying about with the reverse current, a number of gun-shots were fired into the air to announce our arrival. The show went on for some time before we came to a stop and selected our camping site.

Our father's huge tent was quickly erected before nightfall and instead of the hosts honouring the group by slaughtering bulls, our father quickly had two bulls slaughtered not only for his group but also for the village and visitors from neighbouring areas. Father soon got up for a walk to the pools and lagoons in the area where a variety of birds assembled. Combining his hobby of shooting, with the intention of impressing those remote villagers with the power of the shotgun, and providing them with the delicacy of foul meat, the shooting walk added a special flair that could only be appreciated in the context.

The following morning, the hunting continued. Later, we moved to another village where the group would be accommodated in huts and where the marriage negotiations were to be conducted. It was there that Chief Awich Ayuel and the leading personalities of his tribe called on our father for courtesy. Chief Awich attended Father's assembly for the whole of that day, socialising, but saying nothing directly connected with the wedding, except perhaps to prepare the ground. He and his companions were entertained with delicious food and gallons of tea, which was considered special in those remote areas of the rural Southern Sudan.

Awich Ayuel seemed to have been won over and became a friend to count on. But Father was discreetly active in winning people: women, men, individuals and groups. Selected persons were busy distributing the gifts of clothes and other town items which we had brought with us. It soon became evident that our possessions would not suffice, for the circle of those to be won over was rapidly enlarging. That was when my father decided to send me to a shop that was some distance away, owned by an old friend of his, Deng Kiir.

Luckily, Chief Awich's clerk had come to see my father on a bicycle and I was asked to take the bicycle, hoping to be back before they had to leave. This was late morning. I rode for what seemed to be a long time without any sign of the place. Then I came to a village located on an elevated spot. There I saw a lady advancing towards me. She was dressed in long elegant leather skirts trimmed with beautiful beads on all sides. She wore white metal coils on her arms and legs and was otherwise decorated with various ornaments on her neck, ears and head. She was clearly a woman of status by Dinka standards and despite her decorated appearance, she was not young; indeed, she looked like what the Dinka would call "the mother of a girl", or *man nya*, whose daughter could be old enough to be a bride.

As I approached the lady, I stopped the bicycle in order to leave her the way. As we passed one another, I said in a typical traditional fashion of respect, "Our ways are meeting; may I be excused in passing?" She stopped and looked back to me as I passed. "Son, where are you from?" I said I was from the Ngok Dinka. She asked whose son I was. I said I was the son of Deng Majok. She said, "What you have done has sweetened my heart very much. I used to fear that the education of our children was destroying the good ways of our people, the Dinka. Now, you have shown me that this is not necessarily the case. May God bless you to travel in safety and peace."

I passed the village and cycled on. At one point, while in a grove just before the open space, where Dinka usually build their villages, I asked a passerby where Deng Kiir's shop was. Surprisingly, he asked where I came from. I told him. Then he said, "You still have a very long way to go; you must cycle very fast if you are to get there before sunset." Disheartened but challenged, I exerted my strength even more and peddled as hard as I could. The wide-open area beyond the woods was encircled by homesteads from which came a crowd of barking dogs converging on me. This pushed me to go even faster, looking directly ahead of me to make sure my path was not intercepted by a dog, struggling to outpace them. That way, I crossed the area and was out of danger from the village dogs.

I continued to cycle on until I came to what seemed like an endless bridge, cutting through swamps of treeless savannah. By this time, I had difficulty understanding how people could have thought I would bring back the clerk's bicycle before dusk. At one point, I asked a passerby how far the shop was and he told me it was some distance, but not too far. Then suddenly I arrived at a shop, immediately alongside the road to my left.

I was so exhausted that I felt immense relief at the sight of the shop. It did not bother me to realise that my front tire was losing air and was rapidly becoming flat. That would soon be corrected. I was warmly greeted and seated. Then I asked where Deng Kiir was. That was when I got my real shock of the day. I had not only passed Deng

TENSIONS
Turmoil Beneath the Calm

Kiir's shop, but had gone far beyond the territory of Chief Awich Ayuel into an entirely different tribe, Awan of Chief Chan Nyal. But the people were kind and helpful. They made me tea and mended my tire, then agreed with me that I had to be heading back, if I hoped to reach Deng Kiir's shop before night fall. As I knew the way back, I was not as anxious, even though I was exhausted.

When I reached the area where Deng Kiir's shop was, I realised that it was the same area where the dogs had chased after me and concluded that the man I had asked in the forest nearby had misled me. Why? Perhaps he himself was not from that precise area, did not know Deng Kiir's shop, and was thinking of the shop to which I had gone.

I arrived at Deng Kiir's shop just before sunset. He received me warmly and was very hospitable. As my tire had again gone flat, he had it repaired, but then advised me to spend the night with him and leave the following morning. I insisted that I had to go back the same night, as my father needed the items urgently. So, he packed the items, mostly clothes, onto the bicycle and let me go with great reluctance.

Shortly after I left, it began to shower and I almost regretted not having stayed. I could still have returned to Deng's shop, but I was quite determined to proceed on, believing that I could cycle in the rain. I soon discovered that I was wrong, for even before I went far from Deng's village, the mud frequently jammed the wheels and stopped the bicycle. I would get down, clear the mud off the wheels, give it another attempt, be forced to stop again, and repeat the whole process all over, a truly slow and painful operation. Again, I felt tempted to return to Deng's shop while I was still near, but I dismissed the thought as ridiculous, for I had already insisted on leaving and it would be embarrassing to retreat. In any case, I had to reach my father the same night. So, I struggled on, mostly pushing the bicycle, while I walked.

Even then, I had to stop very frequently to clear the mud off the wheels. I soon became convinced that there was no way I could continue pushing the loaded bicycle back to my father's place. I would need someone to help me carry the load. I approached the next person I saw and offered him the job. He was at first tempted by the offer, but soon withdrew on the grounds that he had to attend to his cattle.

Struggling on by myself, I came to a village where I had met the lady. It had now been raining for some time and water had gathered on the ground. This helped wash off the mud so that the problem of getting the wheels jammed had been considerably reduced. It was beginning to get dark when I suddenly met a group of elders almost exactly on the spot where I had met the lady. They were about four, all tall and stark naked, with clothes folded and tied to their spears. As soon as they started talking to me, I realised that this was Chief Awich Ayuel himself with his followers. Although shocked to see them naked, I quickly decided that such things should be expected in that part of Dinkaland and felt great relief in having encountered them, for I assumed that the least the chief would do was to see me taken home to my father quite safely. It was now darkening so quickly that only the frequency of the lightning helped show the way. Otherwise, the rain, the violent thunder, and the darkness of the night were frightening beyond words.

To my utter surprise and horror, Chief Awich simply enquired as to why I was so late and urged me to rush on if I hoped to reach home that night. I had not even said anything then about wanting to reach home that night. When one of his men expressed surprise that he would send me off under such dreadful circumstances, instead of insisting that I should spend the night in his house, Chief Awich Ayuel said "I have no room; why don't you take him yourself?" I could not believe the words I was hearing the chief say. That was when I said that I did not want to be accommodated, but simply needed someone to carry my luggage and otherwise guide my way back to my father. Awich's companion again talked to him in a murmur, obviously urging him to do something. Awich shamelessly, even loudly, responded that there were no people to send with me, and directed me to go to a nearby cattle byre in the hope that I might find someone to hire.

Infuriated, but challenged by this behaviour that did not conform with what would be expected from a chief, I felt my way to the cattle

TENSIONS
Turmoil Beneath the Calm

byre. As I might have expected, no one was willing to undertake the task. The chief's clerk's house was nearby. When he learned that I was going back under those circumstances and that I had met Chief Awich, he showed clear indignation at the chief's attitude and tried to persuade me to stay with him until the morning. But by this time, anger had driven me into blind courage and determination to continue my way, no matter what dangers lay ahead. The clerk could not help me with anyone and so he watched with astonishment as I left.

What lay ahead was miserable beyond description. So much rain had fallen that the entire ground was flooded and appeared like an endless lake, noticeable only when the lightning flashed. There was no way to tell the path and although frequent lightning continued to guide me away from obvious hazards, I found myself falling into thorn bushes from time to time. On several occasions, when lightning became less frequent, I wandered into heaps of prickly barrages around the gardens and got myself completely entangled. Many times, I fell flat with the bicycle, now heavier than ever as everything was soaked to full capacity. Violent thunderstorm continued as did occasional lightning, even though the rain was ebbing. But apart from the many thorns that had pricked me all over, there was reason to fear snakes, scorpions, and of course, hyenas, lions and leopards. More than once, I broke down and cried in utter despair. I would curse, then pray, and otherwise surrender myself to fate. The world had never, never, been so cruel and lonely.

At least twice, I felt my way into a homestead, knocked on a hut, and implored to be guided and helped with the luggage. But I was told that there were no men in the hut, a clear lie I could detect. Then I came to a hut where the man made the mistake of answering, but refused on the grounds that it was too dangerous an undertaking, as the area was infested with lions and other ferocious animals. Nevertheless, they did not invite me in for the night. All the prejudices we had grown up with against those people that they were greedy, selfish and inhospitable became fulfilled.

I had nothing but contempt and disgust for them all, from their Chief Awich Ayuel, down to the people in the hut to whom I was now talking: "You people, I have heard much about you, but never really knew you. Tonight, I have come to know you. I am a literate person, and I can write things down to be found and read, even after I am dead. My father is Deng Majok and you know what kind of man he is and what he can do. I am going to write down what you have done to me and how you can be found. If I die, it will be found and read. If I live, I shall tell my father all about you. In either case, you will have no way to escape and you will see with your own eyes what can become of a person who behaves to guests in such an inhuman way as you have done to me. You have your choice, either you take me to my father and be rewarded well for what you have done, or refuse and you will pay the price."

That was absolutely my last trump card. There was dead silence; then a murmur. Finally, a voice said, "How much did you say you would pay?" My answer was unequivocal: "Money is nothing. My father will pay you all you want, I promise you. Only please take me to him."

Again, they complained about the dangers on the way, the darkness, the difficulty of recognising the way, the wild animals, and the women they were leaving behind unprotected. But, eventually, they emerged from the hut and we got onto our way with better feelings towards one another. They proved to have been right about the difficulty of telling the way. Several times, we knocked on people's doors to be redirected, and several times we discovered that we had been heading in the wrong direction.

Several times, we heard a lion roar. By this time, our purpose was the same and our fate could be one. We therefore walked in unity and solidarity. We arrived at the village long after everybody had gone to bed. The two men slept in the cattle byre, while I joined my brothers in a hut specially allocated to us. When I told my father the whole story the following morning, it was clear that he was angered by Chief Awich's attitude. However, nothing could be done in the circumstances, but to nurse the grievance and otherwise pretend all was well. My two guides were of course thanked and well remunerated by my father. When Chief Awich Ayuel came to see my father that morning, he was well received, honoured, lavishly fed and otherwise given a good time, with no word said about what he had done to me.

The negotiations went well for my father. The marriage was discussed, its terms agreed, cheerfully celebrated and concluded. On the insistence of my father, we were given the wife to take back with us, thereby bypassing a few steps in the ordinarily lengthy procedure of Dinka marriage. Apiny became sick a year later and had to return home. Since her wedding day, the only time we saw her again was as she was leaving for home on her sick leave to her family. She then walked gingerly and looked very weak. We were indeed embarrassed not to have learned of her illness and to witness the sharp contrast between the one who had been so much sought after and the retreating one whose severe illness did not seem to have drawn much attention at home.

It was no wonder therefore that word was later to come to Father that she did not wish to return to her marital home. Repeated messages from Father to her family did not produce any positive results. One day, Father asked me to write a letter to her chief, the successor of Awich Ayuel (who had since fallen foul with the government to my obvious delight), to say that he should be sent his wife or have his bride wealth cattle returned. I wrote the letter which was carried by two of my father's retainers, tribal policemen. Father then said, rather casually, that if no result came from the letter, he thought I should go myself to demand the return of his wife or claim compensation for the bride wealth. Shortly after we sent the letter, Father went to a council meeting in Rigil el Fulah, our district capital. The retainers returned empty handed, without the wife or the cattle.

Our departure date for the final year at school was approaching; Father was still away, having taken longer than had been anticipated; and we needed both school fees and pocket money. Rather than risk meeting Father on the way without sufficient money on him, we decided to carry out the mission he had wanted me to conduct to return his wife or claim his cattle back. I persuaded Bol and cousin Osman (Kooch), son of Aunt Awor, to come along with me. We went on horseback.

We found the new chief more friendly and hospitable than Awich. He certainly seemed to understand our mission, and sympathise with our mission, which offered the choice of either taking back the wife of our father or claiming the return of our bride wealth. He began to send for the relatives of the girl and in the meantime tried to enlighten a few people about our mission. It soon became evident to us that there was a sharp division within the girl's family. Some, perhaps most, wanted the marriage to survive either because of their desire to maintain the relationship with Chief Deng Majok or because they saw the task of returning the cattle as quite formidable, if not impossible.

Before the court convened, we paid a visit to Apiny's family, where we were shown lavish hospitality and great courtesy. Then we met with our step-mother. In her own gentle and courteous way, she was extremely frank in expressing her determination not to return to our family. She argued that there was nothing for her to return to but a circle of crowded and frustrated wives, suffering in isolation, who did not even see their stepsons. She challenged us to say how many times we had seen one another since her marriage, and we could not argue with her contention that we saw her again just as she was leaving for home. She said that in the entire course of her illness, she rarely saw her husband and certainly never any of her stepsons. "What kind of a family situation was that?" she asked rhetorically. We were deeply moved by her words and felt that it would clearly be in our mutual interest to work on Father's second alternative, that we be given back our cattle, which had indeed been our motivation in undertaking the mission in the first place.

When the court convened, I opened our case, presenting the two alternatives and discreetly concealing our preference for the second choice. There was overwhelming support in court for the first alternative, namely, that we be given our father's wife to take back with us. Of course, we could not oppose that even though it was unfortunately at variance with our secret preference. Luckily, the girl herself and her brother as well seemed determined beyond persuasion to end the marriage. Having stated our case, backed by further statements from Bol and Kooch, we turned into spectators as the family members and their public battled among themselves over the two alternatives.

Suddenly, as soon as the court realised that the girl and her brother were determined and that there was nothing, they could do about that, there was a turnabout in the trend of thought. Instead of trying to persuade the girl and her brother to maintain the marriage, there was a surprising criticism against the idea that we could come to plead a case which might entail divorce. One after another, the elders spoke strongly in praise of our father and his powers of persuasion. They said he could never fail in achieving his aims through the power of his words and that he would certainly have succeeded in securing the return of his wife had he been there personally. They were clearly opposed to the case being argued by his sons who were not even old enough or knowledgeable enough in traditional matters to have their six lower frontal teeth extracted, let alone being initiated into adulthood. This, they felt, was not only a weakness in our father's case, but indeed an insult to their tribe. There was no way they could simply decide to end the marriage and return the cattle unless and until Deng Majok himself went to declare his will in front of them.

We were then reminded of the paramount value the Dinka place on cattle and the difficulty of persuading them to surrender them. The hostile trend of thought was none other than a strategy to deter us away from our case, to prolong their possession of our cattle, and perhaps to frustrate our entire claim to their return. Because we clearly understood the purpose, we refused to be intimidated into withdrawal and we applied all the verbal skills we could command to press our case, which was in any way quite strong. The chief himself remained persuaded to our point of view and at any rate we had become socially so close, giving him as much hospitality from what we had brought with us as we were receiving from him, that it would have been difficult for him to ignore our point of view simply for reasons of material benefit to the members of his tribe.

Eventually, the chief decreed that we be returned our cattle that were still in the possession of the girl's relatives and be compensated for those that were lost. Since the cattle were so many and widely dispersed, the process of reclaiming them would be a lengthy one that could go on for years. Quite apart from our mission to settle the marriage issue, our interest was more immediate, namely, procuring cattle to sell for our school fees and pocket money. We argued that we had no time to wait. We would be content with returning any number of cattle that were easily available, on the understanding that the rest would be fetched later. After intensive efforts on the side of the chief, we were able to obtain some thirty cows, many of them attractive cow-calves that had matured during the marriage, but had not yet given birth.

We rushed back home where people seemed disturbed not only by the quality of the cattle we had withdrawn from Father's marriage, but, even more significantly, by the thought that we could have dared to break his marriage in his absence. What was worse was the reaction provoked by our selling a good number of the best cattle, which most Dinka thought should have been kept for breeding. Throughout the adventure of divorcing Father's wife, starting from the time we had undertaken the mission, through the tough litigation we had eventually won, to our controversial sale of the best of the herd, I personally felt continuous stress and uncertainty about what we were doing. I was convinced that what we had done would not please our father, despite the fact that we were following the instructions he had given me.

It was of course true and unquestionable that Father had asked me to undertake the mission and to present the two alternatives. It was equally true that I knew my father well enough to realise that he was not as interested in returning his cattle as he was in securing the return of his wife. He had never retrieved his cattle from any marriage that had failed. In fact, it was never Father's style to initiate divorce. His most effective punishment for any woman who dared seek the dissolution of their marriage was to abandon taking care of her, but otherwise maintain the strings of the marriage as a restriction on her freedom. It was clear to me that what Father had meant was to exert pressure on her family to return his wife, not his cattle. Our objective was exactly the opposite and we knew it. By achieving that objective, we had deliberately sabotaged Father's purpose. That we had done something very serious was obvious in the way people had already reacted. And I felt that the responsibility was first and foremost mine personally.

All this gave me a deep sense of guilt which I did not explain to anyone, including myself fully, but which made me very apprehensive of Father's reaction and gave me an acute sense of anxiety and insecurity. As we rode to Muglad, I found myself increasingly buried in my thoughts: "What will Father say when he learns of what we have done?" There was no question that I individually shouldered the main burden of responsibility, since it was me, he had requested to take charge of the mission. It was then that the horrible thought of his declaring in anger that I was not his son crossed my mind. Might he be correct if he did?

As we proceeded, we met with people coming from the North and received news of Father's whereabouts. Some of the passersby were close enough to tell us that he had heard of what we had done. While they carefully avoided saying anything that might disturb us, they indicated that there was reason to be apprehensive about his reaction. As I was lost in my worrying thoughts about how Father would react to me personally, we suddenly came across Father and his party. We got off our horses and embraced each other very warmly, indeed unusually so. My immediate impulse on contact was one of deep relief and an unusual depth of love and affection for my father. All he did that day reinforced this mutually positive sentiment between Father and us.

Being anyway a convenient time to stop for the afternoon rest, he decided that we should rest together and talk before proceeding in our opposite directions. Somehow, his questions seemed to be largely aimed at me and we talked about everything, frivolous and important, but all with surprising warmth and affection - no anger of any kind whatsoever. Even when he did ask how much money we had sold the cattle for and I told him, he only remarked: "And the two of you are taking all that money by yourselves?" We argued on the basis of our needs. Things could not have gone better with Father. He had not questioned our actions in dissolving the marriage or in the sale of cattle and was, quite the contrary, much more friendly and loving than I would have expected. He only asked us to give some money to Ahmed, who was in Nahud, still a prisoner, which indicated that his feelings about Ahmed had softened. Despite this friendly interaction with Father, my earlier apprehensions remained. "Perhaps there is something I have never been told. Might it be possible that I am not my father's son?" With that question, I had plunged into a depressive obsession.

The school had been closed before the exams because of a strike. We were expected to sit for the exams immediately after our return and there was no doubt that the school was determined to be tough on the students. Those who failed would repeat the class and might even be dismissed. Bol had done his best to study under the difficult social conditions of our family. I had not even tried to study, partly because I had found it impossible in the social circumstances of Abyei, and partly because I felt there would be enough time to do so after returning to school. There was also a deeper, more dangerous, assumption that I had always managed to do well with only moderate preparation at best. And there I was, so preoccupied with the issue of my very being that it was impossible to concentrate on my studies the last minute as I might otherwise have done.

The exams came and although I managed to pass in most subjects, I failed in two. I do not remember the subjects, but probably science and maths, the subjects I was generally rather weak in. This was enough to put me in the category of those about whom the authorities had to make a decision whether to repeat or proceed. Bol had passed well and would proceed without question. When the results were announced, the combination of the turbulent mood I was already in and the shock of the new situation made the whole thing completely unreal. Never in our entire education had we been separated by examination results. For the first time in our three years at Khor Taqqat, I walked in the shrubby woods of the arid land of Kordofan alone without Bol, to give myself the privacy to reflect undisturbed and unnoticed and to think aloud. "What will they say at home when they learn that I have failed and dropped behind Bol?" But other thoughts would intervene: "Is it possible that I am not my father's son?"

I was absolutely devastated, so much so that when word came that I was to proceed to the final year, it made very little difference to the turbulence of my inner world, which continued to ferment with meticulous analysis of my identity crisis. Because of the complexities involved in the circumstances of my mother's marriage, which I knew in general terms, my analysis kept leading me to different conclusions. I would sigh in relief, proud and happy that I had ruled out being anybody else's son, but my father's. Then suddenly, all the calculations and the logic in front of me would be erased and the crucial question would reemerge, "But what if all this is wrong and I am simply not my father's son?" I would get back into myself, even if I were in other people's company. While harmonising between my inner world and my external appearance, trying hard to satisfy both, I would be that deeply engrossed in looking for the loopholes that had plunged me back into doubting my identity as father's son.

In the classroom, I watched the blackboard, focused on the teachers, and appeared involved in the lesson, but in reality, I was in my own uncertain world of unresolved identity. I would go back to the dormitory, lie on my back, eyes open or closed, and perhaps even go to sleep, but never with tranquility or peace of mind. I remained haunted by the same questions, the same line of thought, the same conclusions, the same doubts recurring over and over again. Whether I was sleeping or awake, showering or walking, in the classroom or in the dining room, in company or in isolation, I never seemed to free myself from the vicious circles of my internal agony.

I then asked myself why it was so important to me that I was the son of my father and how I would take it if the facts turned out to be otherwise. On the whole, I had felt proud to be my father's son, whatever grievances I might have held against my father. Could I face the world as somebody else's son? Well, if I were in fact someone else's son, I would have to face that reality. That would mean recognising my real father, probably joining him, whatever his situation. And leave my present father? Why not? I began to believe that I understood the source of the ambivalence I had always thought Father felt towards me. But then I would suddenly feel a deep sense of appreciation that he had been so good to me despite my not being his real son. I felt I owed him a great deal which had to be expressed in one way or another, if I were to discover and join a different father. The overriding issue for me was not where I would be better off, by whatever criterion, but what my integrity as reflected in the truth of the situation dictated. The fate would be determined by the facts.

In sharp contrast to the turmoil of my internal world, I remained externally composed and secretive about my thoughts. Even Bol was totally in the dark. Although he and I had always been so close that the family thought of us as twins, I believe we have never been as distant in our thoughts as I felt we were then. The only way out of my predicament was to find the answer to the crucial question. But the only people who could provide a reliable answer were not at Khor Taqqat, but back home. I decided to request leave immediately and return home.

Our form master was Mr Jones, a slim sharp-featured Englishman of medium height and friendly disposition. Mr Jones also taught us English and seemed to be especially interested not only in my performance, but also in my future. As he was the most likely to be sympathetic to my point of view, I spoke to him. As I was not about to reveal the full nature of my disturbance, I simply told Mr Jones that something was bothering me a great deal, to the point of interfering with my studies. I needed to go home, I said, but promised to be back as early as possible and would then be able to concentrate on my studies.

Mr Jones surprisingly understood. Whether it was because I was persuasive in my presentation or because he had already noticed something unusual in my behaviour and felt that this was perhaps an opportunity for a remedy, I cannot tell. He thought the problem might be too much of Khor Taqqat and promised to talk to the headmaster. I received the headmaster's approval and was directed to receive my travel warrants from my housemaster, Abdel Azim.

But Zulfu, as Abdel Azim was known in jest, a term I did not understand, said to me that they were responsible for my education and my future and that there was no way they could let me go without the consent of my father or guardian. If I wanted, they would be happy to write to my father, stating my reasons for wanting to go home, and would then permit or prevent my going home, according to my father's reaction. This was understandable, but as good as "No." Even assuming Father's understanding, the mere circumstances of correspondence ruled out a letter getting to him and his reply coming back before the end of the academic year. Abdel Azim's approach was a dead-end which the headmaster, then Bushra Abdel Rahman, sanctioned.

I thought of just leaving, despite everything and everybody, but I felt that would be tantamount to closing the door on my eventual return to school. I also had a deep conviction that the authorities were trying to serve my interest. I decided to reflect further, rather than act rashly. Realising that it would not be too long before the mid-term leave, I eventually resigned myself to waiting until then. The hopelessness of being prevented from going home ironically forced me to shape up and face the hard facts of the coming mid-term examinations, which the school authorities were taking as an indication of how we would perform in the nationwide Cambridge School Certification examinations ahead. The latter would qualify one for the university or otherwise determine one's professional future. Against the odds, I did my best to prepare for the exams, always shifting between studies and worries.

I was in the middle of all this when our student's union decided to go on strike over some political issue, I believe the Algerian war of liberation from France. The strike had been ordered by the executive committee of the national union. Bol and I initially threatened to boycott the strike because Northern students had not supported the Southern students in their opposition to the government's policy of burning villages in the South. When Rumbek Secondary School students, who had been moved to Khartoum because of the widespread violence in the South, had marched the streets of Khartoum in protest against the burning of villages, only the members of the Communist Party, the Anti-Imperialist Front, had joined them. The Northern students, if anything, had stood with the crowds against the Southern demonstrators. We saw no reason to stand in solidarity with the Arab world on an issue which was clearly more removed from us, when they had refused to act on an issue that directly affected our people.

When our position became known to the leadership of the student union, members of the executive committee requested to meet with us. They pleaded that we join the strike, arguing that although the national committee had erred in not supporting the Southern students, that did not justify our not standing in support of the just cause of the Algerian revolution. One wrong did not justify another. They promised us that they would officially present and support our point of view to the national committee. Having registered our position, we eventually agreed to join the strike.

While the strike was on, Bol was admitted to the health care centre with an attack of malaria. The strike was carried out according to plan and then we resumed our studies. It was then time for the school administration to strike back. The rumour was that every student would be given five lashes and that anyone who refused the punishment would be dismissed. We went back to our classes with great excitement as the students anticipated the test of wills. Bol was still sick in the health care facility. No formal debate had taken place on the issue, but the union leaders in the various classrooms asked the students to reject the punishment.

The form masters were the ones to inform and punish the students. Mr Jones came into our class with a whip in a mood of formal confrontation. Having formally informed us of the decision that the students must accept the punishment or face dismissal, he proceeded to read the names of class members, one by one, expecting each student called to proceed to the front of the class and receive his punishment. One by one, the answer came as "No", said in differing tones of emphasis and ridicule. I was located almost four-fifths down the line. By the time the "Nos" came halfway, the atmosphere was still charged and very tense, but it was apparent that the "Nos" had carried the day and that no one would dare say "Yes."

As the reading of the names approached me, I found myself faced with a critical choice. The most obvious alternative was to conform and win the good will of the student body. But going home meant a couple of days by lorry to reach Muglad and then covering some one hundred and twenty miles on horseback from Muglad to Abyei. Communications were so bad that I would be outside the reach of the school and might not learn of the reopening or readmittance in good enough time to be back and sit the School Certificate Examinations. What was more, most of the Northern students were not only within easy reach of the school and with relatively good means of communication and transportation, but were likely to be brought back by their parents within a few days of their dismissal, persuaded to accept the punishment, and permitted to resume their studies. My case was therefore special and had to be handled with prudence.

Only a short time earlier, I had very much wished to be allowed to go home and that was a golden opportunity to achieve that objective. But the circumstances were different, for whereas I had planned to go, resolve my crisis, and return to concentrate on my studies, I was now facing the prospect of being dismissed, sent home too far away to follow the developments in the school, and perhaps remain isolated and uninformed until most, if not the whole of my final year was wasted. I might never return to school. The rational decision was clearly "Yes." but could I face the predictable reaction from the student body?

I had no time to exhaust my thoughts and clarify my position. My name was called and the choice had to be made. It came almost by itself: "Yes," and I rose to proceed to the front of the class. The reaction was exactly as I had expected. There was a sudden uproar and commotion in which nearly everyone took part in some form or another. But the reaction of Mahmoud Gumaa, a light-skinned, muscular fellow, the union leader of the class, overshadowed everyone's. He jumped up in a rage, shouting "traitor, traitor," as he approached me for physical assault. Some students jumped on him to restrain him, but being unusually strong, the struggle was enough to cause absolute disorder in the class as desks turned over and students either joined in the restraining struggle or stepped aside for their own safety. With shouts from Mr Jones and the desire of most that I not be harmed physically, calm eventually settled on the class and I received my punishment.

By now, anxiety had largely diminished and I felt satisfied with the wisdom and indeed the moral courage of my decision. No one else said "Yes" in front of the class, but several students left the class and went straight to Mr Jones's office to receive their punishment secretly. As we were soon to learn, the practice in other classes was apparently the same, all said "No" in their classes, but many went straight and received their punishment in more discreet circumstances. By the time the school was closed in a day or two, quite a good fraction of the school, especially the finalists, had received their punishment and stayed behind. But the situation between us and the strikers could not have been more intense. I chose to ignore all provocations, to remain quietly to myself, except for the visits to Bol, who supported my decision, and otherwise maintained the delicate balance between my studies and my private worries.

As the lorries carrying the students to their homes were leaving, we were booed and called names, while some sarcastically called us "the bright boys" who wanted to be assured of Division One in the School Certificate. The morning the students left, a poster which was abusive of the school administration and those who had accepted the punishment, was found plastered to the headmaster's office. I received a good share of the poster's attention. The writer called me ambitious, not only for university studies, but for a scholarship to pursue graduate studies in the United States of America. He warned that there was no place for my kind in the United States, obviously alluding to my black race from which the Northerners, despite their dark and often black colour of skin, considered themselves different as Arabs.

The school was back to normal within a month. All the students returned except the dismissed ringleaders, who included Mahmoud Gumaa of my class. Although a certain degree of sensitivity and constraint lingered on, relations with most students returned to normal cordiality. My position on the strike had increased my motivation to work hard and succeed well, even though I had not fully recovered from my mental anguish over the issue of my identity. The mid-year exams eventually came in December. The results showed that I had done far better that I could possibly have expected under the circumstances.

We then proceeded home on the mid-term leave. What was surprising was that I was no longer feeling the pressures of determining the identity issue as much as I had felt earlier. It was as though a stormy and thundery rain and lightning was ebbing. I did not stop from pursuing my original lines of investigation, but I was less compulsive and insecure about the possible outcome, and even felt rather silly about the whole matter. The question became whether I should ridicule myself by proceeding to pose the questions. I decided to do so in order to clear every doubt that still lingered. When I discreetly broached the issue with Uncle Ngor and he explained to me the circumstances of my mother's marriage, I had an instinct that he might be telling me what I wanted to hear. So, I decided to ask him a straight question: whether my mother was pregnant when she came to my father's home. I left some room for uncertainty as to whether such pregnancy, if it had occurred, was with my father or the other man to whom she had been betrothed. Ngor was swift and clear, almost angrily surprised, and for the first time, seemed to worry about the state of my mental wellbeing.

With more difficulty than was the case with my uncle, I talked to my mother, trying to get at the truth, but carefully avoiding the naked question of pre-marital pregnancy that I felt would painfully offend her. There was really not much more she could have revealed that Ngor had not told me. I therefore contented myself by simply telling her that I had gone through a difficult period of insecurity which was affecting my academic concentration. She took this as the work of evil-doers who were jealous of my performance. She truly surprised me with her understanding of what was at stake, talked of the many years I had spent in school, and how much Father had invested in our education thus far. The meaning of all those years, she said, now depended on the outcome of the forthcoming exams. She urged me to face the challenge of those envious, evil-eyed people who desired my failure. She then went to my paternal Uncle Biong at Noong, and as my father was away, they agreed that the Dinka rituals of mental cure be performed on me.

The Dinka conceive of mental disturbance as the evil-eyed casting "the spell of the birds" on the persons concerned. The cure for that is to take a chicken, pray over the patient, whirl the live chicken over the patient's head, then sacrifice it and throw it away. I do not know why the concept of the bird is associated with mental problems, except perhaps that the freedom of flight of the birds in space might have a philosophical and symbolic similarity to the free and uncontrolled imagination, fantasies and preoccupations that accompany mental disorders, a contrast to social controls and constraints.

During that brief visit, Uncle Biong and Uncle Ngor performed their separate curative applications on me. Whatever the scientific explanation, all this enhanced visibly my already improved state of mind. I returned to school ready to study seriously, and indeed I worked hard and enjoyed my studies. When the examination finally came, I found the papers relatively easy and interesting. As always, I could not be sure of how well I had performed, but I was optimistic that I had done reasonably well.

We chose to wait for the examination results in Khartoum. Should we not achieve well, it would be best to be far away from home and avoid embarrassment. Besides, we planned to seek temporary employment. We had never been to Khartoum and it proved to be everything I had imagined: full of people, men and women in traditional and modern garbs filling the streets and pressing on one another in the trams and buses, and the taxis, generally representing the affluent face of Sudan. The buildings, the streets, indeed the air proudly revealed the modernity and the sophistication Sudan was capable of offering. I felt humbled and yet privileged to have gone that far from Abyei. And perhaps, within a few months, we might join one of the grandest institutions of learning in the country - Khartoum University.

We met with Uncle Bona Bulabek, the genius who had jumped from one level to another, had caught up with as at Tonj, had passed us at Rumbek, but had been delayed by the disturbance the South, and had therefore graduated at the same time with us. Our cousins, Justin Deng Aguer, the senior son of our Aunt Awor, and Yusuf Deng Bar, the son of Father's maternal uncle, who were then working in Khartoum, accommodated us. Justin was in the Ministry of Finance, while Yusuf was in the Ministry of Information and Labour.

Since our intention was to acquire temporary jobs until the results of the Sudan School Certificate examinations and university acceptance were out, we answered one advertisement after another, and went to one appointment after another. But all our applications were to no avail. We soon learned that nepotism was the rule and that being otherwise chosen was highly exceptional. Such was the privilege Bol received after the interview by the Grand Hotel for the post of a receptionist, in those days a position of notable status. Probably through Yusuf, I found some relief in writing a series of broadcast talks on the special Southern programme of Radio Omdurman, "Southern Corner," *Rukun el Janub*. The programme was supposed to be in Southern Arabic, but I wrote in "standard" Northern Arabic, which was impressive by Southern standards. I cannot recall the precise topics of my talks, but they seemed so successful that I was asked to write as many as I wanted, with the promise that they would all be aired.

After the first six talks, I went to receive my pay, which was five Sudanese pounds per talk, in those days quite a good pay. As I sat waiting to be called to the cashier's window, I found myself sitting next to a Northern Sudanese who had appeared on the same programme. Our chat led to the scales of pay. Despite his having aired exactly the same number of talks in one of the Southern languages, Nuer, he was expecting to receive ten pounds per talk instead of my five.

I was at first surprised and curious, but I soon learned that differences in the pay scale between Southerners and Northerners was the norm. The more facts I learned, the more it became obvious to me that I was a victim of blatant discrimination, and the more I became indignant and eventually enraged, of course without telling my broadcasting colleague what was going on in my mind. When my turn came, I went in and asked a few questions about the scale of pay. It soon became obvious to the person processing the pay cheques that I could be a source of trouble.

He channelled me to his boss, a certain Awad Abdel Razig, who was unknown to me, but whom I later learned was one of the prominent Communists in the country. Whether because he was caught or because he had been a party to the violation of his socialist principles of equality, Awad Abdel Razig was enraged by my complaint. He quoted stories of traditional wisdom to the effect of:

"Never help a needy person, for he will eventually turn against you," implying that I ought to be grateful for the opportunity he had given me.

The matter came to the attention of my cousin, Yusuf Deng Bar. Being both diplomatic and proud of his identity and background, and idolising his cousin, my father, Yusuf was faced with a predicament, complicated by the fact that he was a junior official in the ministry. The more enraged Awad Abdel Razig became, the more insulted I felt, and the more Yusuf felt the need to find a compromise. I went to Southern Members of Parliament to draw their attention to the discriminating practices of the Ministry of Information.

A question was tabled in parliament and the minister was requested to answer. I was called by the permanent undersecretary of the ministry, who was asked to investigate the situation for the minister. From being a sympathiser and a helper, Awad had become a virtual enemy who would not even face me, let alone greet me, as our paths crossed in the corridors of the ministry. Then we both appeared in front of the undersecretary, and with us was Yusuf. The undersecretary tried to intimidate me by reminding me of the seriousness of the offence of which I had accused the officials of the ministry and that if my accusation was found to be false, I would in turn be the offender and liable to serious consequences.

I simply told him the facts, and to my surprise then, though not now, it seemed that the officials had cooked a response. Yes, the Northerner to whom I had talked had been receiving double my pay because of his efforts to have learned Nuer. On the other hand, I was well qualified to give talks in Arabic without unusual effort. That I was non-Arab and therefore had to learn Arabic was not at all a consideration to them. I was therefore blameworthy for accusing the ministry of discriminating against Southerners. However, I would be forgiven on account of the special regard they had for my father.

It was quite obvious that people were looking for a way out. They had discussed with Yusuf and had agreed that the whole matter would be dismissed if I could be persuaded to abandon the complaint. By that time, I knew I had notoriously made my point and that what everyone needed was a way out. As it was not my intention to punish anybody, I felt no need to question their face-saving tactics.

The results of the School Certificate remained for us a subject of speculation and a source of anxiety. As time went, all three of us, Bulabek, Bol and myself acquired a similar psychology of hoping for the best, but fearing the worst, although for Uncle Bulabek, the genius, that fear was totally unwarranted. We kept anxiously checking with the Ministry of Education for the announcement of the results and found no more than the rumours that circulated in the streets of Khartoum. One day, while expecting an announcement any day, we were surprised to hear the results of Rumbek on the special "Southern Corner" of Radio Omdurman. As expected, Bona Bulabek headed the list with distinction in all subjects. When we heard the news, we had just finished lunch and were relaxing in Justin's and Yusuf's house.

The results of the Northern schools would be announced with the evening news. Although we were obviously very happy for Bona, we fell into a sudden shock of uncertainty and insecurity. We did not wait to hear the news at home. So, as the sun was setting, we all parted, Bol to go back to his hotel work, and I to wander into some place where I could listen to the radio unrecognised. I found myself in a popular teahouse on the Blue Nile in Khartoum North. Judging from the looks and behaviour of the people there, none of them was of a secondary level, but all seemed excited about the results that were about to be announced, perhaps because of relatives and friends, perhaps because of the enjoyment of the value of education.

I sat and ordered a cup of tea, absolutely certain that no one would expect this "Southerner" to be interested, let alone fully absorbed, in the results of Northern secondary schools. Then came the announcement, beginning with Hantoub, Divisions One, Two and Three. Wadi Seidna followed, again Divisions One, Two and Three. It would have been torture had my senses not become numbed by the combination of anxiety and helplessness. When the turn came to Khor Taqqat, there was an acceleration of the heartbeat and a climax of anxiety.

Fortunately, that did not last because my name was fourth in the list of Division One. Though relieved, I remained in suspense for Bol. But I did not have too long to wait as his name, though delayed by the alphabetical order of the letter "Z" for Zachariah, was in Division One. Suddenly the weight was lifted and for the first time, I felt the urge to jump and shout with extreme pleasure. But I prudently controlled myself and maintained my calm. To do otherwise would have been a senseless exposure to a totally inappropriate crowd who would never have understood. I left quietly, first to see Justin, Yusuf and Bulabek, and then to go on to Bol.

As I walked the streets of Khartoum, still mesmerised with pleasure, hardly feeling the ground under my feet, and barely aware of the crowds passing by, my mind wandered back through the long journey I had travelled. I recalled my grandfather's prayers and ambitions for me even before I was conceived, how his expectations had grown with my birth and early childhood, and how he had even sacrificed himself to an early death to save my life, about which his son, my Uncle Ngor, had spoken so movingly to me when I had experienced emotional problems that had nearly destroyed my education.

My thoughts went back to my childhood at Noong, an innocently naked boy proudly taking care of cattle, goats and sheep, frequently visiting my maternal relatives several miles away, walking barefoot through a path of gluey mud, barbed with half-buried thorns, and lined with tall thickets of entangled savannah grass. I recalled my first donkey ride to school at Abyei, some twelve miles from Noong, excited, anxious and apprehensive, lest I should fail and disappoint my father, for it was to demonstrate our love for him that we had agreed to be the first in the tribe to undertake the adventure of joining the first school to open in our area. I recalled the miraculous transformation of learning to read and write in a classroom built of sorghum stalks with dirt floors, infested with snakes and scorpions, not to mention the flies.

I recalled our dramatic move to the South and how our mothers and sisters had cried, protesting our being taken to the land of tribes they regarded as cannibals even though some of them were fellow Dinka. I recalled the tough discipline of Tonj Primary School, run by a burly Englishman for whom the British public-school system as illustrated in *Tom Brown School Days* and the army in which the headmaster had served were the models. After what had seemed in comparison to be a less adventurous interlude at Rumbek and Tonj for intermediate education, my tumultuous journey between cultures had taken me through an even more dramatic move to Khor Taqqat Secondary School in the Arab Muslim North, where I had spent four years of precarious adjustment to what had in effect been a totally unfamiliar environment. All that had now come to an end and suddenly seemed so remote as I looked into the future, for judging from the results just announced, I was at the doorsteps of Khartoum University, about to join a faculty of my own choice - Law.

For those in parts of the world where going to high school is the norm and proceeding to college not so significant an exception, the moral boost of the promotion may seem exaggerated. But in the Sudan of our time in the fifties, when there were only four secondary schools in the largest country in Africa then, with only one university whose entire student body was just over a thousand, and the professional faculties such as law and medicine admitting not more than thirty students a year, one can imagine the competition and how significant it was to be one of the selected few.

Bol, Bulabek and I were the only ones from our Ngok Dinka tribe of Abyei to have gone that far. I was elated by the thought that our family, and I hoped our father in particular, must be proud of us. And indeed, when I arrived at the house of our cousins, Justin and Yusuf, who had also heard the radio announcement, the atmosphere was jubilant and festive, for they were exceedingly pleased and proud of us. As for the three of us, Bol, Bulabek and myself, with the university as our next target and challenge, the world could not have been a better place.

CHAPTER ELEVEN

UNIVERSITY
AT THE MEETING POINT

FROM THE EARLY DAYS OF MY CHILDHOOD, MY LIFE HAD CONSISTENTLY been one of transition, getting into new situations and meeting new people. The movement between my paternal and maternal homes was first, followed by the transition between our village and the homes of paternal uncles. Then my brothers and I went to school and away from one home to another. The move to the South was a greater transition into new circles of new peoples and new cultures. Moving to the North was yet an even greater cross-cultural leap. The university was the meeting point, the institution where all the various groups I had met earlier and new groups I was still to meet later converged. Apart from the academic benefits, the influence of Khartoum University on my life was crucial in three areas: it introduced me to the exciting world of women as colleagues; it helped me consolidate my views on the bridging role of our family and our tribe in the South-North relations; and it introduced me to the wider world beyond my country.

In sharp contrast to my expectations, for the first few weeks the only woman in the whole Faculty of Law was a second year student. Then things changed dramatically. Hassan Abdalla el Turabi, the leader of the fundamentalist Muslim Brotherhood and the first Sudanese lecturer in law, told us that two girls would be joining our class. He teasingly challenged the students to the implications of competing in front and with the girls.

I was subsequently confronted one day by two girls. One was dressed in European clothes, well groomed, and urbanely attractive. The other was taller, dressed in the traditional toub, with a natural, beautiful, smiling face. It was the latter who spoke to me first and in Arabic. She greeted me and asked me where the dean's office was. I said I was not sure, but would help find it. I turned back and walked up the stairs with them to the second floor: Where else would the dean's office be since I knew it was not on the first floor of the two-floor building? The taller girl asked teasingly how I could be uninformed about the location of the dean's office! We found the office, but the dean was not there. They stood to wait for him while I took my leave. It dawned on me that they might be the girls who were to join our class. I decided to ask them and was assured. "Welcome to the faculty!" I said. They smiled and thanked me.

As Hassan el Turabi had accurately predicted, the girls had a spontaneous impact on the mood of our class. Things were never the same again. When the first class ended, the tall girl asked me to lend them my notes to copy what they had missed. As I was the first person they had met from the class, it was natural that they would approach me, but in that context, it was an act of moral courage for a Northern Muslim girl to approach a fellow student of a conspicuously different background, a Christian and a Southerner. That girl was Wisal, the daughter of Siddiq Abdrahman el Mahdi, the head of the Ansar religious sect and the patron of the rightist Umma political party. That she was from such a prominent background, yet so natural, soon added to her grace, charm and popularity. The other girl, was Samieha, the daughter of one of the leading advocates in the country, Ahmed Gumaa. Being a liberal Northern Sudanese of mixed Sudanese Egyptian parentage, Ahmed Gumma was said to be a strong defender of the rights of South Sudanese. Samieha's mother was also Egyptian, which also added to her cross-cultural sophistication. Although she occasionally wore the traditional Sudanese toub, she dressed regularly in Western clothes and was quite meticulous about her dress and appearance. Both in her dress and in her social interaction, she reflected a modern and cosmopolitan character, which, while discreet, was as striking as it was rare in the Khartoum context.

There is no denying that the presence of the girls in the class challenged students in a positive way, but it also caused complications that were distracting and even damaging to some. I was considerably less inhibited in my association with our female colleagues than most of my Northern colleagues and my familiarity with the Northern cultural context made me more outgoing than my Southern colleagues. I became good friends with both girls and especially with Samieha. But social attitudes in the Sudan of the 1950s and 1960s were averse to friendships between male and female students, and especially between non-Muslim men and Muslim women. The subject of relationships between boys and girls certainly took the lion share of conversations in many circles.

Socially, more generally, I found Khartoum quite congenial and I had many friends. Among my closest friends at the university was my first-year roommate, Zaki Abdel Rahman, whom I had known at Khor Taqqat. As Bulabek and I had returned home for the university fees and pocket money, Bol had arranged for me to share a room with him, but we agreed that it would be more appropriate for me to accept Zaki's offer of a roommate. Zaki was from Wadi Halfa, in the extreme North, slender, gentle, sensitive and one of the youngest in our class. Furthermore, he was one of the few Northern Sudanese who were sympathetic to the Southern cause, a position he had demonstrated in Khor Taqqat. Another Northern Sudanese who soon became a very close friend was Mussab el Hadi Babikir, a graduate of Hantoub Secondary School, whose father was a tribal chief in the Gezira, the rich agricultural belt whose cotton provided most of the foreign earnings of the Sudan.

Mussab was well-dressed (something I was also reputed for), amusingly snobbish, status conscious, and although a devout Muslim in that he observed the fasting of Ramadan and prayed regularly, quite responsive to worldly pleasures. Within the limits of his context, he was a lot more sophisticated than many of his Muslim colleagues. Mussab was financially well-to-do. I was also reasonably well provided as Father arranged with the Khartoum Municipality for Bol and me to receive a monthly allowance from his salary. I had also won the First Year's Prize for being first in the class, which entailed a financial award payable on a monthly basis throughout the remaining years in the University.

The story of my winning the Prize was rather comic. I was one day approached by a fellow student by the name Nuri, a rather flamboyant and affluent-looking character who, ironically and unexpectedly began a conversation on the impending results of the examination and the Prize. He said that he came from a poor background and needed to win the Prize. I was not even aware of the Prize. What was extraordinary was that he talked as though I was not a classmate and therefore implicitly a competitor. After that encounter, I was surprised by one of our British lecturers, Dr. Oliver Farran, who congratulated me for being first in the class and the winner of the Prize before the result was not yet officially announced. That afternoon at the Students' Union Club, as a number of us sat chatting with Hassan El Turabi, my friend, Tigani Omer El Karib, asked him about the winner of the Prize. Turabi responded, "It has been given to Francis". The students began to congratulate me, but Turabi did not, perhaps because he felt awkward about not having congratulated me in the first place. On the other hand, it is difficult not to read a degree of prejudice, conscious or ingrained, in the attitude of both Nuri and Turabi, which appeared not to expect a Southerner to be top of the class.

This was remarkably made clear to me by a fellow student, Abdel Semieh Omer Ahmed, two years my junior, who became Dean of the Faculty and Attorney General. We were having dinner at the residence of the American Ambassador. Suddenly, Abdel Semieh surprised me by saying that I had liberated him from racial prejudice. "How?" I asked. He said that he used to believe that Southerners were intellectually inferior to Northerners until he learned that the top of the class ahead of them was a Southerner. I was amazed, but impressed, by his candor. Over the years, I heard similar racist comments on my being top of the class. My friend, Tigani El Karib, told me how someone asked him whether I was in his class at the University. When Tigani told him that I was top of the class, the response of the person was 'Billah!?' – 'By God', a version of 'Really !?' Of course since then, many Southerners, including members of my family, have been top of their classes in the University, although I suspect that racist beliefs do not easily get eradicated.

Mussab, Zaki and I formed a trio that acquired the nickname of "The Three Musketeers". I met Tigani El-Karib who would become a lifelong friend under somewhat unusual circumstances. As I stood reading the Arabic section of the notice board, a Northern student came, and, surprised to see a Southerner read Arabic, initiated a conversation in a remarkably outgoing manner that I later realised was not typical of him: "Can you read Arabic?" I was slightly annoyed by his rather presumptuous and assertive character, but I chose to be reservedly polite and answered: "A little bit." Another student who knew me and happened to have been standing by, remarked: "Don't you know that he is a graduate of Khor Taqqat?" Somewhat embarrassed, my new contact faded away politely only to approach me shortly afterwards in a more friendly manner, this time inviting me for a drink at the nearby refreshment stand. I accepted. That was how Tigani Omer el Karib and I met and became close friends for life.

Tigani was then a member of the Muslim Brotherhood. Like Mussab, Tigani came from the Gezira. His father was assistant manager of the Gezira Board, the body that managed the backbone of Sudan's economy - the Gezira Scheme. From these examples, it is obvious that most of my closest friends were Northern Sudanese.

Not long after we joined Khartoum University, Bulabek and Bol left to study medicine abroad. Bulabek had been offered a scholarship by the Catholic missionaries to study medicine in the United States, but when the visa formalities threatened him with a year's delay, he chose instead to go to Padova, Italy, with a Southern colleague, Justo Muludiang. Bol had always wanted to study medicine, but despite his brilliant performance in the Sciences, he had fallen short of the credit level in mathematics required for admission into the Faculty of Medicine and was admitted to the Faculty of Arts and Economics, for which he had no interest at all.

Determined to pursue medicine, Bol applied for a scholarship abroad, and although government scholarships for undergraduates were available only for those who could not enter the University of Khartoum, an exception was made for him, and he went to study medicine in Leipzig, East Germany. I therefore found myself the only member of our family, indeed of our tribe, the Ngok Dinka, in the University of Khartoum. And for the four years in the University of Khartoum, I remained the only student from Abyei.

Before Bulabek and Bol left for Europe, they and I initiated a campaign towards the establishment of a Southern Students party in the student union. We were, of course, propelled by our Khor Taqqat experiences, and especially the lack of concern with Southern issues by Northern students. We thought that a Southern party in the national student movement would cater for Southern interests and help raise the level of awareness among Northern students. The idea quickly caught on and became the subject of intensive debates.

One of the main issues I recall was the name of the proposed party. We had to balance delicately between avoiding being accused of racism by declaring the party exclusive to Southerners and not leaving room for the Northerners to join in large numbers and become the majority. A long debate ensued which, on the advice of Abel Alier, a finalist in the Faculty of Law, ended in favour of an open-door policy, eventually resulting in the name Student's Welfare Front.

Being from a Northern secondary school, Arabic speaking and socially involved with Northern students, my political image stood across the South-North dividing line and although many Southerners did not trust this bridging role, the majority felt that my Northern connections could be an asset in the elections. Southerners proposed to put my name for a seat in the senate of the union, trusting that I would attract Northern votes and improve the chances of the Southern Front. I declined on the grounds that I did not consider myself sufficiently representative of the mainstream Southern viewpoint to occupy the seat. Donato Mabior, then in his second year in the Faculty of Law, was elected instead. And yet, I was not only accepted in Southern circles, but indeed played an active role and was expected and encouraged by the Southerners themselves to represent them in various situations.

Paradoxically, my identification with Southerners seemed to peak at moments of crisis. One such occasion was when the editors of the girls' newspaper, *El Wathba,* and the editors of the Southern Sudanese paper, *The Negro*, got into a conflict that engulfed the leaders of the Student Union. The girls had removed The Negro from the wall where papers were posted and put up their own in its place. They explained that they had been so directed by the Union leaders because the Southern paper was out of date. Provoked by the action of *The Wathba*, the Southerners removed the girls' paper, and put their own back. The Union leaders, specifically the president, Ali Mahmoud Hassanein, ruled in favour of the girls and ordered the removal of *The Negro.*

Ali Mahmoud, a Muslim Brother, light-skinned, short, boney, and with large protruding ears, became the target of Southern reaction. The editors of *The Negro*, Natale Olwak Akolawin, a fellow law student, and Isaiah Majok, an engineering student, wrote an acid attack in an article entitled, "The Insignificant President." The union established a court to try them. I was selected by the Southerners to be their defence counsel. The atmosphere on campus was quite ripe for an even worse confrontation and conflict on account of that crisis. The court members and myself felt that proceeding with the trial could only add fuel to the situation. An informal settlement was eventually reached and the case was dropped. The crisis was averted.

Another occasion was when the military regime of General Ibrahim Abboud decided in 1960 to make Friday instead of Sunday the day of rest in the South. I was chosen by the Southern students, together with my colleagues, Natale Olwak and Donato Mabior, to prepare a protest letter in the name of the Southern students in the university.

As is evident in the three occasions on which Southerners chose me to represent their political interests – the suggestion that I run for the Senate of the Student's Union, my appointment as defence counsel to the editors of *The Negro*, and my membership of the committee that drafted the protest letter to the government – there was no question about my political identification with the South, my own commitment to the Southern cause and the confidence of most Southerners in my representative role as a Southerner. And yet, some Southerners seemed to question my dedication and loyalty to the Southern cause, perhaps because they realised that I did not share the separatist objectives of the cause, but most probably because they did not trust my close association with the Northerners, even though ironically it enabled me to explain the Southern point of view and win sympathy and support from some, without compromising on the principles of autonomy and equality as the foundations of unity.

The political atmosphere in the university was tense beyond South-North relations as the students' opposition to the military government of General Ibrahim Abboud mounted, even though the circumstances under which Abboud had toppled an elected government were relevant to the South. I recall one meeting between the Southern students and the Southern parliamentarians in November 1958, a few days before the pro-Umma head of the Army, General Ibrahim Abboud ascended to power. The new elections had turned up a group of young Southern members of parliament who were determined to depart from the corrupt practices of earlier politicians who had been readily available for grabs. The issue was how the Southern members of parliament were to play their cards to make maximum political gains before committing their votes to the support of any of the Northern political parties. The ruling Umma Party was then in serious trouble and was expected to lose power in the new parliament without a coalition government. It was obvious that Southern Liberal Party votes would make a big difference. As we considered the best strategy to be adopted by our Liberal Party MPs, I got up to speak about the importance of timing. I said that I could not see how the prime minister, Abdalla Khalil, a former military officer, would go into parliament and risk the vote without some indication of how the Umma, his party, would fare with respect to the support of the Southern members.

Apparently, I had said more than I realised about what the prime minister might do. Luigi Adwok, one of the MPs who later became a prominent figure in Southern politics, rose up and after complimenting me for my remarks, went on to say that the possibility I had alluded to was real and that they had reason to believe that if Abdalla Khalil did not feel assured of the majority, he might dissolve the parliament and declare a state of emergency. A few days later, on November 17, 1958, Sudan woke up to the sounds of martial music. Prime Minister Abdalla Khalil had asked his colleague and friend, General Ibrahim Abboud to take over the reins of power. Abboud had accepted and done so. So, disenchanted had the people been with party politics and so ignorant of military rule were they that the excitement with the army seizing power overshadowed any fears of military dictatorship. It was so peaceful a move and so exhilarating a change that life in Khartoum, including the classes, went on normally, only the rhythm was much more exciting.

The initial theme of Abboud's putsch was labelled "White Revolution" and "Peace", but the reality was soon to change radically as middle-aged generals and younger officers began to understand and relish the new concept of military rule and of "bossing" not just over a platoon or a company but a whole nation. In due course, only Abboud remained in his "Marshall's" ivory tower, a dignified old fatherly figurehead who was himself falling captive to his own younger, but more hawkish generals, brigadiers, and colonels. His dear friend, Abdalla Khalil, who had handed him power, was to live to regret his action and even Abboud, when he was thrown out by an unprecedented popular uprising some six years later, was to say: "Why did nobody tell me how unpopular I was!"

While the group of young members of parliament had been a promising development, the military usurpation of political power led by General Abboud brought a sudden end to any discussion of the political problems. The belligerence with which the military regime fought political expression was aggravated by their obsessive fear of a separatist movement in the South. In fact, initially, what made military rule somewhat appealing to the North was that it held the best prospects for silencing Southern politicians. Northern administrators in the South used military rule as a licence for ruthlessness in the suppression of Southern politicians and nationalist tendencies in any quarters in the South.

As the political war between the university students and Abboud's dictatorship mounted, expressed in increasing demonstrations and clashes with the police, the gap between loyalties to the government and to the student union became increasingly unbridgeable. On one occasion, the arrest of the union leaders was attributed to betrayal by fellow students. A judicial committee was established to try the "traitors." I was appointed to the committee. I was then in my third year. I must confess that while I was flattered by the selection, I felt ambivalent about trying people because they had cooperated with the government. There was of course the probability that we ourselves would be arrested and perhaps dismissed from the university. Yet, I could not voice my doubts, far less decline from the responsibility. When we met, the members wisely, but discreetly, saw a number of practical difficulties in our task and by implication preferred a quiet death to the committee and its task.

I was also involved in a variety of extra-curricular activities. One of these was as a member of Saint Augustine's Society to which Catholic members of the university belonged, including lecturers and students, Southerners and Northerners alike. I was elected secretary general during my second year. At first, I refused the honour, but on the insistence of members, I accepted not so much because I felt religiously qualified as for the purposes of administrative contribution and perhaps in order to gain some useful experience. The patron of the society was Bishop Baroni of Khartoum, with Father Philip, the principal of Comboni College, as the chaplain. The president was first Ingledew, a lecturer in English and then Richard Gray of the History Department.

As secretary general of St Augustine's Society, I was instrumental in organising a joint Christmas carol singing of all Christian denominations during one Christmas. In a way, our objective was more political than religious; we hoped to unite all the Christians in a way that could cater for the interests of the non-Muslim community in the university. The occasion, which was well organised, proved very successful. All Christian denominations participated and hymns were sung in a variety of languages: English, Latin, Arabic, Dinka and other languages.

On one special occasion we gave a tea party to honour a young lady from South Africa. She was white, I believe English. She gave a detailed critical account of the racial situation in South Africa, occasionally punctuating herself with emotional silences, gasping as though about to break down. At one point, nearly dropping tears, she said, "Apartheid is such a dreadful system that it is difficult to talk about it. One has to experience it to believe it." I have often wondered what her name was and what has become of her. The experience also left me at least vaguely aware that racism did not necessarily polarise people into two distinct groups, the dominating whites and the subjugated blacks, and that there were whites who felt as strongly as blacks about the indignities of apartheid.

Academically, I found law a most enjoyable subject and in varying degrees I enjoyed all my classes and liked my teachers. My love for law seemed like a natural. After all, although we studied Anglo-American law, with some concession for Sharia, law was by no means an unfamiliar field for me, since I had watched it functioning at home in my father's court from my early childhood. Except for the fact that the law I had observed at home was not being taught in the university, my love for law throughout my years in Khartoum was almost unqualified. As I approached the end of my university years, I hoped for a degree that would qualify me for an academic appointment at the university. This was not only out of some theoretical desire to be a teacher, but also a dream for excellence, since only the top students were offered academic careers and their acceptance for the honour was taken for granted.

I had received the First Year Award as top of my class, which carried with it a handsome sum of money that was spread over the three remaining years at the university. The money from the prize and the monthly allowance which Father had made for Bol and me made me financially well-to-do in the university. Although the results of the intervening years did not show the order of success, it was also obvious that I was doing well and generally understood to be still ahead of the class. Yet, I continued to suffer considerable anxiety about my performance, sometimes shifting emotions between wanting and expecting to be the best, and fearing being a failure.

Part of this was justified by my extracurricular activities, my social preoccupations, and my "adolescent" obsessions. All this, combined with my temperament for extra curriculum activities, never permitted me to be as studious as many of my fellow students. But my anxiety was in part a reflection of an innate disposition towards wanting to excel while worrying about failure at the same time. It was a disposition which had been nurtured by long experience going back perhaps to the contrasting themes represented by the always flattering and supportive attitude of most people at home and in school and the always critical attitude of my father.

Samieha and I studied together and were often seen together which drew significant attention in the university, especially because of the obvious racial and religious differences reflected in her being a Northerner and I a Southerner. But we were both unconventional and were not intimidated by such prejudices. Much of the credit for such liberalism went to Samieha and her open-minded family background. One of the highlights of my time in the university was appearing with Samieha as counsels in a moot trial that was the first the Law Society had ever organised and was to be open to the legal profession and the public. The case was given wide publicity in the national press and by all accounts was considered a major event, not only in the university, but in the city. The court members included a high court judge, a lecturer, and a finalist student.

Although it was held in the largest lecture hall in the university, so great was the attendance that the hall could not take the audience; some crowded outside, blocking the windows as they peeped in, and otherwise lingering around to have a feel of what was happening. The fact that a girl was pleading in a public court was in itself an unprecedented and unexpected attraction. Even senior members of the legal profession attended. Samieha's father was there.

Perhaps even more important than the legal issues concerned was the atmosphere of the simulated court and the method of presentation which could not have been more serious, even by normal judicial standards. So theatrical was the drama that I frequently, though inadvertently, turned my back to the judges to face the audience. Several times, Samieha discreetly directed my attention to the court. I was in effect interacting with the audience, getting reinforcement from the expression in their faces, and rarely consulting my notes. Samieha followed, well-poised, well-spoken, and well-prepared. Her performance made an impact on the audience, not least because it was a dramatic innovation. When it was all over, we had won the case, with all three judges concurring to "allow the appeal."

When I was in my third year, approaching the Final Part I examination, which would count for the degree, my life had become so entangled by preoccupations at home and abroad that I felt distracted and unprepared for the exam. I contemplated not taking the exam and repeating the class. In the end, I decided to seek the advice of one of my lecturers, William Twining, whose subject, Torts, I enjoyed enormously and whom I found to be an understanding, sympathetic and supportive teacher. I told Twining about the situation in general terms without any specific reasons or explanations.

Twining did not push for details, but he argued strongly against my repeating, stressing that however well I performed afterwards, there would always be a stigma. In particular, if I were to be considered for an academic appointment, some people could argue that I had taken five years for a course of four years and use that against me. He also could not believe that I was as unprepared for the examination as I feared, giving the example of his own subject to show how well I was performing.

Twining's advice helped me pull myself together and reassess my chances. Of course, the papers would be subject to the evaluation of external examiners from London, but Twining's judgement of my standing was significant. I decided to try my luck with the examination and to do what I could by way of preparation, working to the final hour, something I had always tried to avoid. The examinations came and went and although I could not be assured of the precise level of my success, I still hoped I had done well enough to qualify for a university appointment for a teaching job. An interview with Twining and the external examiner assured me that I was doing well in Torts. I was also encouraged when Mohamed Omer Beshir, the influential academic secretary, tipped me by urging me quite discreetly to work hard for the Final Part II, if I wanted a university appointment. I took the hint to mean that he knew enough about the results of Final Part I to believe that if I did well in Final Part II, I stood a good chance of being appointed to the faculty.

By the time we approached the examination for Final Part II the following year, I had travelled abroad and my world had continued to expand beyond my tribe, my race, or my country. But I also continued to pay the price, perhaps rendered even higher by the gains. Exciting as it was, my world became a turbulent sea of conflicting currents, a burning desire to succeed and a debilitating preoccupation with relationships that were as distant as they were omnipresent and consuming. As though all that was not enough, I was suddenly seized with high fever and a general physical weakness which the university physician first diagnosed as malaria and Dr Abdel Wahab Zein El Abdeen, who was popular with the Southerners and was said to be half-Southern Sudanese, diagnosed as exhaustion.

He urged me to rest. But of course, I could not turn off the burning fire of adolescent pre-occupations. I also had to make up for lost time, again working to the last hour, contrary to my normal practice. When the exams came, my condition had improved considerably, but I still felt hazy and weak. Several papers came and went without any significant signals of danger. Then came Company Law. To my surprise, I found the questions reasonably easy, the answers rather clear in my mind, but I could not write. It began with a vigorous heartbeat. Then my mind suddenly went into a haze and although I felt knowledgeable, I was completely incapacitated in communicating my knowledge. I sat, watched, tried to calm myself down, but all to no avail. At the back of my mind, the examination clock was ticking away and with it, my chance of success.

After some time, I explained my problem to the supervisor, Zaki Mustafa, the second Sudanese to be appointed lecturer in Faculty of Law. I asked him whether it would be acceptable for me to lie down somewhere and rest for a while without studying or talking to anyone and come back to complete the examination when I felt better. He went and consulted with the dean, then he came to tell me that I should go to see a doctor. Accompanied by Zaki himself, I went to Dr Abdel Wahab Zein el Abdeen. I was, of course, extremely distressed that I would not complete the exam and had obviously missed my ambition, and worse, would end my university years a dramatic failure. Dr Abdel Wahab gave me an injection and suggested that I go back to the examination. He was amazingly calm about the whole situation. I returned half an hour later and to my utmost surprise found myself totally at ease and able to finish the paper with the rest of the students. So pleased was I at having done the exam that I did not at all think of how difficult the paper had been, even though everybody else in the class complained about it.

Gordon Abyei, one of my two Southern colleagues in the class, was later to tell me how one fellow student, a Northerner, Saleh Awad Saleh, had taken pleasure out of my crisis. According to him, Saleh, ironically one of the Northern colleagues I found most friendly, had remarked out loud as I left the class, *"El Abid waga'a"*, "The slave has fallen." Gordon was extremely embittered not only by the remark, but by my seeming inability to appreciate the prejudice Northerners had for Southerners. He said he nearly shed tears at seeing a fellow classmate delight in the fall of his colleague. He hoped I had learned my lesson.

I did not share Gordon's reaction, partly because I was not sure of what had actually transpired and what was Gordon's own projection, and partly because, even if Saleh had said that, it would have reflected a playful way of reacting to the situation, especially as the students found the paper very difficult, rather than an expression of inherent racial antipathy. Furthermore, Saleh did not represent all the Northerners. As it was, I later confronted Saleh who denied having said that, and although I could not have expected him to admit it, the denial itself was a conciliatory way of saying that even if he had said it, his intention was far from deliberate racism or adversity. I accepted his denial and did not press the angle of racism.

For the first two years at the university, I spent my vacations at home, but unlike former years, when time had passed mostly in leisure, I began to utilise my time in field research. Two of my lecturers were instrumental in developing, guidance and encouraging my interest in the traditional law of my people. One was Dr Oliver Farran, who taught us Roman Law, Sharia and later conflict of laws. The other was William Twining who was not only to become a close friend but was to have a profound effect on my future, both in Khartoum and in later years. Under the guidance of these lecturers, I prepared a questionnaire on the basis of which I was to collect data during the summer vacation.

My other Southern colleagues shared the same interest in customary law and received more or less the same encouragement, but political conditions in their areas were less favourable. Our interest in customary law had a two-fold purpose. Objectively, since customary law still applied to the overwhelming majority of Sudan, it seemed paradoxical that the faculty should limit itself to the teaching of Anglo-American and Islamic laws. Subjectively, we saw in the official disregard of customary law a discriminatory attitude which was part of the Southern problem. Our preoccupation with customary law was therefore both professionally and politically motivated. For me, there was the added incentive of my childhood association with my father's administration of customary law.

Although the questionnaire I had developed with my lecturers was primarily in the field of family law and torts, I extended the area of investigation to cover oral tradition about authority and control, including the legends of leadership in which our family line figured prominently but on which we had never been instructed by our elders. My research was therefore a major contribution to the continuing exploration and reinforcement of my identity, which paradoxically also entailed sensitive political dimensions.

No sooner had I begun my research than stories started to circulate that I was being prepared for the position of a judge to hear appeals on customary law. Some even said that I was being groomed for the position of the "supreme chief" over my father's authority. Several prominent personalities, including Matet Ayom, the friend-enemy of my father, came to me to congratulate me and to pledge their support and loyalty. My explanations to the contrary were merely taken as a discreet way of avoiding premature publicity. Matet flattered me by saying that he had always been convinced that of all my father's sons, I was the one best qualified for chieftainship. And indeed, Matet had always called me by the nickname, Bashom, "Fox" which I assumed meant "clever." Uncle Deng Makuei also remarked, "I saw it in your eyes from the time you were a baby."

So widespread were the baseless tales that I began to fear suspicions and tensions on the part of my father himself. My father initially showed considerable courtesy and support in the prominent way he seated me in his court and in the willingness and readiness of his court members to explain to me points of fact and law as litigation proceeded. But in direct proportion to the spreading rumours I began to notice a significant cooling in Father's attitude towards my research. So, I went to him one day and said that I was aware of the circulating propaganda concerning the purpose of my research and that, to avoid any further misunderstanding, I would forthwith end my court attendance and interview individual chiefs and elders discreetly at home. My father smiled with obvious approval and seemed to understand and appreciate my discretion.

The suspicions and tensions provoked by my research were symbolic of the continuing complexities and ambivalences in my relations with my father. There was no question now about Father's dependence on my advice on political and family matters. In particular, he felt that the increasing role of the educated Dinka in leading or instigating opposition against him was a challenge for us, his sons, among whom I occupied a leading position, especially as Bol was abroad. But my role with respect to the educated opposition group was a complicated and precarious one. Naturally, I shared my father's interests and concerns. On the other hand, as an adviser, I could try to moderate his reactions against his political adversaries. My influence was of course limited and depended on Father's own realisation of the dangers or the benefits accruing from any line of action I might suggest.

When I tried to reconcile my father with Ireneo Biong Bol, a cousin who had been sentenced to imprisonment by one of Father's deputies (obviously with Father's acquiescence) after unsuccessfully accusing Father of political and other offences, Ireneo flatly rejected my mediation on the grounds that I was a party to my father's autocratic rule. He said that he had seen me standing with my father and laughing as the police were escorting him to prison. I also failed to help resolve a conflict between my father and one of his young half-brothers, Manau. My father married a girl with whom Manau was in love and whom he continued to pursue even after she had been betrothed to Father. Manau was tried by Abyei court for soliciting a married woman, was sentenced to imprisonment and sent to the district headquarters at Fulah to serve his term, pending his appeal to national authorities. On appeal, the judge thought that the court had been biased in favour of my Father, although my father had not participated in the decision. He decided to send the case back for retrial.

I had the opportunity to discuss the case with the judge at his initiative. He had been a senior colleague in the Faculty of Law. He intimated to me that he saw no cause for punishing Manau and that it was in any case unbecoming of Father to permit such punishment over a family affair. With that background, I tried to persuade my father to quash the case against Manau, hinting only vaguely at what the judge had said, carefully avoiding anything that might challenge him into insisting on the punishment. Reluctantly, Father agreed to forget the matter. In an attempt to reconcile the two, I approached Manau with the help of three uncles, Mijang-thii, Alor-Jok, and Yai, but he flatly refused to be reconciled with Father. Manau left the tribe, joined the Southern movement, Anya Nya, and went into exile in the Congo, later to be renamed Zaire, where, I learned later, he continued his campaign against Father among fellow Southerners, portraying me as Father's righthand son and a supporter of his autocratic rule. It was a flattering, but unwarranted condemnation.

I had better luck in reconciling Father with Lino Wuor, our former headmaster at Abyei Elementary School. Wuor and Father had been close friends and collaborators in promoting education in the Ngok Dinka area, but the two had drifted apart for both personal and political reasons. As I think back now, it was certainly an act of moral courage to convene these two monumental personalities in my childhood experiences and approaching them as though I was their elder urging them to resolve their differences and restore their original friendship and cooperation. But I believe my success lay not so much in what I said as in the mere fact of facilitating their get-together to iron out their differences. I was in essence, a catalyst and an instrument for achieving their common objectives without loss of face.

Although I appeared to be, and was indeed, Father's close adviser on political and family matters, I still felt more valued than loved. For instance, I could not understand it when Father came as far as Sennar and he returned without sending me a letter or even a verbal message. He sent his guns to be repaired in Khartoum, but even that came to my attention, not because Father had asked the messengers to pass the guns to me, but because they came to seek my help when they didn't know what to do. I was infuriated. On my next vacation at home, I requested a private talk with my father. My request was granted.

We sat some distance from his company. I told him that while I appreciated all he had done for my education and support, I felt that something important was missing. Father's love was not simply a matter of providing for material needs, I said, and proceeded to give the example of his going as far as Sennar and returning home without a word to me in nearby Khartoum. I asked him to tell me quite frankly whether he had any misgivings, reservations, or grievances towards me. Had I done anything I shouldn't have done or failed to do something I should have done?

Father responded more tenderly than I had ever seen him do before or ever saw him afterwards. In refuting the suspicion of possible disappointment with me, he restated that Bol and I were his main hope for the future of the family and the tribe, citing a line of administrators, British and Sudanese, in support of his expectations. He went on to say that according to the Dinka ways, any grievances a husband might have against a wife could be transferred against her children, but that in the case of my mother, not only did he hold no grievances against her, but, quite the contrary, he held her in high regard and depended on her as though she were a first wife.

He said that whenever he was away and Achok, my mother, was at home, he felt confident that any problems that might arise in the family would be contained through her wisdom. My father specifically stressed that he attached no difference to the positions of Achok, my mother, and Nyanboldit, his first wife. So, he had no reason whatsoever to be negative towards me but, quite the contrary, had much reason to be proud of me. I was very happy with our talk; Father had expressed more sentiment than I had ever expected.

As I often reflect on my relations with my father in those years, I sometimes conclude that my expectations from him were perhaps too high. I spoke to my father on issues and in a manner that I doubt any of my brothers ever did. More examples are still to come later in this book. What this conveyed to Father about me, I will of course never know.

On my way back to Khartoum, after my second year's vacation at home, I travelled in the company of my father and his chiefs who were going to the district headquarters, Fulah, to attend the meetings of the Missiriya Rural Council. We had stopped to rest between Muglad and Fulah when we heard disturbing news of Bol's illness according to newspaper reports that had just reached Muglad. The reports were rather vague; they simply said that Bol had not eaten or drunk anything for a period, which, by the time we received the news, must have made his condition certainly critical, if he was still alive.

There was no explanation as to why he had not been eating, whether it was a hunger strike and why, or the result of an illness and what illness. When I delivered the news to Father, he was so shocked and distressed that he decided we should proceed immediately to inquire further in Fulah, where contacts with Khartoum would be easier. So, we left, arriving at Fulah in the evening and proceeding immediately to the district commissioner to see whether we could inquire with Khartoum. There, we learned more details of the newspaper reports. Sid Ahmed Nugdalla, a reporter who was studying with Bol in East Germany, had written the article, alleging that Bol had tried to commit suicide by a hunger strike. According to Sid Ahmed, Bol was popular and had many friends among both Sudanese and Germans and seemed so happy that his attempted suicide was most puzzling. Additional reports from Nugdalla had said that Bol's condition had improved, even though his friends still found his attempted suicide difficult to explain. That information only raised more worries; why would Bol try to kill himself? We wondered whether his reasons might be financial, but Bol had a scholarship and I had been saving and sending him his share of the allowance Father had set aside for us. Whether a cause or a cure, Father decided to give me more money to be sent to Bol when I arrived at Khartoum.

I was supposed to spend a month training with the district judge at Nahud where Andrew Wieu, a Ngok Dinka from Upper Nile Province, was the assistant district commissioner. Andrew Wieu was a tall, stern-looking young man, whose administrative competence and discipline, combined with a popular touch, were as feared as they were admired by the Northerners, to whom they were refreshingly reminiscent of the fair and impartial British district commissioner. Andrew Wieu and I frequented *Nadi el Salaam,* "The Peace Club," a fashionable meeting place for the leading personalities of Nahud, where evenings passed in a variety of games.

Shortly after I got to Nahud, we were playing cards one day in the club when an old acquaintance from Khor Taqqat Secondary School joined our circle. As he and I were discussing the newspaper reports about Bol, one of the people there, who had also read the reports, but did not know the relationship between Bol and me, remarked casually, "Is that the Southerner who died in East Germany?" It was as though a bomb had just exploded, shattering me into pieces. I felt a deep sense of emptiness. I remained seated motionless. The cards dropped from my hands onto the table.

After a brief silence that seemed like eternity, the colleague from Khor Taqqat tried to correct the speaker, but our companion, not at all realising the significance of his words, insisted that Bol had died. Others joined in to say they had also read the news, but had seen nothing about his having died. Eventually, he seemed to get the message. He conceded that he himself was not so sure after all. There was sufficient room for doubt and hope, but I still felt consumed by apprehension. Andrew Wieu and I decided to try to reach Santino Deng Teng, the Dinka government minister in Khartoum, for further clarification. We eventually reached him and were reassured that Bol was alive.

Shortly after I was back at the university, letters came from both Bulabek and Bol explaining what had happened. Bol had had another operation on his leg to remedy the earlier operation that had left the broken leg a little shorter than the other. While this had been remedied by a shoe, Bol remained self-conscious about what he saw as a defect. He preferred the operation, even though it was a major one. He remained in the hospital for months, during which he became severely depressed. It is true that he went on a hunger strike, perhaps to end the suffering, but it was not a conscious suicide attempt as had been reported. He had been so affected by the depression that he did not even know what he was doing. He remained on his hunger strike and reportedly lost consciousness until Uncle Bona Bulabek went from Padova in Italy, where he was studying medicine. Once Bol saw Bulabek, he suddenly gained consciousness and ended his strike. He gradually normalised his condition.

Bol reported that he had been advised to come home to rest, and leave Germany to study in a warmer country as the climate in Germany was said to be too severe for his leg. He would therefore be proceeding to Sudan. When Bol arrived, I could not believe my sight: although he was now fully recovered, he had been in bed for a long time, and one would have expected him to be slimmer and leaner than usual. But quite the contrary, Bol, who had always been slim and lean, was now so overweight and burly that I felt strongly suspicious of his health. It was as though some substance was inflating his body to an exploding point. But I did not want to worry him with my suspicions; so, I simply reacted as though what I saw was evidence of good health and affluence.

Bol proceeded home for about a month and later returned to Khartoum, having slimmed back to his normal size. That is when I then spoke frankly about my earlier worries and he explained that his body had swollen up because of eating without exercise for the prolonged period of his confinement in the hospital.

On returning from Abyei, Bol approached the Italian missionaries and the West German embassy for a scholarship. Both were interested in the failure of the East German scholarship and the fact that Bol left East Germany more anti-Communist than he had been before going to East Germany. Since our secondary school days, Bol and I had leaned towards socialism. Now he spoke with antagonism about the system and the attempt at indoctrination even in medicine. Both the Italian missionaries and the West German embassy promised to find him a scholarship. The Italian promise materialised first, even though the German promise remained a probability. Bol decided not to miss the chance offered to him in Italy, which, in any case, would bring him together with Uncle Bona Bulabek. So, he left for Italy. The week of his departure, the German scholarship also came through. Bol would have preferred West Germany, but it was too late; he was already in Italy.

During the short winter vacation of my third year at the university, the Faculty of Law decided to send a lecturer, Rodger Fisher, with Donato Mabior, now a finalist student, to go home with me on a research mission. The data I had gathered on the Dinka had stimulated the interest of the faculty in furthering research into traditional Dinka law, but there was also a desire on the part of Fisher to tour the country. Fisher was a young graduate of Oxford who had never been to Africa, and the opportunity of going into the hinterland was as exotic and exciting as it was academically motivated. We spent two weeks sitting in court, interviewing elders, reading court records, and otherwise hunting and partying. Father once more revealed his secret fear of my study of customary law as a potential threat over his authority when he asked me "Mading, is the study of tribal laws being conducted throughout Sudan or only in this tribe?" I answered in a way that was reassuring to him.

When we came to leave, my father simply bade me goodbye and did not give me any pocket money. He did say that he had nothing on him, but, for me, that was no excuse, for it was not possible for Father to have no money on him or somewhere at home. Although it now seems unreasonable of me, since he had made arrangements for Bol and me to receive a monthly allowance in the university, I still expected him to give me pocket money for exigencies, especially as I had incurred expenses in connection with the trip. I felt hurt, but I betrayed no feelings to my father. For the first time in my entire education, I left him with no money in my pocket. Although I did not complain, this reactivated the ambivalence I had always felt in my relationship with my father.

It also brought back to mind two other grievances which I was still nursing. During one of my vacations back home, Kuol, who had become a policeman, was also back home on leave. A few days before the end of my holiday, Kuol and I were passing near Father's Court Tree when a retainer came and said that Father wanted Kuol. When Kuol returned, he reported to me that Father had asked him how much money he thought I needed for pocket money. I had been pressing Father for pocket money, stressing that I was getting late. His question to Kuol indicated that he was about to give me money. Nevertheless, I was insulted that he would ask Kuol about my needs. But I concealed my anger and did not even betray my thoughts to Kuol.

The other incident occurred during Bol's visit home from Germany. Father had asked him whether I had been sending him his share of our monthly allowance. When Bol answered in the affirmative, Father remarked: "Madiŋ acï a moc", which translates, "Mading has become a man of his word." It sounded as though he had suspected I might be dishonest and do otherwise.

So, when Father visited Khartoum during my last year at the university, I decided to have it out with him one more time. I took an early opportunity to ask for a private talk and went straight to the point:

UNIVERSITY
At the Meeting Point

How was I supposed to feel about my father asking another son how much money he thought I needed? What did Kuol know about my needs in the university? And how was I to feel when my father reacted in surprise about my honesty by sending Bol his allowance?

My father's reaction was surprisingly sincere, but typical in its reversal of guilt. First, he did not remember having done the things I was complaining about. Then he argued that even if he had done them, he could not see anything offensive in that. What was wrong with asking my brother how much he thought I should be given? I should be pleased that he asked instead of giving me whatever he thought sufficient, and which might turn out to be inadequate. As for Bol's allowance, he wondered why I should be offended by the assumption that I might have used my brother's money, which was natural, but had not, which was laudable and appreciated. Being appreciated for resisting a temptation was reason for happiness, not anger.

When I argued back, stressing how disturbed about the matter I had felt, Father got angry and became hostile. Turning to his companions, he pleaded angrily, "Achuil, why don't you people come and advise Mading?" He explained in a fashion what we were arguing about. Then turning to me, he said, "You speak of being disturbed. Well, you are driving me out of my mind, quarrelling over such ridiculous issues as these. I don't think we should discuss the matter further." Achuil and others present rallied to Father's side, not so much to blame me as to stop me from pursuing the issue, especially as I was the host in Khartoum. They argued that a father might say things which might seem insulting, but which, coming from a father, should be taken well and not allowed to affect the relationship between father and son.

I withdrew, but was not persuaded. The next day, I kept away. Father was disturbed by my conspicuous absence and kept asking for me. When I did not come early the second day, he sent for me. But when I went to him, he had nothing to say except to ask why I had kept away so long. He was very conciliatory, which was as much of an apology as could be expected from Father. I had also thought over the matter and had decided that my attitude might be misconstrued as an ungrateful withdrawal from obligations to my father, now that I was about to graduate and become financially resourceful. I recalled the history of the relations between Father and Ahmed and felt that it would be cruel to put him through anything which even remotely resembled that experience. So, I adjusted my attitude accordingly and the rest of the visit proved very pleasant and constructive.

The reason for the visit, judging from his meetings, was primarily political and administrative. Relations between Father and Babo Nimir, the paramount chief of the Missiriya Arabs, had become strained over competition for leadership in the Missiriya Rural Council and the Dinka-Arab relations. Their relations had reached a point of undisguised hostility. On the trip during which we heard the news of Bol, we had driven through Muglad without stopping to greet Babo and his brother and deputy paramount chief, Ali Nimir. Babo and his brother, Ali, had later followed and driven by our resting place and stopped to greet us. Father was lying resting in his bed, with a turban covering his face. Although I believe he was awake, he appeared to be asleep, presumably to avoid talking to the Arab chiefs. They proceeded to rest, under a separate tree. I later followed to chat with them and hopefully make up for my father's presumably offensive dismissiveness.

It was there that I learned the news of Bol's hunger strike in East Germany. Things had since worsened even more between Father and the Nimir family. The Missiriya Council had elected my father as the president in the place of Babo Nimir. Being a minority leader as against the paramount chief of an overwhelming majority of Arab leaders, Father's victory was unexpected. For reasons of their own internal politics, the Arab chiefs had united against Babo Nimir, and turned to Father for leadership. Father had tried to argue that while a member of the council, he was radically and culturally different from the majority of the members, who were Arab. He could not therefore represent the whole council as president, arguing that Babo would be more representative. But the chiefs had insisted on his election and he had eventually accepted.

According to the constitution, Father's election qualified him to represent the district at the province council. But the province authority, that is the military governor, appointed Babo as the district representative, despite his defeat. This infuriated Father and prompted him to come and discuss with the authorities in Khartoum. I accompanied

Father to all his official meetings with ministers, the chief justice, and senior civil servants. One of the meetings I recall was with the undersecretary of the Ministry of the Interior, Suleiman Akkrad, a man in whom Father had great confidence. To my surprise, his comment on the defeat of Babo was, "You and the Arab chiefs conspired against Babo." Although the remark was made in a casual, friendly and joking manner, it then became clear that my father's victory was not viewed by the system as evidence of his popularity with the Arabs, but as the result of intrigues among the Arabs themselves. That was why the authorities exercised their discretion to appoint Babo to represent the district, instead of Father, the elected representative. When we left the Ministry of the Interior, my father was vexed and preoccupied.

Our next visit was to Comboni College, where the principal, Father Philip, showed us around. When we ended in his office and he asked the delegation whether they had any questions, my father spoke immediately as though in response to Father Philip's invitation for questions. In fact, what he had said had no connection with Comboni College, for, still preoccupied with the meeting at the Ministry of the Interior, he wondered what the undersecretary had meant by a particular remark. As I was interpreting, the embarrassment fell on me; I had to say something that would appear to be an interpretation of what Father had just said as a response to Father Philip's invitation for questions. I quickly thought of a question and posed it as my father's. In retrospect, it seems amusing, but in the circumstances, it was a critical situation. But it was a good illustration of Father's political preoccupations.

It was in my last social function for my father and his followers that some of my Sudanese and European friends met my father. I chose to give a tea party at the Mogran, a garden refreshment restaurant recreation complex, located at the confluence of the White and Blue Niles. Among the invited guests were Santino Deng Teng, then Minister for Animal Resources, Bishop Baroni, Father Philip, the cultural attaché of the Federal Republic of Germany (for I had then been to Germany on a study tour) and a number of German and Sudanese students, including my classmate, Samieha. The tea party was a great success, combining a degree of formality with an informal air of friendship.

When it was all over, one of our German guest students, remarked,

INVISIBLE BRIDGE
An African Journey through Cultures

"I had always wondered what Francis' father was like and I must say he absolutely fitted my image of Francis' father." She went on to describe my father as "regal" and "majestic" I could not have been prouder at her observations; I knew she was not talking about resemblances between Father and me, but about mannerism and something deeper and more substantive. I knew that they had all been extremely impressed by my father whom they described in most exhaling terms. I took Father and his delegation to a German International Trade Exhibition in Khartoum. The tour of the exhibition, with its wide array of spectacular modern products, ending with the enjoyment of beverages served by beautiful glamorous German girls introduced them to a European environment that reflected an entirely different world from what they knew and to which I had been introduced a year earlier during a summer study tour to Germany. That visit is the subject of my next chapter.

Professor William Twining, the Author's lecturer at Khartoum University and lifelong friend, with his wife, Penelope.

CHAPTER TWELVE

ABROAD
TO THE LANDS BEYOND

Although my life had been one of transition from early childhood and I had moved around quite considerably within Sudan, Europe seemed like a world far beyond reach. From the earliest days of his period in East Germany, Bol had written substantially about life in Germany, the country, and the people. His description was vivid and Germany sounded quite exciting. Although he wrote once that "These Germans make out of me a moving cinema," I envied Bol and wished I could join the fun, but it was only a dream that I did not seriously contemplate or anticipated.

I was in my third year when I ran into the encounter that would lead to my first visit to Germany, even though I was not aware of that likelihood at the time. One day, a senior student, a Greek Sudanese law student, introduced me to two foreign students at about lunchtime. He was living at home where he was going after classes and wanted me to attend to the foreign visitors. After chatting for long enough to learn that they were law students from West Germany, members of a newly formed International Students Federation, abbreviated as the ISSF, which was organising study tours for German university students to visit foreign countries during vacations. They were at the tail end of their study tour in the Sudan. I invited them to join me for lunch. They seemed rather surprised, but pleased by the spontaneity of the invitation. I soon learned that they were part of a larger group who were accommodated in the university hostels. We had a pleasant lunch followed by a relaxed tea in our room.

They asked questions about the political situation in the Sudan, especially with respect to the Southern problem. I answered them quite candidly and with an objective appraisal which they thought not typical of Sudan. They appeared so absorbed in what I was saying that they did not seem to entertain any thought of leaving for the sacrosanct Sudanese afternoon siesta. At the end of that session, I invited them to the students' union for a late afternoon tea. They gladly accepted and asked whether it would be convenient to bring others along, as they thought their colleagues would benefit from talking to me. Of course, I had no objection.

At the club that late afternoon I was surprised by the number of the German students they brought along with them. I believe there were at least ten, probably more, and they soon formed an enlarged seminar-type circle. Almost immediately, they began to bombard me with questions. They seemed to ask about everything and appeared intensely interested in every answer I gave. It was as though there had been a blackout on the situation in Sudan for the entire time they had been in the country. One of them was later to tell me that they had come to learn more about Sudan in that single sitting than they had learned during their entire stay in the country. I felt flattered, but also sorry for my country, even though I knew that the discrepancy had to do with Sudanese pride and the desire to project a favourable image of the country to outsiders.

Before greater exposure to the world, Sudanese in general, and Northern Sudanese in particular, held a fanatically ethnocentric view of themselves and their country. But, at least on the subconscious level, they also recognised their shortcomings. Foremost of their "dirty linen" was the political situation in the South. The war that raged in that part of the country made the Northern Sudanese so insecure and vulnerable that they tended to conceal the problem from foreign visitors. Nearly all the people the Germans had met had been Northern Sudanese. As a Southerner, I had a vested interest in letting facts be known; as an individual, I believe I was more inclined towards objectivity and self-scrutiny on the North-South conflict than most Sudanese on both sides.

By the end of the evening, the German students had invited me to a cocktail party that was to be given by the German ambassador in honour of their delegation. They also asked me to recommend other students for the party as they had been authorised to invite friends from the university. As they were interested to talk to a girl student, I introduced them to Samieha, who in turn introduced them to other female students. About twelve of us Sudanese students attended the ambassador's party.

Our German friends hinted to me that we would be invited to visit Germany as they intended to institute an exchange programme between German and Sudanese students. All twelve of us who had been invited to the ambassador's reception, including four girls, received invitations to visit Germany. The leader of our delegation was to be Abdrahman, a huge, pleasant light skinned science student.

We were given some evening lessons in German. The classes were stimulating not only because of the jokingly competitive atmosphere among the students, but also because they were an introduction to the exciting trip ahead. They also helped introduce the team members to one another in a closer sense than had been the case before that.

As many Southerners were fleeing the country into refuge abroad and the rebel movement in exile was rapidly gaining momentum, the Government of Sudan placed stringent restrictions on exit visas for the Southern Sudanese. I was the only Southern Sudanese on the student delegation to Germany, and although my own position in the South-North problem was not typically Southern, it was obvious that being a Southerner going abroad was disturbing to the security men in the passport office. This was to confront me with a comical situation. At first, I applied for the passport on my own without any recommendation and obtained one that was marked "Valid for the United Arab Republic only." My argument that I was going to West Germany made no difference whatsoever. When I returned with a letter from the university making the same point, the authorities added, "And also valid for the Federal Republic of Germany."

As I wanted to visit my brother Bol and Uncle Bona in Italy, quite apart from my natural desire to have an open passport to enable me see the world, this was still not satisfactory. So, I decided to go to Mohamed el Hassan Adhaw, the lord chamberlain at of the Republican Palace – the seat of the country's president – and an old friend of my father. He made a telephone call to the man responsible for issuing passports and gave him a hard time, wondering how his people could behave that way towards the son of such a leading figure as Chief Deng Majok. How would my father feel if he knew that his son was not sufficiently trusted by the government to receive an open passport? He was asked to send me over immediately with a note of recommendation. When that had been done, another addition was immediately inserted in my passport, reading, "And also valid for all countries."

This is how that page then looked: "Valid for the United Arab Republic only." "Also valid for the Federal Republic of Germany." "And also valid for all countries." I often wondered why they did not issue me with a new passport. One thing was certain: none of my Northern colleagues went through that amount of trouble to obtain a passport; and I doubt if they even needed more than that the university note to obtain the validity of their passports for all countries.

We went by train to Wadi Haifa on the Egyptian border, then by steamer to Aswan, and finally by train to Cairo. During this phase of the journey, I was simply struck by the bareness, the desolation, and the poverty of the desert-jammed Northern Province. Cairo was to me absolutely overwhelming, not only in its size, but perhaps even more dramatically in the attitude and the spirit of the people. Streets buzzed with the sounds of the performers or trick-players. It was as though life for the Egyptians was a stage performance of comedy. Apart from the jammed annoying harassment of the streets, the Egyptians were excellent hosts, receptive, hospitable, witty and funny.

A programme was organised for us that included visits to the university, the museums, the pyramids, and a tour of the city.

ABROAD
To the Lands Beyond

Otherwise, we explored various aspects of the exciting city of Cairo. A group of high school students approached us one day, as we strolled in one of Cairo's parks. Convinced that we were from any one of many black countries in Africa, still struggling against colonialism and imperialism, they chanted, "Lumumba! Lumumba! Lumumba!" as they followed our steps. Apart from my unmatched black skin, we were a typical conglomeration of the in-between colours of Sudan, from the dark brown Osman to the nearly white Abdel-Rahman. Yet, for one reason or another, the black must have set the tone for the Egyptians: "Lumumba! Lumumba! Lumumba!", they continued to chant after us. We tried to ignore them, but the insult implied in the denial of Arabism made one of us lose patience. "Oh, Brothers," Ali broke the silence as he turned plaintively towards the chanting Egyptian students, "we are Arabs like you." The situation became immediately clear to the Egyptians: "Welcome to our Sudanese brothers", they said without betraying any feeling of inconsistency or contradiction.

Much more modern than Sudan, with men and women moving arm-in-arm without drawing attention, Egypt was for me a transitional station which whetted my appetite for Germany even more. I was eager to get to Germany. When the day came, we all got into our Sudanese national dress, the white jallabiya with turbans for men and the toub for the ladies. Whatever else others thought of our peculiar appearance, it was an impressive sight, no doubt. The Lufthansa flight, being my first, was too unbelievable to be frightening; floating in the air was a miracle.

When I was not marvelling at the technology that could float with such a load so smoothly in the sky, I was anticipating the point of contact that we would soon establish between Africa and Europe and for all of us, the first time. As we disembarked at Frankfurt, with our jallabiyas, turbans, and toubs, we could not have generated greater curiosity or made more impression on the Germans. We were received at the airport by members of the International Students Federation, ISSF, our hosts. The formalities at the airport were smooth and swift, thanks to the German efficiency. Then we checked into our hotel, convened for an informal dinner, and retired for the night.

By the standards with which we were familiar, the hotel was luxurious. The following morning, we had a reception breakfast during which we formally met with members of ISSF, whose leader was Reinhard Spilker, a charismatic dynamic young man who exercised full control of the organisation and enjoyed the unreserved respect and loyalty of the members. We were also introduced to the prominent personalities of our programme, including the families that were to host us in the vicinity of Frankfurt during the week's introductory period to Germany. The programme included every one of the team saying a few words of self-introduction. When my turn came, whether it was because I was the only Southerner, or the only son of a chief (which our team played up), or perhaps because of the flattering consideration people gave my English, my remarks drew considerable applause.

We were then assigned to our host families in the vicinity of Frankfurt. Samieha and I were assigned to the family of the Kuhns in Falkenstein in the district of Taunus, about half an hour from Frankfurt. As we drove with Mr Kuhn through the district of Taunus and into the Falkenstein area, I still remember the almost illusory beauty of the landscape, the intersecting roads, the greenery of the undulating countryside, with wooded interludes, open farmlands, and elegant houses.

I felt a dichotomy that was as unbridgeable as it was fascinating. Here were the Germans and the country, both with whom I almost instantaneously and objectively felt a surprising affinity, perhaps because they too gave me the impression that the feeling was mutual. The Kuhn family was both ordinary and extraordinary, a successful lawyer, with an older son whom we never got to know, a second son who was amicable, and two daughters who were lovely and friendly in their two different ways. The parents were obviously old enough to have lived the German Nazi past, but were astonishingly global in outlook and in their respect for people. They certainly showed no prejudice except, perhaps, in the positive sense of treating us with unusual kindness, deference and compassion. With the exception of our host students and their facilitators, they were my first experience with the contrast between the image of Germany that is associated with the "Nazis," and the good people whom that image overshadowed.

While Mr Kuhn and his sons would be at work during the daytime, we would be in the hands of the female members of the family. That entailed not only hospitality at home, but also pleasant walks in the beautiful nature that surrounded Falkenstein. We walked in the immediate vicinity, and we walked farther away for long distances, and we walked up to elevated altitudes. I was fully mesmerised in the company of those young, exciting, and different sisters. Judged by the standards of Khartoum, with its social and cultural constraints on male-female companionship, it was a dream-world that was real.

We spent a week that passed too fast and were then assigned to places where we were to spend half the period of our stay in Germany, supposedly working in factories. I was assigned to the Black Forest, a small town called Zell-am-Wiesenthal, near Basel in Switzerland. With me were Osman and Ali, who were destined for Lorach, a few miles within reach of Zell, but considerably larger in size. We arrived by train in the nearby Freiburg (in Germany, not to be confused with the Freiburg in Switzerland), were met, and driven by car to our destinations. I realised later that the trip by car would have been a spectacular introduction to the area of Grunewald, "The Green Forest," had it not been night time.

At Zell, I was warmly received by my hosts, Dr Heinz Dieter Fessmann and his wife, in their home, and then taken to a Hotel Lowern, where I was to stay for a month and a half. I was at first slightly disappointed that my hosts would accommodate me in a hotel, for it was my initial understanding that I would live with my host family. I soon realised that they were very warm and hospitable, and that they probably accommodated me in a hotel to give me privacy and freedom.

Zell was a small town located at the bottom of a circle of mountains that provided a commanding view over a far-stretching territory and were in themselves a spectacular scene to the town dwellers. Otherwise, there was not really much at Zell. Most of the town was employed by my hosts, the Fessmanns, in a spinning and weaving factory that had been a family business for over one hundred and fifty years. The other significant feature was the school which provided education up to the junior high level.

My life at Zell was to be significantly tied to these two institutions – the factory and the school. Dr Fessmann explained to me that since the main objective of my work with them was to acquaint myself with the working conditions in a German factory, I could be flexible in what I did at the factory to observe as much as I wanted. In practice, I worked in two sections, first making boxes from cardboards and then filling cans with hair spray chemicals. In both, I tried to work very hard, resisted any special consideration, and as much as possible, identified myself with the workers. This was very successful with both management and labourers.

The workers had a pleasant attitude towards me, curious but not offensively so. They appreciated my efforts at learning German and did their best to encourage and improve my vocabulary. During coffee breaks, we would get out into the occasional sunshine. One older man made a habit of gesturing with his hands, as though removing sweat from his forehead, and saying, "Afrika ganz heiss." I took my work so seriously that some workers kept telling me jokingly not to work so hard. Dr Fessmann from time to time called me to his office to introduce me to visitors, converse on various aspects of the business, visit other factories in the area, or otherwise we would go on trips to surrounding places of attraction. Although I lived in the hotel, they closely associated me with their family life, frequently inviting me to the house for meals and joining them in their recreational activities.

The Fessmanns had two children, a girl of about four and a boy of about six. The first time I went to the house, the girl was scared, would not shake hands, and in fact cried. I was the first black person she had ever set eyes on. I asked them not to push her and to let her take her time. The second time, she shook hands with me, but soon checked to see whether I had stained her hand black. Gradually, she began to relax with me until our relationship became positively affectionate.

One day, we spent time on the water in the large family motor boat. As we got on to the boat, she rushed over to where I sat and said, "The seat next to you is reserved for me, "Ja?" "Yes." I said. Then we sat together playing with our hands in the water. She noticed that the palms of my hands were lighter than the back of the hands. "The black colour has been washed away from this part of your hands," she remarked, startled by her finding. I laughed but did not try to explain. Then I rubbed her face with my hands and told her that I had painted her face black. She rushed over to the mirror and came back beaming with a smile to say, "No, you didn't!" Then suddenly, she held my face between her two hands as though I were the child and she a woman: "*Du bist mein bester Freund*," "You are my best friend," she said with genuine sentiment. I immediately responded "Aber, natuerlich," "Naturally." Then her demeanour turned into that of a child matron: "Aber du bist kein kind!" "But you are not a child!" she said. I have always remembered my interaction with her as an example of both the limitations of social conditioning and the humanising potentials of contact and broadened experience.

Hotel Lowern was what I believe the Fessmanns had intended it to be for me, a place where I could lead my own life and meet people on my own. Not long after I settled in the hotel, a very pleasant, smiling, but serious-minded salesman, apparently a regular visitor, came. He sat at what must have been his popular corner, far enough to be outside our social orbit, but close enough to be within hearing distance. I soon found myself with another German hotel resident, obviously an outsider to Zell who was so extroverted that he approached me as I sat alone at my table. I welcomed his approach, as I was clearly lonely and rather shy to join others. He soon invited me to a drink. I had become quite fond of the "Scholle," a mixture of (red) wine, sugar, and soda water. He had his order of Schnapps, a strong alcoholic drink with beer as a chaser. When we finished the first order, we placed a second order and I insisted that it should be on me. The visitor insisted he should pay, but I would not let him. Then, to my surprise, he asked me what my father did. I said he was a chief of a tribe. "But why do you look so thin?" he said.

We laughed and talked about more serious things, like Germany under the Nazis. He was exaggeratedly anti-Hitler and pro-America. My line of argument was different. I said that Hitler was the product of his social and political environment; there was no way he could be isolated from the German context and the circumstances then prevailing in the world. Having been a student of History with a bias for the period of both the First and Second World Wars, I tried to argue that the prevailing atmosphere in Germany, in particular, the allied treatment of the defeated Germany, had precipitated the German jingoistic reaction that caused the Second World War. It was only human nature for the vanquished to seek vengeance. That was particularly true of a major power, like Germany, humiliated under defeat.

I discussed the situation we found Germany in, the Allied troops roaming all over, and the evidence of defeat that was rampant everywhere. I argued that if things continued the way they were, we were bound to witness another patriotic surge in Germany, with a disposition towards self-assertiveness that could once more endanger world peace. The best approach, I thought, was not to deny Hitler, but to reject the negatives in Nazi policy, while also scrutinising the conditions that brought the Nazis to power, and guarding against their recurrence.

This was to be a popular theme of my commentary on Germany. My German interlocutor at Hotel Lowern simply dismissed the argument about the potential resurgence of nationalism as "impossible." He told me that the Americans were the best friends of Germany. "They have saved our country and nationalism will never again have a place in Germany," he said. Nor would Germany ever get into the struggle for military might. He noted that Hitler was not even a German but an Austrian.

As soon as that man was gone, the salesman who was within hearing distance came and requested to join me. I welcomed him. He quickly introduced his line of thought. He said that he had been listening to our conversation and felt the urge to tell me how much he agreed with my line of argument. He had been a teenager during the war and his task had been to carry messages between military posts. He had therefore been able to observe the Nazi period quite closely. Hitler had never been what he was being portrayed to be. The distortion he thought was because Germany was then going through a period of fear and self-denial. That was bound to come to an end. When that happened, he thought that what I was predicting would come true. Although he talked carefully, looking around to make sure his words were off-the-record, I felt he spoke with conviction, from experience, and with a quality that was enhanced by his gentle, smiling, and apparently humane outlook.

Osman and Ali complained much about racial prejudice in Lorach. They were told that they had initially been booked in another hotel but that the manager on learning that they were black had refused to accommodate them. They were particularly sensitive about German curiosity and always saw it as a gesture of racial prejudice. So intimidated were they by the racialism they saw or imagined that they shied away from contacts, took no initiatives to ask girls for a dance and otherwise avoided social situations, which might generate any racial reaction or tension.

When I visited them, they were surprised to see my interaction with curious onlookers, for I would respond to their gestures and we would soon find ourselves in conversation with strangers. Osman and Ali became convinced that I positively enjoyed the show and even went as far as saying that I was happiest when I was surrounded by spectators and unhappy when we were ignored. That was an obvious exaggeration of significant differences in our response to curiosity. For them that was perhaps the first and most significant cross-cultural encounter. For me, it was yet another horizon in a chain of experiences that had begun much earlier in my life. I had already gone through curiosity even within Sudan.

One day, the Fessmanns took me to a trade fair in Basel, Switzerland. I was reminded of Bol's first letter from East Germany where he had remarked, "These Germans make of me a moving cinema." I was like an animal in a zoo, with people not only gazing, but crowding and following. Even the Fessmanns were surprised that a black man could have been all that much of a novelty. An elderly lady even approached me and asked whether she could touch my hair and feel my skin. With a receptive smile, I gave her permission to do so. But the show was dehumanising and although I took it well, I felt that it was fringing on the intolerable. The Fessmans were obviously embarrassed, but chose not to make a scene in the crowd. Mrs Fessmann was to remark humorously later, "We would have made a lot of money by charging a fee for people to see you."

My experiences within Zell itself were even more dramatic. I was certainly the first black man the town had ever witnessed, at least so I was told. As a result, I enjoyed and suffered the distinction of racial uniqueness. As I got out of the hotel to go to work or for my frequent walks, I was followed by a crowd of children from the nearby school, running after me and shouting, both in fear and excitement. If I stopped to talk to them, they ran away from me; if I ignored them and walked on, they ran after me, encroaching so close that there was no way I could ignore them. What compounded the problem for me was that adults too would suddenly lay eyes on me, stop in shock with hands on their mouths, and perhaps betray a withdrawal reaction that was only different from the children's in that it was slightly more inhibited.

After a while, this got on my nerves; I could no longer tolerate it. I decided to enter the school and ask for the director. I was shown into the director's office amidst crowds of following and screaming children. When I got to the director, there was the problem of the language of communication, as he did not know enough English and would not expose the little amount he knew. So, one of the teachers, a lady, was fetched to interpret. As I discovered eventually, she was one of the very few who spoke English at Zell. She came into the director's office amidst extreme excitement that must have been unique in the history of the school. She was a woman in her twenties, perhaps approaching thirty, quite attractive even with a tragically amputated arm. Marlene Passens was her name.

I gave them the gist of my experience with the children, how much I had tried to dispel their fears by approaching them in a friendly manner, how they had refused to respond to my gestures, how they would run after me when I proceeded and away from me when I approached. I told them that there was a limit to what a human being could tolerate and that I was not there as an animal in a zoo, but a human being with feelings and sentiments. I said I was keen to cultivate relations with the children but, instead, I received only insult and an unwillingness to learn on the part of the children. I said that where I came from, the school was the institution which cultivated manners and the pupils the example for proper conduct in society. I was therefore surprised to find that school was an example of the opposite in German society. I ended by appealing to them to do something about the problem.

The director, Herr Bohler, who, I later learned, came from one of the prominent families of Zell, was enraged by the behaviour of his pupils. He said in a language I well understood even before interpretation, "They will be punished." And judging from his demeanour, he meant it. Fraulein Passens was purely an interpreter, but she reflected an enthusiastic sympathy for me and seemed to share the director's reaction. But I argued against punishing the children. I said that since they were afraid of me, punishing them would only add to their fears. All I wanted was to make them understand that I was a human being, that what they were doing was offensive to me, and that I would not harm them as they feared. The director promised me to look into the matter and to inform me of the action they would take.

A few days later, I received an invitation from Herr Bohler, through Dr Fessmann, to give a talk to the school to be interpreted by Fraulein Passens. I accepted. The talk was well attended and I gave a general overview of Sudan, putting some emphasis on the aspects I thought children might appreciate, but without being simplistic, condescending, or ignoring the serious issues in the Sudanese scene. The pupils asked a number of questions that showed a determined interest within children's preview. The occasion was a clear success.

The next day, as I was having my afternoon walk, a lady came out of her house and tried to gesture me into the house. I responded with hesitation as I was uncertain about the intentions or the implications. She must have understood my thoughts, because she rushed back into her house and re-emerged with her husband and photos of their children, indicating that they had talked about me and gesturing her invitation for me to stop for tea. I went in briefly.

From that time on, not only would the children approach me on the street with a "Good morning," but many would come to shake hands and even follow me to my hotel, just chit-chatting. One small girl was absolutely hooked on our friendship. She would rush to me and hold hands back to my room, staying there and communicating with me non-verbally until it was time to depart, which she would always do with reluctance.

Herr Bohler, the director of the school, agreed with Dr Fessmann to have me receive lessons in the German language from Fraulein Passens. Our initial lessons in Khartoum had not, of course, prepared us for being in a non-English speaking environment as Zell. Private classes in German would undoubtedly be useful, not only in Zell, but also later in other parts of Germany. So, I gladly accepted.

Fraulein Passens was a good teacher, professional, compassionate and tolerant. The lessons were held in her apartment where she went out of her way to entertain me. While I was moved by her condition, so proud was she to do what she did that I minimised any help based on sympathy. Fraulein Passens occupied an apartment on the third floor in the house of the Bohlers whose family I became quite friendly with. The Bohlers had two sons and two daughters. The eldest son was a technician while the second studied medicine in Basel. He and I got to be quite good friends.

But the ones I saw more often were the sisters, one nineteen years old and her younger sister of about twelve, who was eager to practise her English. The nineteen-year-old daughter, Bernadette, was a girl of great compassion. While the whole family was devoutly Catholic, she was even more so, with a touch of missionary zeal which was expressed in the pictures she hung on the walls of her room. She and I saw a great deal of one another and whether our friendship triggered off her missionary zest or vice versa, religion became a significant aspect of our time together. She even succeeded in persuading me to go to church after a significant void in my adherence to religious forms. But we also enjoyed being together, running in the open fields, hiking up the surrounding mountains, walking in the woods, pausing for coffee or tea, and despite the language problem, conversing in a mixture of English and German.

Our stay in Grunwalt, "Greenbelt", eventually came to its end and we were due to move on to Rothenberg on the Tauber River, where the Goethe Institute had one of its language training centres. We spent a month at Rothenberg with half the delegation. The others, including the girls, went to another Goethe Institute. Rothenberg was a Gothic town whose beauty and depth of heritage would have been apparent to anyone with Western roots. But for us, it was too rustic and a banishment from cosmopolitan Germany, except for the rewards of the hundreds or thousands of tourists that poured into town daily. The most spectacular feature of the town was a clock that donged at a certain hour of the day, synchronising with the opening of the window, revealing the hero, drinking the pints of beer with which he saved the town, according to mythology. We were accommodated in different parts of the town, mine being a room in a house of a kindly, elderly lady, who took more care of me than was envisaged in the lease. She provided me with breakfast and meals during the weeks beyond her cultural obligations.

The main purpose of our being in Rothenberg - learning German - went very well. We had an experienced, grey haired, pleasant teacher, the director of the institute, who inspired in us a desire to learn his language. His classes were quite entertaining. Although there were others in the institute, we seemed to fall into a programme of our own, which limited the competition, but also gave the course an intimacy that added to the informality. I took the classes quite seriously, and considering my background at Zell, soon proved far ahead of my group. The fact that I had such a warm, socially sensitive landlady added to my advantage for practising German "at home" and providing an additional human context for deepening the tools for learning the language.

Apart from learning German, Rothenberg was a peculiar experience and a good illustration of how people can be inside a community of tourists who flocked into Rothenberg on a daily basis and yet remain isolated and desolate. In retrospect, it now seems as though the programme suffered from a cross-cultural misunderstanding. The German organisers left us to experience the situation at that phase of the programme entirely on our own, without their direct involvement. The Sudanese on the other hand, applying their own concepts of hospitality to foreign visitors, felt grossly neglected and disregarded.

When the one month for language training was over, the two groups reunited at Frankfurt and met to assess the visit thus far and to discuss any action we might deem fit in reaction to the situation. We had all become critical of the programme, especially the neglect we had suffered from the international students organisation that was our host - ISSF: no visits from any of our hosts, and no attempt to look into our problems, far less to solve them during the two and a half months of our stay in Germany. Most members of our group wanted to express our discontent by terminating the visit and requesting immediate return to our country.

Almost single-handedly, I opposed that reaction, stressing that we were guests in a programme that was still experimental. Rather than permit personal inconveniences, discourtesies or mistreatment to create a crisis that might severely damage the scheme, we should be more positive in our evaluation, voice our grievances, and suggest areas where the programme could be improved in the future. My statement had the immediate impact of provoking a lively, even heated, discussion. Contrasting views on both sides were presented. Then some members began to support my position. Before long, I had shifted the mood of the meeting and moderation became the accepted approach.

We then left on the final leg of the visit, an extensive tour of Germany. I really liked Germany and felt a positive mutual appreciation with the Germans. They seemed to me both rational and humane; sharply contrasting with their reputation as harsh and aggressive, they were gentle, receptive and friendly. I believe they also appreciated in me some of the attributes I admired in them.

Our tour around Germany was guided by a serious-minded, time-conscious young man who was originally from East Germany. He had come to the West as a refugee, but as many Germans I was to know later, had adjusted and integrated into the West German context. He had an acute problem with our concept of time and must have ended feeling ambivalent about the Sudanese. Few in our group fully appreciated what time meant to the Germans and, if they did, they thought it was compulsiveness that was not a virtue to be emulated. We were late in visiting factories, kept the executives waiting, and did not catch up with our hosts, as they showed us the plants. Some of us occasionally dropped apologetic comments, but there was clearly a cross-cultural gulf that could not easily be bridged.

One day, while within the vicinity of his home, a light-spirited German student I had come to know, told me that his family, in particular his mother, did not believe that there were people with truly black skin. Since I was a perfect example of black skin, would I mind coming with him to convince his family? I accepted with pleasure. We got into his house and obviously took his mother by surprise. As we sat in the living room with his sister, waiting for their mother who was totally unaware of our presence, we saw her pass through the hallway going into her bedroom totally naked. I was embarrassed, but they all laughed. She re-emerged in minutes, fully dressed. While his sister spoke some English, their mother knew no English at all and our conversation was limited and brief. The entire purpose was to prove the unbelievable fact that human beings could be that black.

We travelled by land to Berlin, our last stop on the tour. The trip was itself pleasant and jovial, with a great deal of singing and laughter. The barbwire which lined up the East German borders along our route appeared so awesome that it was hard to believe the same people, Germans, lived on both sides. As we approached the entry point into East German territory, which had to be crossed to reach Berlin, we started noticing posters with the words "Achtung", warning us "Beware" that we were about to leave "Free" Germany. The warning was repeated several times before we came to the border post. There, we encountered what initially seemed an insurmountable problem with the border police. We did not have visas for East Germany as we were simply transiting into West Berlin, and the police would not let us go through. The delay was compounded by the fact that there was a long line of other cars waiting. I do not know how we eventually managed to get through, but it was not before losing what seemed like half a day.

In Berlin itself, the programme was initiated with a visit at the office of the mayor, then Willy Brandt, where we were briefed about the status of Berlin. The German position was charged with emotion.

Although West Berlin seemed to be better placed than the rest of West Germany to recognise the existence of East Germany as a reality, West Berliners shared with the rest of West Germany what seemed to me to be an astonishing lack of realism in their attitude towards East Germany. The result was an inconsistent refusal to recognise East Germany while holding meetings with East German authorities to sort out the practical problems of relations between West Berlin and East Berlin. At the briefing, I pointed out this ambivalence and wondered whether it would not be more advantageous for the West to accept the reality of East Germany and to be in a better position to negotiate in their mutual interest. The answer was an unequivocal "No" and a reaffirmation of the West German policy of non-recognition of East Germany.

We toured the city, with its impressive parks and lakes, its depressing division between East and West, and its remarkable record of reconstruction after the devastation of the Second World War. The wide avenue with greenery on both sides that led to the Gate linking East and West had the familiar characteristic warnings of "Achtung Sie verlassen West Berlin." When I left West Berlin, it was not through the Gate, but by the underground. And although the passage into East Berlin seemed relatively easy, despite the massive police barriers at the station, experiences on the other side revealed a marked difference between the two sectors. In sharp contrast to West Berlin, impressively reconstructed and clean, East Berlin was a living reminder of the ravages of war, as though it was intended to make the horror remain convincing. Even the dresses and the faces of the people revealed a degree of need which was either real or only apparent in contrast to the otherwise radiant and affluent West Berlin. The East Berliners were generally friendly, except for what seemed like abject conditions of need in comparison to the West and the ominous presence of police everywhere. I walked into a coffee bar and ordered "Coca Cola." The waitress looked at me disbelievingly and disappeared only to return with her male senior who asked for my papers. After they assured themselves that I was naive, but harmless, they told me they had a local drink not too different from Coca Cola.

ABROAD
To the Lands Beyond

In the conference that followed to present our observations from the trip in Germany, I presented my thesis on the German denial of Hitler, the continuing presence of allied troops in Germany, and what I foresaw to be another nationalist reaction in the end. In particular, I argued that isolating Hitler from the German context and viewing him as an extraordinarily evil man, exceptionally evil to be human, created the artificial situation in which humankind absolved themselves of moral responsibility to explain evil away without recognising the realities that brought it about and finding appropriate remedy. I argued that even if Hitler had been totally immoral in what he had done, only by recognising him as one of us, with motivations and reactions revealing the human weaknesses to which we are potentially all susceptible, did we stand a chance of curing ourselves of the latent Hitlerite tendencies within us.

I found the Germans somewhat ambivalent about my interpretation of their situation. While they seemed to appreciate giving Germany some reason for reacting the way it had and even giving Hitler his due, they nevertheless felt a strong need to disassociate themselves from the horrors of the Nazi era, stressing sentiments of solidarity with their Western Allies, and denying any remote possibility of a German return to nationalism. The days of love of Fatherland were over for the Germans, they unequivocally asserted.

Our stay in Berlin concluded with a period of festivities in the Free University and the Technical University where we spent our last two days. One late afternoon, as we were about to move to a nearby snack bar for a pre-boat social introduction, Fredrich von Bismarck, one of the leading personalities of the ISSF, introduced me to a young lady who had just arrived. She was a very attractive girl of medium height, barely twenty years old, with twirling, longish hair, and a smiling, outgoing personality. Her name was Verena von Trott Zu Solz. Verena and I spontaneously drew towards one another and soon discovered the basis of mutual understanding that would rapidly develop into a deep and lasting friendship.

The following day she took me on an extensive tour of Berlin which ended at the Congress Hall, an impressive display of modern design. By now, I had come to know Verena as a young patriot from a noble family whose father, Adam von Trott, a diplomat-politician, had participated in the underground movement against Hitler. He had been sent on a mission to Great Britain and the United States by the resistance movement. Although many of his friends in both countries had advised him against returning to Germany, he had insisted on returning to continue his work inside. When a bomb planted by his friend to assassinate Hitler exploded on July 20, 1944, Adam von Trott was arrested, tried, condemned to death and executed, leaving behind a young wife and two small daughters, the oldest of which was Verena. Their mother subsequently studied medicine and psychiatry, and raised her children alongside her practice.

It was now time to leave Berlin and Germany. That year, I was asked to be co-leader of the ISSF German team that was to visit Sudan. After interim visits in Europe, I joined the group at Rome airport, flew to Cairo, and then proceeded back by train, steamer and train, the same way we had come before.

Perhaps the most significant aspect of my visit to Germany was not so much that it enabled me to see new countries, experienced new cultures, and new horizons, as it was an opportunity to contact people and establish relationships in those new situations; interactions which, though casual and short lived, gave me new human dimensions that were far richer than their touristic values, relations that opened a new page in my life, with new aspirations, new dreams, and new ambitions. The real irony was that in certain respects, and especially in the relationships between men and women, I felt closer to the Germans than I did to my compatriots in the North, where religious, social and cultural barriers seemed insurmountable. But there was more to it than that: not only did the barriers with the Germans seem more bridgeable in principle, but I also felt even more appreciated intellectually and humanly than I had been in my own country. This is not to say that I had not been appreciated in my country. It is perhaps to say that there was a different quality of appreciation which I found particularly exhilarating. It was therefore no wonder that my tour of Germany had established between me and the Germans, a special bond that was to link me with their country, and perhaps by extension, the wider world.

ABROAD
To the Lands Beyond

Towards the end of my final year at the university, our newly established Sudanese-German Friendship Association, in consultation with the ISSF, designated me as the leader of the next delegation to visit Germany. As interest in the programme was mounting in the university, the selection was by no means easy. To ensure objectivity and fairness, it was decided that the matter be left to a high-level committee of faculty members, with senior students, including me in my capacity as the leader of the delegation.

The second trip to Germany took place shortly after our final examination. As with the first delegation, I was the only Southerner in the group. That was not well viewed by some of my Southern colleagues who became aware of the programme and were showing interest. I had indeed tried to interest the Southern students in the association, but had met with no response, largely because it was perceived as primarily "Northern." although it had, in a sense, been championed by me, a Southerner.

I was one day approached by Daniel Kot, a remarkable Nuer with whom I had become friends in Rumbek after a quarrel, because he had misunderstood me to have commented on his hunchback in Dinka. D.K., as he was known, informed me that there was considerable displeasure among Southern students that I had not included Southerners in the delegation. He said he was informing me as a friend, particularly because he suspected Southerners would probably not convey their sentiments to me with the same frankness with which he himself approached me. I tried to explain to D.K. that only members of the association could be chosen for the trip. But if the criticism was widely shared in Southern circles, explaining it to D.K. could hardly help.

We followed the old route by train and steamer to Cairo and then by air to Frankfurt, and on to Berlin, where we were to carry out the first leg of the programme. The girls were distributed between German families, while the boys were accommodated in Ernst-Reuter Heim, a modern building that was within reasonable reach of the Siemens factories, where the boys were employed. For me, it was a return to a city I really liked; its beautiful nature, its open space, its wide streets, its green parks, and its generally clean environment.

But there was a new feature to the city. The tragic wall separating West and East Berlin had been erected and had a deeply undesirable effect on the people of Berlin.

Unlike the first year, when work had been more an orientation or a means of acquiring insights into German working conditions, our employment during the second year was a far more serious undertaking. We also took it quite seriously, observing the importance of time to the minute, respecting the hierarchy of authority in the factory, and identifying ourselves in every way with the rest of the workers. We even developed a common dislike of the limping fierce-looking foreman, whose appearance, despite relative courtesy to us as students and foreigners, invoked the authoritarian image of the "boss."

A minute's delay had to be accounted for; we stopped instantaneously when the bell rang for the coffee break; and we ended work with the signal for the day's labour, when we went into our changing rooms, discarded the working uniforms, entered into our common showers, and put on our own clothes. When the day was done, we were so exhausted that an early time to bed in anticipation of an early time from bed was the wise thing to do. As the factory was a considerable distance from our hostel, we had to rise as early as five o'clock to be at work on time. The girls were employed elsewhere, but while the nature of their work was lighter as compared to the heavy industry of Siemens, the essence of labour was relatively the same.

As I was the supervisor of my male colleagues, I had to work even harder to set an example. But while we worked as hard as all the rest, I could not help thinking that there was a major difference between us and the German workers. We were there for a brief period, but for most of them, that was the total meaning of life. As I watched those men, some of whom had been there since adolescence, labouring away into old age, contributing to a small piece of a larger machine that they never envisaged as a whole until the end of the production line, I could not help but feel sympathy, even sadness about the injustices of life. One man particularly saddened me by showing me a photograph of his young son, whom he said was in school, but quickly added that he did not think he was intelligent enough to go high in education, and that he would probably end up a labourer like him, his father.

The Sudanese students on the other hand had been conditioned as the cream of society in which education exempted people from menial work. Some members of our team missed the objective of the exercise and considered it inhospitable of the Germans to subject their guests to such hardship. That must have been the gist of the complaint by one girl to her host family, the Lossows, who saw the programme as a bad propaganda for Germany. Professor Lossow, who taught art, was initially from East Germany, had immigrated into West Germany, married a charming lady, who had been his student, and quickly established himself as a distinguished "Herr Professor." For him, the human attractions of the West ought to be more important than making material use of visitors, especially foreign students. Professor Lossow wrote to Bonn a letter that provoked a sharp controversy over the whole programme. But it was not until the issue was brought to my attention by the ISSF that we learned of his protest.

The reaction of the ISSF was compounded by another development that had come to their attention; some members of the group had crossed over to East Berlin and established contact with the student organisations there. As I was to discover, these were the group members with communist leanings. In those days of extreme sensitivity about the partition of Germany, such double-dealing could not be tolerated by the West Germans, for whom East Germany was still an anathema.

The reaction of the ISSF came in the form of a very rude angry letter from their leader, Reinhard Spilker, addressed to me, in which he mentioned the complaints against work and the trip into East Berlin. He reminded us of the purpose of the programme and rudely criticised us offensively by saying that they thought they were dealing with "mature people and not a bunch of children." As might be expected, I was infuriated by Reinhard's letter, not only because of its discourteous tone, but also because he was implying that we as a group were behind the complaints and the contact with East Berliners, even though I was hearing about both for the first time through that letter. The girl might have complained to her host family, admittedly an ungracious thing to do. But the letter of Professor Lossow was his own reaction as a German, and considering that the girl was living with them, so that they could see how hard she was working, no formal complaint was needed from her to make Professor Lossow react the way he did. The visit to Berlin, while not the right thing to do to the West Germans as hosts, was also the result of a personal ideological move from individuals. The German reaction, I thought, should have been to hope that the comparison between East and West would in any case be in their support. Their hostile reaction was to provoke the Sudanese sense of pride in a manner that could only favour East Germany.

I convened a meeting of the group to discuss the situation. After investigating the facts, I discovered that Professor Lossow had indeed discussed the working conditions with their guest student and had expressed strong disapproval of that aspect of the programme. The visit to East Berlin on the other hand had clearly been a spontaneous move by those individuals with communist leanings, suggested and organised by Sudanese students in East Berlin. Obviously, both the Sudanese in East Germany and members of our delegation had been oblivious to the sensitivities of the West Germans, which they should have expected and respected. But none of the arguments for the West German point of view could justify the vulgarity of Reinhard's letter. The general reaction of the group was one of extreme anger. They preferred immediate departure for Sudan. I argued against that as a negative response that was bound to be counter-productive to the basic idea of the exchange programme, which we agreed was on the whole positive and useful. Instead, I suggested writing to Reinhard and waiting to see the developments from there on. That became the consensus. It was the experience of the former year all over again, although this latest conflict pitted me against the ISSF leader personally.

My letter to Reinhard, though measured, was calculatedly not any less offensive than his. Perhaps the strongest attack was that his insulting attitude was sadly reminiscent of the racial arrogance for which the Germans had been known under the Nazis and for which we in Sudan had neither experience nor tolerance. I made it clear to him that the preference of the group was to terminate the programme forthwith and return home, but that I had prevailed upon them to stay with the clear understanding that if such an attitude were ever repeated, we would have no choice but leave and end all association with the ISSF.

On receiving the letter, Reinhard telephoned me, full of cordiality and apologies. Having assured me of his best intentions, he explained the threats to which the programme was being subjected as a result of the complaint of Professor Lossow and the contacts with East German students, which were interpreted as evidence of our disenchantment with the conditions we had been subjected to by the ISSF. He stressed his high regard for me personally and his hope that the provocative tone of his letter did not detract from that regard or from his respect and affection for the Sudanese.

I was reconciled by his conciliatory tone and we quickly re-established our mutual respect and friendship. I took the initiative to contact Professor Lossow and persuade him that the working arrangement had entirely been with our approval and for a more cross-cultural benefit than the financial support of the programme. Professor Lossow was not entirely convinced, but he appreciated my intervention and explanation. I became good friends with the Lossows. And Reinhard and I grew to be very close lifelong friends.

Perhaps because of the crisis over the private visit of some members to East Berlin, the ISSF organised a rather unusual arrangement for us to meet with East German families in a discreet manner and to talk with them very freely about conditions in that part of the country. We were divided into twos and threes. I went with one of the girls. We were to get off the train at a particular station where a person who had been given our description was to meet us discreetly. As soon as we arrived at the station, we were immediately spotted by a man in his fifties whom we quickly recognised as a pastor from his outfit. Asking to assure himself of our identity, but speaking in a disguised manner, he directed us to follow him to his car. Then we dashed off to his house.

His home was modestly comfortable. With him were several ladies, including his wife and three other relatives. We sat, had tea, and conversed for quite a while about nothing significant. We were rather reluctant to initiate a serious discussion, not least because I assumed that being a pastor, his anti-communist position was quite predictable and did not need digging into. Realising that we were probably too discreet to initiate the discussion for which we had come, he himself opened the subject, urging us to feel free to ask any questions we wanted. We did.

I was surprised by what they, in particular the pastor, said in response to our questions. He was far from being the stereotypical reverend I had assumed he must be. He gave an in-depth analysis of the situation, pointing out plusses and minuses, and even more significantly, ended on a note that showed the East German system in a better light than obtained in West Germany. To him, the socialist system that obtained in East Germany was in principle the correct approach to the problems of the people; what it needed was reform. He himself had chosen to be constructively and openly critical, making his views known to the leaders, rather than opt out of the country or work to overthrow the system. He said the authorities, realising that his objective was largely corrective and reformative, not counter-revolutionary, tolerated and even respected his ideas. I wondered whether the West Germans who had organised the visit were aware of the pastor's ideas. I immediately developed great respect for the man. I was particularly impressed by his desire to integrate his spiritual ideals into a deeply- entrenched Communist system.

We later met to compare notes on our experiences and discovered that in sharp contrast to our rational discussion with the pastor's family, some of our colleagues had dramatic encounters. Our female colleagues who visited one family were reported to have been so affected by the discussion of the situation in East Germany that they broke down and cried.

Verena was not in Berlin when we arrived there. She had explained in a letter that she would have to be in Hamburg for a family occasion at the time of our arrival, but would come as soon as she could. Her arrival was for me the highlight, as we began to sightsee the city of Berlin, West and East, and the neighbouring areas in greater depth, going from buses to trams, from buildings to parks, from the city to the surrounding lakes, and from scenic views to the Berlin Wall. We went for leisurely walks in the woods, visited friends, attended political discussions, and deepened our friendship.

I soon met the Poelchaus whom Verena had described as her second parents. Harold was a minister of the Church whose role during Nazi Germany had been to assist and comfort prisoners, including those condemned to death. He had a quiet, gentle, spiritual personality that seemed to promote faith more vividly by living example than by preaching. What he left unarticulated in words, his wife, Dorothy, complemented with her sweet smiles and compassionate style. Having been close to Verena's family, and in particular after her father's execution, the Poelchaus were very dear to Verena, supportive and comforting at moments of her greatest needs. They also treated me with great favour and I could say, even affection. From Verena, I learned much about the racial slurs which the Germans made and which I would naturally never have spotted by myself. While no one ever confronted us with a look of disapproval, and indeed the opposite was often the case – people smiling happily at seeing young friends of different races –Verena overheard some racially charged comments. Verena overheard some racially charged comments: one said, "She must go through a lot of soap," another added, "They probably change sheets every day." Verena would interpret all that with a natural sense of humour that disarmed me and left no room for any offence; quite the contrary, we laughed a great deal about it all.

Verena once invited me to a meeting of an informal East-West discussion group including a Soviet diplomat. Although they talked as though they represented Capitalism and Communism, it was my assumption that those young Germans had some socialist leanings, but disapproved of the Soviet system and the repressions entailed in that system. As they discussed, mostly in German, I could not actively participate, but I was quite content to witness the occasion. Perhaps desirous of involving me, they decided to pass the controversy on to me for an impartial opinion. They asked me which of the two systems, Socialism and Capitalism, I thought would triumph in the end. In response, I said there would probably be an alternating role for both. The conditions of capitalism and the social and economic stratification they created were bound to generate a socialist move for equality. But once socialism was established, the pressures for the individual to develop his or her own social and economic potential would also generate a move towards capitalism. I argued that while people resented inequalities, once you gave people an equal starting point, individuals were bound to utilise their means in varying ways and differences would soon manifest themselves into inequalities that would again generate a move for equality. The pendulum would keep swinging between the two systems. They laughed and declared me a "born diplomat."

Perhaps the most significant event in Berlin from the Sudanese standpoint was the visit of General Ibrahim Abboud, the president of our country. Just a few days before his arrival, we were told that his programme would include a visit to the Siemens factories. The management requested us to turn up for the president's visit on a day which would otherwise have been free. I do not remember whether it was a weekend or a special holiday. Whatever it was, the Sudanese students, who had just had a confrontation with the Abboud regime before our departure, were not about to honour him in Germany. I was of a totally different opinion. I told them that whatever our internal differences, as long as we were abroad and the president was visiting in his official capacity as a symbol of our nation, to refuse to meet him would be insulting to our national pride.

But the members of the group would not be persuaded. In the end, many of them bargained; they would receive him if they would be compensated for the day of the reception. I called the management and secured their approval for another day off, which made it impossible for the students to resist any further. So, despite their political opposition, they turned up largely as a result of my pressures. We lined up to meet President Abboud, with me standing in the front of the line. We greeted the president and began to follow him as the Germans led him on the tour of the factory. Among his companions was the lord chamberlain of the palace, Mohammed Hassan el Dhaw, the very person who had facilitated the validity of my passport for all countries. After I met both the president and the lord chamberlain, he must have said something to the president about me, for Abboud stopped, turned back to me a few steps behind him, and said, "So you are the son of Deng Majok? He is a great patriot and a dear friend. I saw him only a few days before I left the Sudan. I am very pleased to meet you."

Everyone, including the president's cabinet members, must have been stunned to see the president interact with me so personally. Behind the president was, among other people, his foreign minister, Ahmed Mohamed Kheir, who, on seeing the president's attitude, turned to my friend, Tigani Omer el Karib, and asked him, "Is this Samuel with you?" The name Samuel was the minister's fictional generic name for any Southerner, supposedly a Christian and an undesirable product of missionary education. Tigani's response, according to his version to me, was, "He is the leader of our delegation"

Tigani did not tell me all this until the president and his delegation had gone. Then he told me in a joking manner, adding that I deserved what I got by persuading the group to venerate unworthy people. I was absolutely enraged, not with Tigani, of course, but with Ahmed Kheir. I thought of writing to him to say that if he, the foreign minister, could use such language about his Southern countrymen, what was the ordinary man in the street expected to say? The group persuaded me not to write, for, as they argued, he is "a madman" and no logical or rational argument would impress him. Of course, Ahmed Kheir was not mad, but he was widely known as eccentric. I decided to let go of the issue, and eventually even accepted the nick-name "Samuel" from a number of friends in the group. Many years later, while I was Sudan's ambassador to Scandinavia, I had a cordial conversation with Ahmed Kheir, as I interviewed him for a book I was writing on the human dimension of British rule in the Sudan. As we talked, my mind wandered back to that incident in Berlin and I wondered what he would say if I recalled the episode. Of course, I did not.

It was while I was in Berlin that I first realised the significance of an eye disease whose symptoms I had felt several years earlier. From my high school days at Khor Taqqat, I would notice rainbow colours around light-bulbs and would occasionally, when strained, see smoke in the air. Under certain strenuous circumstances, my reading capacity would almost entirely diminish. In one English test, which was given in the evening, my vision was so blurred that I could not see the questions nor the lines of the paper on which I was writing the answers. Afraid that I might be accused of finding excuses, I decided to continue with the test, closing my eyes to rest for a moment, reading the question, and then writing my answers almost blindly on the paper, not caring whether or not I was following the lines. Otherwise, every eye test under normal circumstances revealed perfect vision.

The doctors continued to dismiss my complaint as sensitivity of the eyes that would diminish with age. For the four years at the university, I kept checking, but to no avail. Then in my last year, the assistant ophthalmologists at the eye hospital, who were technicians and not professionals, suggested that I use glasses. One day, as I was sitting with Emil Nosseir, a Sudanese medical student whom I had met in Germany and with whom I had become friends, I complained about my diminishing vision, especially in my right eye. Emil asked to see my glasses and discovered that the lenses had been reversed. Once that was established, it became obvious to me that the harm to my right eye had been caused by the glasses from the National Optical Company.

I decided to sue them and engaged the only Southern advocate, Joseph Garang, who would later play an important role in the politics of the Sudan, to be my attorney. Joseph in turn suggested that we should have a proper professional assessment of the actual damage done by the glasses. Mohammed Ibrahim Khalil, a part-time lecturer from the attorney general's chambers, was kind to recommend me for examination by the top ophthalmologist, Dr Abdel Gadir Hassan. Dr Abdel Gadir discovered that my eye problem had nothing to do with the glasses, but was the result of glaucoma, which had not been detected and treated for some five to six years, and had therefore begun to affect the field of vision. At that time, glaucoma did not mean anything to me. I asked the technicians who had failed to detect the disease in the first place whether glaucoma could cause blindness. They answered in the affirmative, but reassured me that it could only do so if not arrested and that once detected it could be stopped. Dr Abdel Gadir told me that I would have to use eyedrops several times a day until an operation was done which, if it were successful, would mean ending the use of the drops. He said he could perform the operation himself, but on learning of my plans to visit Germany, he suggested that it would be better to do it in Germany, where facilities were more advanced. I did not understand much of anything, but I felt disposed towards the operation, preferably in Germany, because I was averse to the thought of having to use eye drops several times a day. In fact, while in Germany, I soon abandoned the use of the drops, waiting with leisure for my timetable to permit an operation, feeling nothing whatsoever about the seriousness of my condition.

Towards the end of our working period, I decided it was time to look into the problem of my eyes, but still feeling quite relaxed about the situation. Even when the eye doctors discovered the eye pressure to be unusually high and could not understand why I was not suffering from headaches on that account, I was not the least disturbed. The ophthalmologist decided to operate as soon as possible. A date was fixed.

The Professor of Ophthalmology who took care of my case was the leading specialist in the hospital. He was a kindly elderly man who inspired confidence. The first eye was operated on and declared a success. About a week later, the operation on the second eye was carried out. But on the operation table, I noticed that the professor was not with the team. I was shaken with fear. After I recovered from anesthesia, the first thing I asked was where the professor was. I was told he was on a trip. My disappointment was obvious, but everyone tried to reassure me that his assistant was just as good and in fact, being younger, had steadier hands. Since the real issue was not an objective assessment of merits, but a psychological state of mind, the arguments were futile and not convincing.

When the bandages were removed the following day and I could not see with that eye, I had no doubt about the cause. The operation had obviously been a disaster and my left eye, my best, was forever gone. I fell into a deep shock. I had suddenly become one-eyed. The head nurse was called in. After examining me, she said that while it was not very frequent, it sometimes happened that internal bleeding after an operation might cause a temporary blockage of vision that would clear in two to three days. She sounded confident, but I was not entirely reassured. The doctor came and repeated virtually the same assurance the nurse had given me. I began to count the hours and the days. The second day came and went, and so did the third day, but my condition remained the same. I continued to panic; but the nurses maintained their optimism, and so did the doctors.

With every additional day for over a week, I began to feel that I was only being consoled by the medical opinions, but that I had in fact lost my sight. I could not imagine the blood remaining in the eye for that long and then flowing away. Yet, the nurses remained decidedly reassuring. The head nurse even playfully made a bet with me on a bottle of champagne that it would clear. I happily jumped on the gamble as though it would give the nurses added incentive to perform a miracle on my eye. Eventually, the eye began to clear, but only gradually, taking at least ten days before I could see clearly again. Verena brought the bottle of champagne as promised.

I was very well cared for in the hospital and although I displayed considerable anxiety over my eyes, the hospital staff took me to be a good patient. A few concessions were made to ease my situation. Visiting hours were also relaxed for me and I had a good flow of visitors, Sudanese and Germans, men and women. Verena intimated to me later that the care and attention I was receiving from her brought twinkles to the eyes of the nurses.

It was while I was in the hospital that we received the good news that I was top of the class in the examination results, was appointed to the teaching staff of the Faculty of Law, and admitted to London University for postgraduate studies. I later learned that Natale Olwak Akolawin, one of my Southern Sudanese colleagues in the class, was also appointed to the faculty and was also admitted for graduate studies in England. I also learned that the appointment of two Southern Sudanese did not sit well with the Northern Sudanese authorities. So, another colleague, Mohammed el Fateh was appointed to make us three.

Of course, heading the class in the exam was itself sufficiently elating, but, beyond that, I saw in my appointment to the faculty a significant step, indeed a breakthrough into a new phase of life. I looked forward with great anticipation to my further studies abroad, specifically in England, which in itself would be an introduction to another world, a widening of my world vision, and an opening to greater opportunities. Being in the German environment, where the concept of professorship was highly honoured, the setting was most appropriate. My German friends began to address me as "Herr Professor," and even the senior ophthalmologist called me his "colleague." All this, though premature, indicated the sudden elevation that came with the appointment.

After leaving the hospital, the Lossows kindly invited me to stay with them in their house. As I had grown to like both of them very much, I welcomed their invitation, especially as they lived close to the Poelchaus where Verena lived. I enjoyed my recuperation period at the Lossows. Although I still had to be careful about my eyes and had to go back for several check-ups, the operation on both eyes was now declared successful. That meant that I would no longer need to use the drops several times a day - a prospect that had appeared gruesome to me and about which I felt very happy to have left behind. The doctor was even to congratulate me for having escaped blindness - a wonderful thing to know.

On both visits to Germany, I transited on my way back through Italy to visit my brother Bol and my Uncle Bulabek. I went to Padova on an express train from Rome where I parted with the Sudanese delegation at the airport. It was not so much the image of Padova as the oldest university town in Europe, nor the theatre of Galileo Galilei, where he had secretly performed the condemned postmortem dissections, nor even the ancient Cathedral of Padova and its immortal art that fascinated me the most, exciting as they all were. Rather it was the contemporary air of the place, the buildings as they looked, the lanes, the coffee-bars, the clubs, the people, the real life in its entire embodiment of past, present, and possible future, all blended, melted, and dynamically forging on.

Venice fascinated me precisely for what it is: a city without cars, the narrow streets, the romantic networks of canals, the gondolas, the islands, and even the tourists. It all seemed enchantingly unreal.

Bol and Bulabek lived in a Catholic student hostel where rooms were relatively modest but comfortable, food simple but tasty, and discipline strict, especially about the gate-closing time at night. I relished the pleasure of being with Bol and Bulabek and did not bother about the limitations of the place. We had a great deal of fun chatting, laughing and meeting people. At 6 feet 4 inches, Bol seemed the tallest person in Padova and all we had to do was step into the streets and we needed no introduction to anyone. People stopped, gazed in amazement, and often commented. We sat in cafes, sipped cappuccino, and discussed many issues.

My first visit also coincided with the decision of St Augustine's Society that I represent Khartoum University at a Pax Romana Conference to be held in Freiburg, Switzerland. When I arrived at Freiburg, a beautiful town in a picturesque mountainous setting, I was well received by the organisers of the conference, comfortably accommodated, and as we got to the conference centre, introduced to a Belgian lady who was said to have sponsored me. I was surprised and rather embarrassed, since I had thought that having paid my ticket, I would not be classified among those who needed charitable sponsoring. Of course, there was more to the conference than tickets: conference services, accommodation and board, social activities, and the like, all of which might have necessitated a fundraiser on the part of Pax Romana.

On the other hand, to have obtained contributions in our names without our knowledge, far less consent, offended me. Nevertheless, I received the information with a contrived air of appreciation and thanked the lady concerned as though I had known of her charity. She was pleasant, modest and discreet about her contribution. The matter ended there. Although the subject of the conference was "University Student as a Pioneer for a Better World", the delegates, who came from all over the world, comprised a large percentage of senior people, including representatives of the Holy See, the Vatican.

The conference was to become memorable to me because of the explosive role I played. After a restless, soul-searching reflection, listening to long statements on why Catholic students were losing their faith, I raised my hand and spoke. I said I was speaking for the

Africans, more specifically the Sudanese converts into Catholicism, whose situation I thought reflected something of the broader picture. The reason for why Catholic students were losing faith, I argued, was because Catholic religious instruction did not prepare students sufficiently for a rational, scientific response to the challenges of intellectual growth. We had been told that our traditional societies, even our parents, were not only without religion, but immoral. Then we discovered how truly religious they were and perhaps more so than many of those who considered themselves religious. We had also been disposed to view other religions, such as Islam and the Protestant Church, with simplistic condescension which, with education and intellectual development, we discovered to be misleading. I said that there were also dogmas about the Church as an institution which were not scientifically explained to students. The result of all this was a scrutinising reaction to the teachings of the Catholic Church.

As soon as I finished talking, impressively robed, high ranking representatives of the Vatican responded. One said he was amazed that a Catholic student could accuse the Church of lacking rational interpretation of the faith. He went on to expound what he saw as the rational bases of Catholicism, speaking emotionally and almost angrily. He was followed by more speakers, evidently senior in the Church hierarchy, all repeating the same arguments against me.

I listened undisturbed and unchallenged, for theirs were the dogmatic responses that simply reinforced, rather than demolished my argument. No one spoke in support of what I said. I felt betrayed and abandoned by my younger colleagues, particularly Africans, who must have understood what I meant. I, however, excused them for the same reasons of dogmatism that I was fighting. Considering the rank of those who attacked me, the large forum in which the attacks were made, and the lack of support I received, I was unusually calm, and composed. Indeed, I considered the attack a victory; my views had been provocative and therefore effective.

When the meeting was adjourned, I was very surprised by the massive support I received from the audience as individuals. Young people, Europeans and Africans alike, and some elderly people, came to congratulate me and to express support for my point of view.

Some went as far as admitting that they could not speak publicly, but wanted to assure me privately of their agreement with my views. A number of delegates invited me to a festive evening to discuss further and otherwise enjoy ourselves.

On the day of the reception, I chose to wear a jallabiya with a turban, and although I had not intended it that way, became the centre of attention. The following day, an enlarged photograph of me was prominently displayed in the window of a fashionable photographic shop. Years later, I was to learn from Lawrence Wol Wol, a Southerner who was then studying in Freiburg, but was away at the time, that he later heard of a Southern Sudanese who had attended the conference wearing Arab clothes. He confessed feeling embarrassed and scandalised, and even went as far as denying me, arguing that I was a Northern Sudanese, not a Southerner. We simply laughed it off.

After my second tour of Germany, Tigani and I agreed to visit Bol and Bulabek. While Tigani was to follow by train, I flew with the group to Rome, intending to proceed to Padova and surprise Bol and Bulabek by arriving at their hostel unexpectedly. But as I exited the transit lounge to enter Rome, I was astounded to see Bulabek in the receiving crowd. Could they have heard of my arrival through some other means? Bulabek was with Justo Muludiang. But where was Bol? I soon learned that Bulabek had been there to see off someone who was about to take a plane to Sudan.

With Bulabek was Joseph Oduho, the co-leader of the Southern movement in exile. Joseph Oduho and William Deng had just established the Sudan African Closed District National Union Organisation, SACDNU, which was later renamed the Sudan African National Union, Sanu. They were then in Italy campaigning for support and finalising the conceptual details of the opposition organisation. In this, they were aided by some Southern students in Italy; foremost among those students was Bona Bulabek. Bulabek gave me the new constitution of SACDNU, which he had helped draft, to take back to Sudan and give to Isaiah Majok, one of the student representatives of the underground Southern movement in Khartoum University. It was a very risky and politically dangerous assignment for obvious reasons, but one I could not turn down. I accepted the risk.

Bulabek decided that we spend a few days in Rome before proceeding to Padova. I stayed with them in the Youth Hostel. We had three days in Rome during which we saw most of the tourist attractions of the city. Some of these were most impressive, even overwhelming, on their face value. But they were all part of a deep and long cultural and historical perspective that was alien to me. So, while the museums, the buildings, and the ruins made a considerable impression on me, it was more the squares, the doves, the people, the concept and reality of the Vatican, the nature and the historic walls blending with it, that gave me touristic pleasure.

Of course, we had learned something about Europe in our general education, and History was one of the subjects I loved most. But the depths of European heritage as evidenced by those monumental Roman antiquities, could not easily be appreciated and enjoyed by a cultural outsider. If the outsider had a parallel experience providing a common ground for mutual appreciation, that might be different. There was none in the perishable cultural materials of my Dinka background to support appreciation for such monumental material symbolism. But of nature, we had a fair share, and of human relations, we had deep roots and a disposition to broaden our horizons.

This theme, although highlighted by Rome, had pervaded my experiences in Europe and to a lesser extent, in Egypt. Although there had been something intriguing about the island of ancient Nubian civilisation at Abu Simbel near Aswan, the stone monuments had appeared stark, weathered and remote from my Dinka world. But inside the awesome dark narrow caves, I had been struck and even fascinated by the drawings on the wall which resembled Dinka figures of people and animals, with cattle horns shaped in much the same way the Dinka still shaped them to grow into desired shapes. At the Valley of the Kings and later in the Cairo Museum, I had seen other antiquities which looked identical to some aspects of contemporary Dinka culture. While the technique of preserving dead bodies was unknown to the Dinka, their burial rites and religious conceptions shared some similarities with ancient Egyptians. Otherwise

I found that the historical, artistic and architectural expression of a heritage was too deeply rooted and culturally conditioned to be adequately appreciated by an outsider or at least by me.

Back to my visit with relatives in Italy, Bol and Uncle Bulabek had already made arrangements to go to Germany, purchase a Volkswagen car, and then drive through Europe into Czechoslovakia, where they hoped to visit Toby Maduot, an old classmate of ours, then studying medicine in Prague. They were all involved in promoting the cause of South Sudan in Europe. Although Bulabek could not change his plans because they were connected with important matters involving other persons whose programme had long been drawn up, it was decided that Bol should stay with us, while Bulabek proceeded with his friend, Justo Muludiang.

Bulabek and Justo left some time after Tigani's arrival and we were able to spend a few pleasant days together with Bulabek, which gave Tigani and even myself a deeper insight into Bulabek's unique attributes as a genius, an indisputable leader, and yet a man who reflected remarkable modesty. This did not in any way compromise the dignity he radiated in his bearing, his self-confidence, his deliberation, and his command of language. By that time, he was entering his final year as a student of medicine and as always in his entire educational experience, he was consistently top of his class and had already been offered a teaching position by Padova Faculty of Medicine after his graduation. That was, at least at that time, an unprecedented honour for an African. Bulabek was also very popular with the people in Padova, students, professors, the clergy, and the ordinary Italians. While in effect younger than us, admittedly only by a few years, he appeared as an elder to us, clearly deserving his status as our uncle.

After doing a great many things together in the few days Bulabek spent with us, both in Padova and in Venice, he departed early one morning, leaving a note for me to the effect that I should proceed home under any circumstances to see the family before returning to England for my graduate studies. In his words, as I recall them, "You must visit your loved ones at home before returning to Europe, no matter how difficult the conditions." It was an extraordinary request considering that it would be the rainy season during which travelling was difficult and Uncle Bulabek knew it. By a remarkable coincidence, Verena had also made me promise that before returning to Europe, I should go home, primarily to see my mother, for whom she had developed a special admiration, obviously based on what I had said about her, and whom she criticised me for not showing her my love. Bulabek's message especially sounded like a sacred call that added to my determination to fulfill my promise to both my young uncle and Verena.

In Cairo, I learned that the Nile was not yet navigable and that the first steamers to go through after that were fully booked. I therefore contacted the embassy to cable Khartoum University for an air ticket. The university responded positively; I received the air ticket to Khartoum and left as soon as I could by Sudan Airways. I carried with me the constitution of SACDNU, which Uncle Bona had entrusted to me to take to the underground Southern opposition in Khartoum. As I have already noted, although I was deeply concerned about the consequences of being found out to carry such a seditious document at the airport, or, for that matter, any time afterwards, I simply could not refuse the assignment. I inserted the document inside the lining of my overcoat and prayed that I should not be detected. Once I was inside the country, I passed the document on to Isaiah Majok at the earliest opportunity.

Back at the faculty, I found an office prepared for me and felt the tangible difference between my years as a student and my new status as a member of the faculty. That was when I learned that two other colleagues, Natale Olwak Akolawin and Mohamed el Fateh, had also been appointed to the faculty and would be proceeding with me to London for the LL.M. degree course.

A few days after my arrival in Khartoum, I received a cable. Something about that telegraphic message terrified me. I had, of course, received messages on previous occasions that turned out to be purely idiosyncratic, such as a birthday greeting from Verena, but something about that cable told me that it bore distressing news. It was from Italy. I hurriedly opened it and saw the tragic news. Uncle Bona Bulabek had died in a car accident near Prague.

I could not contain myself. According to Dinka principles, a man must not shed tears whatever pain he undergoes, whether such pain be physical or emotional, including the death of a relative, however close. I had cried when Bol nearly died in a car accident, but I was then still a child. I was now an adult. On the other hand, no principle could stop me from breaking down. Burying my head in my arms on my desk, tears streaming from my eyes, I sobbed in the privacy of my office.

Many things were rapidly flashing in my mind: the picture of the man with whom we had just been, his unique attributes, a genius whose potential contribution to the family, the tribe, the South, Sudan, indeed the world, we had felt no doubt about. And now, suddenly, he was no more. What was the logic of it all? Why was he permitted to distinguish himself so much, if it would all end up so purposelessly? Was there really a power and a reason behind all that? If so, what did it mean? I could not see Bulabek just dying and disappearing without any reason behind his death.

Uncle Bulabek's death contributed significantly to the diminishing of my faith in the conventional concept of God, for I failed to see a goal-oriented architect, a designer, a builder, or a creator behind it all: Bulabek's birth, his academic success, which the Dinka explained in mythical terms as willed by his father, a spiritual leader, and now his sudden death! All those thoughts crossed and flowed in my mind as did my tears.

I did not want to attract the attention of sympathisers, for according to Bol's message, I was to contact the authorities in the Ministry of Education to arrange for the body to be transported home to Sudan. As some days had passed since the death, the issue was of utmost urgency. So, I hurriedly contacted Santino Deng Teng, the minister for Animal Resources, in the hope of cutting through red tape and securing the immediate sending of a message to the embassy to arrange for the transportation of the body to Sudan.

Santino Deng was of course responsive. He telephoned Ziada Arbab, the minister for Education, and arranged to see him, taking me along with him. I will never forget the manner in which Ziada Arbab received us. In a callous way, smiling cynically, maliciously, almost viciously, he said to Santino, "What is the matter, Brother Santino, is there no work to do in the ministry?" At first, I could not believe my ears. Then I thought that he had perhaps not been told of the reason for our visit. But it also occurred to me that he was making the remark precisely because he knew the purpose of our visit.

Even after Santino Deng had explained the reason, Ziada was not any less revolting in his insensitivity. Indeed, he became worse, inhumane, and hardly Sudanese in the values he espoused. First, he explained that the embassy in Prague, in fact the government, had no funds for such situations and that the burden for returning bodies home was strictly a family affair. I suppose he thought that we would thereby be intimidated into surrendering to the official position that Bulabek be buried abroad. When we said to him that the family would pay, but that in view of the urgency of the situation we wanted the government to help on the understanding that it would be reimbursed later, Ziada Arbab then reached his worst: "Brother Santino," he said, "let us be frank and realistic. Our people are poor and need every bit of money we possess in order to meet essential needs. Why would the government or for that matter the family pay some four hundred pounds just to return a dead body for burial at home? Let us stop being sentimental and face realities. We should have him buried there and be over with the problem."

That was more or less his final word, rational-sounding, perhaps even persuasive to some, but totally hypocritical, in fact racist, because we knew he could never have said that to a Northern Sudanese family. Even more important, he was absolutely ignorant of the person involved, the sentiments of his people about him, and the pride and weight of his family. We left his office with more determination than ever to face the challenge to the very end. But then, we learned that the instructions had already gone from the Ministry of Education that the body be buried in Europe. Judging from the lapse of time, the body must have already been buried by the time we were struggling for the authorisation to bring it back home.

Nevertheless, I refused to be forced into submission. So, I contacted the Czech embassy to enquire into the law and practice pertaining to the exhumation and exportation of human remains. They told me that it would take about three to six months after burial to exhume and that the body could then be exported under certain conditions.

Having established the principle of eventually exhuming and patriating Bulabek's remains, I decided to leave for home immediately, despite the fact that the road had closed and I would have to travel on foot or on horseback from Muglad to Abyei. I recalled Uncle Bulabek's message that I had to visit the family before leaving for England and could not help seeing some prophecy in his words. I left Khartoum for home.

Before leaving for Abyei, we generated a campaign of awareness in Southern Sudanese circles about the treatment which the government had given a distinguished son of the South, an instrumental, though little known, leader for the cause of the South in Europe. I recalled the role Bulabek had played in promoting William Deng and Joseph Oduho and his overall activity for the Southern cause - the very reason for his going to Prague. Then I wondered whether Bulabek's accident had really been natural or had perhaps been planned. The attitude of Ziada Arbab began to raise doubts in the minds of the Southerners, foremost my own, as to whether Bulabek had not indeed been murdered by a hired truck driver. That was the thought I left with on my way to Abyei and that was the sparking thought I left among the Southerners in Khartoum.

A political movement around Bulabek's death, focusing on the return of the body, had begun as I left, infuriated and challenged by Ziada's attitude, which I took to reflect the considered and concerted position of the Sudan government - the official, racist attitude of the ruling Arab North.

I left for Muglad and quickly found my way to Abyei on horseback. I had deliberately sent word ahead so that my time in Abyei would not be wasted on the devastating reaction to the news or the inertia of the mourning rituals. By the time I arrived Abyei, the family had just received the news and was in mourning, with Father still sitting on the ground according to custom. But the atmosphere had sufficiently settled down and was ripe for a serious talk about the circumstances of Bulabek's death and the challenge that the family must face. My father was most attentive to everything I had to say and his response was swift and clear. He convened a meeting of the leaders of the clan and presented the situation, discreetly insinuating some sinister reason behind Bulabek's death, but understating the political angle, and emphasising the challenge to our dignity involved in bringing back the body. The message was very well received and cattle were quickly collected and sold. Within ten days, the required amount was raised and I was ready to return to Khartoum.

Although my visit home was prompted by Bulabek's death, it was something both he and Verena had requested me to do and as it turned out, it provided a rare opportunity for a significant contact with the family that was to be my last for seven years. Needless to say, the circumstances of Uncle Bulabek's request were mystically moving, especially in retrospect. It was as though he had had a spiritual insight into the importance of the visit. Things were to happen which did not then seem so important, but were later to prove to be of vital significance to my life.

The news of my operation in Germany was both a shock and a miracle to my family. My sisters nearly cried - one did indeed shed tears - on hearing my account of the operation. Had their consent been required, they would certainly have opposed the operation. From their point of view, the eye was too delicate an organ to risk with an operation. "What if something had gone wrong with the operation?" they reasoned. Father on the other hand, being the progressive innovator, was impressed by the outcome. He was to remark, "This shows how the things that normally blind us, the Dinka, could be controlled."

Perhaps the most significant outcome of the visit, apart from the fund-raising for the return of Bulabek's remains, was my daring to record a variety of Dinka songs, arguing that as I would be far away from home for at least two years, these songs would provide me with a useful cultural link with my people. I asked my father whether he saw any objection to my recording in the mourning circumstances. My father fully appreciated my reasons and dismissed any other considerations as secondary. I borrowed a tape recorder from the Italian missionary, perhaps the first and only one in Abyei.

As the recorder lacked batteries, we used the generator of the local government radio communication system for electricity. That meant recording in the small office in which the generator was located. My father not only invited prominent singers, both groups and individuals, but also attended the recording sessions himself.

It was perhaps the first time the process of recording had been publicly conducted among the Ngok Dinka and the response was quite enthusiastic, far more than I could possibly have anticipated in the circumstances. Another reason was probably the degree of interest my father demonstrated in the project. I recorded samples of virtually all forms of Dinka songs, including group songs, that are professionally composed, and personal songs, that must be composed by the individual singer. My father even saw fit to record a message for President Abboud, which unfortunately, I knew I could not deliver, but accepted and appreciated as adding a certain dimension that enhanced the significance of the recording. I was later to cite Father's message in my doctoral dissertation that became my first book: *Tradition and Modernization: A Challenge for Law Among the Dinka of the Sudan*.

After the recording session, as my father and I were walking home, surrounded by a large crowd, I heard a man saying to his companions, "What an intelligent machine! It listens briefly and immediately learns the song, repeating it exactly the way it was sung." I then realised that for most of the Dinka, the recording was a miracle never before performed. Little did I know then that those recordings would be a vital link with home at a most crucial period when I was not only threatened with blindness, but with political persecution, and the prospect of an asylum abroad, which entailed the possibility that I might never see my people again. The other area where the occasion offered a useful opportunity for cross-fertilisation with the family was discussing with my father the issue of mixed marriages.

Stories presumably surrounding my friendship with Verena which was known to my colleagues who had been to Germany with me had reached home that I was engaged to be married to a German girl. My mother and sisters were the first to ask me about that. I told them that those were untrue accounts, but discussed with them the principle of mixed marriages. There was a hostile reaction to the possibility of my marrying outside Dinka society. Ayan, my second sister, went so far as to say that she would never visit my home if I were married to a foreign girl. My mother argued quite logically that she would not feel sufficiently as a mother-in-law to my wife or a grandmother to my children if I were married to a foreign girl with whom she would not speak the same language. I would be depriving her of something of vital importance to her as my mother, if I did not marry a Dinka girl. I presented my case to my mother in terms of the changes I had undergone through my education and experience abroad, arguing that I had become more distant from Dinka girls than I was to foreign girls, and that they could not expect me to lead a happy life with a woman simply because she was Dinka. After considerable discussion of the issue, my mother suddenly surprised me by saying, "Let it be as you wish; whatever will give you happiness will also give me happiness." That was a testimony to mother's unqualified love.

My Uncle Ngor was a lot more adamant, only conceding, "Let us leave the matter for now; we shall see when the issue arises on your marriage." Ironically, all three - my mother, my uncle and my sister - who had opposed my marriage to a foreigner as a matter of principle, were to become very close to my American wife, coincidentally of German ancestry, and my mother was to say that what she regretted the most was that my father did not live long enough to see Dorothy and our four sons, of whom she was obviously very proud.

Perhaps the most understanding person on the issue was my father, probably because of his individualism or innovativeness. He began by telling me that he had heard rumors to the effect that I was planning to marry a German girl. Was there truth to the reports doing the rounds? I told him I was not engaged to be married, but that as I would be abroad for at least two years, with the possibility of involvement with foreign girls, I would be interested to hear his views on the possibility of my marriage to a foreign girl. That was when he questioned me about my colleague, Samieha, whom he had met on his visit to Khartoum, wondering whether the relationship was merely a friendship or whether there was more to it. I said it was merely a friendship and that it could not be otherwise, as she was a Muslim. "And what are you?" my father asked. I was surprised by the question, for I was sure my father knew I was a Christian from the earliest days of our schooling and our eventual baptism, which had to be with his consent.

Father obviously had reasons for asking that question. One was that he obviously liked Samieha; the other was that he thought I ought to be flexible with my religious affiliation. I told him that the issue for me was how he viewed the possibility of a marriage to a European girl. My father responded in a serious manner of speech. He said that in principle, he did not object to his sons marrying whomever and wherever they pleased, provided they did not compromise their standards of choice. He said that we should be very mindful of the family into which we chose to marry. Many years later a fellow South Sudanese diplomat would tell me the way what my father had told me was distorted to a comical degree: "My son, as you are going to America, I hear of the Rockefeller and the Kennedy families. Should you want to marry abroad, those are the families into which you should marry." I do not know whether the story was based on some serious belief that Father said that to me or a caricature of his presumed status consciousness. I must say that it was reported to me in an amusing manner. Ironically, after I became friends with the David Rockefeller family, I told the story to one of his daughters with her husband, and he wittily responded by saying, "Too late!"

Another topic that proved to be quite controversial was the issue of my going into teaching instead of becoming a judge. Uncle Ngor was sitting quietly at a periphery when the issue was raised and discussed in my father's court in the open area outside our Abyei home. Some members of the family, chiefs and elders, were wondering about the news that I was going to become a teacher instead of a judge. My father tried to explain to them the significance of my position in the university, ultimately summarising that I would be teaching judges instead of being just a judge. Many saw the point and recognised the hierarchical importance of my position.

Then Uncle Ngor got up and asked me to see him off. As we walked away from Father's seated circle, Uncle Ngor remarked,

"What is this about you not wanting to be a judge and choosing to go into teaching?" I explained to him that teaching at a university was a recognition of my academic performance, that I was appointed to that position because I was head of my class, and that financially, that position paid better than being a judge. The first set of arguments did not seem to register with Uncle Ngor for whom the catchiest and obviously questionable argument was the one pertaining to salary. He was scandalised: "You mean that you, son of the paramount chief, whose concern should be the welfare of your people, would choose a job because it pays more, instead of asking yourself how much it will help your people? Mading, being a leader is a sacrifice that must subordinate one's personal interests to the greater interest of one's people. Money should be the last thing you consider in determining your future."

Uncle Ngor then proceeded to tell me of what he saw as my destiny for the leadership of our people: "Let me tell you what you might not have heard. I have been approached by many people, common men and even members of your clan. They have all told me that their hope for the tribe rests in you. They know you are a son of a middle wife, but they think that you are the one who will deliver this tribe when your father goes. I have heard this said by even your uncles like Biong Mading and Arop Kuol. They tell me, 'Your daughter has produced our hope; but for Mading, we would not know what would become of this tribe after Deng Majok.'"

Uncle Ngor's words brought back to mind a conversation I had had with Father's younger brother, Uncle Arop, during one of our vacations at Noong. Uncle Arop had proudly explained to me the extent to which he had supported my father's marriage to my mother in the face of my grandfather's objections. He ended his story by saying how the family had been blessed with my birth and what a loss it would have been had the marriage not taken place. Arop had obviously said the same thing to Uncle Ngor.

"Mading," Uncle Ngor continued, "I cannot believe that you would choose a job for its material worth. You are a sacred son chosen long before you were begotten; that destiny requires sacrificing for the people of your father. Do not forget that your father married your mother against my personal wish. That was because my father saw in the marriage a prospect for a son who would not only give us access to the leading circles of this tribe, but would provide leadership for our people. You are the son, Mading; do not let small things deflect your destiny, the destiny of your ancestors."

Tears nearly flowed from my eyes as I heard my uncle talk. He had always been a great orator, a leader in his age-set, believed to be an inherited verbal skill. I knew there was no room for doing what he wanted me to do. The choice had already been made.

But there was an embarrassingly penetrating wisdom and power in what he was saying, except that he did not fully realise that there was also a gap between what he wanted me to be and the limitations of being a judge in terms of achieving the objectives he espoused. Being a judge was a mystic concept of power which the Dinka confused with political authority and control, contrary to what was implied in the separation of powers, a concept that Sudan espoused and tried to follow.

I do not recall what I said to Uncle Ngor as an argument beyond my initial reaction. But I recall being impressed by his arguments, enough to keep retelling them to friends throughout my time abroad. Of course, Uncle Ngor had no idea about the limitation on the opportunities and choices which were then open to me in the complicated and complex context of Sudan's politics. "Complicated" and "complex" were indeed the words, not only about Sudanese politics, but also about domestic rivalries.

I could not help noticing the difference between Father's understanding attitude towards my professional choice and the hostile reaction of Uncle Ngor. Although Father promoted my position as teacher of judges, I felt that he was more comfortable about my not being a judge than he was elated by my being a teacher of judges. It was a continuity of the old research scenario which had brought us close to confrontation, happily evaded by my withdrawal. That, in a way, was always the story of relations with our father, withdrawing at the right time or risking a head-on collision with the probability of Father's adversary perishing or retreating in defeat, as a consequence. Ironically, three years after Father's death, when I was offered the option of being a Province Judge (Chief Justice of the Province or State) or Ambassador, and I chose to be Ambassador, my brother Bol said that he was sure I would have taken the position of the Judge if Father were still alive. We never discussed why he thought so, but I believe his reason was that I would have wanted to impress and please our father.

The issue of tribal leadership was already bubbling when I visited home. The prospect of a deputy for Father, which he himself had initiated by recommending Kuol (Adam), was now open to debate and competition, primarily between Adam and Abdalla. The tension between the brothers was clearly mounting, with each one beginning to build his own constituency. I had already been approached by the women, the mothers of the contenders, each promoting her son for Father's deputy, with eyes obviously on the ultimate succession to Father's position. While both sides offered information and arguments, and Abdalla was particularly keen to present an objective assessment of the situation, I received more pressure from Nyanbol Amuor, Adam's mother, and her junior wives, to talk to my father about the choice of Adam as the deputy.

I remember the issue being discussed in my mother's presence by Nyanbol Amuor and her associates, and my mother's response to them: "You people are bothering yourselves for nothing on the issue of the deputy," my mother began her argument. "You are not going to see Deng with your own eyes selecting a deputy. That would be a declaration that his days in the leadership are numbered. He would not want such a thing to happen. You are just aching your heads for nothing."

Just before I left to travel the distance of 125 miles on horseback in a rainy season, my father came with me to Noong to finalise the family collection for the repatriation of Uncle Bulabek's body and to give me a last-minute farewell. When I was actually ready to depart, my horse saddled and ready, my father pulled me aside for a private family talk which focused on the choice of his deputy. Father asked me which of his sons, Adam and Abdalla, I thought he should designate as his deputy. He proceeded to summarise the history of the issue with which I was already familiar. As though to apologise for not designating me or Bol, he explained that he did not have his eyes on us, as we had become children of Sudan and no longer of the Dinka. He explained that he had initially thought of Adam as his deputy, but the elders had recently been arguing that he should designate Abdalla, being the son of the first wife, according to Dinka tradition. He said that he had argued with the elders on the grounds that both were his sons and that the issue of the mother's seniority should not be such an important consideration. He wanted to know which of the two sons in my judgement would be a better choice for his deputy.

It was a difficult question to be confronted with, especially in view of the history of the issue to which I had already been a party, if only by writing Father's letters, and the intensive politicking which was already under way among the brothers and the wives. And indeed, I was in a vulnerable position to judge between the two brothers. I belonged to Adam's mother's section and that entailed a certain assumption of bias for him. But Abdalla and I had been very close and shared a common approach to Father, combining filial piety and diplomacy with frankness and honesty. Abdalla had once said to me that whenever he contemplated an important action with respect to Father or otherwise, he would ask himself, "What would Mading do if he were faced with this situation?" He would then proceed to do what he thought I would do, a most touching compliment.

As I reflected on the two brothers, I decided to be very discreet in my evaluation, perhaps too much for the purpose Father had in mind. I told him that I was not going to give him a definite answer because whatever I said might be circumspect by other considerations. As a member of Adam's section of the family, if I spoke in his support because of age, seniority, and experience, I might be accused of partiality. As a person who was personally fond of Abdalla, my suggestions that he be the choice might also have an element of favouritism. All things considered, I felt that the best thing for me to do was to provide a neutral plus and minus evaluation of the two and leave the choice to my father. I argued that Adam was older and more experienced with the law by virtue of being a policeman. Abdalla as a person had a deep sense of responsibility, and though younger in age, was more likely to take advice from his elders. I told Father that as a son of a middle wife, I was perhaps prejudiced on the issue of mother's seniority as a basis for selection. But I stressed that whatever his choice, it should be on the grounds of relative merits and not on the mere fact of mother's seniority. I also suggested that he should move to orientate the Dinka to his preference. Waiting for long would only augment polarisation and make it difficult for the family and the tribe to unite behind whomever became the leader eventually.

Father listened to me and made no further commitment on the issue, and only concluded with: "Very well." But my mother was absolutely correct in predicting that Father would not surrender to the choice of a deputy. He never did. Perhaps he was afraid that what he himself had done to his father could be done to him by a son.

As I was heading back to Khartoum, indeed from the time I left Khartoum, developments were already under way towards placing the issue of Bulabek in its correct political perspective. Southerners in Khartoum began to mobilise both politically and for the purposes of fund raising to ensure the repatriation of Bulabek's body. By the time I was heading back, the pressure had been sufficiently mounted and the government had been alerted to the political risks that were potentially buried under the drive for funds. They had to act in time to defuse the potential bomb, not only by deciding in a cabinet meeting to exhume and return the body, but also by publicising the decision to ensure that it was heard in Abyei and throughout South Sudan. This was clearly aimed at countering any political movement that might be provoked by Ziada Arbab's initial reaction.

So, on arriving in Khartoum and confirming the news of the government's decision, I simply handed over to Santino Deng Teng, then the only cabinet member from the South, the sum of money that had been collected by the family, to be used for any activities that might be associated with the return of the body, when that eventually materialised.

As it turned out, Bol had taken the body from Czechoslovakia to Italy and after going through the dreadful experience of opposition by the Catholic clergy that Bulabek not be buried on the Church property because he had gone to a Communist country, he had secured a plot in a private burial ground of a family that were Bulabek's friends, and had proceeded to bury him. The body was to be exhumed several months later and sent to Khartoum where it was buried with all the formalities and dignity of a repatriated leader. He now lies in the grounds of the War Cemetery, appropriately named even for the peace-loving civilian that he was. After that problem had been resolved, I left for England.

Tigani Omer el Karib, the Author's classmate at the University of Khartoum and a lifelong friend. He is the one who informed the Author of the Government's decision to recall me to be tried for supposedly leading South Sudan opposition in Europe.

The Author with his friend, Verena Onken von Trott and members of the Khartoum University delegation to Germany.

The Author with Reinhard Spilker and Khartoum University students.

ABROAD
To the Lands Beyond

Dr. Godfrey Lienhardt, Anthropologist, specialist on Nilotic Studies and Author's friend.

Natale Olwak Akolawin, Author's colleague in Khartoum University and London University.

Lawrence Wol Wol, who was the clandestine representative of South Sudan Liberation Movement in London when the Author was accused by the Sudan Government of masterminding the Movement in Europe.

Mary Trevelyan, who was host to the Author, Foreign Students Advisor, London University.

Clarita and Adam von Trott zu Solz, the parents of the Author's friend, Verena, in 1944.

INVISIBLE BRIDGE
An African Journey through Cultures

A close friend of the Author in London, Frances House (née Hills).

James Glassmam and Jane Glassmam, my host family at Yale.

The children of the Glassmans, the Author's host family, from left to right, Peter, Nancy, Sallie and Andrew.

CHAPTER THIRTEEN

TRIALS
A Period of Reckoning

Although the trip to England was yet another international flight, with a stopover in Cairo, there was something special about this occasion, for it not only marked a new phase in my career, but was my first visit to England, the land of our rulers that were, where I would spend two years of what in retrospect was the most critical turning point in my life.

We arrived in the late afternoon and drove into London in a bus, almost too casually for our anticipation. With all its historical and cultural majesty, London was simply a crowded city whose distinction had been somewhat robbed by my earlier European experiences. A number of places, of course, had a special appeal to me: Trafalgar Square, with its Nelson Statue, splashing fountains and hungry pigeons, was one. The Hyde Park Corner, with its conspicuous, though frivolous democracy, was another. The greenery, with beautiful flower beds and spacious landscapes of London parks was yet another. The double-decker red public buses were both functional and interestingly unique.

Otherwise, it was the underworld of London with its complex

network of railways and the automated "stand clear of the gates" recorded commands of the elevators at the underground stations, that dominated my view of London. Even such great places as the Parliament Building, the Law Courts at Aldrich, London University, the cathedrals, indeed the historic architecture of Old England, were simply a reflection of a distant past that was too foreign to my quest for "modernity."

I preferred the open space and the clean modern buildings of Berlin to this archaic conception of man's existence and accomplishment, the very thing we had been taught to break away from. Nelson's Column in Trafalgar Square evoked in me a historical sense of monumental heroism. Even Madame Tussaud's heroes, with all their diverse claims to fame, invoked in me a more vibrant reaction than those architectural monuments of British heritage that lacked any tangible human expression that was culturally recognisable to me.

On the other hand, since my failure to appreciate the depth and wealth of Roman architectural heritage, I had learned to value people and bring a human dimension to any situation above the antique symbols of man's material legacy, demeaned by guides and manipulators of the tourist trade. So, in a way, people, combined with my infinite love for nature, and the interaction of the two, were to be the essence of my period in England.

We were registered at King's College, although we took courses in other colleges and schools of London University. For my first year, I took Jurisprudence with Professor Graveson at King's College and African Law with Anthony Allott and James Read at the School of Oriental and African Studies. I was particularly delighted at the thought that African customary law, about which there had been so much prejudice in Khartoum University, was now a subject of dignified learning and research in one of the famous and respected institutions of learning in the world – London University. Furthermore, I found African law most entertaining, perhaps because of the way it was taught or perhaps because it was a subject which was already in my experience and knowledge – thanks to my background and my field work while in Khartoum University.

TRIALS
A Period of Reckoning

Socially, the Goats' Club provided the first opportunity in London for contacts not only with the British, but also with other foreign circles. The Club was founded and directed by the Foreign Students' Advisor, Mary Trevelyan. Abel Alier, a fellow-Dinka law student at Khartoum University, three years my senior, had spent a year in the Institute of Advanced Legal Studies of London University, and had been a member of the Goat's Club. Abel Alier had suggested our joining the Club and had introduced us to Mary Trevelyan in a letter. A quota system limited the number of nationals from any one country, which increased the number of nationalities and added to the international atmosphere of the club. Elizabeth (Liz) Ware, who assisted Mary Trevelyan, was herself an institution of generosity, patience and understanding. Combined with Mary's "maternal" love and affection, the two formed a rallying point for the international students' community.

Otherwise, London appeared to be a vast context that lumped together infinite varieties of peoples, races, and cultures, but gave them room to choose to remain separate, distinct, and insulated. It was a context of relative isolation in multiple togetherness. Very often, I was to find myself the only Sudanese, the only African, indeed the only foreigner, at British social events - parties. And yet, there was really no obvert racial discrimination to explain this segregation. In fact, I hardly felt any racial problems in Britain in those days of the early 60s. A notorious exception was the area of accommodation, where racism was strikingly conspicuous. Real estate agencies openly displayed such signs as "Sorry, no Coloured," "Europeans only" or "Whites only."

The Poelchaus, Verena's host family in Berlin, had written to introduce me to the Hudsons who lived in East Finchley, North London. On their invitation, I went to tea and we had a spontaneous liking for one another. The Hudsons were a middle-class English family with international connections. When they learned that I was renting temporarily and looking for a more suitable accommodation, they indicated that they would keep their eyes open for any opportunities. Shortly afterwards, the Hudsons invited me for dinner. Also invited was their neighbour and friend, Lady King, who looked much younger than her seventies.

Lady King was originally French. She had met her late husband, Sir Edwin King, during the First World War. She herself had been knighted for her voluntary services in the Second World War. Despite having lived in England for some forty years, Lady King still spoke English with a heavy French accent and seemed very proud of her resistance to cultural assimilation. A few days after the dinner, I received a note from the Hudsons informing me that if I were interested, Lady King would be pleased to have me as a paying guest in her house. It then dawned on me that the dinner had been primarily aimed at discreetly introducing me to Lady King. If she didn't like me, the matter would end at that. Apparently, I had passed the test and they were now willing to reveal their intentions.

After having lived with her husband in a large mansion with several servants, when her husband died, Lady King moved into what she named, "The Little House," to contrast with her past fortunes. Initially, she kept one maid who later passed away, leaving her with the services of Flora, who came daily, but lived with her own family.

Flora was a pleasant person, very English and yet cross-culturally curious. I once asked Lady King whether she minded my playing tapes of Sudanese music and she responded diplomatically by saying, "Flora likes it very much." Flora herself revealed her admirable simplicity and sincerity on another occasion. We had been honoured by the Queen Mother at the Goats' Club and she had stopped to talk to me about a private tour she and her husband, King George, had made to Dinka country. When I told Lady King and Flora about the conversation, Flora could not conceal her excitement: "How I would love to meet a member of the royalty," she said plaintively.

Apart from Flora and myself, Lady King's family included Ackie, an old cat, and Lassie, a dog. Lady King would later end her letters to me with the words, "The children send their love." The children of course were Ackie and Lassie. Lady King never had a child, but she loved children. There was clearly a vacuum to be filled. So, it was no surprise that she "mothered" me in the ambivalent sense of the word.

I occupied a room next to hers on the second floor, quite sizeable, comfortably furnished, with a large king-size brass bed, antique chests, a marble topped counter, and two leisurely chairs. A family bond that superseded the tenant-landlady relationship soon developed. Breakfast and dinner were part of the rent, but whenever I was at home, Lady King happily provided me with all the meals, including the afternoon tea and that vital last drink of hot Ovaltine, which she insisted guaranteed a good night's sleep. Lady King would also see to it that my bed was warmed up with a hot water bottle before I went to bed. Apart from the physical comforts of the Little House and Lady King's motherly care, I found East Finchley well suited to my personal likes. It was relatively quiet, clean, and greenish, more a suburb than an integral part of the city of London.

The pleasure of settling into the pleasant East Finchley environment was soon interrupted by the need for an eye check-up, as directed by the doctors in Germany and Sudan. The danger signal I saw flashing on the screen of my life was soon confirmed by the shattering results of the checkup. The pressure had returned and was high in both eyes. I was back to the original problem. But worse, I was now less naive, indeed rather well informed, about the dangers of glaucoma and the threat of blindness associated with it. I was put on the pilocarpine drops, the daily use of which I had thought traumatic and from which I had been supposedly rescued by the Berlin operation. A series of tests further revealed that the pressure on the right eye could not be controlled by the drops. Another surgery was necessary.

I began to ponder a great deal on the ultimate outcome. The doctors had congratulated me for having escaped blindness with the success of the operation in Berlin. The reverse was obvious; if the operation had not succeeded, I would again be under the threat of blindness. That the operation proved after all to have failed indicated that the threat of blindness was back, perhaps imminent. But what did that really mean? Would I be blind in a few years or at a later stage of my life? Or was it even possible that I could delay the fate into old age? Any of these possibilities was simply dreadful. Whether the blindness was an immediate threat or an old age eventuality, it was almost equally frightening. The mere thought of blindness was a timeless tragedy.

However, time was significant, if only as a matter of degree. Here I had the choice between being fully informed and leaving room for doubt and perhaps hope. I vacillated between the two positions as I weighed the medical evidence already given me and looked for comparisons with glaucoma patients. I learned that King Saud of Saudi Arabia had been suffering from glaucoma for some forty years, and although he was not seeing well, at least he was still seeing. On the other hand, I rationalised that he was availed of the best care money and position could afford from anywhere in the world. The examples of the Sudanese who were suffering from glaucoma unfortunately confirmed my dismissal of the King's case as irrelevant; all the Sudanese patients of glaucoma were rapidly losing sight.

Whether blindness would come sooner or later, what was the purpose of ambition if the dead-end was already in sight beyond which there would be no sight? Above all, how could I think of marrying and raising a family, if my destiny was blindness? Yet, what would be the meaning of life if I could not marry and have children, the Dinka idea of immortality? Was all my effort throughout life, all my successes in the face of immense obstacles and challenges, all the promises of a fruitful future, all the great expectations for myself and my contribution to my people, my country, and perhaps humanity, all a fantasy, a myth now shattered by the reality of blindness?

I lay back absorbed in my sorrow as though to discover a meaning to life that was different from what I had known in the desperate hope that I would still emerge relevant, useful and significant. The alternative threatened me with total negation, except in a form and status that contrasted sharply to anything I had known and expected. I could not face, let alone accept, what I feared would be my fate. So, in desperation, I lay down and absorbed myself into an inward vision of the past without a future. I played the tapes of Sudanese songs, Dinka and Arab alike, to accompany my thoughts and feelings.

The songs I had recorded during my last visit home on the occasion of Uncle Bulabek's death were now serving a purpose far more significance than I had anticipated. Dinka songs brought me the security of returning to my roots where I belonged and where I was sure to be accepted in whatever condition including that of blindness. The melancholy of the Arab songs gave me the empathy that seemed to express emotional support by the sadness of their tune and words of frustrated love.

In the class, apart from wandering away in mental anguish, I closed my eyes and opened them, gazing at the blackboard, as though to assure myself that I could still see or to alert myself to what could be a daily deterioration. Sometimes, I could read the writing on the blackboard, sometimes I couldn't without straining my eyes; sometimes I could not read even with contracting the eyeball to focus vision. The reason could be the handwriting; to me it was indicative of the deteriorating condition of my sight.

There was also the question of what was meaningful to study and towards what professional objectives. Should I choose subjects that did not require much reading not only for the purpose of the examination, but also for the purpose of teaching? Should I even continue to plan to teach or would my failing vision make that inadvisable? If the latter were the case, what alternatives were open to me? Would legal practice be more in tune with the condition of blindness? How should I orient my life to meet the threat?

I decided to face the truth. On my next check-up, I told the doctor that I wanted to know the prognosis so that I could plan my life accordingly. What did he think were the odds of my getting blind and what time span was involved? His answer was the straw that broke the camel's back: "If you think you will be blind in two or three years, no, you won't. You will probably see as you do now for three years, perhaps up to five years. Beyond that, it is difficult to tell." I took his answer to be a licence of clear vision for three years definitely, five years possibly; beyond that, unlikely if not improbable. In posing the question, I had clearly overestimated my ability to take the news. My situation turned for the worse, which had seemed impossible. The focus was now on juggling with the years and giving practical significance to anything I might choose to do.

But what would I, indeed could I do? Was there need to study if I could not make use of the results in any professional sense? Should I go back home and entrust myself to the unfailing care of my family? But under what kind of conditions? Could I possibly stand that kind of return in helplessness to a people who had always seen an immense purpose to my life? Could I conceivably live in virtual death, a recipient of charitable affection and care without any meaningful contribution? Father had told Bol when he was taken to faraway Nahud with a broken leg not to accept amputation, even if that meant death. What would he say about my being blind? Of what use was I? As I lay on my back, going home with Dinka songs, feeling a strange affinity in the sadness of Arab songs, I felt a deep fall from great heights and from the even greater heights of a future that had seemed so reachable, but now clearly beyond my reach.

Perhaps the evening I went to the Astors for dinner epitomised the feelings of diminishing value under which I was labouring in those days. Verena had written to David and Bridget Astor to introduce me. Bridget had written to establish contact with me and to say that as soon as David, then travelling abroad, was back, they would have me for dinner. As David's timetable became rather intractable, she decided to have me alone. Immersed in self-pity and doubt, I felt an intimidation and an apprehension I had never experienced about social contacts. I knew David owned and ran *The Observer*, that the eldest brother was in the House of Lords, and that the family was upper class. Surely it was an important contact. But towards what? And more important than that, was I in a situation to offer a sound basis for a meaningful, mutually respectful relationship?

In sharp contrast to the confidence I had always found in the combination of my background, my own accomplishments, and a vision of greater achievements in the future, I felt a deep sense of insecurity and deprivation. I could only invoke, and perhaps receive, pity with nothing to offer. I felt uncertain about my poise, my appearance, my conduct, even my potentials for social companionship. Yet, this was all internal. I do not know how I looked externally. After all, I had always been able to conceal my internal world from external appearance.

It was a weekend. Flower shops were closed. After driving around in a taxi, frantically hunting for flowers and finding none, I arrived quite late, wishing I had flowers and feeling rather nervous about the whole situation. I remember Bridget Astor as a very attractive lady, slim, of medium height, soft spoken, ladylike and very charming. She escorted me to the elegant furniture in front of the fireplace where we sat and had a glass of something before dinner. Then dinner was served. The setting could not have been more romantic. The table was reduced to a small size. Light was dimmed and candles lit.

The table setting was overwhelmingly elaborate and my cultural preparedness limited. There were several forks, several knives, several spoons, several glasses, several plates, and several possible usages. Observing Bridget discreetly, I soon noticed that I was using the wrong fork and knife for the wrong course, I believe fish. I discreetly put them back and picked up the appropriate ones. Like an ostrich with a head in the sand, I convinced myself that Mrs Astor had not seen me. No sooner had I got out of that situation than I committed another blunder. I overlooked the salad plate and placed my salad on my main plate. With each of these errors, I felt I was sinking deeper and deeper into self-devaluation, more so in what I thought would be her estimation of me than in my own self-conception. I had never, until then, and never since then, felt more awkward in a social situation.

I do not fully recall what Mrs Astor and I talked about that evening. It must have involved politics, particularly the South-North conflict which no Southerner could ever manage to keep out of any context, political, social or otherwise. From what I was to learn from David Astor later, the size of my family must have been quite prominent in our conversation. It always was. By way of similarities, we also talked of the leading Botswana family of the Khamas, also friends of the Astors. Verena had talked about Tshekedi Khama, the son of Seretse Khama, the president of Botswana, whom she had met through the Astors.

Mrs Astor lent me a book about the Khamas which I read with enthusiasm, not only because of its inherent interest, but particularly because of the striking similarities in the experience of both families, the struggle for power within the families, the feuds resulting from the power struggle, and the colonial support for one party resulting in the banishment of the opposition leader from the tribe. All that combined with the similarities of the social systems and the cattle cultures of both peoples made the book immensely relevant to me. I was later to read Schapiro's works on Tswana law and was also struck by the similarities with Dinka law. Placing that knowledge in the context of family relationships and rivalries was most stimulating.

When I later received an off-print of Paul Howell's article on the Ngok Dinka in the journal, *Sudan Notes and Records,* nicely bound in the form of a booklet, I took great pride and pleasure in sending it to Mrs Astor as further evidence of what I had said about my family and its leadership position in the Ngok Dinka tribe. The article not only gave some details about the social and political organisation of the Ngok Dinka and some principles of authority and control, but also included a thorough account of the power struggle between my father and Uncle Deng Makuei. It could not have been more pertinent as a reciprocity for the Khama book. In those days, seeing an off print of an article, a booklet, containing so much about my tribe, my family, and my father was exhilarating.

Verena was perhaps the closest friend in the depths of my agony. She wrote with deep perception and strong emotional and intellectual support, giving analytical comments on me as a person, the qualities I possessed, the destiny which lay ahead, and the necessity of overcoming the obstacles through faith and will. She sent me books: the Bible with underlined passages, *Faust* by Goethe, Fyodor Dostoyevsky's *Brothers Karamazov,* and a host of other books, which she hoped would both entertain me and give me strength. Citing her aunt, she spoke of the similarities between me and her father, a man whom I knew she held in great esteem. It is peculiar how words, even from a distance, reflected only on paper, can be such an effective instrument of support and strength. Such was the nature of Verena's contribution to my spiritual resilience against all the ills that threatened my survival as a full functioning person.

Indeed, despite the turmoil of my inner world and the ineptness of my social conduct with Mrs Astor, there was a surprising dichotomy between the crumbling world inside me and the appearance of serenity, even happiness which I still radiated to everyone who came in touch with me. Not even Lady King was aware of my inner turmoil. Certainly, the Sudanese community saw my life as one of relative luxury, flamboyance and a smooth ride in British society. It would never have occurred to them that I was perhaps at the lowest ebb of my self-esteem.

It was at this time when I did not seem to have much of a future that I received the greatest compliment I had ever received from my father. A group of province judges were visiting England and one of them carried a letter from my father, introducing him to me as a good friend and one of his principal allies in the politics of Kordofan Province. My father asked me to do all I could to facilitate his visit in England. His letter then went on to tell me about the turn of events in his relations with the North.

Ali Baldo, whose very name was synonymous with South-North animosities, had been transferred to Kordofan as governor. Apparently, he had been too used to mishandling Southern chiefs to live up to the treatment my father had been used to in the North. They soon clashed. In the process, Ali Baldo told my father that he was free to join his brothers in the South, if he wanted. My father was severely insulted by the remark, which he saw as racist. Being the shrewd politician that he was, Father would not let Ali Baldo get away with that racial slur. Realising that it had dangerous political connotations for the unity of the country, he reported to President Abboud who, I understood later, not only reprimanded Ali Baldo, but also decided on his early retirement, bringing an end to an administrative career that claimed a lion's share of the devastations following of the Southern disturbances.

But my father had not been reconciled by Ali Baldo's punishment; he said he now knew who his people really were, implying an emphasis on his South Sudanese identity. He said that he wanted to inform me because I was "the High Dam of the Dinka." Father had often praised us, Bol and me, but never had he been so forthright about his expectations from me or the burden of responsibility he saw resting on me as a future leader of my people.

I had heard from Abdalla describing the rift that had taken place between him and Adam, which he could not understand, although he of course realised that it was the result of rivalry over the leadership which opportunists were fanning. I had written to my father urging him to make a decision on the matter and foster the unity of the family behind one of the brothers, rather than allow the rift to continue. Father had never replied to my letter. Now he was calling me the High Dam of the Dinka, when my potential worth for my people had diminished.

I was as deeply moved as I was severely pained by the limits now flashing before me. But I did not betray my agony to the bearer of the letter. I honoured the group with a dinner party and accompanied them on their visit to Oxford and Cambridge. When they came to leave for Sudan, I did not reply to my father's letter, but from their observations, I was sure they would report positively to my father about my living conditions.

One of the people who helped me free myself from the doom psychology and discover constructive purposes to my life was a lecturer in Anthropology at Oxford University. I was one day standing, talking with a group of students in the Senior Common Room of the School of Oriental and African Studies when a man presumably in his late forties walked over and patted me on the back, while I was in the middle of whatever I was saying. When I turned to him, he said in an almost blasé manner and as though he had not interrupted our conversation, "Are you a Dinka?"

In the circumstances, the appropriate reaction might have been to be dismissive, if discreetly. Somehow, I was surprisingly cordial. "Yes, I am a Dinka," I said smilingly. He went on asking in the same spirit: "Which Dinka?" he asked. "Dinka Ngok," I said. "Oh! I have a rather nice photograph of your chief," he added. "Who?" I asked, just to be sure. "Deng Majok," he said. "That's my father."

I had a glass of coke in my hand. In a manner quite consistent, and which I was becoming increasingly intrigued by and responsive to, he said, "Put that down and let us go for a drink." I did exactly as he commanded, smiling with surprise. We left the room without even excusing ourselves from the group. I soon learned that my companion was Godfrey Lienhardt, whose doctoral field work in anthropology had been carried out among the Western Dinka of Bahr el Ghazal Province.

I later received a proposal from Godfrey Lienhardt that we jointly present a talk in the BBC Third Programme on the subject of "Man in Society", in which he had been scheduled to speak on the Nilotics. I liked the idea and quickly recalled the moving Dinka songs I had recorded with my father's assistance. How marvellous it would be to illustrate whatever I would say with the live voices of the Dinka singing about their religious devotion, their spiritual concept of authority, their material and aesthetic dedication to cattle, their loyalties to family ties, their pride in their Dinka ways and concerns, the worries and agonies they felt about the disintegrating effect of disruptive change. Godfrey liked the idea and so did the programme director. Naturally, the material in the songs would be even more enriched by translating the excerpts into English to be read immediately following the voices wherever appropriate.

The BBC programme thus introduced me to the treasures of my song-collection which eventually went far beyond the pleasures of listening to the tapes. I had initially recorded the tapes for expected nostalgic reasons as a prospective link with home. Now, they were playing an educational role and evolving into a source of information on various aspects of the Dinka. I was now making use of works translated into English rather than merely listening to the sounds of Dinka songs. Godfrey soon realised that the quality and the quantity of my collection offered a significant potential and suggested that he and I work on producing a volume of Dinka poetry for the series of the Oxford Library of African Literature that he himself co-edited with E. E. Evans-Pritchard and W. H. Whitely.

The opportunity could not have come at a better time, for even as my academic and professional future seemed dim and doomed, I could see some salvation and lasting value in the production of a volume that would embody a vital expression of an important aspect of my people's tradition. Highly motivated by this opportunity, I worked industriously on transcribing and translating the songs and found solace in the process.

My periodic checkups entailed an aggravating subjection to examination by medical students, not for the treatment purposes, but as part of their training. What I found especially objectionable was that the professor under whose care I was supposed to be, hardly ever examined me. He would merely glance at my records, which had been prepared by his assistants, and then say a word about the state of my eyes and the date for my next appointment. Otherwise, he displayed me to his students as though I was an object of demonstration. Every one of them would pose the same questions regarding the history of my case and I had to go over the same answers I had just given over and over again. When I suggested that they might consider looking into my records, which were right in front of me and in which all the relevant facts were recorded, they told me that they were professionally required to ask the questions and record the answers themselves.

Once, I was examined and discussed with another patient, a young girl in her teens, the main issue being the age when to suspect glaucoma. We were a good example, so said the professor, of how erroneous it was to associate glaucoma only with old age. As they discussed in front of us, I felt a sense of despair that we were more useful as medical cases for educational purposes than we were curable and valuable as individuals whose sense of privacy should be respected. Taking us as rare cases of young people with a disease otherwise associated with the old only accentuated the sense of doom which I was nursing.

Neither the professor nor the students approached us with respect or the courtesy of asking our permission even as simply a matter of formality. I sat there passively available to every one of them as though I were their property or as though they had a right over my body. I had become tired of that demeaning treatment and in particular for the inadequacy of the care I was receiving. I came to the conclusion that this was the outcome of the national health service which lacked the personal or individual touch normally associated with private medical service. I decided to request Sudan to authorise me to receive private ophthalmological care rather than continue under the national health service.

My request was granted with surprising speed. I then asked the embassy doctor to recommend another ophthalmologist, for I did not want to continue with the same man whose care had been clearly inadequate. Professor Greaves was recommended. When he approached my former ophthalmologist, the latter offered to take me into his private practice to continue under his care. The issue was thrown back to me, but I flatly turned down his offer, for I could not see how he could change just because my category had changed from national health service to private care. I reasoned that if he were to change, that would be sufficient indication of the kind of person he was and with whom I would not want to be involved.

Professor Greaves was a totally different kind of person, very pleasant, very sensitive to the needs of his patients, and luckily for me, an optimist, but without falsifications. It is hard to tell whether that was in the person or in the private care I was receiving. But Professor Greaves appeared so natural that I could not see him behaving otherwise to his patients, even though being a private patient perhaps enhanced the quality of the services I was receiving from him. From the time I went into his care, I ceased to be an object of study and became a human being deserving respectful attention. Greaves' prognosis on my case was also much brighter than that of his colleagues.

When I mentioned the time spectrum of three to five years which I had been given, he dismissed it flatly as sheer nonsense, for he said that even if the pressure was to be difficult to control by drops, there was no limit to the number of operations that could be performed to help remedy the condition. He encouraged me to plan my future without consideration to my eye's condition. I was, of course, pleased by what he said and I felt considerable relief in consequence, even though I was suspicious that he was simply trying to give me hope and strength and that what he said was at best partial truth. In any case, there was no way I could derail myself from the track of blindness on which I had set my course of expectations. Yet, as I entered the hospital for an operation on my right eye, which had been more damaged by the disease, I felt a sense of tranquility, a breathing space in time, and at least two spectrums of expert opinion to maneuvre my hopes, aspirations and expectations.

The operation went smoothly without complications and my week in the hospital was quite relaxed and rather pleasant. I occupied an excellent room in the private wing and I was permitted visitors without restriction. One of the people who had been taking care of me, an attractive, pleasant, and soothing nurse, came in one day to say she would be leaving and wanted to bid me farewell. I wondered where she was going. "South Africa," she said. "On vacation?" I asked. "No, I come from South Africa." She had been on a nursing course in England and was now returning home. I tried to look natural, but that she should be from South Africa, the land of apartheid, was white, yet so friendly and without the least trace of visible racial prejudice in her treatment of a black patient was intriguing to me. All that unexpected combination made it quite irresistible to raise the issue of the racial situation in South Africa. To my surprise again, I found that she was a true believer in the policy of apartheid. Her father owned a large farm on which he employed blacks. She had therefore grown up among blacks, but was segregated by the apartheid system which she strongly supported. Yet, here she was, taking excellent care of me without the kind of instinctive reaction I would have expected from a person so obviously conditioned towards racial consciousness and prejudice.

Her reasons for supporting apartheid had something to do with the difference between the blacks and the whites, the value of developing along their own lines, and the need to protect the white minority civilisation against the onslaught of the black majority that would result from a policy of an open society.

That was not my first encounter in London with a white South African who believed in the policy of apartheid as a policy and in practice. Earlier, while my colleagues, Natale Olwak, Mohammed el Fateh, and I were having a drink in a pub or public house as bar is known there, I went to make a phone call in a booth outside the pub. I found a man standing at the door of the booth, apparently waiting for a call. He realised I wanted to use the phone, but rather than let me in or explain his need for leaving the phone unengaged, he stood, resting his back against the door, his legs stretching across to the other end and his body blocking the doorway. After acknowledging me with a greeting, he asked, "Where are you from?" "Sudan," I said briefly, clearly resentful of his condescending mannerism. "How are things down there?" he asked with an air of arrogance. "Fine," I said, and went on to ask, "And where are you from?" "South Africa," he said. "And how are things down there?" I asked with a slight air of malice. "Fine," he said and went on to elaborate a defence of his country. It was the best in Africa, the most democratic, with the highest standard of living even for the blacks. I realised that we had just embarked on a highly controversial road and were in fact feeling less hostile towards one another as we spoke.

Since he seemed eager to talk, I said, "Why don't you join us for a drink?" He received his call, I made mine, and we went into the pub with him joining our table. We had a fascinating conversation in which he vehemently defended the policy of apartheid, stressing that Africans were different from Europeans and needed to be developed along their own indigenous lines. "Remember," he said, "these people are not as civilised as yourselves; they are primitive." Being the first to have gone to school in our areas, and bearing in mind that black South Africans had a longer history of contact with the West, his distinction could not have been more comic, if contrived. "How do you know when you are separated from them?" I posed a question which I knew he could not really answer. But although we did not influence one another, our discussion was cordial.

After the operation, I was able to resume normal social life, especially as I had reconciled myself to my condition. At a Goats' Club dance, I met a person who became one of my closest friends in whose friendship I found solace and strength. Ironically, her name was Frances. At twenty, approaching twenty-one, Frances was slender, of medium height, delicate in mannerism and attractive in a natural way. Her humane qualities had presumably been nourished by her family religious background, her father being a clergyman and the vicar of a reputable Oxford parish. They often had African Anglican priests as guests in the vicarage, sometimes with their families, as her father promoted partnerships with African dioceses. Frances' aunt, Helen, worked as a nurse at a mission hospital in South Africa, training young African women as nurses, and Frances had aspired to go and work with her.

We saw much of one another and did many things together, went to parties, walked in the parks, and enjoyed being together. Frances was in her final year of anthropology, at the University College of London, where the students studied the customs, laws, religions and social structures of African societies. As I later experienced with anthropologists elsewhere, I was a source of information on the Nilotic people, everywhere a focal subject of the discipline.

Frances mimicked and teased me about my English intonation, flattering me that I spoke better English than many English. I can say unequivocally that my friendship with Frances was a major factor in my overcoming or coping with my health problems, even though I do not recall that we ever talked about the condition of my eyes. Strangely enough, I do not even think she knew I had an eye disease; I did not tell her until much later in the friendship and it never came up naturally. She later recalled, "You did briefly talk about your eye problem, but you didn't make it a big thing, so I didn't either. Now of course I read that it was a huge worry hanging over you, quite understandably. And yet with me you hardly mentioned it!!".

So, Frances' help was indirectly expressed in the pleasure her company gave me and the way it detracted from my obsessive involvement with my problems. What made things so much easier was that Lady King liked Frances whom she regarded as a very nice, obviously well brought up girl. Such social or class considerations were always very important to Lady King. My eye problem came up towards the end of my time in England when we discussed the future and the challenges I was facing. Frances got married to Simon House, an Anglican pastor, shortly after I left England and we reconnected many years later.

Bol visited me after my operation. Seeing Bol again after my traumatic experience with my eyes was a moral boost for me. He continued to be the optimist, taking advantage of his medical qualifications to assure me that I would see practically into old age. I knew he was motivated by his desire to help me emotionally, and although I did not give much credence to his opinion, I felt the strength of his moral support. And then, there was that everlasting preoccupation with our family affairs, now given new dimensions and significance by my condition. We continued to discuss the future implications of the large family size, but we also enjoyed reminiscing about our childhood days, which, considering all the turbulence we had gone through in change, now seemed one of great happiness and tranquility.

That was the year Bol revealed to me aspects of his own self-image in the family that were surprisingly similar to mine. First, I broke the ice by telling him quite candidly all about my identity crisis of Khor Taqqat. He was astonished that I could possibly have entertained such absurd thoughts, adding "You must have been mad." But then he gave me an account of his own experiences at approximately the same time, when he was so preoccupied with problems that he would get up in the middle of the night and walk around our home in Abyei, absorbed in his own worries. He never told me what precisely had preoccupied him nor did I ask.

But Bol revealed another angle which I thought reflected the thrust of his concerns then. He suddenly turned solemn and dead serious when he introduced the subject: "Mading, I want to tell you something very important and confidential." I allude to the story here, though without elaboration, because after all these years, I had considered these incidents to be part of our shared experience from which I believe much can be learned about our family. Bol told me accounts of events which had taken place early in his childhood which he took seriously to explain how he had grown up nursing a deep sense of grievance against the inadequacy of Father's love and the inequities in his attitude towards individuals and factions in the family structure.

In a way, despite the variance of our respective positions on specific issues, and although our reactions on details were different because the particulars of our individual circumstances were not identical, we were both driven by the same forces, reacting to the same basic needs, revitalising our shared identity, clarifying the sense of purpose that had always been associated with our education, and working to meet the challenges that we saw facing us at the juncture of our cross-cultural experiences. Bol and I were clearly the closest friends. We held no secrets from one another even though some things had to wait for long before being revealed.

That year, I spent my summer vacation in Sweden at the invitation of a Swedish writer, Perceval Bucklund. It was on the Nile steamer on my second visit to Germany that I first met Percy and his wife Margaretta. Percy was a lean man in his late thirties, with a beard-mustache combination linked to a medium length hairdo, and a somewhat mysterious, but intriguing personality. He took the initiative to introduce himself. I did the same and soon found an enthusiastic companion. He had been to Sudan, had travelled down the Nile to the South, and was now back guiding a group of Swedish tourists visiting the Egyptian and Nubian antiquities on which he had become an expert. That evening, Percy asked me to join him and his wife on the deck of the boat. He started to speak about his disenchantment with the Western civilisation, his discovery of the spiritual wealth of Africa, the Middle East and the Orient, his desire, through his writings, paintings, and music, to educate the West about those spiritual and cultural values.

I was a ripe captive for Percy's ideas as I was on the brink of cultural revival, reacting to an educational process that had denied the dignity of our people's heritage in every aspect of modern life. Of course, I was excited about going to Europe, but I had begun to recognise and respect my background in a more substantive sense than personal identification with my father and family background. My response to Percy was one of enthusiasm and the more I discussed with him the more he seemed to feel that he had tapped the African of his dream. Unbelievable! So excited was he that he invited me to visit Sweden, travel together with him and co-author a book on his country, as viewed from the perspective of an African. He even suggested that I abandon my mission to Germany so that we could immediately start our work on the project. Of course, I could not abandon the German tour, but I promised to visit Sweden on the earliest possible opportunity. My first summer vacation in England was such an opportunity.

Percy had formulated a broad-based programme of extensive

travel around the country, to the extreme north, visiting the Lapps, detouring into Norway, to the east into the Finnish border, to the west as far as Goteborg, to the south as far as Lund and into Denmark, with Stockholm as the base to which we returned from time to time. The programme itself was varied, comprehensive and intensive. We visited town halls, newspaper offices, academic institutions, factories, paper mills, mines, homes for the elderly, hospitals, prisons, reformatories for juvenile delinquents, churches, remote villages, private homes, farms, parks and forests. We talked to government officials, business executives, editors of provincial newspapers, journalists, writers, artists, architects, professors, students, doctors, patients, prison governors, juvenile delinquents, housewives, old people, young people, important personalities and ordinary people. An audience with the king was even suggested, but I modestly turned it down.

We lived in youth hostels, in rented rooms, in private homes, in cabins, and sometimes at the stations. We talked intensively with the people we met and either took notes as we talked, which Percy preferred, or wrote later, which I preferred. We were continuously on the move, and constantly at work. Even social functions were part of the work. Wherever we went, we saw anyone we wanted to see and received considerable courtesy and hospitality. In most places, our visit was covered in the local press whether or not we met with the editors of the local papers. And the image of me which Percy had half seriously and half humorously promoted was that of an African prince, which somewhat disturbed my sense of humility, but evidently helped open doors.

As our tour of Scandinavia was approaching its end, Percy suggested that we proceed to Paris, where he had made an appointment for us to meet with the renowned American-born British poet, T.S. Elliott. By then, I had been away from my studies for too long and I also wanted to visit Verena and her mother in Hamburg, the Fessmans in Zell Wiesenthal and a Dutch friend I had met during the Pax Romana Conference in Freiburg. Percy and I agreed to part and reunite in London.

I had only been back in London for a few days when Percy

joined me most excited about his meeting with T.S. Elliott, to whom he explained that the "African prince" had to change his plans at the last minute due to unforeseen circumstances. I kept my commitment to Percy that I would write a report on our visit. I did that with a sense not only of duty but also of purpose and pleasure since it crystalised my own views on a variety of important matters. Indeed, I wrote with considerable depth of reflection and expression, summarising my observations under five main categories: an introductory chapter providing the background to the project and four other titles: "The Impact of Alien Religions in Africa", "Racialism at the Meeting Point", "The Family as a Symbol of Human Solidarity" and "The Paradox of Contemporary Civilization". Although I did not know it at the time, these would become my first works to be published.

Almost from the moment of its commencement to its very end, my tour of Sweden was an intensive experience from which I emerged exhausted, dizzy, and hardly able to stand on my feet, far less distinguish between what was real, what was a dream and what was a nightmare. Yet, the experience had a cathartic effect. As I reflected on that reality, that dream, or that nightmare, I felt the strength of a new education that was relevant to the reality of my critical situation.

With that strength, I had more or less been reborn again and was prepared to plunge into the challenges that my new life posed for me. But my world was a complex one, with twists and turns, entailing seemingly endless challenges, and no easy answers. I was soon to be confronted with political problems which made the last phase of my stay in London a traumatic year of reckoning. With the turn of 1963, the political situation in Southern Sudan continued to deteriorate. The Southern insurgency abroad was intensifying its struggle. All this was reflected in the United Kingdom and to a certain extent in the relations between Southerners and Northerners.

My position in the Southern movement was a precarious one. Of course, I shared the position of all Southerners and campaigned for change in the government's Southern Policy, but there were differences in the political objectives of the movement. Southerners generally professed separation, either as a means to achieving satisfactory compromises, or as a serious political objective. I stood for a united Sudan in which the South would enjoy full control over its own affairs, combined with equality in the sharing of national power and wealth. But whatever the objectives, there were different ways for attaining them and there had to be different roles for those concerned with the problem. I chose for myself the individual role of discussing, lecturing, and writing as an advocate of the Southern cause to Northerners and foreigners alike. I did not engage in any organised political movement, though participating in Southern meetings and strategy planning. As Southerners and Northerners seemed to believe in a clear-cut position, where one had to be either a Southerner or a Northerner, in support or against the status quo, my position was confusing to both. But I made my views known to both sides, hardly concealing anything about my convictions or my actions. And often, this provoked a negative reaction from both sides.

This was perhaps most marked when William Deng Nhial visited London, and all of us, Southerners, met him in his hotel room. The news of his presence in London was in the British press. One day in the midst of a heated discussion with Northerners, I was asked by Osman Sid Ahmed, one of the senior Sudanese colleagues, a Muslim Brother, whether I had met William Deng. I said I had. Amin, a graduate student of history, surprised me with his emotional outburst and display of hatred, even calling me "a traitor." I was most surprised because Amin had been very friendly towards me and had visited me at the The Little House on numerous occasions.

That confrontation revealed to me that to most Northerners in London, I was probably more dangerous than any other Southerner in the United Kingdom. I was an active member of the Executive Committee of the Sudanese Students Union in the United Kingdom and, as always, I associated with all Sudanese, Southerners and Northerners alike. But to those who did not know me well, my close association with them, my open discussion of the political situation, and my frankness in voicing my views, probably made me seem particularly cunning. Indeed, although I did not realise it at the beginning, it began to dawn on me that most of the graduate students were senior government officials, who had not known me before. They did not know my political background in both the secondary school and the university education, nor my family position on provincial and national politics. Taking me simply as a Southerner, they probably concluded that if I could be so critical in their face, I must be even more hostile and dangerous behind their backs. That was precisely the gist of Amin's accusations: that I pretended to be a close friend, while I was in fact an enemy.

Although Natale Olwak was politically very active, he generally kept his distance from the Northerners in so far as discussion of the Southern problem was concerned and gave little evidence of his political involvement. This was of course the attitude of the Southerners in general and one I had used to criticise at Khartoum University. Natale had been present in the heated discussion which provoked a hostile reaction from Amin, but had largely been silent. He later expressed his surprise and even anger at my admitting to having met William Deng. He said he could not believe I would be so naïve as to admit meeting a political dissident who had been sentenced to death in absentia. I told him that I could not lie, nor could I see how the Northerners could expect us not to meet a Southern nationalist who was promoting a cause we must obviously share; if they did not think we were lying by claiming not to have met William, they would not respect us for being indifferent to a leader who was championing the cause of our people.

Natale's own manner of handling South-North relations was demonstrated by a small incident involving Lawrence Wol Wol, the graduate of Freiburg University in Switzerland, who had denied me as a Southerner for wearing a jallabiya. Lawrence was the editor of the Southern movement's publication: *The Grass Curtain*. He was a frequent visitor to our places and Natale worked with him very closely on *The Grass Curtain*. Once, our Northern colleague, Mohammed el Fateh, visited Natale and found Lawrence Wol with him. Not wishing to be identified with Lawrence as a

Southern activist and Lawrence desiring to conceal his identity from the Northerners for security reasons, they both pretended that Lawrence was a Congolese, who spoke only French.

The ambivalent attitude of the Southerners towards me was manifested when Bishop Edward Mason, who had been expelled with other missionaries from the South, came through London on his way to the United States to promote the Southern cause. All the Southerners, including my cousin, Michael Deng Abiem, who was then putting up with me in The Little House, went to meet him at the airport. I was left completely ignorant of the whole situation until cousin Deng Abiem felt morally obliged to inform me about the incident and the general attitude of the Southerners towards me. When I confronted my Southern colleagues on the issue, Natale Olwak was forced to explain that the situation involved the life or death of many, and that I was dangerously close to Northerners.

Professor Allott, pleased with my performance in his African Law class, offered to sponsor me for the Ph.D. programme, and bypass the LL.M requirements. The only requirement was the approval of Khartoum University, my employer. I was pleasantly surprised and exhilarated. I wrote to the Faculty of Law, supported by ample medical reports, arguing that I needed an extension of my course period because of the interruption imposed by the eye problem during the first year and also because of the opportunity offered by Professor Allott, that I proceed with the Ph.D. course in African Law. A short time after my letter had gone, I was called into the office of the cultural attaché, Bushra Abdel Rahman, who had been the headmaster of Khor Taqqat Secondary school during our time. A letter concerning me had arrived from Khartoum, and he wanted to convey the contents to me personally. I was impressed, but surprised that Khartoum had responded to my request so promptly. The question in my mind was whether they had approved or rejected my request. I went.

Bushra Abdel Rahman was remarkably detached when he conveyed the message that was to change the course of my life – I had been recalled and should return to the Sudan immediately. The letter was from the minister for Education, and not the University of Khartoum. That in itself was surprising, but not very much so, since the independence of the university had been curtailed by placing it under the minister of Education, who was then Talat Fareed, a military officer, and one of the pillars of General Abboud's dictatorship. Naturally, I wanted to know why I was being recalled, but Bushra Abdel Rahman had no answer. Why was the recall from the minister for Education and not the university? I wanted to know many things about the meaning of the recall, whether it had been initiated by the university, whether it had something to do with my request for extension, whether the university was repudiating my appointment, whether! Whether! Whether! My mind was suddenly streaming with questions. But Bushra knew nothing or at least played being ignorant, continuing to reveal a detachment that began to look suspicious to me, especially in view of my long association with him as my former headmaster and my expectation that he would show interest in my future.

It then began to dawn on me that there was probably more to it than my request for extension. It was even possible that the recall was decided in ignorance of my request for extension. Might it be political? The answer seemed obvious to almost everybody, particularly Southerners, except me. My political position in favour of self-rule for the South within equitable national unity had always been considered so moderate that Southerners viewed it as pro-North. My criticism against the status quo had also been so open that it could never have come to any one as a surprise.

So, what could possibly have provoked the regime to consider me subversive? How could I be suspected of subversion when one of the most active Southerners, Natale Olwak, my colleague, remained completely unaffected? Natale and the other Southerners found an easy explanation in what they saw as my naively close association and frank discussions with Northerners. Although it seemed possible, especially in view of the violent discussions I had just had with some Northerners, it also seemed unbelievable that out of all the Southerners in England, the government would single me out for anti-North activities, when I was also considered the least extreme or the most moderate of them all.

TRIALS
A Period of Reckoning

Be that as it may, what was to be my response? On the one hand, it seemed quite obvious that if the reasons were political, then to go back would be to risk persecution, especially as the Southern problem had intensified and was driving the Northerners into a political hysteria. And it should be recalled that I had taken the first constitution of the opposition SACDNU to Sudan from Europe. On the other hand, to refuse to go would be to become a political refugee for the duration of the Southern problem, to which there was no end in sight. And then there was the problem of my eyes. To go and risk being locked up in jail without the care I so badly needed would be certainly to accelerate blindness. But, to remain a refugee abroad would mean that even if the problem of the South was eventually solved, I would be almost certain to have become blind in exile. It was a predicament for which there did not seem to be easy answers.

I decided to play delaying tactics, aimed primarily at refusing to go without saying so. First, I sent a message to the Sudan through the cultural attaché's office enquiring into the reasons for my recall. A message quickly came back saying the reasons would be given on arrival and repeating that I should proceed to Sudan immediately. I sent another message in which I raised a series of questions about the recall: whether it had been initiated by the university or by another institution or someone else with the university's knowledge and consent, and whether it was a termination of my employment with the university and the associated scholarship. If that were the case, I should feel free to seek alternative employment and opportunities for scholarship.

I was trying to view the situation from the perspective of contractual relations and deliberately ignoring the political angle, so that my refusal would not be interpreted as a political reaction, but only as a response to the termination of the contract and its implications for my career. To my surprise, they instructed the cultural attaché to terminate all payments to me, including the scholarship and the transferred part of my salary. Their action made their motives even more obvious.

Natale and I had already begun to gather bits and pieces of information which substantiated our suspicion that the recall was politically motivated. But perhaps the most direct evidence I received in London was in a telephone conversation between a Northern colleague and the military attaché, Colonel Muzamil Ghandour. The Northern colleague had come to visit me in The Little House and learned for the first time the news of my recall and the termination of my scholarship. He insisted on calling the military attaché, and although I tried to discourage him from doing so while with me, he would not be dissuaded. What was more, he insisted that I should listen to the conversation, even though I argued that I did not consider it proper. Of course, I only heard what he said, but it was not difficult to construct what was being said on the other side and, in any case, he himself told me the whole truth.

As soon as he heard my name, the military attaché responded with "Oh, him; I know of his hatred for Northerners. He is very active against the government." My friend said to him, "Are you sure you know the person you are talking about? That cannot be Francis; in fact, he is a Northerner from Kordofan. You really ought to meet him and you will see how wrong you are." The conversation went on and it seemed that the military attaché was convinced about his judgement. They ended the matter inconclusively and my friend undertook to pursue it with the military attaché, whom he said was a childhood friend.

Although the political motives of my recall were obvious to all those in London, it was the letter from my colleague and friend, Tigani Omer el Karib, which clarified the situation from within. Tigani gave me the full account of my case in Khartoum, the intelligence reports that had gone to Sudan about me, the instructions of the Minister of Education to the university that I be recalled, the initial refusal of the vice chancellor to act in accordance with that instruction, as there were no academic grounds for doing so, and the final decision by the minister for Education to recall me himself. Tigani made it clear that the whole issue was political and that I was clearly being accused of subversive activities. But he left the decision of whether to return or not to me personally and implored me not to be influenced by others in making the decision. Tigani's brother, Salah, an educationalist on a postgraduate course in London, was, ironically, the only Northerner to advise me openly against going back. As he was to tell me years later, he found himself under heavy attack from the other Northerners.

What had seemed inconceivable had become a reality and I was once again plunged into a crisis which was so acute and unexpected that I continued to be torn between doubting and believing. It was as though I was in a nightmare from which I hoped to wake up any minute. Obviously, I could not go home and risk imprisonment, blindness and even possible execution. But the thought of being a political refugee horrified me. It would mean not going back to my beloved country, perhaps forever, and almost certainly not before my getting blind. This meant that I would probably never see my people again. My world had radically changed, darkened both by the threat of blindness and by an injustice that I never believed could be so blatant, so arbitrary, and so ruthless. The magnitude of the Southern problem and its impact on individual lives now came so clearly to me.

The Little House became an active meeting place for the Southerners as they pondered over my predicament, showing me sympathy and solidarity, but also secretly, and not so secretly, relishing the idea that I, who had always seemed so friendly and politically close to the North, should be the victim of the North. Their attitude was not so much a result of ill intention towards me as it was pleasure in the lesson I was learning, and the hope that I would now be provoked into becoming more militant in the struggle. With this set of ambivalent calculations, their concern over my problem did not seem to me a spontaneous gesture of brotherhood and solidarity; rather, I saw it as largely a tactical political opportunism. Nonetheless, I appreciated the fact that they were after all Southerners and that it was that common bond which made them particularly interested in my crisis. Whatever their ulterior motives, they were part of what united us behind the common struggle in which our differences were more in the form and the degree of our militancy against the system rather than in the essence of our struggle.

Chief Anthony Enharo of Nigeria had just been extradited back to Nigeria and was very much in the news. Although the British Government was being subjected to extreme criticism for permitting extradition for alleged political crimes, a precedent had been established which could be successfully invoked by the Sudan Government against me. I went to Oxford to see Godfrey Lienhardt's brother, Peter, who also taught Anthropology at Oxford; Godfrey was then away in Ghana, teaching for a term. Peter was of the opinion that I should of course not return to Sudan. He suggested that he and I should go to the British Foreign Office to see a friend, Willis Morrison, later ambassador to Cairo. Ambassador Morrison met us and was friendly and sympathetic, but understandably noncommittal.

Peter and I went to see Mary Trevelyan and found her most sympathetic and helpful. Indeed, she impressed us by reaching for the phone and saying as she did so, "The home secretary is a good friend of mine. Let me give him a call." A positive conversation went on after which she put the receiver back to announce, rather casually but reassuringly, that all was well: "I am assured by the home secretary that nothing of the sort will happen to you." Even Peter, an Englishman, was most impressed with how simple it all seemed because of knowing the right people.

That issue more or less resolved; the next problem was financial support. Here again, Mary Trevelyan was to prove most helpful and effective. Even before I took any steps in that direction, she had invoked a grant request from a foundation or a fund that included Lord Euston and I later understood, Lord Twining, William's father, on its board. Before that, and on learning of my crisis, Lady King had told me to count on her continuing to provide me with room and board for as long as I needed and without worrying about payment. The grant through Mary Trevelyan came through speedily and I was able to backpay Lady King.

My natural reaction was to publicise my case as a typical example of the injustice and political persecution prevailing in Sudan over the case of the South. This was very much the wish of my Southern colleagues, who in fact geared me towards such a reaction, certainly encouraged it, and clearly intended to reap political fruits from my crisis. Natale Olwak and I drafted a statement in which we gave a factual account of my recall, summarised the circumstantial evidence which indicated political motivation, and gave my reasons for refusing to return. We presented the significance of the case as an example of what was going on in the country against Southerners. We then went to see David Astor of *The Observer* and Colin Legum, then the well-known commentator on African affairs, who was also with *The Observer*. The two men convinced me that it would be wiser to avoid reacting emotionally and putting myself in a position which would then be used by the Government of Sudan to justify their unfair treatment of me. Instead, it would strengthen my case to react calmly and allow time to unravel the facts and expose their mis-judgement of me. I thought it was a wise advice. A number of developments were to prove them right.

During those critical days, I spent a weekend with the family of Michael Tibbs, the last British district commissioner in my home area. They lived in the village of Haselmere, in the county of Lynchmere in Surrey, a lovely countryside. That weekend, I went to church with the Tibbs on Sunday morning and was introduced to the pastor who was not only close to the Tibbs as members of his parish, but held them in high esteem as their family had been in the clerical leadership of the area for many years. During the sermon, I was astonished to hear the pastor preach a message which seemed to be directed to me personally and to give me consolation. The preacher spoke of the spiritual values of endurance, of the strength of faith to counter suffering, of the virtue of forgiving our enemies, and in the continuing hopes for God's blessing to overcome our difficulties. Even his prayer seemed clearly intended for me. Whatever the facts, I was absolutely convinced that Michael Tibbs had agreed with the pastor to hold that Sunday's sermon for my sake and to pray for me. I was deeply moved.

It was during those days that I was also invited by K.D.D. Henderson, who had served in the Sudan Civil Service for a full career term during which he was a district commissioner, assistant civil secretary, editor of *Sudan Notes and Records*, and governor of

Darfur Province. Mr Henderson had been district commissioner in western Kordofan when my grandfather Kuol Arop, was still the chief. Henderson had a great admiration for Kuol Arop, whom he was later to describe as "a great leader and ruler of men." I had first met Mr Henderson in Oxford where they then lived. They had since moved from Oxford and settled in a beautiful house on lovely grounds in the tiny village of Steeple Langford, near Salisbury in Wiltshire.

On hearing about my problem, Mr Henderson went into deep reflection, pondering over the issue of whether I should return or become a refugee. It was clear that the considerations he was making were extremely difficult. On the one hand, he had known my grandfather and had held him in great esteem. He had also known my father even before my father succeeded my grandfather. To see me abandon the country which my forefathers had served so loyally as leaders was an idea he found extremely difficult to accept. Mr Henderson also loved Sudan and hated to see a situation develop that would polarise the country even more and perhaps to confront him with an even more critical choice of political position over the Southern Problem that he had resisted in the past.

Mr Henderson had a strong belief in the tradition of justice which the British had established in Sudan and this provided the basis for his eventual advice. He said I was not the kind of Sudanese who should be a political refugee and that he was prepared to write to the chief justice, Abu Rannat, whom he considered a close friend, to tell him that he knew me personally and was sure that any political accusations or suspicions against me were totally unfounded. Most surprisingly, Mr Henderson went on to tell me about the case of Adam von Trott Zu Solz, Verena's father, not realising my connection with the family. He recounted the story of Adam von Trott's return to Germany against the advice of his friends in the United States and Britain, because he felt that Germany was where he belonged. I knew that Adam von Trott had returned, had worked to overthrow Hitler, had eventually been arrested and had been tried and executed.

It was ironic that Henderson should invoke Verena's father's case at a time when Verena was perhaps one of the closest friends on whom I depended for advice and consolation during that difficult period and who often saw similarities between me and her father. I was soon to receive a most moving letter from Verena which stressed the importance of my making an independent assessment and judgement uninfluenced by political and impulsive decisions. She wrote words of great praise for what she regarded as my unique qualities, emphasising reasoning, moderation, consideration, and soundness of judgement. She pleaded with me not to give into the easy temptation of reacting emotionally out of anger; nor should I allow myself to be persuaded by others to take a line of action that was more their own than mine. Somehow, her letter invoked in me the belief that difficult situations presented a challenge and a test for the strength of one's character. It was as though she were on my side giving my individuality both a challenge and a boost to pursue its own course against the distortions of foes and friends alike.

What Mr Henderson wanted to stress was of course not that I should go even if I were to be executed, but rather that I came from a noble and patriotic background which he thought would be compromised by my becoming a political refugee, an understandable but unduly optimistic view of the postcolonial Sudan, which was radically different from the country they had governed. By pledging to clear my name with the chief justice, he eliminated in his mind the possibility of danger, while emphasising the positives of a heroic return. I was of course not persuaded by Mr Henderson, although I did not say so. But Henderson's view of my family gave me an even greater conviction that we did indeed have a bridging role to play in the history of Sudan and that I should not be driven into extremism or factionalism by anger.

It was while I was with Mr Henderson that I met for the first time Sir James Robertson, who, as the civil secretary, had been the architect of the change in Southern Policy which, in 1947 abandoned the separatist trend and led to the independence of Sudan, under a unitary system. As district commissioner of our area in the 1920s, Sir James had known both my grandfather and my father. As we discussed the developments of South-North relations since independence and especially the civil war, Sir James surprised me by saying that he felt personally responsible for the tragedy that had afflicted the country in its South–North relations, for "I should have known that the two peoples were too different to constitute a unitary state." I found myself defending his policy, that unity was an ideal to which people should aspire and that the assumption he had made was that both sides would accommodate one another; there was no way he could have known that they would fail to do so. I doubt that Sir James ever stated publicly what he told me privately, that he regretted his decision over the future of Sudan.

I wrote to William Twining, then dean of the Faculty of Law at Queen's University, Belfast, to inform him of my situation in the hope of receiving some advice and support. William responded promptly. He gave me the names of two professors from Yale Law School in the United States, then visiting professors at the London School of Economics, whom he said were his friends. He asked me to discuss the situation with them quite frankly; he was also writing to them to introduce me and to ask them to get in touch with me. He himself would be in London by a specific date and I should telephone him on the evening of that date. We would then get together and discuss the situation further. He also informed his father about the situation and to expect a call from me.

I received the expected call from Professors Quinton Johnstone, an American, and Robert Stevens, an Englishman with a tenured position at Yale. We met at a corner in the faculty lounge of the London School of Economics. I spoke very frankly and in details about my health situation, the impact on my studies, the political crisis confronting me, and my desire to proceed with graduate studies to the doctoral level. It was Professor Johnstone who asked, "How can you be sure that your worries over your eyes will not reoccur to frustrate your academic performance in the future?" I replied that I felt certain that I had gone beyond the worry and that my objective was to accelerate my academic advancement to achieve appropriate qualifications to be of value, even if I were to lose my sight in the future. He also pointed out that the prognosis of my eye situation was also a consideration, for while I was highly recommended by Professor Twining, and my academic qualifications were not in question, the required medical care and the prospects for the future had to be weighed against the value of my graduate training. Then he said in conclusion that although they were influential at Yale and their recommendations would carry weight, it was very late in the year and even those on the waiting list had been considered and final selection made. The chances of my admission were therefore very slim; they would nevertheless do their best and keep me informed. In the meantime, he advised me to proceed with my plans as though Yale was not a viable alternative.

Ironically, although initially cautious and understated, Quinton Johnstone was to pursue the matter of my admission to Yale with diligence and was to become a source of unfailing support, but with an always sincere and a realistic, almost pessimistic, approach to problems, the type who would overstate a problem to find an appropriate solution. I received several calls from Professor Johnstone to give me an up-to-date information on the chances of my going to Yale. The first gave a glimpse of hope in that I was to fill in an application form and my application would be considered at a forthcoming committee meeting. The second was more optimistic: the committee had met and, despite all the odds against my last minute application, had approved my admission in principle, but wanted assurance that I understood the terms, especially regarding financial arrangements and medical care, and that I accepted them. Essentially, all it meant was that I would receive the amount normally granted to unmarried graduate students which Yale feared I might consider inadequate and that Yale would pay only up to some eighty per cent of the medical bills of any eye operation that I might have. The final decision of the committee would be made on receipt of my response to their conditions. Of course, I accepted their terms which implied that my admission to Yale was virtually assured.

In the meantime, I was toiling with the question of whether I should sit for the LL.M. examination. My eye problem had interfered with my studies during a large part of my first year. In addition, political crises had made it virtually impossible to study during my second year. And yet I saw academic qualifications as a form of licence, a ticket, a membership card into opportunities that I did not know, but hoped existed. I chose Islamic Law and Civil Litigation for exactly the wrong reasons, that they required largely cramming and not such a great volume of reading. I had never been a crammer. I had always depended on logic and reasoning, supplemented by a photographic memory which was never meant to memorise quantities of facts.

I rarely went to Islamic Law classes, where I was mostly bored by mathematical calculations of succession and inheritance. I hardly ever went to the Civil Litigation classes also, for I presumed it was a matter of memorising the formalities of procedures. And when I went, I worried about being called upon and having my utter ignorance exposed. So, I decided to adopt a relaxed attitude towards the whole thing, to attend when the mood required attendance, to keep away when I felt like it, to work on those areas which interested me, and to leave open the question of whether I should sit for the LL.M. examination or not. I decided not to sit if I had the alternative of going to Yale, but to give it a trial if I were not admitted to Yale. And yet, even if I were accepted to Yale, how would I account for the financial help I was receiving? That, together with the possibility that I might pass, made the question worthy of consideration.

I posed the issue to Professor Johnstone. His immediate response was that if I sat and failed, it might be a matter of record which I might find unpleasant; I should perhaps consider avoiding that possibility. Professor Allott, who had kindly recommended me to Yale, was reluctant to advise, saying that he thought it was a matter I should decide for myself. William Twining came after my Yale position was virtually clear. I telephoned him the night he had specified and found his father, Lord Twining, who told me he had heard much about me, not only from his son, but, I learned later, from the committee of the fund that had awarded me the grant and of which he was a member. Lord Twining informed me that William had been delayed for a day but had told them to expect my call. He would call me back the day of his arrival. He did.

We got together in a cafe near Dillon's Bookshop. I filled William in on all the details concerning my eyes, my studies, the recall, the financial support I had received, Yale's admission, the prospects for the future not only in terms of studies but also employment. William listened carefully, now and then posed a question, with much sympathy, understanding and support radiating from him. We even discussed teaching and practising from the point of view of the amount of reading required, bearing in mind the progressive weakening of my eyesight and eventual blindness. He was at once idealistic and practical, which left all the avenues open for speculation. He, of course, had been kept informed by the Yale professors and his father had already mentioned to him about the grant I had received.

While we were discussing mundane problems of my life, immediate and long-term, William suddenly surprised me by saying, "You know, Francis, you ought to write your autobiography." It was a big sound on my ears; I wasn't sure I heard him correctly and if so, what he meant. I must have conveyed that essence in the gestures I made for he quickly added, "I mean it seriously!" And then he tried to say something that sounded so complimentary that we both felt somewhat uncomfortable. By that time, my whole system was melting with a combination of great pleasure, embarrassment, and confusion. I could hardly follow his words. I took William's suggestion as a flattery, perhaps aimed at lifting my spirits under demoralising circumstances. But I took note of it as significant, especially because of the way in which it was said and the sincerity which William radiated as he spoke. But the matter ended at that: positive, relevant, encouraging, but otherwise not to be pursued.

William and I also discussed the prudence of my sitting the examination. His view was that I should take the exam. If I passed, well and good; if I failed, he would be willing to certify that he had made me sit an examination for which I had not prepared. But he also argued that it might in fact be a good thing to sit and fail, for I should not take life as a series of successes and become intolerant of failure. It was Khartoum all over again, except, in Khartoum, Mr Twining was more convinced that I would pass. In London, he probably thought I might pass but also rationalised that failure might also prove a blessing from a negative lesson.

My own feelings were complex, I felt unprepared and would probably fail. But I also thought that for whatever reasons, talent or luck, I might pass. After vacillating between apprehending failure and hoping for success, I eventually decided to proceed along the lines of Twining's advice. Despite my decision, I did not get to the work of preparing for the exam until very close to the examination date. Instead, a coincidence of circumstances filled my life with things to do which in retrospect had a liberating effect on my condition.

Developments in the circles of the Northern Sudanese in England seemed to indicate an increasing disapproval of the way I had been treated. Hassan Omer, a Law Faculty member, then at Oxford, was to write a letter to our colleague and mutual friend, Mohammed el Fateh, in which he strongly condemned the political hysteria that was prevailing within the ruling military junta. He wrote that if I could be suspected of anti-North activities and victimised on account of that, then something was seriously amiss with the government's policy in the South and that it was time for the genuinely patriotic Northerners to appreciate the dangers to national unity posed by that policy. I was moved by the letter and in a way, it was an effective reinforcement of my long-held position of moderation. More reactions were to come from the North. Sayed Mohammed Saleh el Shengeitti, a prominent nationalist and a highly respected political figure in the country, the first speaker of parliament, the most pivotal individual in the shift of the separatist Southern Policy in support of unity, came on a visit to England and learned about the case. He and others undertook to work towards correcting the situation. Beshir Mohammed Said, a prominent journalist and owner of the most influential *Al Ayyam* newspaper, telephoned and invited me to lunch to discuss the situation. He entreated me not to overreact, but to patiently await the results of the efforts which were being exerted by men of good will, including himself. Even the Sudanese Students Union in the United Kingdom, of which I was an executive committee member, met and resolved to write to the authorities to protest my recall and the withdrawal of scholarship. An anti-government attitude among

TRIALS
A Period of Reckoning

the Northerners was clearly evolving over my case and that helped to reinforce my faith in the bridging role of my political stand.

Despite this encouraging development, I was totally taken by surprise when I received a telephone call one day to learn that the military attaché, Colonel Muzamil Ghandour, was on the line. After introducing himself, he suggested that we should meet and talk about the problem, for, he said, "I believe no problem is beyond solution if there is the will and the people are prepared to talk." I told him that I had nothing to hide and that I would be happy to meet with him and talk anytime he suggested. He invited me to lunch in an Indian restaurant where we had a good meal and a long talk. I was extremely relaxed about the whole situation, whether it was because I had gone beyond caring or because I was so sure that the truth was on my side and that the mere fact of talking could only help uncover the truth, I cannot be sure.

Colonel Muzamil Ghandour told me the whole truth which, unveiled him as the source of my entire problem. He said that as soon as he had suspected me for the anti-North activities, he had had me followed everywhere and full reports had been furnished to him about all I had done or said. He said I had gone regularly to Oxford to meet Richard Gray, the professor of History who had written on the Southern Sudan and was sympathetic to the Southern cause, presumably to confer on the strategy. Richard Gray, in fact, lived in London and not in Oxford.

According to the military attaché, I had gone to Richard Owen, the ex-governor of Bahr el Ghazal, whose sympathies for the South were well known, presumably for the same reason. I had indeed visited Richard Owen for Christmas and had a pleasant time. But although he had been the most vocal of the British administrators in support of the cause of the South, and was the one who had tried to return Abyei to Bahr el Ghazal Province, we had not talked politics at all, which I had in fact found rather surprising.

The military attaché alleged further that I had also visited many other places in England supposedly to promote the cause of the South and raise funds for that the struggle. He also said that I had toured Sweden for the whole summer for the same reason of promoting the Southern cause and raising funds. I have already discussed my tour of Sweden during which the issue of Southern Sudan surprisingly never arose. The military attaché also alleged that I had gone to Italy at least twice to confer with the expelled Catholic missionaries and to raise funds. My visits to Italy had been solely to my brother Bol. He also alleged that I had gone to France, Germany and other countries in Europe for the same reasons.

My activities, both in England and on the European continent, had convinced them that I was masterminding the Southern movement in the whole of Western Europe. He said that they had been monitoring every move I had made and had given it a political significance. He even said in jest, "If you raised your hand to scratch your head, our man following you would pull back in fear that you were about to hit him!"

Then he said that while he kept Khartoum closely informed, he frankly had never thought that they would act so foolishly as to order my immediate recall. "They could have waited until you returned normally and then make you to account for your acts. In any case, whatever else I might have suggested they did, I would not have endorsed this stupid action, had they consulted me. As it were, they simply ordered your recall through the office of the cultural attaché."

He went on to say that he had since been hearing a great deal of positive things about me which had begun to raise doubts in his own mind about the accuracy of the reports he had been receiving. He therefore wanted a frank discussion with me to clarify the situation, at least to himself, and to see what could be done in the circumstances to correct the situation.

I listened with absorbing interest to everything he said, not believing my ears at times, laughing at times, but clearly pleased that the whole thing was so ridiculous after all. I told the military attaché the whole story from my point of view, explaining away every area of doubt that his account had raised: my visits to Oxford to meet Lienhardt and not Gray; my cooperation with Lienhardt that took me to Oxford so frequently; the Christmas with Richard Owen, the total lack of reference to the Southern Problem during my stay with Owen, and my suspicion that Owen had wanted to avoid the subject because he had remembered my father's refusal to join the South so that he probably had considered me "Northern" in outlook and had not wanted to embarrass me; the trip to Sweden, both in its background and its outcome; my visits to my brother in Italy; the visit to my German friends; and the detours into France and Holland.

I stressed to the military attaché my opposition to the government policy in the South, my views on the Southern problem, and the approach I had chosen for myself and which entailed a frank and open discussion of the Southern Problem in all circles, Sudanese and foreign alike, as an individual and without involving myself in any organised political movement. I told him that since my secondary school days up to, and through, Khartoum University, I had never made a secret of my political stance on the Southern Problem and that my views were an open book to all those who came in touch with me and cared to hear them or otherwise discussed the problem with me.

Just as I had listened with great interest to his side of the story, so did he to mine. By then, we had clearly established contact and were communicating most effectively and surprisingly with considerable understanding and sympathy for each other's position. His informants were of course grossly wrong about me. They might have been sincere in their mistakes or might have felt it necessary to lie in order to justify whatever they were receiving. He himself was simply doing his duty as he thought it best and was clearly convinced about me. I too held political views that were understandable to him and if I pretended not to entertain such views, it would have been impossible for him to believe or respect me. But none of those views necessarily implied organised political movement or supported the validity of the allegations against me.

Deep into our conversation, the military attaché recalled a Sudanese proverb to the effect that those who have shared a meal must no longer fight. He said he had been completely won to my side, although he had been responsible for my problem. The issue was how to undo the harm he had done. He would do his best, but he suggested that the most effective way of remedying the situation would be for him to try to arrange a meeting between me and President Abboud during his forthcoming official visit to the United Kingdom. That way, they would also test for themselves his new opinion about me.

Several days after my meeting with the military attaché, I returned to The Little House to find Lady King very worried; an officer from Scotland Yard had come, asked for me, and said he would return. None of us had the slightest idea of what the visit was about; I too joined Lady King in worrying. What on earth could it be? I knew I had not committed any offence, at least not that I was aware of. And it had been a long time since the prospects of extradition had been speculated upon and dismissed. In any case, there was now contact between me and the Government of Sudan; they could not try to reconcile with me and at the same time enforce extradition. Nor could extradition be simply a matter of the police coming to tell me to leave the country. Whatever it was, Scotland Yard was a name I associated with "crime" and I had never expected to be sought after by an officer from "Scotland Yard."

The officer came again, this time accompanied by a colleague of his. When they did not find me, they left word that I should go to see them at the Headquarters - Scotland Yard. To get the matter over with, I rushed there at the earliest opportunity specified in the message. I found the whole issue both simple and perplexing. Scotland Yard was concerned about the security of the president of Sudan during his forthcoming visit. They wanted me to assure them that I would do nothing "embarrassing to Her Majesty's Government." I told them the gist of the problem with the Government of Sudan, that I had been wrongly suspected of engaging in an organised political movement in England, but that the officials had realised their misjudgement and were working to correct the situation. In any case, I told them to be assured that I would do nothing against the president of the Sudan, far less embarrass Her Majesty's Government. They did not do anything beyond that relaxed conversation and verbal assurance. But I left both relieved and disturbed; relieved that the matter was after all nothing serious, but disturbed that Scotland Yard would check on me and interrogate me as though I were a potential assassin or criminal. The whole thing seemed absurd and painful, but I decided to dismiss it.

My initial suspicion of Southerners as finding some political advantage in my crisis was confirmed when Lawrence Wol Wol, clearly speaking on behalf of the Southerners and in the presence of Natale Olwak, requested me to lead a demonstration which was being organised against President Abboud by the East African students. According to Lawrence, since most Southern students were government officials on graduate courses, for them to join the demonstration would be risking dismissal and the withdrawal of their scholarships. As for Lawrence himself, since he was permitted into England under the pretext of being a student who would not engage in political activities, for him to join the demonstrations would also be to risk expulsion from Britain and endanger his covert activities in promotion of the Southern cause. I was therefore the only one who had nothing to lose, for I had already refused to obey orders from Khartoum, had lost my scholarship in consequence, and had chosen to be a political refugee.

I was outraged at the attempt to exploit my difficulties unscrupulously and in total disregard to the principles involved in my political stand, which were very well known to them. I restated the obvious, that they were grossly mistaken if they thought I could deviate from my objectives and act out of tune with my character because I had been victimised by the Government of Sudan. My response simply opened the door for a heated and angry discussion of my whole attitude towards the Southern Problem, with Lawrence Wol making incriminating arguments and I becoming even more enraged. He dismissed my pledge to Scotland Yard by stating firmly that they had no right to require such a pledge, that any student was entitled to exercise his political rights of peaceful demonstration. Yet, he maintained that he was in Britain on a student permit and that engaging in political demonstrations might lead to his expulsion; it was a puzzling contradiction.

Natale Olwak on the other hand sat through the discussion, quiet, solemn, head bent down, occasionally biting his lips, obviously very uncomfortable with the whole situation, because he had probably given each one of us a reason to believe that he might be on our side. He avoided taking a position, but made it rather obvious that Lawrence Wol should not expect me to do what I did not want to do, thereby hoping to give the impression to me that he appreciated my point of view and to Lawrence that I was not committed to play such a role.

We parted that day after having decided to put the subject aside and turn to something else about which we could smile. But our differences had clearly sharpened and seemed impossible to bridge, not because I disagreed with whatever they were doing in the interest of the South, but because I felt they were totally incapable of seeing my point of view or appreciating my role in the struggle. I resigned myself to the confidence of my own convictions and loyalty for the South and dismissed them as people who could not reach the depth of my conviction, which was in itself the result of a long chain of experiences, some due to the geo-political location of my family and tribe between South and North, some being the outcome of personal experiences in Southern and Northern academic institutions, and some being the result of my own personality. Reinforced with that faith in my individuality and my undoubted commitment to the ultimate interest of our people as I saw it, I remained very much at peace with my line of approach, even though I deeply regretted our failure to communicate and appreciate each other's position.

About a week before President Ibrahim Abboud's arrival, I was once again visited by officers from Scotland Yard and I soon discovered that all the other Southerners in London had also been contacted. Essentially, they let us know that our names had been given them by the Sudan embassy as among the people who posed a potential threat to the president during his visit. They talked to us individually and requested us to sign an undertaking that we would neither harm the president nor act in any manner that was politically hostile during his visit. What we did before or after was not really their concern; they were simply keen on the visit not to be negatively affected by anything we might do. The same embassy which was trying to arrange a meeting between me and the president was giving my name as one of the people who posed a potential threat to the security of the Sudanese head of state. How paradoxical!

President Abboud came and the appointment for me to meet him was made. I received the word to that effect from Muzamil Ghandour, the military attaché, who received me and escorted me to Talat Fareed, the minister for Education, who would then introduce me to President Abboud after the initial discussion of the situation. Talat Fareed greeted me very warmly and offered me a cup of tea. We were then alone in the room. As we sipped tea, we engaged in an informal friendly conversation about matters not related to my problem. They had just been to China on an official visit and I asked him how they had found China. Talat spoke very positively about China, the organisation, the spirit of the people, their hard work, their enthusiasm, and the progress they had made, at one point, he remarked, "If that is Communism, then we ought to welcome Communism." Now feeling relaxed and almost uninhibited with him, I said spontaneously, "But did you think the people were free?" "Free?" he shot back at me. "What do they need freedom for when they are so happy?" I must have just laughed.

Then he made a remark, which like the one he had just made, was typical of him: "You seem like such a nice person, why did you do what you did?" I laughed and could not help saying, "What did I do, Mr Minister?" "I mean your activities against the government!" The knowledge that I had acquired from Muzamil about the suspicions and accusations against me gave me the upper hand. I told Talat what I had told Muzamil, with the advantage of rehearsal and repetition. I emphasised the fact that my position on the government policy on the South was not a secret and that I would be delighted to make it known to whomever cared to know.

Then I went on to draw a distinction between my own views on the government policy, my own way of making my views known, and the allegations of my involvement in an organised political movement. While emphasising that I was not a member of any organised movement, I also stressed that I was not in agreement with the policy of the government over the South, but that this was very different from leading an organised opposition movement abroad. From the start, Talat Fareed appeared to be rather conciliatory towards me. I knew a great deal had to do with whatever Muzamil had said to correct the picture, but the chemistry of our interaction was also helpful.

With conviction and seeming faith in the justice system, Talat Fareed still argued that I should have gone to Sudan, defended myself against the accusations, and returned free to pursue my studies. He said that as a military man, what had offended him the most was my disregard to orders; that had angered him even more than the subversive activities which I had been reported to have engaged in. The minister then summarised his position. He said he could see in me and in my words that I was an honest man. He believed that I had been wrongly accused of subversion and anti-government activities. His main problem was how to convince his colleagues about me in the first place and persuade them to withdraw a decision which had been reached by the council of ministers. But he said all that would simply be a matter of procedure and time. Then he said the president wanted to see me. As a word of advice, he asked me not to get into the unnecessary details of saying I did not agree with their Southern policy. "All that you need to say is that you did not do what you are alleged to have done."

So, he got up to join President Abboud and then sent word for me to go to the president. President Abboud received me very warmly while Talat explained that I was the Southern student who had been alleged to have led anti-government activities in Europe. It seemed to take a little while for the case to crystalise in Abboud's mind. That is when he said to Talat, "Do you know that he is the son of our brother, Chief Deng Majok? In fact, just before I left, his father sent me a message asking me to look into the case of his son in England. Until then, I had not been aware that the student about whom we had talked was Deng Majok's son. Now that I see him, he is clearly his father's son, both from his looks and from the way he speaks. Sit down, my son". Abboud then offered me something to drink and proceeded with a flow of nice sentiments and a humane air that truly typified the qualities of a Sudanese elderly statesman. Talat proceeded to summarise his own findings about the case and the fact that I had been erroneously accused, adding his own impression that he did not think I had done what I had been accused of having done.

Displaying a degree of cordial impatience with the explanation, President Abboud said, almost interrupting Minister Talat Fareed, "His father is a great patriot. He is one of the leaders of Sudan most committed to national unity and to the service of the country. Even if his son had done the things he is said to have done, for the sake of his father, let us forget it all. It is clear that he is his father's son. Even the way he smiles is his father's." After a brief exchange of polite, friendly, and patriotic remarks on all sides, the president gave us permission to leave, saying "Go with your Uncle Talat to work out the details. All is well! Let us forget the past. Just discuss the details with Talat as your uncle, not as the minister."

That was of course not my first time to meet President Abboud, for, as will be recalled, we had met during our study tour in Germany when he had also displayed considerable warmth and had been lavish in his praise of my father. Now that I saw him even more closely, I could easily see that there was a great deal to the generally held view that his dictatorship did not reflect his personality as much as it was a reflection of the personalities of a number of his subordinate clique, military officers who were the effective dictators under his umbrella.

After the president's return to Sudan, I received a letter from my father saying that he had met President Ibrahim Abboud after his visit to London, that he had been promised that all charges against me would be dropped on account of my father's loyalty to the country, that I must promise him not to engage in any political activity, that I should watch his own steps at home and follow suit, and that I should pass the message on to Bol to do the same. He asked me to write to him at the earliest possible opportunity to assure him that I was acting in line with his directives.

It was very rare for my father to write to his sons. In fact, I don't remember ever receiving a letter from him before the one that called me the High Dam of the Dinka. This was the second, and like the first, it touched me enormously, not so much for what it said, as for the mere fact that it had been written and sent. Nevertheless, it angered me because I felt betrayed by the president or whomever had transmitted the message to my father. I had been of the opinion that the government had realised its misjudgement of me and that it was correcting itself by undoing all that had been done on the wrong premise. Now, I was being told that I had in effect been "pardoned" on account of my father. I realised, however, that President Abboud must have said something courteous to my father about their change of position. To me he had said that the matter should be dismissed even if I had done what I was said to have done. To my father he had probably said that I had done what I was accused of having done, but had been forgiven on account of my father. One made me innocent; the other made me guilty but pardoned. I felt reasonably sure that the president did not fully realise the distinction and that in both cases he had acted in good faith. But I felt the difference to be very significant. Anyway, I never responded to my father's letter.

Word eventually came from Khartoum giving the final signal for the restoration of my status and approving resumption of my monthly entitlements with back payments to be fully affected, which Talat Fareed, with characteristic humour had called forced saving. As soon as I received the money, I repaid all the grant money I had received through the help of Mary Trevelyan and got a very appreciative response from the foundation.

Now that the situation with the Government of Sudan was fully normalised, the alternatives in front of me seemed considerably improved but by no means simple. I could pursue my original request for extension, even leading to a doctoral programme, and decide to remain in London instead of proceeding to Yale. Going to Yale for me was a new horizon fraught with risks, some foreseeable, others still part of the mystery about the United States. If Khartoum were to approve my request for continuation in London, it would be morally wrong and indeed disloyal to disregard my commitment to them and proceed to Yale. Yet, there was something exciting about adventuring new horizons and despite all that I had heard about racial problems in the United States and my long-held prejudices on account of that, I had come to know a number of Americans, both in Khartoum and abroad, who had influenced my view of their country very positively. Indeed, fears of racial prejudice among the Americans had ceased to be a matter of concern to me. So, I found the prospect of going to Yale to be quite appealing.

To clear my conscience, I wrote to Khartoum once more suggesting three alternatives: to grant an extension for both master's and doctoral degrees in London, grant me study leave with my salary to continue graduate studies on the Yale scholarship, or grant me leave without pay, salary or scholarship. This last option essentially meant abiding by our employment commitment with one another and retaining my seniority. I received a letter rejecting my request and explaining that I would have to relinquish my position on the Faculty of Law if I wanted to proceed for graduate studies at Yale. I could then reapply after completing my studies and my application would be considered on its merits as a new application. I decided to proceed to Yale, implicitly opting for the last alternative, but without responding to Khartoum University in writing.

The examination came and went rather smoothly, with me feeling vague about the whole thing. I could not tell whether the exam had been easy or difficult or even how I had performed. I was surprisingly "cool" about the whole thing, which raised in my mind the possibility that I might prove my theory correct: that the less knowledgeable one is the less self-effacing one is likely to be. From experience, I had found out that scrutinising one's performance and discovering one's mistakes after an exam often reflected the degree to which one had prepared and was knowledgeable.

Some days before my planned departure for the United States, I was having lunch at Soho with an English friend when a lady came from behind us and said, "Excuse me, I was not eavesdropping, but did I hear you say you are going to Yale?" "Yes", I said. "Well, we are from Yale," she continued. "My husband is professor of Medicine at Yale Medical School." Milton Senn was his name. We exchanged pleasant sentiments about the coincidence and made quick acquaintance. In the end, the Senns gave me their address and offered to meet me and put me up in their house until alternative accommodation was made by the Law School. They were leaving that night, but before they left, they dropped me a line repeating their invitation. I sent off a response immediately, once more expressing appreciation for their warm approach, letting them know that accommodation had already been reserved for me at the Law School, and that I would get in touch with them as soon as I arrived at Yale.

Lady King told me that she had been so happy with me as a paying guest that she would welcome any Sudanese I would recommend to take my place on the same terms. Lawrence Wol was interested and I recommended him. Because I felt that Lady King's house had become for me a second home and because the person succeeding me was a fellow countryman, indeed a fellow tribesman, I thought it would be better to minimise my weight by leaving most of my belongings there, including my correspondence, my diaries, my notebooks, and my entire library. After attending the auspicious annual dinner of the Goats' Club, where I spoke on behalf of the outgoing Goats, and giving my own farewell party to say goodbye to my many friends, it was at last time to leave England.

I would like to end this chapter on my time in England with a comment on another member of the Goats Club, Barbara Anderson, a tall, warm, smiling, and very dignified medical student, whom I got to know and who became one of my closest friends. I frequently socialized with Barbara and her friend Brenda, who was also studying medicine. I was deeply moved when I recently received a message from Barbara in response to my request for a photograph of hers to include in the book. She wrote, "I am very touched and honoured that you would like to include me in *The Invisible Bridge*. This, surely, will be an important book for future generations. Your life has been almost unique in the huge spanning of cultures – an era that could never be repeated. You have reminded me of Goats days!! Do you remember, I think it must have been 1964, when, at the end of term dinner, you proposed a toast to leaving Goats and I responded to it? I also remember going to occasional concerts at the open air theatre at Kenwood in North London — you, me, Natale and a medical student friend of mine who I was sharing a flat with, Brenda. (Bren is now a grandmother and I am godmother to her daughter). Barbara's brother, Andrew, developed the negative of the only available photograph of my grandfather, Chief Kwol Arob, K.D.D. Henderson had given me, and also enlarged the photograph of my father with Bishop Baroni of Khartoum. These two photographs have now spread widely and have been included in several of my books. As a physician, Barbara later accompanied Mary Trevelyan on a visit to South Sudan and both became close friends of more individual South Sudanese. In her message, Barbara included a photograph of herself with Mary Trevelyan, Abel Alier, Natale Olwak and Peter Gatkwoth "when we came to Sudan to celebrate the 2nd anniversary of 'Unity Day' in 1974. You were the key person in inviting Mary Trevelyan and me as her medical escort. That was a truly memorable visit". And so was my time in the United Kingdom from 1962 to 1964, when I left for the United States. .

Barbara Anderson, Author's friend in London, was a student of Medicine in London University.

INVISIBLE BRIDGE
An African Journey through Cultures

As I left by Alitalia for New York, I felt I was leaving behind two years loaded with experiences, both negative and positive. It was a period during which I had suffered much, but had also grown and emerged somewhat traumatised, yet largely unscathed. And now I was entering a new phase with a new page and a new challenge. The objectives ahead were rather vague and cloudy, but I was determined to make use of the new opportunity, to give meaning to my life, to be of some value not only to myself, but hopefully to my people at home and perhaps to humanity. The precise form, the method, and the nature of the end result were part of the mystery of the future that made the undertaking adventurous and exciting.

March 1974. Natale Olwok, Abel Alier, Barbara Anderson, Mary Trevelyan, and Peter Gatkuoth, in Juba during the second anniversary of the 1972 Addis Ababa Agreement.

CHAPTER FOURTEEN

SALVATION
IN THE LAND OF REFUGE

Although my problems with the Government of Sudan were now resolved and I was no longer technically threatened with political refuge, there was something refugee-like in my leaving behind all the traumas of London and opening a new page which would determine much of the meaning of my future. In a peculiar sort of way, all my earlier prejudices against the United States on account of racial problems and cowboy type violence and coarseness suddenly vanished as I speculated on the opportunities of self-realisation. My emphasis suddenly changed to an anticipation of a continent where technological advancement had transformed nature with monumental symbols of humankind's capacity and achievement. I recalled a concluding line of a film about the United States which I had seen when I was a student at Rumbek Junior Secondary School: "New York: a wonderful city." New York and its wonders symbolised the United States in my expectations. But I had already been warned that New York, like all big cities, did not really represent the United States.

Some American friends in London had advised me to proceed to

New Haven straight and then return to visit New York after having first seen something else of the United States. Nevertheless, I felt sure that the technology that had built the skyscrapers had affected the whole of the United States in a way that was splendid and pervasive. My only concern, which was quite faint and remote, was whether the Americans, being extremely allergic to Communism, would hold my high school days' sympathies for Communism against me. Those sympathies had long vanished, but I did not expect the Americans to be reasonable on the subject. Otherwise, I approached the United States with a positive frame of mind that sharply contrasted with my past outlook and I felt almost intuitively that my last chance in life was to make this new adventure a success and a key to the realisation of the hidden meaning of my life. The attitude of the immigration authorities at John F Kennedy International Airport was reassuring. The immigration officer looked at my papers and remarked, quite casually, "Yale Law School! Do you realise that you are going to our best law school?" He spoke in a friendly manner which I appreciated as a welcoming gesture. I am smiled with satisfaction. Having cleared the customs, I got onto a bus for New York Grand Central Station where I took the train to New Haven.

It was late afternoon and it was rapidly getting dark so that I could not see much of the countryside as we rode to New Haven. I had written to Joe and Margo Onek, American friends who had been fellow members of the Goats' Club in London. They were now at Yale, Joe studying Law and Margo Medicine. Once I got to New Haven, I telephoned them at the station and Joe drove over to take me to the Law School dorm. Joe knew my room number and my roommate who was expecting me that evening. My roommate opened the door and introduced himself in a mid-Western accent that struck me then as very American. Alan Cullison was his name. Al soon revealed his kindness and generosity by offering me bedsheets, pillow cases, a towel and a soap, all of which had to be obtained privately. As it was late, we did not have much time to talk and in any case, Al was a shy person, not at all prone to initiating conversation with strangers. But the following morning, we sat and made each other's acquaintance over the coffee that Al had made.

SALVATION
In the Land of Refuge

A few days later, a reception was organised by the foreign students' association to introduce the students to one another and also to provide an opportunity for meeting host families. It was a late afternoon garden party, in which people met casually and without introduction. I was standing with a group of people engaged in a light conversation when a man, probably in his forties, walked over and joined us. He smoked a pipe, and had a cool, understated but effective sense of humour. I do not remember precisely what he said by way of introduction, but he conveyed to me in a joking manner that he was my host and was there to look for me. His name was Jim Glassman. I reciprocated with a joke, and our first contact was marked with jokes and laughter, a delightful way of suddenly becoming not only host and guest, but friends. After conversing with us for some time, Jim took leave, saying he would be back. He soon returned to say I was invited to dinner in their house the following day.

Jim was in the shoe business, and, judging from his house and his lifestyle, must have been doing well. The Glassman residence was in a fashionable part of what was in effect a border spot between New Haven and Hamden. It was a rather large three-storey house on a sizeable plot of land that surrounded the house with attractively spacious grounds. The house itself was charming and spacious. My favourite spot was an impressive two-way glass-doored fireplace separating a good size living room from a cozy sunny library. By American standards, the Glassman family was sizeable. with four children, two sons and two daughters. Peter and Andy were teenagers in high school, Nancy was about ten and Sally was a few years younger. Their mother, Jane, was an attractive lady of great charm and intellectual stimulation. I was to learn later that she had been a bright student, had graduated with a distinction from William's College, had been admitted to graduate studies at Harvard University, but had to abandon her plans to get married and raise a family.

The Glassmans received me with warmth, friendliness, and hospitality. From our first encounter, it was obvious that they intended to draw me close to them. I took an immediate liking to all of them. I do not recall fully what subjects we talked about that night, except that they were both serious and light-spirited. We touched on my experiences in England not only from the political point of view, but also from the angle of my eye problem. It was in that context that I was casually informed of Jane's mastectomy. Although it never showed in her sprightly personality, she was suffering from cancer. At the time, cancer did not mean much to me, nor did I have any idea of the nature of the operation Jane had had. But there was a solemnness in the casual way they spoke about her case and the sympathy I felt from her about my eyes was already that of a person who knew the pain of affliction with a serious disease. This, as much as shared views on political issues, must have contributed towards the strong sense of mutual understanding that seemed to spring up between us from the moment of contact.

The story of how I came to be a guest student of the Glassmans was rather amusing. For a number of years, the Glassmans had Japanese guest students with the last student introducing the next, thereby maintaining a continuous flow of Japanese. Then they decided to broaden their horizon beyond one nationality. So, they requested the International Students Office to assign them a national of another country. They were assigned an Arab Muslim student; I believe from Egypt. Concerned about potential religious and political problems, they declined the student, explaining that as they were Jewish, the situation might be difficult and embarrassing to both sides. They were told that there were no more students to be assigned, but that they would be placed on the waiting list, in case a suitable student turned up. About half an hour after the conversation, the office called to report that they had an African candidate from Sudan by the name of Francis Deng. The Glassmans gratefully accepted the assignment, not knowing anything about Sudan beyond being in Africa. They then rushed to a copy of an encyclopedia only to learn that Sudan was an Arab country. Surprised and disturbed, but too embarrassed to complain again, they accepted their fate and waited for me with apprehension. So, when I turned up clearly an African, blacker than anyone they had ever seen, a Christian, and with my people at war with the Arabs, it was certainly a pleasant surprise to the Glassmans, as their expectation of an Arab had been a source of some anxiety.

SALVATION
In the Land of Refuge

From the time of my arrival at Yale, the most preoccupying issue for me and my sponsors was the problem of my eyes and the need for the best care available at Yale. Here, Professor Senn proved to have been a most appropriate contact. After inviting me to dinner, he soon made an appointment for me to see the top man in the field. Later, when I saw the attitude of the ophthalmologist to be impersonal and lacking individual attention, very much the same experience with the first ophthalmologist I had in England, I complained to Professor Senn and he soon sent me to Dr Philips, another specialist on glaucoma, who was then associate professor in a second position to the specialist I had turned down. Dr Philips proved well suited to my personality as a patient and he also happened to develop a more optimistic outlook in me. Nonetheless, I remained pragmatic in assuming that the worse would probably be the eventuality and that I should prepare myself psychologically and practically. Professor Senn seemed to share my approach and even suggested that I should train myself in the use of dictation machines.

The news of the result of the London examination eventually came. I had failed Islamic Law and Civil Procedure, had just passed Jurisprudence, and was top in African Law, but the gist of it all was that I had failed my LL.M examination. The news was of course not altogether unexpected, and yet it came like a bomb-shell. Knowing the attitudes in the Sudan and indeed Anglophone Africa, England was the place to look to for higher education abroad. Just as success to obtain an English degree was considered prestigious, so was failure likely to be viewed as degrading and humiliating. And why did I allow myself to ever face such a prospect when the problem was not one of lacking intelligence? Why did I ever listen to Professor Twining's advice that I should sit the examination and risk the failure? Now that I had failed, what would be the use of a letter from him to explain that he had indeed urged me to sit unprepared? Was it even necessary to contemplate such a letter: To whom would it be addressed and towards what objective? How would I ever face my people in Sudan with the stained mark of a failure? How would Yale view me as someone who had failed to obtain a degree from London? In particular, had not Professor

Johnstone warned me against the possible damage of such a record? Even socially, when asked about my period in England, what could I point out as the outcome? Would I have to admit that I had failed to obtain the intended degree or would I brag as I understood some Asians and Africans did about being a "London Degree Dropout?"

The immediate instinct was to work towards achieving that which I had failed to achieve. I wrote to Professor Allott that my failure had motivated me more than ever before to work for a London degree and that I would appreciate his assistance towards preparing for a master's degree from London alongside my work at Yale. I never received a response from Professor Allott and I soon accepted that my letter was probably viewed as a spontaneous and an understandable reaction of a disappointed student that did not need serious consideration. After all, every person who fails an examination has some reason to give for the failure and people have learned to take reasons as nothing but ego cushions for students to fall back on and be patted for their failures. I felt immersed in agony and self pity.

In my loneliness and agony, I found solace from Joan Baez in one of her classic albums of folksongs which included old English ballads with lyrics full of tragedy, compassion, and the challenge of ultimate triumph, despite everything else. I found in the lyrics the strength of the unbeatable spirit of human's destiny. But above all was the music of Joan Baez itself, her guitar and even more, her voice which was tender yet forceful, compassionate yet objective, so deep in history yet so present and relevant. She was able to bring together a complex of positives and negatives in the three situations with which I was identified: first, the United States, where I was immersed in a mournful mood, but with some promise of a brighter, challenging, though yet unknown future; second, England, where I had just suffered a series of grave misfortunes in health, politics and now academics, but for which I felt a sense of historical association from the colonial past and in education, and which was in many ways closer to home and, therefore, a form of a second home; and third, Sudan, my homeland, which was not only far geographically speaking, but from which I had been sentimentally separated by reasons of mistreatment that remained bitter, despite some correction, and about which future corrections seemed tenuous and doubtful.

After a brief holiday in the Caribbean, the Glassmans returned with an album of Caribbean folk songs that were also ballads about old England. The music, the words, the voices, the rhythm of those songs were all magic to me and the focal point was again the strong sentimental or romantic association with memory. It was the memory of England that was prime in my nostalgic association, and yet there was a somewhat undefined linkage with my background and a vague notion of sweet home, despite the pains and sorrows the memories of both England and home invoked in me because of the misfortunes that had plagued my life since I had set foot in England. The song "Island in the Sun," which was on the Caribbean album and which Harry Belafonte also sang magically, was a direct expression of the home component involved in the complex sensation I am attempting to describe.

Having assimilated my thoughts and pains into the catharsis of music and songs, especially of Joan Baez, and having developed wider and closer relations around New Haven, the misfortune of the London failure began to ebb and recede into the darker corners of my psyche, surfacing in sleep as nightmares, or lingering on in a faint consciousness of a recent, but awesome past that I decided to discard; instead, I was determined to open a new page at Yale, in New Haven, and in the United States of America. The result was that I withdrew from most of my British connections. Lady King was to complain not only to me in letters but to Lawrence Wol about lack of news from me, concluding: "Oh, Francis, he is always surrounded with too many new friends to remember old friends," at least so wrote Lawrence Wol who accused me of breaking Lady King's heart. But somehow, I needed everything to help me forget what I had gone through in England, and above all, the failure.

Hilary Logali, who had been in the final year at Rumbek Senior Secondary School while I was in my first year of Rumbek Junior Secondary, was also at Yale, working for a master's degree in economics. He lived in a single room at the Graduate Hall across the street from the Law School. Hilary visited me frequently and in due course with my roommate, Al Cullison, we became a circle of three very close friends.

Developments in the Sudan soon brought about dramatic changes. On October 21, 1964, a popular uprising erupted against the Abboud regime which soon resulted in the overthrow of the military dictatorship. An interim government was established under the leadership of Sirr el Khatim el Khalifa, an educationalist with considerable experience in Southern Sudan, a long-time friend of the South, and a sympathiser with the Southern cause. Prominent Southerners and fighters for the cause joined his government and very soon the attitude over the Southern problem had shifted from confrontation to negotiation. Three months after the overthrow of the military regime, the transitional government convened a Round Table Conference that brought together the Northern and Southern political parties, as well as the leaders of the armed insurgency headed by SANU. Hilary Logali was invited to attend the conference.

The interim government of prime minister Sirr el Khatim el Khalifa led the country through elections which returned to power a coalition of traditional parties. Mohammed Ahmed Mahgoub, the new prime minister, adopted a hardline policy towards the South. In implementation of his policy, about 1,499 persons were killed in Juba on the night of July 9, 1965. Two days later, 76 government officials in Wau were massacred at a wedding party. Carroll Brewster, who had provided legal expertise to the attorney general in Sudan and was now back in New Haven and associated with the Law School, telephoned to inform me and proceeded to read from the Southern newspaper, *The Vigilant,* some of the names of those killed. One after another, they were colleagues, friends and relatives, people who had been very close to me. When eventually the list came to people like Joseph Lok Aguek, a colleague from the Tonj Elementary School to Tonj Intermediate School, Salvatore Mawien Ariik, my room prefect and friend at Tonj, Lino Ayong, a first cousin, and Mekki (Miyar) Deng, my half-brother. I slammed down the receiver as I could no longer contain myself.

Alongside my academic work at Yale, one of the most determining elements of my education in America were people. Our room became the meeting place of many students, Africans and Americans alike, graduates and undergraduates, former Peace Corps volunteers with African experience and those interested in African studies, and many others we came to know as individuals and who became friends. But by far the most significant relationship I had at Yale was with the Glassmans. From the first encounter with Jim to the delightful dinner with the family, the relationship continued to grow. I soon became a familiar face in the Glassman household, whether for the daily family dinners or for special parties. Both Jim and Jane loved to entertain. I was invited along with them to social functions with their friends. We drove around Connecticut sightseeing and visiting homes of historic architectural or artistic value. We went to the folk festival in Newport, Rhode Island, attended concerts by Ray Charles, Harry Belafonte (with Miriam Makeba) and Bob Dylan. We went to the theatre both in New Haven and New York. We visited Washington D.C. where Izzeldine Hassan, an old friend and colleague from Khartoum University, was studying for an LL.M. degree at Howard University.

In due course, I was seeing the Glassmans on virtually a daily basis and it is simply impossible to attempt a summary of things we did together. They even hosted a Sudanese weekend, attended by the cultural attaché from Washington, Mutawakil el Amin, and Izzeldine Hassan, and a number of other Sudanese, including the Sudanese folk singer, Hamza Alladin, who performed very successfully. Jane and I became particularly close. I found her socially and intellectually stimulating and engaging; defying cancer with an enchanting zest for life. Initially, I could not believe that she was the mother of her children. And this was not only because of her looking so much younger than her age, but largely because of her youthful spirit. She would talk, and act, and play, and sing, and dance, and sled just like a little girl.

That went a long way in cutting down the age difference between us. Jane became progressively involved in my work, contributing invaluable editorial assistance on my papers, and otherwise playing the constructive role of a critic and a sounding board. When she died eight years later, her contribution to my work was one of the highlights in the Rabbi's eulogy, and he did have a great deal to say about the incredible Jane as a mother, a wife, a humanist, and an intellectual. My first book, the result of my doctoral dissertation and years of academic preoccupation, is dedicated to Jane Glassman, jointly with my parents.

I do not recall exactly when Jane's grandmother, Mrs Ginns, first visited. She was then 94, a tiny old lady who was still surprisingly alert, sharp, and very articulate. I had long and informative conversations with Mrs Ginns. She told me her exciting personal story and that of her family, including their struggles as immigrant Russian Jews amidst prejudices, and the way they supported one another to make a breakthrough economically. She spoke of her community efforts among the Jews, their help to the blacks, and the development of Black-Jewish relationships in their community. I encouraged Mrs Ginns to put her memories on record as she was a living history; she was both flattered and challenged by that, for she was by no means a modest lady.

Mrs Ginns visited again a year later. I made myself again available for long conversations with her. Suddenly, she surprised me by saying, "Francis, I am willing to bet you that you will never return to your country." "Why?" I queried in a joking tone. "Because it is obvious that you like it here," she replied. "I think you like the American way of life and the good things it has to offer. I don't think you will give them up to go back to Africa." I took her judgement in light spirit and told her that I was willing to bet high so that I would use the money I would win from her to improve my living conditions in Sudan to make it possible to go back. I admired her too much to be offended by her condescension about Africa and her skepticism about the extent of my commitment to my country.

My first opportunity to return to Africa came through the conference planned to be held in Ibadan, Nigeria, on the Concept of High God in Africa, to which I had been invited on the recommendation of the leading Oxford anthropologists, Professor Evans-Pritchard and Dr Godfrey Lienhardt. I was requested to prepare a paper and I chose the topic of the Impact of Alien Religions on the Dinka. The preparation of the paper had an effect somewhat comparable to working on the songs or on the cross-cultural essays, following my visit to Sweden, with the exception that I had to do a great deal of library research for the paper on religion. That itself was a source of both pleasure and stress. I went back into the early nineteenth century world of missionaries and travellers, treading the sacred soil of our ancestors and working to mould our spiritual outlook into their image in competition with the Muslims. Both sets of aliens not only took our forebears as heathens, who needed to be delivered from evil, but by implication, assumed a spiritual vacuum that they felt had to be filled. As the deadline approached, I worked for long hours late into the night, resuming early in the morning, with Al as both my editor and typist. It was one of the times when Al unmistakably established his selflessness and dedication to the service of a friend. At least once, we worked right through the night without sleep, enjoying the challenge and suffering the strains of working under pressure.

The Nigerian experience was pleasant. It was my first time in the country and after having been in Europe and the United States for years, it was almost like a return to my own country. Both the conference and the social functions were most entertaining and enjoyable. I was not only the youngest person at the conference, I was also the only non-specialist on the subject, all the rest being theologians, academic clergymen, and social anthropologists of considerable scholarly reputation and experience, nearly all from the United States, the United Kingdom and Nigeria. But I was not intimidated because I felt, if anything at all, my age and the fact that I was a lawyer and not an expert on the subject gave me a distinctive status and won admiration for the perspective I was contributing. Because of the high level of participation and because the conference was under the auspices of the vice chancellor of the University of Ife, then still located in Ibadan, a great deal of attention was given to the comfort and enjoyment of the contributors. The ruggedness of the surroundings of the otherwise comfortable hotel and the brightness of the sun made the return to Africa excitingly real.

I came back from Nigeria through England and made a surprise visit to Lady King, a bundle of flowers in my hands, together with gifts of artefacts from Nigeria. Lady King was exhilarated, crying with joy at seeing "My dearest Francis." But it was then that I got a shock of my life. As will be recalled, I had gone to the United States, leaving in Lady King's house all the belongings I would not need urgently, including my entire library, my diaries, and notebooks, my tape recorder, tapes and records, and all the correspondence I had received during the two years I had spent in England.

Later, while in the United States, I had requested and received a few of the law and anthropology books I thought I might need and otherwise left everything else still in Lady King's house. All those things had vanished, never to be found again. Lady King admitted to burning my letters and notebooks, thinking I did not want them anymore. Lawrence however intimated to me that Lady King had become addicted to gambling and had sold the tape recorder and my books. Whether all this happened because Lady King was becoming senile, which she was, or whether it was because she was in desperate need for money, which Lawrence intimated to me to be the case, or whether it was because she had been nursing some grievance against me for not keeping close contact, which I could somehow understand, or against Lawrence Wol, which I suspected from what he had said, and chose to express her hostility by disposing of my valued objects - I was never able to determine. The loss was impossible to value and the pain beyond description. All the documentation of my life through a most critical period had gone forever. On my part, this was to give me an ambivalence towards Lady King which virtually obliterated the sentiments of appreciation, gratitude, indeed affection that I had felt for her. I was to minimise, and over the years terminate, all contacts with her because they reminded me of the tragedy of the loss with which she had inflicted on me and for reasons I could not understand.

Back at Yale, my work was going through a critical phase during which Quinton Johnstone proved to be both a constructive critic and a source of reliable support. On his recommendation and facilitation, Professor Harold Lasswell undertook to supervise my work for the J.S.D., but of course I first had to obtain the LL.M degree and be admitted to the doctoral programme, hoping that it would come with financial support, both of which would depend on my performance. Although Professor Johnstone always had encouraging and even flattering things to say about me, he impressed upon me in no flattering terms that far from taking the outcome for granted, I would have to work harder to prove that I would be able to meet the doctoral requirements. While he himself maintained that he did not doubt my abilities, there were skeptics who wondered about the feasibility of the project which they regarded as quite ambitious and the material available at Yale perhaps inadequate. I would have to persuade those skeptics that I was up to the task and that there were enough data both in my possession and in the various Yale libraries to substantiate a thesis.

The immediate test was of course the work for the LL.M. It now became absolutely important that I had to concentrate on completing my papers and meeting the deadlines. But as I said, our suite was the common room for many students and since we provided coffee and other refreshments, it became an alternative place for coffee breaks. Al and I eventually felt that it was endangering our own work which we conducted mostly in the room. Towards the end, as we were feeling pushed with the preparation of term papers, Sally Glassman offered what seemed the solution. She designed a notice which I was to place on my door, saying, "I must produce or perish." Even that proved futile. The reaction of two of my African colleagues, Sam Asante and Sam Gyando, was amusingly illustrative. Asante saw the note, but knocked all the same, and when let in, said "Obviously you do not include me in this." Gyando did the same, saying, "I love this because it assures me that you are in!" How could one quarrel with such friendly attitudes? I had to do my best under those conditions.

Despite the distractions, all my papers were completed and submitted in time, the last-minute struggle being the crucial paper which was to lay the foundation for the J.S.D. dissertation. As it had to be submitted before a certain date in order to be graded and considered by the Graduate Committee for both the LL.M. degree and the admission to the J.S.D. programme, Jane Glassman and I worked day and night, and even solicited Jim's assistance in proof-reading during the final hours of the deadline. Professor Johnstone's outlook had developed into one of cautious optimism. He now thought I had considerable support in the faculty and that as long as all my papers were in on time, I stood a good chance of admission to the J.S.D. programme with financial support. When the results were out and I had been awarded the LL.M. and admitted to the J.S.D. programme, Quinton Johnstone was to inform me that my admission had been unanimously approved. My committee, as predetermined, was to be chaired by Professor Harold Lasswell with the membership of Johnstone and Robert Stevens. But later, Professor Stevens was to excuse himself from the supervision, although he agreed to be one of the readers. Mary Alan Caldwell became the third member of the committee.

My success for the LL.M. degree and acceptance to the doctoral programme was a great triumph, as I felt that only a doctorate could remedy my London fiasco. I was later to receive a letter of congratulations from Lawrence Wol who was then in East Africa, reminding me that I would be the first Southern Sudanese in history to obtain a doctorate in any subject and that the distinction carried with it special responsibilities for the guidance and leadership of our people in the South. Coming from Lawrence Wol, who had been so critical of my role over the South, this was a welcome and most appreciated courtesy. It is so easy to forget; for it was not until recently, when I came across Lawrence Wol's letter that I remembered being the first Southern Sudanese to obtain a doctorate in any subject. The Glassmans celebrated my LL.M degree and admission to the J.S.D. candidacy with a party to which they invited my colleagues and faculty members. I then went with them for a relaxing holiday in Maine.

Shortly after I had been admitted to the doctoral programme, William Twining arrived in June 1965 as a visiting professor, expecting to remain at Yale until December. As might be expected, with both his own interest in my work and Yale's need for his expertise in Jurisprudence and African Law, he was asked to help develop the approach. A precise topic for the thesis had yet to be settled. Indeed, a clearer view of the dissertation, including the format and the methodology, was to emerge after an initiation meeting with

Lasswell, Johnstone and Twining. My main objective was to use law, broadly conceived, to guide social change in a manner that would balance tradition and modernisation to maximise the advantages of development, while minimising the cost in terms of human values.

After William Twining left, Godfrey Lienhardt visited me at Yale, following a conference in Chicago to which he had been invited by Charles Long, a professor of Comparative Religions, who had participated in the Ibadan Conference. Godfrey went through the vast materials Jane and I had worked on towards the volume on Dinka songs. So moved was he that he immediately wrote me a note, I believe for the records, since he could have just communicated the same to me verbally. Among the many nice things, he said in the note was that it was then clear I would in the long run be the person who would do the most to promote knowledge about the Dinka to the outside world. I do not have the document at hand now and all this is a reconstruction in which I have tried not to be immodest in my restatement; Godfrey's own words could not have been more flattering and encouraging. He suggested that since I was so advanced in my work on the volume of Dinka songs and since I seemed to have sufficient material for the book, I should proceed to produce it alone, instead of having him as a coauthor as we had initially planned. He himself had a good collection of Dinka songs, but he argued that it would serve me more to have my name alone on the book than with him as a coauthor and that he would in any case render to me whatever editorial help I would need. I appreciated his sentiments very much and also realised that coauthorship would prove extremely difficult, with Godfrey all the way across the Atlantic. Producing the book alone would probably be more practical.

During the second phase of my time at Yale, I moved into an apartment. As the rent was high, my monthly allowance modest, and my entertainment immodest, I took part-time employment in the university to supplement my allowance. Arie David, an Israeli friend, and Peter Mutharika, from Malawi- who would rise through being professor of Law to becoming president of Malawi decades later- worked at a medical care centre. They both recommended me to take the position of another student who was leaving. I got the job.

Of course, it did not pay much but it also did not require much. In fact, it was a convenient job to combine with studying, for there were few calls and visits to interrupt one's concentration. I also found another employment at the Sterling Library on the recommendation of Mr Charpentier, the librarian of the Law Library. The job entailed collecting books from the reading tables and returning them for re-shelving.

When Edna Castle, with whom I had become good friends, went on leave with her family and asked me to housesit, I decided to sublet my apartment. Housesitting was also an opportunity for accommodating a fellow Dinka, Ambrose Ahang Beny, and his American wife, Mary, with their baby son, John, who were about to visit me on their way to Sudan. Next to the Castles was an Italian American family. Their house seemed elegant and their grounds better maintained than Edna's. Our neighbours had small children who initially seemed curious but polite and pleasant. As soon as we moved into the house, they would come over and engage in a friendly conversation blended with innocent curiosity. For instance, they approached Mary and wanted to know how it happened that her baby was black while she was white. She explained to them that his father was black. Another day they approached me in the morning, while I was in my long white Sudanese robe, the jallabiya; "Excuse me," one of them ventured to say, "Are you a human being or an angel?" I smiled and told them I was a human being. "A male or a female?" she asked. I answered in a matter-of-fact manner, with a sympathetic smile.

All that innocent and beautiful exploration suddenly stopped and we could not explain the development other than as a result of the attitude of the father, a rather heavy man of medium height in his late forties or early fifties. He was often seen in the garden, looking fierce and hostile, or heard in his own house shouting loudly or angrily at someone, perhaps the children, perhaps his wife. One day, standing conspicuously for us to see and speaking in a voice loud enough for us to hear, he told his children never to come to us again. "Communists should be shot at, not talked to," he said. It sounded so strange that we never even took it to be seriously aimed at us, although that seemed obvious. The children suddenly stopped coming or talking to us, even when they were within talking distance. They would approach our side, come close, but rather than talk, merely gaze with a combination of curiosity and fear.

More was to come. If anyone visited me and went into the driveway, my neighbour would stand keenly watching the car. With the slightest touch of the edge of his lawn, he would scream, telling the person to get off his lawn. If the person visiting happened to park his or her car on the street, my neighbour would telephone the police that there was a strange car in the neighbourhood, supposedly alerting them to a possible burglary. If I had people in the house for a party or even a small get-together, he would telephone the police to say we were too noisy and a nuisance to the neighbourhood. The police would come, find the situation to be different from what they had been told, apologise, and leave. Next time, the same situation would be repeated again and again and again. The police would apologise and leave; others would come, and yet others would come. There did not seem to be any coordination among the different policemen who came or else they agreed to use the pattern of being a nuisance to me and my friends and yet acting surprised and apologetic. Somehow, I believed them when they apologised and I only took it to be a lack of coordination.

As though all that was not bothersome enough, my neighbour made telephone calls frequently only to hung up on me or maintain a dreadful silence when I answered the call, with only his heavy, hateful breathing reaching my ears. I went to the police station about all that, but not only did I receive no help, I was frustrated by the lengthy, time-consuming formalities, with a dismissive, almost rude attitude from the police who made me feel as though I was wasting their time for nothing. In the long run, I would be told that nothing could be done, although I could of course initiate a procedure by filing a complaint that no one could tell as to where it would eventually lead. Even though a graduate student of law, I felt helpless because I realised that there was a lot more involved than the law.

I contemplated talking to the man, but my friends, themselves all white, advised me against the idea. They said he was a bigot and that talking to him would only expose me to an even more painful experience, without resolving anything. So, I just suffered at the hands of the man. Some friends suggested that I should leave the house, but I refused to do so because I had committed myself to Edna that I would take care of her house. Besides, I could not accept such defeat. In fact, I could not make myself believe that what was happening was truly happening on racial grounds, for I could not believe someone who did not know me could hate me so much simply because I was of a different race. I was itching to explore the real reasons in case there was something else of which I was unaware and which could be corrected. But the unanimous position of all my friends was not to venture.

Edna came and I moved back to my apartment, feeling a sense of remorse at my failure to dig deeper into the situation with my neighbour. Of course, I explained the situation to Edna and all she could say was that they had never had anything to do with him and that they always heard him sounding loud and aggressive, even to his own family. Edna shared the attitude of all my other friends that it was not worth discussing the matter with him because one would not get anywhere with his kind of attitude. A few days after I had moved back to my apartment, I came to visit Edna, riding a bicycle she had lent me. As I was going through the driveway towards the garage at the back of the house, I saw the neighbour sitting in the garden. It was a beautiful sunny day. As I walked back to the house from the garage, I felt an impulse to talk to him, despite all the advice to the contrary. I walked towards him. Standing in front of him, I said, "I would like to talk to you, may I?" "What do you want?", he said in a rude voice and manner that clearly indicated I was not welcome. But I decided to persist, "It will take some time, would you mind if I sit down?" "Sit down," he consented with apparent disdain. "Would you please tell me what wrong I have committed to deserve the way you treated me," I said calmly in a calm manner of speech.

He immediately became defensive: "If you think I am racially prejudiced, you are mistaken. If you go into my house, you will see many pictures of black musicians hanging on my wall. Some of them are very good friends of mine." He then went on to explain what he held against me. "I object to one thing, and that is marriage between races. Aren't you people proud of your own race? I am a good Catholic and I believe in God and respect God's work. God created man in different races and it is not right to change what God has done. I am an Italian and I am proud to be Italian and Catholic. I perform for rich Jews and Protestants, but as soon as I finish my performance, I go back to my people, the Catholics, the Italian Americans."

Hearing him talk made me feel a sense of relief that I was dealing with a case of dogmatic racism that posed no significant moral or intellectual threat to my position, but indeed placed me in an advantaged position. So, I relaxed and interacted with him in an almost patronising fashion. "You, of course, know that I am not married, don't you?" I said with an almost frivolous sense of detail. "I know you are not married," he explained, "but you accommodated a black man who is married to a white woman. That means that you approve of their marriage." My response was more substantive, although even more patronising: "You say you are a Catholic and a strong believer. I am also a Catholic and one of the principles I remember the Bible advocates is giving accommodation to the needy", I began to preach. "Are you telling me that your objection to mixed marriages is so strong that it overrides other Christian principles, such as providing accommodation to those in need?" That seemed to provoke him even more. "Don't tell me that your friend was destitute", he said, "I know about you both. You are a law student, working for your doctorate, and he is a graduate from Indiana and a university teacher. He is no destitute to need your accommodation."

I began to relish the sport of arguing with him: "But all the same, the Christian faith teaches us to observe many principles of behaviour towards our fellow human beings. Is the issue of mixed marriages so paramount in your evaluation that it outweighs all those moral principles governing social attitude towards neighbours and fellow men in general?" It seemed that I was simply provoking him even more. "Look, I told you that I consider races to be God's creation and we should not mess around with God's work." I decided to assure him that his attitude was not exceptional to his race, but was also shared by my own people. "I had an uncle," I said. "He was a genius; always top of his class even after jumping classes. He was about to graduate from a very famous Italian medical school, Padova, when he died. He always maintained that one should marry from one's own people. Although he was Westernised and had spent many years abroad, and very popular wherever he went, he always insisted that he would go back and marry from amongst his own people." That intrigued him. "That uncle of yours would certainly have been my friend," he interjected.

I resumed: "In fact, he is no exception. Most of my people feel exactly the same way. I would even venture to say that most people throughout the world feel the same way. It is only a few people who do otherwise. Mixed marriages constitute a negligible exception, compared to the overwhelming preference for marriage within the group. So, you are absolutely right that people should marry within their groups, because that is the norm."

Having established a base of agreement, I then introduced my own line of thought; "But my disagreement with you stems from the fact that the norm reflects a situation where people were somewhat isolated from one another and the chances of meeting and marrying across the border were not only limited but they also threatened the individual with separation and isolation from his group. This situation is now changing. People are mixing extensively across all kinds of group lines. And when individuals meet in these interracial situations, there is no way of controlling their feelings. Love knows no boundaries, especially when people are able to know and understand one another across those boundaries." My interlocutor seemed to be listening intensely.

I continued my sermon: "It doesn't mean that it is easy or that it is preferable; it is just a fact of our changing world that mixed marriages will continue to increase as contacts between races continue to expand." My words did not of course register significantly to him, but he listened rather attentively and patiently. Then he responded: "That is your opinion; I certainly do not share it and I pray to God that our world does not get off the track that way." I resumed my lecture, feeling so relaxed that I was not even diplomatic: "You see, unless you approach future realities with flexibility, you are bound to clash with them and could harm yourself. There are certain developments that we can only predict but cannot prevent or control. To stand against such an uncontrollable current would be only to drown yourself. Take, for instance, what you were telling your children, that Communists should only be shot at and not talked to. You were calling us Communists simply because we are black. When your children grow up, they will certainly realise that being black does not make one a Communist. What do you think they will feel about what you had taught them? You will be discredited."

On this issue, he had a rigid point of view, which he put in the form of a rhetorical question: "Are you telling me that the civil rights movement is not infiltrated by Communists?" "I am not telling you that," I said, "nor do I know enough about your civil rights movement to judge. What I am telling you is that I am not a Communist."

By now, although we had not agreed on anything, we were arguing quite amicably and with hardly any hostility towards one another, only a realisation that we genuinely disagreed. "Let me go back to what you did to me," I continued. "Do you know that every time you called the police, they came and apologised when they discovered the truth? Was that in itself not enough to convince you that you were being hard on me for reasons that were unfounded, at least to the police?" Again, he seemed certain about his position: "If you think they are on your side, you are mistaken. There are many phoney liberals who go about giving the blacks the wrong impression that they support them, but I know them and I also know how hypocritical they are - I will tell you, all those policemen will not admit to you their feelings, but they not only share my point of view, some are angrier than I am. Don't let them fool you with their apologies. It is just a put-on."

He was now speaking in a manner that almost made him seem sympathetic to me for being so naive about such a strong hatred towards my racial group. Perhaps he felt that if I were that naive, I could not be all that bad, and certainly could not be a Communist. He even seemed friendly. "Let me introduce you to my family," he said as he called his wife and children. After meeting them he asked me whether I would want to have a cup of tea or coffee. By now, we had been talking for over an hour and I felt that I should not stay any longer. So, I thanked them and excused myself, but only after some concluding remarks: "I would like to ask of you one big favour." His response was friendly, "Sure, what?" I said, "Next time you find yourself in a similar situation with anybody, would you allow contact and exchange of views rather than cut him off and display hostility towards him? At least you will give him and yourself the opportunity of learning each other's point of view and you may find that he can be convinced to your point of view or you may see some sense in his point of view. In either case, you will have promoted understanding and reduced tension and animosity." He did not commit himself, but he did not dismiss the point either. We seemed to agree without words on this last point and although we had disagreed on all other points, a spirit of mutual understanding and a degree of respect for each other's point of view had evolved between us. I still realised he was a bigot; he probably saw me as one of those intellectual dreamers. I left feeling very proud that I had resisted the unanimous advice against talking to him. My faith in the traditional values of my people which had propelled me to do so was enormously reinforced and consolidated.

My academic work was progressing well. I was turning out volumes of written material for my dissertation. And what was more, everyone had come to realise that I had developed my own perspective, which utilised Lasswell's and McDougall's theory of Law, Science and Policy, but with its own originality and distinctiveness; this was becoming appreciated. Even the use of songs to substantiate the legal culture of the Dinka became an intriguing innovation to many. Quinton, in particular, formerly rather reserved on the use of the songs, was won over. He even joked frequently, not only about the way people had been converted to the song material, but especially about the global significance of the Dinka.

I felt not only privileged to introduce the subject of customary law as a respectable subject for my doctoral dissertation, but also found new intellectual tools to build upon in my expanding study of African customary law. Through the jurisprudential school of "Law, Science and Policy," I learned that law was not an abstract objective concept to be unscrupulously upheld, but an outcome of a constitutive competitive power process in which people, individuals or groups, guided by overriding goals, seek value-objectives, through institutions, using resources. Before I went to Yale, I would have been reticent to talk about "Values" as antithetical to the "Positivist" or "Command Theory" of English jurisprudence, or the American "Realist" school, through which I had been introduced to the study of law. When I mentioned to Professor Quinton Johnstone how my English legal education was against value judgement, he said with a sense of affirmative humour, "Tell your English professors that at Yale, we force you at the point of a gun to take a value position".

As I was approaching the end of my doctoral work and feeling reasonably confident of obtaining the J.S.D., I wrote to the registrar of Khartoum University, recalling the history of my relationship with the university and the commitment to return which I had made to the university. The dean, Mohammed Ibrahim Khalil, had visited Yale Law School shortly after my admission and had argued that the negative response I had received in London from Khartoum University had not been authorised by the academic leadership, that I should forget all about it and that I should undertake my position on the faculty when I completed my studies at Yale.

Mohammed Ibrahim Khalil was now minister for Foreign Affairs and was therefore no longer directly involved in the decision, hence my writing to the registrar. In my letter, I informed the registrar that I was near completion and wanted confirmation of their intention to have me back. My letter was replied to by a junior official in the office of the registrar, sending me application forms and additional literature about the university, the city of Khartoum, and Sudan. He clearly took me for a foreigner wanting to apply for a job in Khartoum and probably interested in some information pertaining to such matters as the cost of living and the available facilities. His letter ended on the note that he hoped I would apply and join the University of Khartoum "and that you will like our beloved country, the Sudan."

I was so offended by the material that I decided not to respond or even consider employment with Khartoum University any more.

Whether they had done this intentionally, which I didn't think was necessarily the case, or they had been simply careless about my case, which was bad enough, I felt I deserved more recognition than that.

An alternative employment opportunity soon came from Singapore. One of my colleagues in the Law School was Jayakumar, a bright young Singaporean of Indian origin who was assistant dean of the faculty and later rose to prominent positions in the government. I got to know from him that Bartholomew, who had taught the Law of Contracts in Khartoum University, was the dean of the Faculty of Law in Singapore. I asked Jaya (as we called Jayakumar) to pass my regards to him. Bartholomew's response was an enthusiastic invitation for me to join their faculty, once I obtained my J.S.D. degree. I responded happily.

Now assured of a job, my task was to complete the thesis, receive my degree, and head for Singapore. The remarkable thing about this prospect was not only that I had known and admired Bartholomew, and had come to be friends with Jaya, but that as a high school student, I had been fascinated with the location of Singapore in the international transport network and had also liked the name. Once the prospect came up, I had no doubt that I wanted to go there.

My old friend and colleague, Izzeldine Hassan, had obtained the LL.M. at Howard University and joined the Legal Department of the United Nations Secretariat in New York. One morning, after I had attended a party and stayed overnight in New York, I went to pay a visit to him at the United Nations Building. As I had not communicated with Izzeldine about my intended presence in New York, he did not realise that I was in town. When I arrived at his office, Izzeldine was attending a meeting somewhere else and there was no chance of his being available before lunch.

I thought of visiting Gouri, Godfrey Lienhardt's Indian friend, a director at United Nations Industrial Development Organisation, UNIDO, whom I had met during Godfrey's visit. As soon as he received my call, Gouri warmly welcomed me to his office. As we chatted, I casually asked him what the service at the UN Secretariat was like, not at all speculating on anything other than sheer curiosity and little talk. Gouri talked about the United Nations in a way that began to engage my interest beyond what I had actually intended. Then he said, "If you are interested to know more about the service, the chief of the personnel section is a good friend of mine. I can ask him to tell you more about it." "Sure," I said, still not fully grasping Gouri's thoughts. I thought that I was going to receive a briefing about the UN more or less as a matter of information. Little did I know that I was being interviewed for a UN post and perhaps my inadvertence was a factor in the relaxed spirit with which I faced the interviews.

My meeting with the chief of personnel was very successful. It soon became apparent to me that they were operating on the premise that I might be interested in joining the UN and while that was not really my goal, I did not discourage their line of thought, particularly because it all sounded very interesting. The chief of personnel eventually asked me which division I would be interested in if I joined the United Nations Secretariat. The question was no longer unexpected, but I was quite elated by the invitation from the United Nations for me to join the international civil service, especially when my country was involved in a civil war and I belonged to the dissident minority, which unfortunately had little or no place in the politics of the United Nations. I said that if I were to join the UN, it would either be the Legal Department or the Division of Human Rights, with a preference for the latter.

Although I was not very conscious of my motivation, I vaguely felt that coming from the war stricken Southern Sudan, human rights would be particularly pertinent. When the question came as to whether I would mind working in the Section on the Status of Women, where all the other staff would be women, I said with enthusiasm that far from minding it, I would almost certainly find it most interesting. I was intrigued by the thought of working in the Status of Women Section because I wanted to pursue the issue of the emancipation of women from a cross-cultural perspective, hoping to develop my thesis for a balanced approach that would consider the various interests involved in the process of change.

By the time I left the United Nations that day, I had virtually been offered a job. I soon heard from the UN to the effect that the director of Human Rights, Marc Schreiber, wanted to see me. Sitting with him when I went into his office was Mrs Margaret Bruce, the chief of the Section on the Status of Women. The conversation was not so much an interview as a meeting of introduction to the division and the section. Although no clear promise of employment was made, it seemed quite apparent that I was going to receive an offer. The only question was whether I should join the Section on the Status of Women or another section of the division. Schreiber seemed more inclined towards the latter while Mrs Bruce wanted me and I was more curious and interested in her section.

I was subsequently informed by the office of personnel that although I was to be appointed on my own merits and not as a government nominee, it would be convenient to obtain a reference from the Sudan government to ensure that my country did not oppose my employment with the United Nations. Mamoun Hassan, a counsellor in the Sudan Mission, willingly accepted to be my reference. I also gave the name of Ambassador Fakhreddine Mohammed, not knowing what his position would be. I had met the ambassador only briefly, but I was confident that we had felt a spontaneous mutual admiration for one another. Indeed, Fakhreddine and I were to become close friends for life.

In the meantime, after sending an optimistic medical report on the state of my eyes, according to the request of the authorities of Singapore University, I received a cable urging me to respond by cable to their offer. I asked the United Nations to give me a final decision. Within two weeks of my meeting with the UN recruitment officials, I received an offer for a job that had never been in my calculations until that visit to Mr Gouri. The status was probationary, which meant that after two years, unless my performance was not satisfactory, it would be converted to a permanent, pensionable service. I was required to join as soon as possible since there was an urgent need for my services.

With the UN offer firmly in my hand, I sent a cable to Singapore explaining the situation and expressing the hope that I might in the future still have the opportunity to join their faculty. I received a very nice letter from the dean, virtually making a standing offer of a teaching position whenever I so desired. By the time the UN offer came through, which was July 1, I had already secured the extension of my fellowship to December. But on balancing all the relevant factors, the UN urgent need for my services, my financial difficulties, and the advanced state of my research, I opted for taking up my new post immediately, thereby foregoing the fellowship.

Work on the dissertation continued after I joined the UN. To avail myself of the editorial assistance of Jane Glassman, I shuttled back and forth between New York and New Haven by train, leaving after work, and returning early for work, using sleeping pills for a few moments of rest and "no-dose" pills to facilitate my functioning through the working day. The manuscript was ready for submission by Christmas. As Quinton Johnstone was then in Ethiopia, as Dean of Law at the University of Haile Selassie, and Harold Lasswell was off on his winter holidays, Professor Robert Stevens, who had declined being an active member of the Committee, preferring the role of a reader in the end, was the first to read the completed work. He approved it with enthusiasm, and even urged me to have it published.

Harold Lasswell had been any way familiar with the progress and was not expected to come forth with surprises. Yet, on reading the final version, he reacted creatively, opening an avenue for a substantial, much more enriched, concluding chapter. Professor Johnstone also made suggestions for editorial improvements and otherwise approved the dissertation. When the dissertation was considered by the Faculty Board, Quinton Johnstone was back from Addis. As though to inject that element of anxiety which makes any test worthwhile, he intimated to me that the Board had added another reader to my committee and that a copy was also to be made available to the Chairman of the Graduates' Committee. Harold Lasswell himself had no doubt about the outcome. Indeed, his main concern was to begin revising it for publication.

When the crucial day came, I was told that the decision had been exaltingly unanimous. McDougall, together with Lasswell, were later to write a strong recommendation for the publication of the dissertation by the Yale University Press. It eventually came out in 1971 under the title: *Tradition and Modernization: A Challenge for Law Among the Dinka of the Sudan*. A year later, it won the Herskovits Award for the best book published in African studies the year before and was described by the Award Committee as "scholarly, well-written, original and theoretically stimulating."

For me, receiving the J.S.D. degree was the culmination of a long held dream so essential that if it were not achieved, I would have considered my life a failure. My cousin Justin Deng Aguer had written to report that he had literally shed tears over the news of my failure in England; he had urged me not to return to the Sudan without at least an LL.M. and preferably a doctorate. It was the latter which I would accept as adequate remedy for the shame of the failure in London. It was also to be a license or a card for preserving some scholarly or intellectual worth beyond the value of my vision. Now, the dream had become true under even better circumstances where I was employed with the prospects of permanence, a decent job, and a respectable status as an international official. I would be able to move in and out of any country, including my own, without being considered a refugee, a dissident or even an expatriate. In a way, the award of the doctoral degree symbolised, indeed represented, a clear demarcation line between the uncertainties and worries of the past and the security, the confidence and the relaxation of the present and the prospects for the future.

There was a deeper benefit than the licence, the club card, or the document called the degree. Yale was for me perhaps the most crucial formative experience. It was not a period in which I went on absorbing quantities of legal knowledge for the sake of knowledge. It was a period of sharpening my tools, of processing much of what I had already learned, of deepening my perception of things, of acquiring the selective technique of learning, of molding vast masses of materials into models of recognisable shapes and attraction, of retracing and clearing the path which change meant for me, of fine-tuning my concept of the invisible bridge I had crossed, and through all that, of being able to move to and fro more securely at levels of greater human heights and depth.

William Twining, with whom I first met when he was a young lecturer of law in the University of Khartoum in the late 1950s, in his

2019 memoire, summarizes my journey through cultures in deeply moving words: "Francis Deng was in his second year in 1957-8, one of only four or five Southern law students. He was one of the favoured sons of Deng Majok, the well-known Paramount Chief of the Ngok Dinka, the only Nilotic people to live in Northern Sudan. Francis was quite short for a Dinka, only about 6 foot, but he was recognizably Nilotic and, without putting on airs, had a dignified aristocratic bearing. He spoke very good English and Arabic and, in some respects, became a leader of the whole class, not just the few Southerners, for instance, leading an expedition to Germany during a long vacation. Oliver Farran and I encouraged him to gather information about Dinka customs and this turned out to be the beginning of his life-long involvement with writing about Dinka culture. In 1965 in New Haven, I helped to record his memories of his childhood and education from his father's compound, through village, primary, and secondary school, to universities in Khartoum, London and Yale. This became an intimate memoire, the publication of which awaits his retirement from public life. Francis later followed a very distinguished academic, political and diplomatic career as well as publishing about forty books. After sixty years, we are still close friends.

Implicit in all this has been the extent to which my education has been so therapeutic because it has given me the most unusual opportunity to analyse myself through a deep and comprehensive understanding and analysis of my own society, it's culture, its values, its interaction with the outside world, and the pluralistic values of that world. In doing this, I have never felt any inhibitions because I have not been studying myself but my society. Yet, I have consistently realised the extent to which my identity issues, indeed my very being, its meaning, and its dimensions have always been tied up with my own social background and all the situations the path of change inside and outside the Sudan have taken me. In a sense then, I had been studying and analysing myself by proxy and in the widest possible context. I feel almost embarrassed about the comprehensiveness with which I have studied the Dinka, both in tradition and modernity. Yet every one of my numerous books, in one way or another off shoots of the seed I had cultivated in my doctoral work, has been a revelation to me and a great source of joy.

Over the years my interest in Dinka culture continued to expand as I addressed questions related to my new understanding of law within the theoretical framework of law, science and policy: What are the overriding value-goals on which the system is based? What are the specific value objectives whose pursuit law regulates? What are the institutional structures for the pursuit of values? What resources are used as base values? What are the sources of information for identifying those values? How are the values transmitted to the next generation? What is the Dinka worldview in which the value system is embedded? And how has that worldview been historically impacted by the changes the society has undergone? To me, as my numerous publications on Dinka culture suggest, answers to these questions reflect a sustained quest for a culturally oriented system of governance, constitutionalism, development and nation-building, approaching the Dinka in the pluralistic context of the Sudan and beyond.

So, the value of Yale to me is more than the document called the degree; nor does it lie in the few years I spent at Yale. It was in effect a crucial phase or stage in which the investments of the many years of my life until then, of the informal and formal education I had received at home and in schools, of the study of customary law in Khartoum University, of the continuation of that study in London, of the many songs I had sung under showers or as I had walked the streets of Southern and Northern towns and even of London, of the childhood dreams I had cherished and remembered, of the future that was still to be witnessed but the logic of which had already been laid, in short, of all the things that were significant to the meaning of things, were all brought into focus and conceptualised into powerful, motivating, guiding principles of thought and action. While I was now "permanently" employed in New York, I was psychologically prepared to return home. The occasion would come barely a year later with tragic news.

SALVATION
In the Land of Refuge

Professor Qintin Johnstone who, while Visiting Professor at London School of Economics, facilitated the admission of the Author to Yale Law School.

Professor Robert Stevens who, together with Quinton Johnston, facilitated the admission of the Author to Yale.

Professor Myers McDougall who, jointly with Harold Lasswell, taught Law, Science, and Policy, and was a member of tge Author's Dictoral Committee.

Professor Harold Dwight Lasswell who taught Law, Science and Policy with McDougall and was the Chaurman of the Author's Doctoral Committee.

CHAPTER FIFTEEN

RETURN
HOME TO TRAGEDY

THE WORLD WAS TURNING AROUND. EVENTS WERE TAKING PLACE IN RAPID succession; some of them positive, others tragic. There had been a revolution in Sudan and a new government under the leadership of a young officer, Colonel Jaafar Mohammed Nimeiri, had taken over on May 25, 1969. It sounded promising, especially coming after a renewed determination by the government of liberal democracy to crush the Southern movement. Joseph Garang, a prominent Communist Southerner, was appointed minister of State for Southern Affairs. Within two weeks of taking over, specifically on June 9, the government had announced that they would grant regional autonomy to the South. They had declared amnesty to all political refugees to return home. Some did; most didn't.

One day I received an unexpected cable from Bol. He had received a cable from home; our father was seriously ill, perhaps dying; he was proceeding immediately to Khartoum. How strange! Why had I not received a message to the same effect? Was it somebody's decision that Bol's presence at the death of our father was more important than my presence? And who would that person be, Father or someone else?

And why? Because he was the son of the first wife? Was he perhaps wanted for reasons of succession? What reasons would exclude me? Of course, I had no answer to any of these questions.

By a remarkable coincidence, although I had only recently been on a mission abroad, I had just been assigned a mission to Cairo. It would be possible to combine leave with the mission. Since the trip was to be in August and we were then in July, I could leave at any time. I chose to leave immediately.

The journey to London and on to Rome seemed incredibly long, but was crammed with thoughts and reflections that made time fly. The reality of my life story, and with it, the close association with my father's life, ran and ran in front of me. The focal point was what the significance of all that long history of projections, speculations, and expectations was now going to mean. It was as though the crucial test of life was at long last at hand. It seemed that everything, literally everything, had only been a preparation for this final hour. Was my self-image, and its relevance to my family and my people, allegedly fostered in me by the society, only an illusion and self-delusion or was it a reality about to take form? But if that were so, why would I not receive a cable urging me to come home immediately because Father was dying and I was needed? And Bol had received the news. Nor had he been asked to transmit a message to me. Quite the contrary, he had simply announced to me that he was immediately heading for home because of the message asking him to proceed. He was probably already at home by our father's bedside. He had not even suggested to me that we should proceed together. Was it even right for me to be trying so hard to reach home as fast as I could? Well, I never questioned that; I obviously had to go and perhaps I would find out the answers to my many questions.

In a strange way, the scene of my grandfather's death which I had read and heard about came to my mind. I recalled Uncle Deng Makuei being informed and described as impatiently galloping with his horse to our dying grandfather, while my father remained behind to be given a car ride by the district commissioner the following day. Then I would rest back feeling a deep sense of trust in the divine justice from Providence. Truth would eventually reveal itself. My father had always said that a person loved by God was far better off than a person loved by his father.

What principles was I going to promote in the family? I told myself that my role should be absolutely committed to the interest of the family and the tribe as a whole. On the issue of succession, unless our father solved the problem before his death, the competition would of course be between Kuol (Adam) and Monyyak (Abdalla). I was clear in my mind that I would only back the person who would be most valuable to the collective interest of our people. I must not be with or against Adam simply because he was from my section of the family, nor should I be with or against Abdalla because he was from the section of the First Wife. I should judge objectively with the collective interest as my only yardstick. But even with that yardstick, which of the two brothers should it be? There, I would stop, reflect, and balance pluses and minuses.

Adam was certainly older, probably more mature, and with a knowledge of some law from his police experience. He was not only more impressive looking, better dressed and more meticulous about his social image, but also very generous, hospitable and cross-culturally astute, especially with the Arabs. On the other hand, Abdalla was more intelligent, more concerned about substance than appearance, more committed to higher values than to pragmatic advantages, more inclined to learn than to dictate, more progressive in the deeper sense than in the superficial show sense of the word. Adam, because of his age and temperament, would be more inclined to resist our advisory role, while Abdalla would be almost certain to depend on our advice. After all, he had said to me that whenever he considered a course of action, he would ask himself what I would have done under the circumstances and then try to emulate me.

To complicate the picture even more, the things that enhanced Adam's standing seemed to be the things that would provide for relative continuity in our father's image. Adam's virtues were only copies of what he admired and followed in his father's ways and therefore lacked authenticity or profundity. There was also another major weakness: Adam drank heavily. Attributes that were pluses for Abdalla as a leader of independent image, who would be likely to go beyond his father in the long run rather than merely continue his image, were the things that would be his short-term weaknesses. He was modest when his father was far from modest; he was democratic when the word had no meaning to his father; he was prudent with money when his father was lavish; he was simple-looking when glamour was one of his father's distinctive features; he was extremely honest when his father's handling of public funds was controversial; he was a lad of ideals and great dreams when realism and a firm grip were the means by which his father governed.

Father could of course solve the problem of succession himself, but he hadn't thus far and might not. To our father, there was one major subjective consideration to make him ambivalent towards both sons: Adam was a preferred son, who, by never committing adultery with any of his father's wives remained clean, clear and dear; but then Father could not care for a drinking chief. Abdalla was a wise promising young man, who had given up drinking, and in many ways could be entrusted with the interest of the people; but I had come to learn that he had committed adultery with two of Father's wives and that was something for which Father would never forgive a person.

I saw shortcomings on both sides, but on balance, I decided my vote should go to Abdalla. There was a problem of the family size, the women, their children, their maintenance, their education: what should we do? It all went back to Father. He had done it; only he could manage it. All my thoughts would fade in the hope that Father wouldn't die; he couldn't. How could he die and leave all those problems to whom? I reflected and speculated and despaired and hoped and stopped thinking with a sigh.

We briefly landed in Rome. There were passengers getting off and others to be picked up. When it was time to reembark, new passengers joined us as we were entering the plane. Suddenly, Bol and I confronted each other as we were about to embark. It was unbelievable. He had stopped for a day or two in Rome to see old friends. That surprised me, considering the circumstances, but I never said anything about that to Bol. After all, it was perhaps the Providence's will that we return together. And there we were surprisingly, indeed miraculously, with boarding cards that seated us next to one another, heading back together, soon to be on the bedside of our obviously dying father.

We lost no time in discussing the issues. The first question I undiplomatically had to pose was why on earth I had not received a cable and why Bol had stopped short of expecting us to proceed together. It was Bol who first suggested to me that he was probably being asked to go because of his medical expertise. As for his not telling me to join him and proceed together, he said that he had not known my circumstances, whether I could leave or not, and in any case had not stopped to reflect.

We then turned to the family situation and specifically to the issue of succession, and got into a disagreement. Bol was more interested in the conclusion than in the process and the reasons, citing the most obvious of explanations. Who should succeed our father? He thought Abdalla. Why? Because Dinka customs required that the son of the first wife should succeed. I could not let him get away with that. I argued that the principle was only a convenient guideline which had been bent and even abandoned before to permit the succession of a person best suited for leadership. I told him that my evaluation of the two brothers threw my support for Abdalla, but for more substantive reasons than his being the son of the first wife. Once I had concluded for good reasons, I would then be prepared to back my choice with the argument of the principle of primogeniture. Bol was happy with my conclusion although he did not share my logic, and indeed, did not stress his disagreement. He even said that if I was interested in succeeding our father, he would support me. Of course, he knew very well that neither of us was in the equation.

Even as we talked rather lightheartedly, the prospects of our father's death were too awesome to anticipate. We sighed back in the hope that our father would not die – at least not yet. Only he could cope with the challenges of the situation. While there remained many unknowns and we left precise approaches to evolve with time and circumstances, by the time we landed in Khartoum, we had consolidated a united front which we hoped would in turn guarantee the unity of the family.

RETURN
Home to Tragedy

We arrived at the airport, mindful of the fact that we had been away for very long, that the new government was military, that there was a political past next to our names, and that the civil war still raged in the South. But we were undeterred and the purpose for which we had returned loomed highest in our consideration. Nothing at the airport gave us reasons to be fearful, but as we emerged from the main airport building, we were invaded by taxi drivers, each virtually grabbing our arms and pulling us towards his car. The air was echoing with their shouts "taxi, taxi", or the names of the specific locations to which they were offering rides. It brought Cairo to mind, certainly uncharacteristic of the Sudan I had left seven years earlier.

We went to Hotel Shark-pronounced as "Shareq"- which I remembered only because our German friends - the ISSF students - had put up there and it had seemed reasonably pleasant. The sight of it from the outside and the rubbish flying about inside its compound as well as the shabby looks of its residents told us that it probably no longer had the same number of stars next to its name and whatever it had was visibly undesirable. We went to another hotel where some Germans had also stayed and checked in not so much because we found it suitable but because we wanted to settle and get to our father as soon as we could.

News of our arrival had already gone around and by the time we had checked into the hotel, visitors from our family started to pour in. The first arrivals took us to the hospital where our father was. As we walked through the corridors of the crowded, filthy, and odorous Khartoum Civil Hospital, engulfed with the breath of death, it was difficult to believe that our father was only scores of metres away from us. When we entered his large rectangular hall, crowded with beds of very sick and sickly people, we realised that things had truly taken a turn for the worse, at least for our father and all those who sat around his bed. But the worst, though also the best, was still to come with the sight of our father.

As Father heard it announced that Bol and Mading had come, he leaped off his bed, trying to stand straight, repelling any attempt to assist him to his feet. He stood up, frail, stooping, wearing an inner-garment that was soiled and dirty, his head shaven with sprouting grey hair, his eyes large sockets of deep holes from which glowed his never diminishing intelligence, dignity, pride and a deep sense of individual superiority. It was as though he was rising from his grave with a renewed zest and hope for life. Bol and I were like hatchlings under his arms as he embraced us together, clearly full of love, joy and hope. Our names, Bol, Mading, Mading, Bol were pouring incessantly from his mouth. And again, and again he would pull us closer to him, both under his arms, as though to assure himself that our presence was real. It was a scene to produce tears, but we did not cry, knowing that what was needed the most was a renewed sense of confidence and responsibility to act.

Father then sat back on his bed. "Have you really come my sons?" he would say unbelievingly. "All is well! Nothing is bad! Even if I should die now, my heart is full of joy if you have come back and I have seen you. All is well!" And then he would again reach for us, embracing us or just touching us and calling our names Father then chose to be a little more light-hearted. "Mading, have your people (the Americans) really set foot on the moon?" I assured him they had.

Something very touching was still to happen. One of the boys with our father raised the question of whether it was any longer necessary for "the letter" to be taken to the leader of the revolution, Jaafar Nimeiri. They all seemed to agree that it was not necessary. "What letter?" we wondered silently. Then they explained, handing us a sealed envelope. Our father had just had a letter written to Nimeiri about us - Bol and me. We opened the letter and read it. In the letter, our father gave an account of his long public service to Sudan. Now he was old and maybe dying. All he wanted to request from the government was one thing: to please bring back his two sons who were abroad, Bol and Mading, so that he could see them once more before he died.

Nobody explained anything beyond that, but it then occurred to me that Father probably thought we were still abroad for political reasons and would not return on our own because of possible political persecution. In particular, he and perhaps others had thought I was still in the bad books of the Government of Sudan since my "rebellious" days in London and would be in danger if I returned without political clearance. Perhaps that was why I had not been sent a message about my father's illness to proceed to our dying father. Bol on the other hand had not been confronted with such a problem and at least in theory faced no political persecution. There was however another reason for the modesty of our father's tone. Among the objectives which the revolution had announced was to do away with Native Administration- created and left by the British rulers for managing tribal communities all over Sudan- of which people like my father were obvious targets. Native administration had indeed been abolished in the North, though not in the South which was considered not ready for such reform and Abyei, being recognized as culturally part of the South, was also exempt. Father however felt the atmosphere of the regime somewhat antagonistic to his position and whatever he requested of them had to be dependent on their good will and not on the weight of his status.

Symbolically, I saw his reduced status reflected in the room he was in, amidst a crowd of other patients, under those dreadful conditions, filth and lack of adequate attention. "Why is our father not in first class?" we inquired from the brothers. "There is no room," was the answer. Incredible! A person acknowledged as the virtual king of his people, descendant of a long line of leaders, acknowledged even by British records as kings, traced by the Dinka to the beginning of creation, looked to by millions of the Dinka, South and North, as an exceptional leader, even by the long-tested standards of his lineage, a man who almost single-handedly believed himself the crucial bond, the needle and the thread, as he himself had put it, that bound the North and the South, the African and the Arab together. There he was lying low, unappreciated, the entire meaning of his life depreciating in front of his very eyes.

I was to learn from our brothers later that the issue of the abolition of the Native Administration was a worry Father constantly expressed. They assured him that it would not affect him, but he was too intelligent to be fooled; he knew sooner or later, in his life-time or after his death, it would reach home and deeply so. Some were to tell me that these worries that loomed heavily on him probably aggravated his illness and accelerated his death.

We went back to the hotel and telephoned Abel Alier, the minister for Supply, one of the two Southerners in the cabinet, to announce our presence in the city. He told us that he would inform Bona Malwal Madut about our presence. Bona was the son of Madut Ring, the chief of the Kuach Twic Dinka, south of us, one of the latest tribes to be carved out of our jurisdiction by the British and affiliated to the South. Bona had been elected representative in the recently dissolved parliament and had also been a prominent person in the Southern movement. He and Abel Alier had been senior members of the Southern Front of which the latter was its secretary general before the parties were banned by the May regime on coming to power in May 1969. He had also been the editor of *The Vigilant*, the influential and only Southern paper that had published the names of those massacred at the Wau wedding. Bona was an impressive, dynamic young man, dedicated to politics and the public service of his country.

Within a short time of Abel's telephoning him, Bona came to our hotel and insisted that we should move to his house. After the dissolution of parliament, he had moved into a more modest house in Khartoum North, one of the Three Towns with Khartoum proper and Omdurman that constituted the capital city. But while it had an old-fashioned pit latrine and bathroom, with only two bedrooms, a sitting room and an open verandah, Bona's house was quite comfortable by Sudan standards and his generosity in asking us in was most appreciated, especially as none of us had until then really known him so closely. Though out of power, Bona's personal influence was considerable and pervasive. A fast driver, with an old model Opel car that he kept meticulously neat, Bona whizzed us through the streets of Khartoum in and out of offices, enabling us to quickly reestablish contacts with old friends and meeting new ones.

Our immediate concern was to find for our father the best possible accommodation in the hospital or take him out of there and place him in one of the private nursing homes. We met his doctor who not only seemed vague about Father's illness, but informed us that there was no room available in the first class; they would of course move him as soon as one became available. In looking for a nursing home, we found a general bias among Southerners for Dr Abdel Wahab, who had a Dinka background somewhere back and catered especially for the Southern community, giving the best care possible with minimum concern for self-enrichment. It was Dr Abdel Wahab to whom I had gone during the crisis in the examination room and he had miraculously enabled me to complete the exams. We went to him and he immediately secured excellent premises for our father.

There was only one problem. It had come to our father's attention that a relative had died under Abdel Wahab's care and according to Dinka customs, a lamb should be sacrificed before he, our father, could enter the same premises. Bol was initially opposed to the idea as superstitious. I, on the other hand, argued that it would do us no harm, but, quite the contrary, might be of significance to Father's psychology and health. After some discussion, we agreed and procured the lamb. It was slaughtered by the elders, and our father was then moved to Abdel Wahab's nursing home.

One day, as we were visiting him, Father sent everybody out, including his other sons, requesting that only Bol and I should remain. He said he was not sure whether he would live or die: "Should I die, you know what your people, the Dinka, are like. They may say that the conditions of the rainy season do not permit taking me back home to be buried there. They may want to bury me here. But I am not a person to be buried anywhere and anyhow. I am a man who must be buried on my own ground at home and even have a tomb erected on my grave. I am a man known throughout the country, South and North. But, what do you see in these people, called the Dinka? They come and cluster in my room and laugh even as they see me dying. Is my death something that should permit laughter?" Father talked in a sad, deeply moving, yet ridiculously conceited manner that confused our own reaction. Once we were out of the nursing home, we could not help laughing out loud. It was however true that the crowded visitors had entered into a conversation and some had laughed rather loudly. I had even caught my father's disapproving eyes turn towards them.

Bol and I chose to encourage our father by saying that he should not think of death when the doctors were clearly working to ensure his recovery. He should dismiss that thought. Bol was speaking on our behalf. Father got impatient. He reminded Bol of his own experience. "When you broke your leg and thought you might die, you asked me to have you buried straight instead of being folded the Dinka way, did that kill you?" It was a rhetorical question for which Bol's reply was obviously silence. "If God does not want me to die, what I am telling you will not kill me. But should I die, I want you to carry out my wish. That is all I am saying."

Taking care of Father was to prove difficult and most strenuous for Bol as he was required to display both the passion of a son and the professional objectivity of a physician. Having made his case about where he should be buried in the eventuality of his death, once I was alone with him, Father turned to me and said, "Mading, you have studied law and you have looked into the books, do you think chieftainship will be taken away from my family? Do you think that Deng Makuei could claim chieftainship again?" I assured him that Dinka law governing succession to chieftainship and which was recognised by state law dictated that chieftainship should descend from father to son, down. Once he had acquired it, there was no way Deng Makuei could claim it.

Father was very pleased to hear what I was saying. I too felt elated because I could see that what I had been doing nearly ten years back – recording Dinka customary law – the very activity which had threatened my father then, now emerged as an asset in the interest of the family and was identifiable by my father as such.

I took advantage of that situation to clear my conscience on another matter. I had decided to make use of my time in recording songs from some of the elders who had come with our father, and who were famous for their singing talents. So, at Bona's house, I had organised singing sessions in which I had recorded those individuals and others whom Bona had secured for me from among the singing talents of his own Twic Dinka group. My recording programme was still underway.

I realised that what I was doing, recording songs, when the kind of songs I was recording were associated with happiness, might be viewed by some as improper in the circumstances of our father's illness. Bol had actually confronted me with the argument that I should not be recording songs under those circumstances. Nevertheless, I chose to take the risk of violating an aspect of Dinka code in order to promote what I thought was an even more important purpose – the survival of Dinka culture. In fact, I recorded elders, who included Uncle Arop, Father's youngest brother, and Chan Dau, a chief of a section, one of Father's closest associates. The two of them were known to have been among the best singers during their youth. None of them indicated any objection or discomfort about the circumstances of my recording being inappropriate.

But since the issue had been raised, I decided to clear it with Father directly. So, as I sat talking with him alone, I told him that he might have heard that I was recording Dinka songs and oral tradition. Before I even argued my case, Father injected his comment: "That is very important; record as much as you can; that is truly important." With that comment, my father not only made my day, he made my life. Since I heard my father say that, I have been doubly more convinced that what I have been trying to do about promoting Dinka culture in my books, is not an elitist Westernised exercise, but an objective I share very deeply with my people, my father, as well as the ordinary Dinka.

Although close to the end of his life, Father still retained not only a clear mind, but also his characteristic wisdom of judgement. One late afternoon, as we sat with him on the open deck next to his second-floor room, we heard the voices of demonstrators. There were a number of visitors sitting around him. Father asked me what that was. I told him that it was a demonstration against Israel. The Arab world was still recoiling from the agony of the 1967 defeat. I added a critical comment to my reply: "Our brothers shout louder than they fight." My father reacted immediately and sternly: "Mading, I simply asked you what the voices were, not what you thought about them!" I realised at once that Father was concerned about the political situation and feared that someone there might report on me. He was protecting me.

On another occasion, Izzeldine Hassan, my friend and colleague who had been at the United Nations, went with us to the hospital to visit Father. Izzeldine's father had died and the family had urged him to return. He was then posted to Khartoum as a judge. I introduced Izzeldine to my father as an old friend and colleague to whom I had been close not only during the university days in Khartoum, but also in the United States. I also explained that Izzeldine was now back as a judge in Khartoum. Later on, Father recalled Izzeldine's visit to him and said, "Mading, that friend of yours who visited me, was he not with you in America?" I said "Yes." "And has he not returned to his country?" "Yes," I said. "Did you not find him among his own people?" Again, I said "Yes." Then he got to the point: "Where is your country and where are your people?" And before I could respond, he said, "If I survive this illness, I intend to have a serious talk with you!"

I understood him; he wanted me back in the Sudan. I chose to explain the situation immediately: First, the political and health crises when I was in London, then the imperative of continuing my studies in the United States, my attempt to rejoin Khartoum University, and the offensive response I had received from the registrar's office. I was not sure my father would find my arguments to be a convincing explanation for my decision not to return to Sudan. He however surprised me with his response: "I understand your words", he said. "Among the Dinka, when a man leaves his tribe, offended by his people's treatment of him, he returns only when they realise their wrong and they go after him to request his return with respect and show of dignity. So, I see your point. Wait for Sudan to call on you; they will." I was very pleased with his understanding. I was also surprised by the confidence with which he made his point that Sudan would call me to return with honour and dignity. I sought to raise Father's spirits by saying that when he recovered, I would like him to visit America, his response was, "I would like that very much." And I really meant what I said and wished it could be realised.

One day, as Bona Malwal was visiting with us and we were leaving, Father called me back and said, "Mading, remain close with Malwal; he is a man." That was my first time to realise my father's admiration for Bona Malwal. I later realised how mutual their admiration was when Bona told me one day that his friendship for me was in part based on the fact that he saw a lot of my father in my ways of doing things. By now, I had almost dismissed my earlier concerns about not having received a cable about Father's condition. Cousin Alor Deng had admitted that he was largely to blame because he had sent the wire to Bol, feeling that Father was particularly concerned about Bol's presence as a doctor. I had also confided in Uncle Arop that I had been offended by not receiving word of Father's condition while Bol received the news. Uncle Arop response was flattering; "My son, never hold such thoughts in your mind. You are the one on whom the hopes of the family and tribe rest. If this illness of your father should result in his death, it will be in your hands that the people will place themselves. Dispel such negative thoughts from your mind."

Initial tests and X-ray pictures showed that Father's lungs contained fluid. It appeared as though it could be pneumonia. Some of the fluid was drained from time to time to give him relief. Then, when more of the results had come in, Dr Abdel Wahab called Bol and me and told us the truth, which he said he had suspected all along, but had kept to himself until he was sure. Father had cancer of the lungs. It was terminal. It was far too advanced to be arrested. He was clearly dying. Nothing could be done, except perhaps to ease the pain. We had of course come with the expectation of death as a serious possibility, but now that it was to be a fact, we received the news with a combination of shock and stark realism.

We had to decide whether or not we should let him know the truth. There was some advantage in letting him know. He could settle the affairs of the family and the tribe and in particular the problem of succession. But then the shock of the truth would be dreadful for a person whose will to live seemed so strong. In fact, we learned that some tribal elders had tried to persuade him in El Obeid to be taken home to settle the affairs of the land, die and be buried in the manner fitting of the paramount chief. But he had simply dismissed them as ill-motivated and lacking in compassion and decency. We could not tell him. Why put him into agony for the convenience of others, the living?

We decided to protect him to the end. We also decided that as long as there was still a breath of life, there was some hope, and, in any case, it was important not only to our father, but also to our family and the people of the tribe, that we were trying to do everything possible to save our father's life. We approached the Medical Commission to arrange for Father's transfer at least to Cairo, if not London. The Medical Commission's verdict came, medically sound but humanly unexpected. Father was a dying man; nothing could be done to save his life. The government could not spend money on the proposed trip which could not be expected to produce any positive results. In short, the government would have nothing to do with taking our father to Egypt.

That was yet another evidence of the changing times, for, while the decision was medically justified, such a dismissive treatment could only have been possible under the circumstances of the new regime where the image of the chiefs was rapidly dwindling. Yet, Joseph Garang, the other Southern minister in the cabinet, and the one in charge of Southern Affairs, although an avowed Communist, was very courteous to Father, visiting him in the hospital and keeping close contact with the situation. When the government declined to send Father abroad, we had to decide whether to take him nevertheless or to abandon the idea.

However, we did not have the money to afford it and the rainy conditions would not permit sending someone home to sell cattle for the required amount. Yet, we felt we must take him to Cairo both in the hope that something might be possible with the better facilities in Cairo and also for the practical reason that I had to be in Cairo for the UN's conference. We decided to borrow money from somewhere and proceed with the mission. My circle of friends came in handy and I was able to borrow a substantial amount from an Indian lecturer in the Faculty of Law, a friend of Izzeldine, who was eager to be paid abroad in US dollars.

As we were making plans to leave, I thought I would subtly gear Father towards naming a successor without appearing to be talking about succession. I said to him that as he was leaving the country and no one could tell how long he would be abroad, it might be a good idea for him to name someone to head the tribe in his absence. At first, he did not seem to understand what I was saying, or perhaps he understood it too well. He kept looking vaguely, and inquisitively at me, obviously wanting further clarification. When I made my point clearer, but more tilted towards a case of interim representation, intending to counter any suspicion that I was talking of succession, Father said, "But did I not leave someone at home when I left? Is not Monyyak (Abdalla) at home? Or are you trying to tell me something else?"

Father seemed to have understood my motive, but I could not pursue the matter further. We ended there. Father was however to indicate his ambivalence by talking to me on his own initiative about the two sons, Adam and Abdalla. He criticised Adam's heavy drinking, praised Abdalla's sense of responsibility, but also condemned him for having coveted his wives.

One day, Father got into a mood of so much fear or compulsion that he insisted one of us should sleep near him in the nursing home. The idea did not appeal to us and we dragged our feet about obliging. But Father was adamant; one of us had to sleep next to him. He did not explain why, he just demanded it. "I do not care which of you stays, but one of you must stay". I wondered what his intentions were. It crossed my mind that he might want to make his dying declaration under the most discreet and private conditions of the night. But why one of us and not both of us? And why did he stress that he did not care which of us stayed, as long as it was one of us? On the other hand, he might have been simply afraid of dying at night and needed one of us by his side. In either case, I thought Bol should be the one to stay both as the senior son of the most senior wife and as the medical doctor. Of course, the reason I gave was the latter. That indeed should have been obvious, although Father kept stressing that it did not matter which of us stayed. I do not know why we did not offer to both stay. I urged Bol, who was clearly resistant, that he was obviously the right person to stay. He eventually grudgingly agreed.

The following morning, Bol had nothing to report. Both he and Uncle Arop said that at some point Father sat up in bed and started to speak in a way they thought sounded like a dying declaration, his will, but then he suddenly changed his mind and said nothing.

Leaving for Cairo was not without a crisis. At first, all seemed to go well. Father was taken to the airport in an ambulance, walking in and out by himself, refusing to be carried and rejecting any helping hand. He was clearly in great pain which he acknowledged only by a bite of the lips, the agony in his eyes, and the sternness on his face. At the airport, it turned out that we had overlooked the international health card without which the Egyptians would not let us into the country. All efforts to obtain one at the airport failed. Abel Alier, the other Southerner on the cabinet, intervened to help. But even his intervention could not secure Father's travel that day. We were forced to return to town, with Father infuriated without words. He was later to say that he saw no point in going to Cairo anymore. He preferred to wait for his death in Khartoum. That was how angry he was. But he was eventually persuaded and we left the next day.

With us was Achier, a frail Arabised Dinka whose Muslim name was Beshir, otherwise nicknamed Mongour. Achier was Father's court clerk, the equivalent of a personal secretary. Father's condition seemed to worsen during the flight. Several times, he was short of breath and had to be assisted with oxygen. It was a most precarious journey during which we expected the worst to come at any moment. But he survived the flight.

After a night in a hotel, we checked Father into Maadia Military Hospital where the Shah of Iran was to struggle for his life and died, and where President Sadat was pronounced dead - assassinated. While Achier remained in the hospital with Father, Bol and I shared a comfortable room in a fashionable hotel where the UN had made arrangements for my accommodation.

I was shuttling between the conference and the hospital, sometimes going with Bol and sometimes going alone. The conference was well under way and heading towards its end. Bol and I began to discuss what to do once the conference was over. How long could we afford to wait in Cairo and towards what objective? The doctors gave us an elastic frame of the time it would take. The end could come within days or might take weeks. Perhaps we should take Father back to die at home. How would he take that? There would be no way to conceal from him the facts of the situation. We wondered and pondered.

Suddenly the telephone rang. It was Achier - Father was getting much worse. We rushed to the hospital and found him considerably worse, but he was not dying. Or perhaps to be more accurate, we did not absorb the fact that he was dying. I, for one, had had no experience with death and Bol told me nothing from his experience. Nevertheless, his condition seemed most agonising, certainly to him and also to us as we watched him. We stood around his bed watching him gasping for breath. From time to time, his breathing was aided with oxygen. His voice had disappeared and at best only his mouth would move with faint hardly audible sounds. But his eyes were still glowing penetratingly from his deep sockets, looking at us almost frighteningly and seemingly scrutinising.

At one point, as though it was the last stroke of strength he could muster, the final hope of expression, Father pulled himself up miraculously, put his arms around me, and pulled me towards him, half sitting and half falling back. It happened so suddenly and so fast that I did not reflect on how to react. Achier immediately interceded and disentangled Father's arms from around my neck, as he said, "The doctors say you should not move." Father, still looking intently at us without words, fell back on his back and remained motionless. That was sadly the last scene with our father.

Then Bol and I left the hospital and Achier remained. As I reflected back to Father's embrace, for that was exactly how it had appeared, I felt terrible about what Achier had done and worse at my having allowed him to separate my father from me. I wondered what Father was trying to do or say. Was it just an affectionate embrace? That was a flattering but unlikely thought. Was he trying to take me close to him so that he might tell me something? That was quite likely the case, but what did he want to tell me? Recognising that he might die soon, perhaps that was an attempt to make his dying declaration, probably about his successor or the management of family affairs. As he could not speak loud enough to be heard, he wanted me to get closer to him, especially as he felt a strong sense of ambivalence towards Bol at that moment. What a terrible thing to have done to him, to have repelled and rejected him that way, a man whose touch had always been an honour, a joy and a blessing, I wished another opportunity would arise when I could compensate for my wrong.

I shared my agony with Bol, of course. Probably to alleviate my guilt, Bol dismissed the whole thing as just a dying man's erratic actions, with no significance whatsoever. Whatever Bol's motive, I did not agree with his dismissal of what I saw as a very significant incident and gesture from my father, whether of love or of trust in carrying out his will. But of course, I did not tell Bol my disagreement with his opinion which I respected as a professional viewpoint.

We continued to discuss the situation deep into the night; what should we do? We had barely slept when the telephone rang. I could tell on Bol's face as he answered the phone. Father was dead. He had died only a few hours after we left. Although we had expected death sooner or later, and indeed he had died at a most convenient timing, it was impossible to believe that Father had died and that the world was now without him.

I was suddenly seized by a sense of unreality, not even a dream or a nightmare, just a state of disbelief in the tangibility of things I knew were otherwise real. How could Father be dead? What did that really mean? Could the world possibly function without him? Impossible! I felt particularly bad about the events of our last meeting with him. Now, it was too late; I could never again remedy the wrong I had done to my father and to myself, depriving him and me of the last wonderful gesture of an embrace between father and son. But all that was an exercise in futility.

Then, we were suddenly seized with the formidable burdens he had been shouldering. Could we carry them? We had always known the answer - impossible. But the test was now before us. The purpose for which we had been born, bred, educated and expected to achieve was now at hand. The very meaning of our being must now manifest itself and we must wake up and face reality, if we were to meet the challenge. Father was no more; he was dead and in Dinka thought he had then transfused into ourselves. And we too had now been transformed into Father. We were no longer what we had been. We had now matured into Deng Majok and must fully live up to his towering image.

We got ready and went to the hospital. They asked whether we wanted to see the body. I said we should, but Bol thought differently, arguing that it would be too painful; it would simply make us feel worse. I thought it was wrong for us not to see the body, but did not push my point of view. After all, Bol was the doctor who was more knowledgeable on such matters. But had I reflected more objectively I should have understood how traumatic the experience must have been for Bol. I was also secretly afraid of seeing my father truly dead. Ridiculous as it might now seem, it was as though I thought mystically that there might be hope he was not really dead. So, we simply went ahead to make arrangements for the coffin and for the transportation of the body back to Sudan without a clear image of our father dead.

I handed over my notes to a colleague to prepare the reports and with the help of Sudan consul general in Cairo, Al-Shazzali, we got the body onto the plane and flew back. Our first preoccupation was how to fulfill the only wish our father had expressed - to be buried at home. Since it was the middle of the rainy season, August-September, flying the body home was out of the question. The alternatives were to fly it to one of the nearest towns, El Obeid, Nahud, Kadugli, or thereabouts, and then proceed with the heavy military trucks that could travel in the mud. But that could take many days and there was the question of whether the health authorities would permit such a delay in burying the body.

We landed in Khartoum and quickly took the body to the hospital, where it was kept in a refrigerated room. Then we proceeded to Bona Malwal's house and started passing the news around. We informed Uncle Arop and left him to inform the Dinka. But our focus was on seeking the appropriate means of transporting the body home, beginning with a plane. We went to the house of Joseph Garang with Bona, although the two were political adversaries. Joseph acted promptly, making contacts up to the top. President Jaafar Nimeiri instructed that everything possible should be done to fly the body home. Telephone calls or telegraphic contacts were immediately made with all the towns in the area, beginning with Abyei, to see whether a military plane could land there. We anxiously awaited the replies the following morning. As they came in one by one, it seemed impossible that the plane could land anywhere in the whole province of Kordofan, including the capital town, El Obeid. That was how severe the rainy conditions were.

We began to consider taking the body by train to El Obeid and then on to Abyei by military trucks. At just about the point of despair, word came from Abyei itself that it had not rained for some time; the airstrip was quite dried up and with work to flatten and level the animal and human footprints, it could be improved to land a plane, hoping of course that no rain would fall in the meantime. With orders from above, it was decided to risk the flight straight to Abyei. We would leave early the following morning, the second day in Khartoum.

In the meantime, the Ngok Dinka in the three towns had gathered and started on the performance of the rites of chiefly burial, booming with choral singing of their funeral hymns, forcing the capital city to come to the understanding that Sudan was truly multi-cultural. The morning of our departure, as we proceeded to take the plane, we could not believe the scene from the hospital right to the airport. The Dinka filled the street, tossing the coffin above the crowd as they all struggled to have a share of pall-bearing thundering impressively with their spiritual songs of chiefly burial. In due course, Khartoum airport was literally taken over by the crowds, either participating in, or attracted by, the choral singing and the show of cultural vitality and self-assertiveness of the Dinka. Most of the cabinet turned up at the airport to pay respects and bid farewell. But the only way to do so was for each minister to push his way individually through the crowds, among whom there was only one person who seemed to matter, Deng Majok, now lying breathless in his impressively long and shining coffin.

Bol wanted to sit in the cockpit with the pilot. I knew and let him enjoy the show of his mother's seniority at the point of departure, having agreed that I would take over from El Obeid to Abyei. Many relatives and elders who had waited in Khartoum wanted to come with us, but the only other person the plane could take was Uncle Arop, now the only surviving son of Grandmother, Nyanaghar. We stopped to refuel at El Obeid where the commissioner, the top military brass, and all the notables turned up to meet us and pay their respects to Chief Deng Majok, of whom the province was very proud. They gave us their authorisation and blessing to fulfill whatever Dinka rituals of burial and succession were required. The security chief gave us a written note to that effect. A number of relatives also turned up at the airport and as we approached the crowds, some women started to wail and were hushed into silence, as tradition forbids people crying over the death of a chief.

Then we flew on with me now sitting in the seat next to the copilot, having a commanding view of the panorama, the Northern desert gradually giving way to the blooming green of the Savannah. The Nuba Mountains rose so high that at times the plane meandered around them, piercing through the clouds below the mountain top. Beyond that, the landscape again flattened into an impressive dark green, with rivers, streams and lagoons snaking their way into a network that muddled the sense of direction. That was the first time for us to fly over that territory low enough to observe it from above and even the sadness of the occasion could not distract admiring the scenic beauty.

Uncle Arop urged us not to engage the pilot too much in a conversation, lest he should lose his way. We laughed at his remark, thinking him too naive. But he was right; the pilot lost his way. I first became aware of that fact when I noticed the seriousness on his face and the anxiety in his eyes. At one point, it became so obvious that we were in some kind of trouble that I preferred to speculate than to ask and learn the truth, thinking that it was more with the plane than with the plain. We had been lost for about half an hour before the pilot suddenly beamed and asked, "Can you locate Abyei?" He had identified the Western railroad well into the Bahr el Ghazal Province, had retraced his way back to the Abyei area, and had in fact located the town of Abyei, which looked so rurally blended that it was easy to give it a cursory look as one might a cluster of anthills.

Once he had located Abyei, the pilot sought to show off with acrobatic maneuvers, making a sharp turn at the landing strip, almost tilting the plane upside down and evoking in us a dramatic false alarm. The biggest shock of my seven years away from home was about to reveal itself. At the airstrip, we were met by a crowd which included chiefs, elders, family members, government officials, soldiers and security men, all mixed in a conglomeration that was novel in our experience.

The faces of the Dinka were perhaps the greatest shock of the occasion. The crowd was singing hymns and war songs, the same ones we had heard sung in Khartoum. But the people in Abyei were obviously miserable, dressed in rags or in dirty looking garments, with faces that were not only sombre in mourning, but also yearning for survival. I could not tell whether change within the seven years of my absence had dragged the Dinka downhill or the loss of their chief had shocked and traumatised them into physical and psychological depression. Everybody, Abdalla, Uncle Deng Makuei, and other uncles, elders, women and children looked devastated and downcast, as though they were from another, and evidently lower planet, on which we had landed by mistake. But no, this was home, the very spot Father had insisted he should be brought to, and we had succeeded in bringing him by our efforts to bring the body home, when the idea at first appeared would be futile. His own mission was successfully accomplished. Ours had just begun.

The whole Khartoum experience, the Dinka display of traditional rituals and the courtesy of the government not only in providing the plane but also, and especially, in the cabinet turn up at the airport all showed a remarkable irony of acknowledged importance contrasting with the oblivion and disregard Father had experienced in his final days. What a pity that he could not see all that was happening to him in Khartoum. But perhaps that was the essence of Dinka culture that he typified in many respects - our continued significance to the living rather than our importance to ourselves - we being the dead. Only the true value lies in the dead understanding the potential, preferably the fact of their significance to the living. I think Father did, but with uncertainties, and in the end, very negative uncertainties, happily now reversed, but only too late for his strong sense of pride and dignity to witness. Let us hope he saw it all, after all. Had he seen it, his pride would have been immensely reaffirmed and reinforced by how needed he was; how destroyed Ngokland would, and indeed had, become without

RETURN
Home to Tragedy

him; how miserable everyone looked at seeing the coffin of their protector at the peak of the civil war.

It was clear that Bol and I accompanying Father's casket was a surprise to the people. They had received the news of a plane that would come if the airstrip was levelled. They had worked feverishly at levelling the strip, thinking that some senior government representative was coming. When the name of their chief was mentioned, they thought he was coming back cured and well, fit to resume control. Then they learned the truth only a few hours before our landing. The civil war between the North and the South had crept into Ngok Dinka land and its devastating effect on the people's lives had worsened with the absence of their chief. We saw the people in their worst moment of dire despair, tormented, intimidated, brutalised, and victimised by the ruthless, unscrupulous, and pitiless security forces with their scavenging informants.

Miserable as they all looked, there was a twinkle in their eyes, a reaction to the hopeful surprise of seeing us. The Deng sons had come to take over from their father. Suddenly, their miserable faces, initially at the brink of shedding tears, were beaming with optimistic smiles, as they greeted us, shifting from the solemnness of mourning to the brightness of hope. With the coffin floating over the heads of the crowds, as they boomed with hymns towards our home, we managed to motor our way first, rather discreetly to our collective destination. As it was the rainy season, Abyei was lush with green but slushy with mud. The way from the airstrip on the southern-most tip through the market place towards our home to the north, all less than a mile, seemed a long journey by the roaring pickup that was one of the few still managing the mud.

We were barely recognising the people. Seven years of absence had added unfamiliar dimensions to people's faces. Children had become young men and women; those we had left in the prime of life were getting old; the old had become very elderly; and all were disfigured by grief, want, and fear. We had to focus on familiar faces for a while before we could guess or were told who the people were. Even brothers, sisters, and mothers were both insulted and amused by our inability to identify people. We were failing the test of "Do you recognise me?" if we politely answered in the affirmative, a follow up question would be, "Who am I?" We decided not to even attempt an answer.

Initially, even the physical conditions of Abyei appeared unrecognisable. Things had changed, seemingly for the worse. Even though there appeared to be more buildings, they all seemed exposed, enclosures broken down, streets smeared with mud and looking depressingly dark grey. Even the green lush vegetation seemed overwhelmed with muddiness. This was our first rainy season in Abyei since our childhood; so perhaps it was because of the season that Abyei looked different. However, the cool climate contrasted marvellously with the heat of Khartoum, and as days passed by, the beauty of nature increasingly reasserted itself, until we were once again in love with Abyei in a way that was reminiscent of our childhood memories.

Going back to the scene of arrival, we were directed towards a ritual ceremony, before we could be officially welcomed home. While Bol and I stood facing East, with the Dinka family hierarchy dictating that I should stand on Bol's left hand side, we received the appropriate blessing, which cost a lamb its life for sacrifice, before we could be permitted to enter our home. The coffin arrived and was taken into the cattle byre for the night, attended to by the senior wives. The burial must await the morning, not only to give time to the tribe to assemble and participate, but also because among the Dinka the chief must not be buried after midday, and certainly not in the dark.

As we sat among the tribal notables and the government officials in the open space next to the cattle byre, one of our paternal aunts came and posed a question: "Are you sure that the person in that coffin is my cousin Deng Majok?" It sounded like the voice of the devil putting us to the test, only she was amazingly correct: Were we sure? Bol and I exchanged embarrassed, indeed guilty, glances and discreetly smiled. We said the obvious: "Of course." But objectively and rationally, could we really be sure that Father was in that coffin? I wished we had seen our father's body, if only to convince ourselves that he was truly dead. For about five solid years, I dreamed almost every night about my father, seeing him in varying conditions: at his best, in illness, and as he was in his last days, sick and dying, or coming back after death. For a very long time, my relations with my father remained mysteriously vague – metaphorically, but also really, was he alive or dead?

The following morning, the traditional burial rites began. Among the Dinka, the burial of a chief, unlike that of an ordinary person, is characterised by singing and dancing which, except for the special hymns that mark the occasion, do not differ from the ordinary dancing of happy occasions. The idea is that while the individual chief will have died, the institution of chieftainship continues. Indeed, before the intervention of the British Government, the chief was not allowed to die completely before he was buried. Whether on his own initiative or on that of the elders, a chief who was seriously ill and near death would make his last wishes known and be buried alive to continue living in the memory of his people, if only through his successor, usually his son. According to Dinka burial and succession, a new chief is raised towards the sky and installed as chief the moment the dying or dead chief is lowered into his grave.

This also means that the issue of succession must be determined before a dead chief is placed in the grave. So, the following morning, as the grave was being dug and the tribes were booming with war songs and funeral hymns and dances, the assembly of elders and government representatives met inside a huge tent, which had been erected for shelter during the official days of mourning. But even before the meeting began, the politics of succession were already under way.

No one could believe that our father had not expressed his wishes on the issue and many elders, men and women, would pull us aside to question us in the hope of getting some information on Father's will. It was obvious that everybody had expected Father's word to be conclusive and the only way out of what was feared to be a bitter struggle for power among Father's sons. For a while, things seemed calm on the surface and it even appeared as though we were after all going to avoid the kind of rivalry which had marked the succession to our grandfather. As it turned out later, it was only postponed by the absence of most of the senior brothers, and in particular Adam. Even then, the compulsively competitive Dinka found it necessary to fan tension between the few of us who were present.

A public meeting was then convened to debate and settle the succession problem. For the Dinka, who relish speech-making, that was a solemn occasion on which to display verbal skills. Arabic translation was available and I was using my tape recorder to record the proceedings. The police officer spoke first to assure the Dinka that they were free to follow their traditional ways, both with respect to the burial and the succession. He took out the note we had brought with us from the provincial authorities and read it out loud to assure them of the official support for their customs with respect to both burial and succession. The province authorities had envisaged the protection of the security forces with respect to burial customs, but succession was a logical step which became controversial later only because the outcome, the succession of Abdalla, was not welcomed by the authorities because they suspected him as supporting the Southern rebellion.

During the debate on succession, many elders spoke by way of eulogy to Chief Deng Majok, to glorify his memory as a leader who had established and guaranteed peace, stability, and security in a difficult border territory, and to argue that according to custom, his authority should automatically pass on to his son. Since Abdalla had already been his father's representative while he was away on treatment, speakers argued that he should be acknowledged as the natural successor. To save face for any other son of Deng Majok who might have wished to compete, it was important to stress that Abdalla had already been acting during his father's absence.

Most, if not all, spoke in that vein except one crucial voice, that of Uncle Deng Makuei, who surprised, even shocked, everybody by recalling the conflict between Father and him, claiming that chieftainship had been extorted from him by Deng Majok with the support of the government, and that it should naturally revert to him; he would be happy to continue working with Abdalla for the time being until the issue of seniority was reexamined and his natural leadership over the tribe restored to him. As he spoke, the crowd booed with negative utterances that were very effective. Some even shouted him down, urging him to stop talking.

One of the elders asked the authorities whether the government would allow the tribe to choose one of us, Bol and me, to succeed our father. Bol spoke explaining that we did not want to be considered as contenders. He wisely refrained from mentioning Abdalla as our choice. I spoke, stressing that I regarded myself as not partisan in the competition between the "Houses" and that I was only interested in the unity of the family and the collective good of our people. I also endorsed Abdalla as the son who had already been in charge during Father's absence. The decision was made; Abdalla was to succeed.

The singing and dancing were now at their peak as the grave was nearing completion. There was a suggestion that the coffin be opened so that the body could be adjusted into the folded position of Dinka burial, but we ruled that out, citing health regulations. When all was done and ready, the ceremony reached an emotional peak as the coffin was fetched by a crowd and brought close to the grave. Then they lowered the body as they sang the hymns, and at precisely the same moment, Abdalla was lifted off his feet and pointed towards the sky, his right hand raised even higher above his head. We had been summoned to mark the grave before it was dug and now, we were called to initiate the filling-in of the grave. After throwing in a symbolic amount of earth, the grave was then filled in with the people facing away as they pushed the earth into the grave.

Throughout the burial rites, I had been tape-recording the war songs and the hymns, and of course, the rhythms of the dance. I was somewhat concerned that people might think it was inappropriate. But, having already confronted that issue on the occasion of the death of Uncle Bona Bulabek in 1962, when Father supported my recording songs, and in Khartoum during Father's last days, when I had again received his blessing for recording songs, I was not about to be intimidated into inaction. The only thing I regretted was that I had not brought with me a team of photographers to film the occasion. That had occurred to me in Khartoum, but it was too late to make appropriate arrangements.

Tape-recording was the least I could do. To my surprise, not only did I not find any objection whatsoever, but quite the contrary, I received complaints from tribal sections who said that their songs had not been recorded. Since songs are a means of competition among warring groups, to be outdone, even with respect to the attention of the tape recorder, could be viewed as defeat. Of course, it was always my pleasure to correct the shortcomings. I was proud to produce some years later among several records a long-playing album of funeral songs from the tapes of my father's burial, published by Folkways Records of New York, together with two other albums of Dinka songs.

After Abdalla had been installed as chief, we were approached by Uncle Yai who intimated that by the strict traditional rules of succession, Abdalla could not be considered qualified for chieftainship, if he did not know the secret hymn of Dinka leadership. The hymn was supposed to be passed on from the chief to his heir, and was probably one of the ways of ensuring that the successor met with the approval of his predecessor. It was supposed to be known only to the chief and then passed down only to his successor. The hymn was used as the ultimate resort, the final prayer to supernatural powers, which the chief was to invoke whenever he felt he needed their help. Uncle Yai said he had heard his father, Chief Kuol Arop, sing it in the middle of the night in a solitary prayer where he happened to be near and listening. He had memorised it and would be happy to pass it on to Abdalla.

The fact that Uncle Yai knew the hymn was a novelty; that Abdalla did not know it was part of the crisis of transition. Yai's offer was a gesture of good will because being from Uncle Deng Makuei's section of the family. I suggested that we should record the hymn, and have Abdalla learn it privately at night. Uncle Yai agreed and Uncle Arop, now the elder of our section, also concurred, but with axes to grind because he could not swallow the idea of Yai, a junior son, knowing the secret hymn, which he himself had not been privileged to learn, when he had thought himself the son most beloved of their father.

When Uncle Yai came to record the hymn, Uncle Arop asked to be involved in the recording session. It was a fascinating situation.

RETURN
Home to Tragedy

The hymn was so ancient that the language was totally unintelligible beyond individual words. We had to question Yai a great deal. But Uncle Arop was particularly absorbed, completely mesmerised by the fact that he now had total access to the hymn directly from his father. Uncle Yai occasionally betrayed a sense of guilt for the way he was exposing a secret of hundreds of years, but cherished the sense of unique importance he thereby enjoyed. Tired, exhausted, and still nursing a cold, I handed over the tape recorder to Abdalla at the end of the recording session and fell into a deep sleep.

Shortly after the burial, the rest of the brothers began to arrive from all over Sudan, where they had been working or living with other brothers. There were a number of urgent problems to be tackled. First and foremost, we had to consolidate our position in support of Abdalla as the chief. In other words, we had to foreclose any ambitions for chieftainship on the part of any other brother. Adam Kuol was the other contender.

He was one of the first to arrive after the burial. Impressively dressed and with a bearing that made him look as though consciously acting the role of his father, Adam appeared to be the natural heir to the throne. To reinforce his image, he surrounded himself with an assortment of people, some quite prominent. They followed him wherever he went and made him believe that he was the man the people wanted to be the chief. Of course, he had no doubt that Father had wanted him to be the chief. Indeed, he could not believe that Father had not made a dying declaration to that effect. As though we had been driven by political expedience to misrepresent the facts, Adam once pulled me aside and questioned me closely: "Mading, did Father really not say anything about succession?" I assured him that Father had not said anything. He believed me, I am sure, but he could not understand how that could have happened. Nevertheless, he was certain that Father's intentions, expressed or not, were for him to become the chief. His followers reinforced that belief and also made him trust that if the issue were put to the vote, he would win.

Adam also soon discovered that the authorities, the Northern security complex, were not happy with Abdalla. He therefore calculated that his chances were promising on a number of grounds.

So conspicuous was Adam's political activity or campaign that his ambitions were by no means secret. So, when the family met and we called for a unified stand behind Abdalla, Adam reaffirmed his already evident position. According to him, the traditional need to install a chief the moment the deceased chief is lowered into the grave was what had necessitated the inauguration of Abdalla as chief; because of the absence of other contenders, and because the rainy season had not permitted the presence of national government representatives, the choice of Abdalla had to be considered as temporary. The final decision would have to be made during the dry season, when the national authorities could attend, and the will of the people could then be sought in the presence of all the contenders.

I worked hard, both in public and in private, to convince Adam, but he would not concede. His brothers from the same mother, Ali (Monylam) and Osman (Mijak), accepted my advice that we should not back Adam as members of his House, but should instead stand behind Abdalla to reinforce the unity of the family. They were unequivocal in their agreement with me. Adam's sisters felt differently. One time, as I was trying to convince Adam to concede, Achai, Adam's second sister, far older than ourselves, voiced strong objections to what she saw as exaggerated objectivity on my part. She said that my commitment to family unity was blind to the realities of disunity and that I was unwittingly harming our House in the name of a family unity that did not exist.

The irony in the situation was that Adau, Bol's and Abdalla's eldest sister, came passing by, saw me in the company of Adam and Achai, and immediately concluded that we were conspiring against her brother, Abdalla. Making somewhat apologetic comments for intruding, Adau of course intruded and the subject automatically changed. The change naturally confirmed her suspicion that we were plotting against her brother. She left to spread her own word about where my loyalties really lay and the double-dealing game, she thought I was playing. Before I knew it, word was going around that I was not really behind Abdalla, but was only making a show of support for him and in fact promoting a strategy in support of Adam. The unverified report reaching me seemed to imply that I was perhaps a much more dangerous adversary than Adam himself because I appeared supportive while I was in fact planning the opposite.

My own sisters were embittered by this mistrust which they saw as ingratitude. I tried to ignore them, but I also felt quite indignant about the way my intentions were being distorted. While I could not show my anger to the members of the family, I let my feelings known to Bol, who took me lightheartedly and made no obvious effort to correct the misreading of my role, not because he agreed with the suspicious elements, but simply because he did not see the need to be concerned with unsubstantiated speculations.

Despite all the misunderstandings, I continued to work feverishly to convince Adam and his sisters to respect the family decision. To win Adam on the grounds of his own vanity, I argued that even though he would formally occupy a second position, his age, combined with his own personal qualities of bearing, generosity, and hospitality, could win him greater influence and power than would be implicit in his official status. Of course, I was not trying to undermine Abdalla, but simply to win Adam's support.

But, no matter how much I worked on Adam, I could not persuade him to give in. He even requested me to try to be neutral with the central government authorities and to report the facts of what had happened, without advocating any particular position or line of action by the authorities. I stressed to him that I was committed to family and tribal unity, that a choice had been made, and that there was no way he could persuade me to take his side. I hoped that he would reconsider his position and join the family line. That was the position when we parted.

The issue of chieftainship was only one of the complex family problems that we had to grapple with. Perhaps the most critical question was what to do with the over two hundred wives of our father, most of whom were within childbearing ages and many of whom were still quite young. According to tribal custom, they were to be inherited by us, senior sons, with our cousins and uncles. Father had never cherished the thought of the custom being applied to his wives. Because his sons were all either Christians or Muslims, whose religions did not approve of the custom, he had probably entertained a vague hope that they would not inherit their stepmothers. The time of reckoning had come and only Bol and I were to prove resistant to the temptations of inheriting sexual rights. All the rest of the brothers proved more than willing to shoulder that pleasurable responsibility. Some were quite enthusiastic, and were eventually to demand their inheritance of Father's widows or, in Dinka thought, wives.

The meeting over the inheritance issue was restricted to our brothers and the sons of our full paternal uncles, Biong and Arop, and Aunt Awor. Uncle Arop himself attended. In other words, it was decided to limit the issue to the descendants of Grandmother Nyanaghar, rather than open it up to the whole family of Kuol Arop. There was a general fear that the matter was sensitive and that involving the wider clan could be scandalous. It would imply that the section immediately concerned had failed to live up to the duties and obligations of widow inheritance. Besides, since many people in the wider family saw the inheritance of Deng Majok's widows as a potential for gratuitous sexual gratification, opening up the opportunity might lead to a disgraceful race and rivalry that could result in lead to the wives rampaging for suitors. From this logic, a consensus soon emerged that the inheritance itself be restricted to the immediate circle of Nyanaghar's family.

I was the first to speak out of tune with the trend. I said that marriage had been the single most important subject on which Father had been criticised. Our criticism had been based not only on the economic burdens his marriage imposed on the family, but also because of the injustices and the hardships it inflicted on the wives. The least we should do would be to give those women, especially the ones without children, the right to leave, if they so desired, and without any demand on our part for the return of the bride wealth. I argued that any wives without Father's children who decided to remain within the family and were inherited by relatives should cease to be Father's wives and become wives of those inheriting them. Consequently, the children they would beget would not be considered Father's children but those of the men inheriting them. Those men should be responsible for the maintenance, the rearing, and the education of the children. I also stressed that in all cases the inheritance of wives had to be by mutual consent between the wife (widow) and the man concerned. Under no circumstances should a woman be forced to live with a man she did not desire to live with.

When I had finished, there was dead silence, then a laughter, not of amusement or understanding, but of surprise and bewilderment. Then one voice after another began to oppose my position. The theme was that to let the women go freely would be to disgrace the name of our father and we would be exposed to the scandal of failure to fulfill the most sacred of traditional obligations to a deceased patriarch. As our father together with our ancestors and the deities were watching our performance, failing to meet their expectations would be to invite their curse, quite apart from the worldly shame and insult to which we would be subjected. As those assembled spoke, it appeared as though my viewpoint would receive no sympathy from anyone.

Then Bol spoke in support of my position, but unfortunately chose a highly explosive line of argument, the overpopulation of the family. He said that children were not like chickens to be brought into this world en masse without concern for their livelihood, education and prospects for the future. In some countries, he argued, people would even be "castrated" in order to control the population. My proposal, if adopted, would have the advantage of controlling the size of our family, rendering it more manageable from the point of view of the maintenance and the education of the children.

Uncle Arop, who had been listening with an obviously critical, but absorbed and controlled attention, lost his patience and temper. "You people better stop talking," he said, addressing himself to Bol and me. "You talk like people who have been too long in the lands where they castrate men." His remark was greeted with roaring laughter. Our case was brought to rest, closed forever. The only line of argument which received some sympathy and support was that allocation of wives for inheritance should put into consideration the wishes of the wives so that the mutual consent of both the men and the women be ensured. Even then, this was to be a discreet process in which the freedom of choice should not be viewed as absolute. No woman, for instance, was to choose outside the immediate circle that had been agreed upon and even within that circle certain broad principles of distribution were to be observed. We, however, insisted that those women who wanted to leave, especially those without children, should be let go and we should not demand the return of our bride-wealth. That was a thorny issue, but also not negotiable for Bol and me.

Having exhausted our family affairs, we then held an inclusive meeting with Father's wives to report on the decisions we had taken on family affairs and to counsel them on how to conduct themselves and the principles that should guide their conduct in life. We stressed the importance of maintaining family unity and continuing deference to the name of our father. We should ensure that every one of them had her conjugal needs met, especially with respect to the choice of a partner and requirements for maintenance. On their part, we hoped they would remain loyal to their deceased husband and the integrity and dignity of the family. However, those wishing to leave, and especially young ones without children, could leave and we would demand the retrenchment of the bride-wealth paid for their marriage. And although we would be living abroad, we would follow their interests very closely and would not default in meeting our obligations towards them.

When they spoke in descending order, beginning with their middle seniors, Nyanawai, Amel and Amou, down to some of the young ones, their voices were united in their commitment to the family, their dedication to their deceased husband, and their loyalty to us as his successors. I was surprised by the conviction in their words and tone. Perhaps for the first time, I felt the relativity of the moral and cultural issues we had considered about their status and condition in such a crowded family. A number of the younger wives we had thought would be least likely to remain loyal to our father and his memory stressed the theme that if they had endured some hardships and remained loyal to him in his lifetime, they could not dream of being disloyal to him and leave him after his death. That would not only be morally wrong and unthinkable, but would also be to invite a spiritual curse.

Family and tribal affairs were intertwined and both were extremely demanding. We worked, or rather talked, continuously from sunrise to midnight and often much later. But although the family problems were critical and complex, it was the public interest, the security situation of the tribe, that received the lion share of our preoccupations in Abyei.

Grandfather, Kwol Arop standing next to the first car to go to Abyei area.

Dr. Mansour Khalid, Minister of Foreign Affairs, under whom the Author served as an Ambassador and State Minister.

Author's father, Deng Majok, during the last days of his terminal illness, with the Author, Deng Majok's Assistant, Bashir Achier, and Bona Malwal standing behind him.

INVISIBLE BRIDGE
An African Journey through Cultures

Joseph Ukel Garang, lawyer, first Southern Sudanese to graduate from the University of Khartoum, and a leading member of the Sudan's Communist Party executed for involvement in the attempted internal coup in 1971 against Major General Jaafar Mohammed Nimeiri, initially an ideological ally of the President.

Abel Alier, Southern Sudanese politician, Minister in Nimeiri's Government and First President of the Southern Sudanese Regional Government under their 1972 Addis Ababa Agreement.

Chief Abdalla Moyak Deng, who succeeded his father as Paramount Chief in 1969 and was assassinated in 1970 by the security forces.

Adam Kuol, Author's half brother who competed for succession to their father as Paramount Chief. He was later suspected of having had a hand in the assassination of Abdalla Moyak who succeeded their father. Installed by the security forces as Paramount Chief after assassination of Moyak, he was later dismissed by Nimeiri and replaced by Kuol Adol, who was also assassinated by the Missiriya Arab militants.

General Ibrahim Abboud, President of Sudan, who came to power in 1958 through a military coup. His government was overthrown by the first mass uprising in 1964, partly because of the Southern Problem.

Justin Deng Biong, Anya-nya leader with his cousin Osman Kooc Aguer who were operating in the Abyei area at the time the body of their uncle, Chief Deng Majok, was taken by the Author and his brother Dr. Zachariah Bol, for burial at home.

Jaafar Mohamed Nimeiri, who seized power in May 1969 and ruled until he was overthrown by popular uprising in 1985.

Kuol-Adol, Paramount Chief of the Ngok Dinka, assassinated by the Missiriya Arab extremists on May 4, 2013.

Bona Malwal Madut Ring, a prominent South Sudanese politician and friend of the Author.

CHAPTER SIXTEEN

DESOLATION
PLIGHT OF A PEOPLE

The time for facing the challenge of stepping into Father's shoes could not have been more momentous and critical. There we were in the small and isolated post of Abyei, in the rainy month of September, 1969, amidst a civil war and a population desperate for leadership and redemption. There was no room for uncertainty; we had to take over immediately.

Uncle Anyiel, late Bona Bulabek's elder brother, had just been killed by the security forces the night before our arrival. We had not heard of that before our arrival at Abyei. His widow had said something about being "on the grave of the man who was killed", but I had no idea what she had meant and chose not to question in view of the crowds and the confusion. Bol, too, had heard about it. And Aunt Awuor Kuol, Justin Deng Aguer's mother, who many years back had urged us to advise our father against disaffiliating Ahmed from the family, and whose other son, Osman Kooch, was a rebel leader in the area, had been arrested, detained and tortured to the point where her arms were incapacitated. She was released the day we arrived, and was literally crippled when she met us. Everything was confusion, except Father's death, people's misery, and a big question mark on the future.

Abyei seemed so incredibly removed from the world that it was impossible to believe that we had only a few days ago been in Cairo, attending a UN Human Rights Conference. Far less believable was the fact that I lived in New York City in the United States, working for Human Rights at the UN Headquarters. But all that was remote and far removed. I belonged to Abyei and the meaning of my entire life was now in a delicate balance. Would I make a difference? That was the question. And it had better be in the affirmative.

Although I didn't recognise it at the time, there was a directive from Khartoum that we should be given full protection and courtesy, for, being from the United Nations, as I was, and in particular from the Division of Human Rights, failure to protect us could result in an international embarrassment for the new regime. Whether for this reason or for reasons of their own local security situation, we were barricaded with security forces, paradoxically the symbol of oppression and insecurity among our people.

After we had arrived at our home, undergone the rituals of blessing, and rested a bit, we got up to go to the government resthouse where we chose to stay. We found it to be a rugged frame, beds half broken, the roof infested with bats, and otherwise a habitat of undesirable earthly creatures. But that was not the reason we abandoned it in the end. First, our cousin, Alor Biong, Uncle Biong's eldest son, whispered to us that they would have to place Dinka warriors around the resthouse to guard us and protect us against the security forces - the government army that was supposedly safeguarding the security of the area. Abdalla followed Alor to brief us about the insecurity of the area, posed primarily by the security forces.

Then came the local government officer, Hereika, an old acquaintance and the son of Chief Izzeldine of the Zurug Missiriya tribe, urging us to go to his house. A tall, frail and tired Hereika seemed powerless and helpless amidst the crowds of soldiers and policemen. We declined his invitation politely, but surely. Yet, even as we turned down his generous offer, I was having second thoughts about the place we were in. We were obviously putting ourselves between clearly drawn positions of the army and the people. Quite apart from being conceivably victimised by the army, perhaps misunderstanding our divided loyalties, there was the issue of how effective we could be with the people in charge of security, if we placed ourselves in a position of suspicion and doubt, being guarded by the warriors of a people they considered rebellious?

Then came Ali Sid Ahmed, the military officer in charge of the security forces, a young, newly commissioned officer, a typical city boy, refined, delicate and deceptively smiley. Looking somewhat impatient, he said standing that he would rather have us reside with him in his house, for security reasons, arguing convincingly that he was single and with ample room. I immediately decided that we should accept his invitation. Of course, we did so with typical cultural ambiguity of wanting, but hesitating, until persuaded, all carefully calculated to avoid being seen as eager, and being cornered into an irretrievable rejection. We went to the force commander's quarters, which was modest, but evidently more comfortable. Bol and I shared a room, the officer in a room, with a screened-in verandah in between. The building was secured by a brick wall.

As expected under such circumstances involving a Dinka chief, the forces above had poured down their blessings and it had started raining heavily, almost immediately after our plane had taken off on its return flight. The rest of the evening was therefore spent indoors. Being accommodated by the military officer freed us rather early from any family or tribal social obligations. Even then, Ali, the officer, threw a loaded pistol onto my bed and said, "Have this, you need it here!" How ironic! Our people wanted to provide us with the protection of traditional warriors against this man and his men and there was the commanding officer warning us against our people who feared he was a danger to our security. Again, this indicated the void at the crossroads. I was shocked by the sight of the gun, but having had an exhaustive day and being on the verge of a severe cold, I placed the gun at a safe distance away from my bed and fell into a deep coma of sleep.

The day after Father's burial, I was still nursing a cold and we had been tape-recording the hymn of spiritual leadership for Abdalla late into the night. The sleepless nights of the preceding days were also beginning to take their toll. I fell deeply asleep with a debilitating sense of exhaustion. Bol was apparently having difficulty going to sleep and was trying to wake me up for some pressing reason; I managed to open my ears if not my eyes. "Mading, do you hear what is going on?" I really had not heard and probably could not hear. "What is going on?" I asked drowsily. "Listen!" he said. But I was too tired and too sick to hear, let alone listen. So, I fell back and slept. Bol woke me up again, "Mading, listen!" I listened and heard some movements. "So what?" Again, I fell asleep. Bol woke me up for the third time and said, "Mading, something serious is going on. You heard what we were told about the army and how it has been terrorising the people. I fear something is happening!"

The seriousness of Bol's tone now woke me up fully. We listened and heard some movements, commotion, and murmurs. We listened as much as we could and eventually faded back into sleep on the understanding that we would certainly face the issue in the morning. We woke up very early in the morning, as one does in that part of the world, and began to discuss the events of the night. Even before we deepened our discussion, I suggested that the best way was to talk frankly to the officer about our observations and offer our help in handling the security situation.

The officer joined us for the morning tea. We told him that by virtue of both being the senior sons of Deng Majok and among the educated of the area and indeed the country, we had a natural interest and a special responsibility in the public affairs of the area. We had heard some things said about the situation, for instance the death of Uncle Anyiel Kuol. But we thought we should hear from him, the man responsible for the security of the area, what exactly was going on and whether we could be of any help to him and the authorities to reinforce their security efforts.

Ali's response was far more positive than we had expected. He said he was most appreciative of our frankness and our obvious sincerity, which he thought spoke highly of our patriotism as educated sons of the country, with a national view of things. Then he proceeded to tell us about the state of affairs with remarkable openness. With respect to Anyiel, he said that he himself had shot and killed him. He was convinced that Anyiel had been a rebel leader, who had not only accommodated rebels, but also provided them with medicine. According to Ali, medicines and Anya Nya uniform with the insignia of his rank as an officer were found in his home when it was raided by the security forces for inspection. Anyiel had then been arrested, but he had tried to run. He, Ali, had then felt duty-bound to shoot him.

In his view, there was a dangerous collaboration between the leaders of the tribe, who were from our family, and the local Anya Nya leaders, who were also from our family. Prominent of these local Anya Nya leaders were our cousins, Osman Kooch Aguer and Justin Deng Biong. Word had reached the officer that our cousins were expected to come at night to pay their respects to their late uncle, Deng Majok. The officer had the whole of the Abyei cordoned and our home surrounded and had given instructions that they be shot on sight, if they were spotted. He dramatised the situation by saying, "I gave orders that they be shot dead even on the funeral carpet."

So, what Bol had heard were the activities surrounding our cousins and had they turned up, another family tragedy would have been raging that morning. As the officer spoke, it was difficult to decide how to respond. It was clearly a mad scene and the officer seemed to typify that lunacy. When he had finished speaking, we told him that we appreciated his frankness. We said the man he had killed was a very dear uncle to us. We were naturally aggrieved and felt a deep sense of loss. However, the real issue in front of us was not to dwell on the dead, but to promote peace and security for the living. We should therefore see what we could do in cooperation with one another to achieve that objective. We then proposed a plan of action in which we would first call a public meeting to discuss the general security situation and to acquire insight into the way the Dinka themselves viewed the problems. We would then reconsider the appropriate measures to take.

Ali appreciated the approach and even suggested that neither he nor any of his security forces should attend. He hoped thereby to facilitate maximum freedom of expression without fear. I was not entirely convinced by his reasoning because we wanted everyone to know what everyone else thought about the situation in the hope of exploring the common ground for a comprehensive resolution of the conflicts. The security people, the critical elements in the situation, to be absent, was to reduce the value of the meeting considerably. But all the same, Ali's point of view was valid that their presence might inhibit free expression of views and in any case, we would convey to them in a constructive manner whatever would transpire at the meeting.

The meeting was one of the best attended in the history of the Ngok Dinka. For one thing, all the subtribes were still in Abyei after the burial. Besides, the issue was one of the most critical in living memory. The shade of the tree under which the meeting was held overflowed with people: elders, youth, men, women, children, and the Arab traders who had settled in Abyei and could claim to be local inhabitants. As I got up to open the meeting, I could not help recall that we were there because our father was dead and that we were his heirs, "standing Father's head upright" in Dinka metaphor, and symbolising his continuity or immortality through his progeny, what Harold Lasswell had made me dub as "permanent identity and influence". The picture of my father getting up to talk in public gatherings came to my mind. I could see him clearly tantalising his audience with the expectation of what he would say as he got up, hoisted his head high, adjusted his shawl over his jallabiya, turning his head majestically left and right, or right and left, as though to size up his audience, and then speaking with confidence, almost arrogance, but also with overwhelming wisdom and verbal talent. It was as though I were putting myself into a state of trance and turning myself into a medium through which my father himself could come back from his grave and address his people. As I spoke, I felt an inward satisfaction that I succeeded in projecting Deng Majok. In the words I uttered, the way I stood and the wave of my hands, even the twist of my lips, I felt truly as a reincarnation of my father.

I cannot reproduce with precision what I said at the meeting, but it was essentially to impress upon the audience our awareness of the grave security situation the area was in; how much we had heard from various sources about the causes of the problem; and our desire to learn from them what exactly was going on and how they themselves appraised the situation. I told them that although our father was dead, it would be seriously wrong for anyone to assume that Father had left a vacuum that could not be filled and therefore to behave in a way that would endanger the security of the people which had been Father's preoccupation, especially in his last days. We were there as his children to fill that vacuum and we were determined to get to the roots of the problems and find solutions that would restore security for every person. I urged them to speak their minds, to tell the truth, and enable us to make a sound assessment of the situation and develop appropriate remedies with the security authorities. Bol spoke, endorsing and re-affirming what I had said.

People began to speak, substantiating the theme of a "spoiled world" that had already impressed itself upon us. Their voices were those of a people tragically squeezed between two formidable forces they could not confront, far less combat, the security forces in Abyei and the rebel forces in the forest. The focus of their bitterness was on the handful of opportunist "informants" at whom they pointed their fingers, of course without names, as the people "spoiling" the land, subjecting them to terrorism and oftentimes, death. One Arab trader, Babo Ali Beshir, the eldest son of the head merchant, Ali Beshir, was there. Married to a Dinka girl, fluent in Dinka, one of the most integrated of the Arabs, Babo spoke, fully, identifying himself with the Dinka point of view. He likened Abyei to a ship adrift at sea, the captain lost, the passengers exposed to a dragon, whose deadly hands would emerge from the waters and grab a person, then submerge with the person only to reemerge again to grab another person. The people in the ship were being helplessly exterminated. He saw us as god-sent captains who would assume the command of the ship, restore a course of direction, identify the source of the dangerous dragon and hopefully rid the passengers of that danger and guide the ship ashore.

Our younger brother, Osman (Mijak), got up to speak. He said that he did not agree with our encouraging the people to speak their minds. We should remember that our people were exposed to imminent dangers from the security forces, that even as we spoke with supposed freedom, their informants were probably there listening on their behalf. They would soon be fully in the picture as to who said what and dreadful consequences would almost certainly befall those voicing objections to the manner in which they were handling the security situation. He said that we ourselves would soon be leaving Abyei while the people would remain exposed and defenceless. He advised the people not to be frank, adding that he himself was saying all that because he did not care what would befall him; he would rather warn his people even if that led to his arrest or death. He also spoke about the death of Uncle Anyiel, saying that when the dry season came and the road opened, he would proceed to the central authorities to pursue the case against those who had killed him. In the meantime, he said, he hoped we would help present the case when we returned to Khartoum and met with central authorities. When Osman finished talking, he received enormous applause from the audience. It was quite obvious that he had said what was in their hearts and minds but could not voice.

We assured the people that we had agreed with the security authorities that they be allowed full freedom to speak their minds and that they should continue to be very frank, completely uninhibited by fear. The lengthy meeting continued almost indefinitely for, as in all Dinka meetings, almost everyone who counted wanted to be heard and as all Dinka feel they count, one speech followed another until the end came almost by exhaustion rather than by decision. As our concluding remarks, we gave them the gist of our work plan. We would conduct intensive contacts with all concerned, develop a comprehensive formula for tackling the security problems of the area, and then reconvene again to present our formula for a general consensus. We however stressed the importance of working through the established institutions and the official channels of tribal authority. Anyone who saw personal advantage of being a self-serving carrier of information, often erroneous and unsubstantiated, yet with severe risks to the freedom and lives of others, was not only discrediting the legitimate authority and the tribal code of conduct, but living on other people's blood. By any ethical standards, eventually carried a curse, perhaps entailing death.

We impressed upon them that our presence was a confirmation and reaffirmation of our father's authority, now descended upon us. We were not going to permit self-seeking, unscrupulous opportunists to endanger the security and life of our people, and in asserting our sacred duty, we were not simply dependent on the support of secular authority, but primarily on the ultimate sanctions of the divine forces behind us, including those of our ancestors, the chiefs who had parted, but were still watching over us and safeguarding the interests of their people. It was anthropology at work, applied in the true sense of the word, delivered in the best fashion of my father that I could recall, muster and project.

When the meeting ended, I could hear the people around me uttering, "Spoken exactly like his father". "What a perfect standing (continuation) of Deng Majok's head" and the like.

Achuil Bulabek, who had always been very close to Father, and was one of the elders whom I held in great esteem, was later to say to a group of people within my hearing distance: "Listening to Mading talk, could one say that Deng Majok is dead? Was he not truly a living image of Deng Majok? I can say that he spoke even better than Deng Majok. His education made him excel over Deng Majok." I was obviously elated to hear such words being spoken of me, particularly by such a prominent personality as Achuil Bulabek. But I was startled to hear him say that I excelled over my father; that was un-Dinka, for, except for my father, who believed he outperformed his father, the Dinka never claim to do better than their fathers; they always uphold a strong bias in favour of a father, in particular when deceased. Yet, I recognised that they also accepted the superiority of modern education and its advantages over traditional knowledge. Achuil was simply reiterating a truism of modern thought among the Dinka. But, in comparing himself to chiefs who could write while he himself was unable to write or read, Father was popularly known to have said that things may be written down on paper, but will ultimately be said by the mouth.

The superiority of education and the power implicit in it were indeed seen by the Dinka in the mere fact of our having brought our father's body back in an airplane in the near-impossible rainy season and at such a timely moment of greatest tribal need. The whole situation seemed incomprehensible, especially in view of the fact that we had been away for seven years, and almost presumed forever lost. Bol's mother was to say that she had never really believed in the value of education, but that our returning with our father's body by plane and in a season where no one could expect a plane to land in Abyei had convinced her that modern education was indeed of sacred value.

We went and met with Ali, the officer, briefed him in considerable details and began to work on a comprehensive plan of action. There were three main facets to the line of action we envisaged. One was to reinforce the authoritative line of communication with the legitimate leadership of the tribe. The other was to enter into contact with the local rebel leaders and achieve some understanding that would remove their threats which provoked reactions from the security forces, all of which contributed to a vicious cycle of instability and insecurity. Then there was the final phase of mobilising the people of the tribe behind one line of approach to the political and security situation in the area, to ensure full cooperation with the legitimate tribal leaders and the security authorities.

With respect to the channels of communication, we stressed to the officer the concerns of the tribe about his unofficial and faceless informants who were considered by the people as selfishly motivated to win individual advantages without the interest of the community in the peace and stability of the area at heart. We reminded him of how our father had been the only point of contact with the government authorities in the tribe, representing the government to the people and the people to the government, thereby leaving no room for unscrupulous opportunistic volunteers and sellers of contrived information.

Ali in turn voiced concern over what he believed as the uncooperative or at best ambivalent attitude of Abdalla, whom he said was suspected of cooperation with the rebels. He said that unless Abdalla was unequivocally committed to cooperating with the security authorities, not only would it be difficult to operate through him, but worse, his own security would be endangered. Ali was extremely frank on the issue, intimating to us that he had found in the confidential files, strong statements against Abdalla and that we should advise him quite seriously on the implications of his conduct. We agreed on that line of action.

On the second issue, contact with the local rebel leaders, Osman Kooch Aguer and Justin Deng Biong, we suggested getting in touch with them and inviting them to meet with us in any place of their choice, under full guarantee of their safety. Our intention was to try to persuade them to take advantage of the amnesty law which had just been declared by the government and return to the tribe to assist in shouldering the burden of leadership which Father's death had placed on our generation. If they refused to surrender, then we would ask them to move their activities further South, away from the border area of the Ngok Dinka, which was too exposed and vulnerable to the government security forces. Under no circumstances, however, would they be subjected to any danger or arrest, even if they should choose to remain rebels. Ali initially opposed our suggestion.

According to the army officer, contact with the rebels was illegal and he could not enter into any agreement with us to see them. We argued with him vehemently, pointing out that his viewpoint was contrary to the amnesty policy already enacted into law and that in any case our objective was to secure their surrender and pacify the situation. After a prolonged discussion of the issue, he ultimately agreed. I drafted a long, strongly worded letter in which I described the dreadful situation our people were in, under continuous threat of death from both the Anya Nya and the security forces. I spoke of the policy of evolving a regional autonomy for the South announced by the new regime, the amnesty law that had been passed to ensure safe return for the Anya Nya, and the current constructive thinking of the Southern leadership in Khartoum. But above all, I stressed the tragedy of our people, the vulnerability of their location as a border area, how the situation had been aggravated by Father's death, and the challenges that required the younger generation to assume control and provide constructive leadership. I pleaded with them to come, or meet us to discuss further, or failing that, to remove themselves far away from our desperate people to let them breathe the air of relief in security.

It was a deeply moving letter. When Ali read it, his eyelids heavy with concealed tears, his emotions beyond himself, he announced, "This is the most patriotic statement I have ever seen. It is a historic document and if you will permit, I would like to translate it into Arabic and have it sent to the Army headquarters in Khartoum, for it ought to be preserved as a historic document." We worked on its translation and made two copies for Osman Kooch Aguer and Justin Deng Biong.

The question now was who should carry the letter to them. No one would admit to knowing their whereabouts, let alone accept being sent to them. Everyone was afraid that whatever assurances the Arab officer gave us, he would never keep his word. Anyone who exposed himself by confessing knowledge of their whereabouts or by undertaking to meet them was destined to suffer torture and perhaps death, whether immediately or later. Several people were thought best suited on account of acceptability to our rebel cousin leaders, but they all declined and could not be persuaded otherwise. In the end, only Arop Biong, the full brother of Justin Deng Biong, and Kolkech, the paternal cousin of Osman Kooch Aguer, accepted the risk of the mission. So, they went with the letter, having ascertained the whereabouts of our cousins.

In the meantime, the officer had also been trying to trail them through his informants, but without much result, as the Dinka were all acting totally ignorant. His informants had, however, learned that the rebels had spent a night in the home of someone ten miles north of Abyei. The man in whose home they had stayed had slaughtered a bull and made a feast for them. They were said to have moved on, heading for another area. The officer had given instructions for his men to go to the home of the man who had accommodated them and given them hospitality and to have him arrested and brought to Abyei.

That same day, we went to our home, as we always did during the day time, to conduct our contacts with elders and to also look into our own family affairs. As we were about to get into the car to return to the officer's house, my mother told me that Uncle Ngor had just arrived and wanted to greet us. Bol and I went to meet him. I was delighted to see Ngor again looking healthy, strolling towards us with the bearing of pride and quiet dignity which was characteristic of him. Then he said he had just arrived having looked after "the young men" who had spent a night in his home. "What young men?" I asked quite innocently, out of natural curiosity. "The Anya Nya leaders, Kooch Aguer and Deng Biong", Ngor explained. "They were in my home a day ago and I had a bull slaughtered for them and offered them hospitality." He was obviously proud of what he had done. I could not believe the casual calm manner in which he spoke. To call it frankness or honesty would be to give it a consciousness or awareness of the danger to which he was exposed and to which he was absolutely oblivious. It was a true case of naïveté at the door-step of death. "So, you are the man the officer was talking to us about!" I said, fully realising that my uncle was in an imminent danger.

Without reflecting any further, I said to my Uncle, "Get into the car." "What is the matter?" he asked, sensing that something was obviously amiss. "Where are we going?" he asked. "Don't ask questions, just get into the car." I was feeling the drama of the situation. But then I felt I had to explain, for Ngor was genuinely in the dark and looked puzzled by my conduct: "We have to take you to the officer; his men are right now looking for you and may find you any minute. If they saw you and arrested you, they would take you to a place where our protection might be too late or too remote." Despite the explanation I offered, I was acting more out of intuition than on reflection.

On getting back to the officer's house and finding Ali, my stream of consciousness or intuition continued to operate: "We have brought you the man your people are looking for; he is not only my maternal uncle, he is one of the people dearest to me. We brought him so that he could tell you his own story." Ali was flabbergasted. They entered into a dialogue and I assumed the role of the interpreter:

"Was it in your house that the rebels spent the night?"
"Yes!"
"And you slaughtered a bull for them?"

"Yes!"

"Why did you do that? Did you not know that they were rebels?"

"I knew that they were rebels, but I also knew that they carried guns and they were many; I only carried spears and I was only one. They wanted food and accommodation and I knew that if I didn't offer them, they would take them from me by force and maybe along with my life. As soon as they were gone, I took my spears and came to Abyei. Knowing that my nephews were here, and they being responsible men, I came and told them about what had just happened."

Uncle Ngor was brilliant in his performance. We had not even prepared him to speak the way he did. Besides, throughout the interview, he remained calm and confident as he told the truth in the best possible way.

Ali appeared totally disarmed by what he heard. When he spoke, it was simply to say, "You have broken the law by accommodating rebels and giving them food. What you have done is enough to put you in prison for a long term and could even end your life. My men are right now looking for you. If they had found you, they would have arrested you or even shot you for having done what you have done. Because of your nephews, who are responsible people helping us to maintain security, I will leave you."

I sighed with relief. We averted a tragedy. But Ali had another idea. "I am leaving you on one condition only, and that is that you join us to be our informant on rebel activities in your area." I interpreted everything factually until he came to his condition of making my uncle his informant. That is where I injected my own opinion. I said that my uncle was a respectable man in the community and that he, Ali, should be realistic enough to know that the role of the informant was not respected in the society. I could not see my uncle assume such a demeaning role which we ourselves hoped could be replaced by the more respectable role of legitimate tribal authority.

Ali did not argue against my position. He only suggested another alternative, that Uncle Ngor should move into Abyei to avoid the dangers of being squeezed between the rebels and the security forces. His suggestion sounded reasonable and acceptable. Ngor was willing to abide. In the end, Ali spoke rather lightheartedly, "You are a very lucky man to have had this happen in the presence of your nephews. Otherwise you would probably be a dead man." Ngor, still in control of the situation, would not be outwitted: "It is not luck; it is just that God knows the truth." When I interpreted his words, Ali laughed and said to my uncle "You are clever devil!"

The second line of action that we had agreed upon with Ali was to unify the channels of communication and to restrict his source of information to the tribal chiefs on top of whom was Abdalla. We scrutinised Abdalla very closely to ascertain his mode of operation with the authorities and the rebels and found that while he was obviously poised in a delicately dangerous situation between the security forces and the rebels, the suspicions against him were largely due to misunderstandings, some of which had deliberately been fostered by the unofficial informants who were also members of the opposition to our family.

The fact that the leaders of the bush army were members of the same family as the leaders at home made the latter quite vulnerable to suspicions. Indeed, in his later years, Father had become increasingly suspected for harnessing both leaderships in a cleverly orchestrated fashion, dealing with the rebels covertly and with the security forces overtly. But whatever the suspicions against Father, his authority had been so overpowering that the security officers could not confront him critically. Abdalla was in a more vulnerable position and an easy target of both tribal opposition and official security suspicions.

We tried to clear the air between Abdalla and the officer and reestablish a sense of mutual confidence and cooperation. Judging from the later events, this was by no means an easy task, but we managed to achieve a workable formula whereby Abdalla and his subordinate chiefs would maintain close contact with the officer as the official channels of communication. The officer was to terminate dependency on the unofficial informants who had clearly proved to be a source of tension and misunderstanding between the security authorities and the people. We recommended Omda Achuil to both Abdalla and the officer as a man whose experience as a close associate of Deng Majok could prove invaluable in dealing with the people.

Our third line of action was to hold a final meeting of the entire tribe after having made a thorough evaluation of the whole situation to present a comprehensive security strategy for the area. The response from Osman and Justin was negative in the sense that they refused to surrender. The messengers said that they had very carefully considered the letter and had been so moved that it seemed quite apparent that they would surrender. But their colleagues had persuaded them at the last minute that they should not give in as the Arab force commander could not be trusted to keep his word for their safety.

With their position made clear, we had no alternative but to urge the people to cooperate with the security forces, and pray and hope that our cousins would remove themselves further south away from the Ngok zone. We therefore agreed to call the public meeting in which to announce our findings, primarily focused on the fact that the presence of "the people of the forest" in Abyei area and the role of the unofficial informants were the central causes of the security problem. We would then recommend that the leaders and the people of the tribe should unify their front to distance themselves from the people of the forest – or as the anti-government rebels were locally known – and work through the recognised legitimate leaders of the tribe in their communications with the security leaders to remedy this dualistic security problem.

Those removed from the situation prevalent in Abyei at the time may read into our attitude a letdown to the people of the forest, but a close understanding of the problems confronting our people at the time would dispel such accusation. The Dinka were truly terrorised, exposed to imminent dangers that might result in death on the most trifling security grounds conceivable. An arrest and a path leading to the military as opposed to the police headquarters, were all that were needed to expect torture and sure death. It was a reign of terror in its true definition and we were soon to witness evidence of that even as we all seemed to agree on a plan of action and were awaiting a general meeting in which to announce the plan.

We had stayed late at home and were returning to our sleeping place at the officer's residence close to midnight. Our relatives felt that we should be escorted back by tribal warriors, but we refused, insisting that it was not necessary. In any case, what use would their spears be in the face of guns. So, we went alone, Bol and I, going through the market place. We were not aware of any soldiers as we walked, talking and reflecting on the events of the day. Suddenly, in the death-like stillness of the night, we heard a loud, but mysterious voice which seemed to come from the dark verandahs of the shops, but without any clear sense of the direction from which it came: "Who goes?" shouted the voice, which we recognised to be that of a soldier on guard. Startled, but calm, we said, "We", hoping that he would read into that a message of confidence and authority. But he was not impressed: "Who are you?" I said, "Zachariah and Francis!" But even that did not seem to impress him. "Who?" he asked again, as he emerged from his darkness with the gun well-adjusted in our direction. We repeated our identification with an increasing sense of concern. He stood looking at us, gun in hand, presumably loaded, and pointed at us. It was as though he was considering a decision he had made to shoot to kill. In the circumstances of Abyei, and indeed in the conditions of the civil war in the South, that would have been the natural thing to do. And the explanation that would then be given would be more convincing to the authorities than any allegations against the security forces. For one reason or another, he refrained from executing the sentence of death against us. "Go," he said very rudely, but much to our relief.

It was the morning of the same day of the planned general meeting; we were having breakfast at the time. Ali was with us. Suddenly, a soldier came and drew his attention. Ali stepped into his office, which opened into the sitting-room-verandah combination, where we were having breakfast. We thought that he was involved in some routine work of little consequence to us or our plan. We wondered whether to wait for him or proceed with breakfast. But we did not have long to wait. Shortly after he had withdrawn, one of our brothers entered the room, breathing heavily, almost out of breath because he had been running. In between halts, gasping for breath, he announced that our brother, Osman Mijak, who had spoken at the meeting, had been arrested and taken to the military headquarters.

To be arrested was bad enough; to be taken to the military quarters was tantamount to a death sentence. The execution would be immediate. After listening to the hysterical brother, a dead silence fell on us. Now, it all figured. Ali had withdrawn to meet his new prisoner. And there he was, next to where we were eating, probably interrogating our brother or perhaps signing a death sentence, the execution of which might soon be under way. I felt an urge to jump up, bang his office door, push it open, and have a last-minute showdown with Ali, come what may. But then I remembered that we had a role beyond the demonstration of fortitude and that utmost patience could do better for more people than an ill-conceived emotional outburst.

So, we sat patiently as we reflected deeply. We seemed to have waited forever and yet Ali could not have gone for more than fifteen minutes. Suddenly, almost unexpectedly, he resurfaced, a fake smile on his face, acting as though nothing at all had happened. "Why aren't you eating?" he asked casually, as if to assure us that all was well. "Come on, go ahead!"

He sat and acted so natural and so gratified that it was impossible to detect that there was any problem, except for the fact that we knew there was a serious problem.

I broke our tense and scary silence: "Ali, you do not really expect us to proceed and eat while our brother is your prisoner for reasons we do not know, do you?"

He said, "You mean Osman?"

"Of course, I mean Osman, unless someone else has also been detained since Osman's arrest!" I answered with a tone of angry sarcasm.

He answered without emotions: "I have sent him over to the police station for investigation. It is for the police to determine the gravity of his offence."

We were beside ourselves with anger, indeed fury, "What is he arrested for, may I ask?" I said.

Ali, still lighthearted, wholly oblivious to the degree of anger he had provoked in us, said, "He has committed a serious offence, but we better leave that to the police to determine. All I have done is committed him to the police investigation."

"Ali," I said, making no effort to conceal my indignation, "I am a lawyer by training and one of the cardinal rules of criminal justice is that you are presumed innocent until proven guilty by a court of law and you cannot be arrested unless there is a *prima facie* criminal case against you. Can you tell us what *prima facie* crime Osman has committed?"

Ali, again talking playfully, said, "Are you telling me that you do not know?"

"Of course, we do not know," I retorted, "What are you talking about?"

Then he suddenly retreated, stating, "Well, the case is with the police; we better leave it there until they determine their case."

By now, all measures of tolerance or self-control were rapidly evaporating. "Ali, if you think we can go and face our people and talk to them about cooperating with the security forces, while our brother has just been arrested for reasons we do not even know, you are utterly mistaken. In fact, by this conduct, you have just confirmed all the things we have been hearing about the security forces in Abyei. All that is left for us to do is leave and report honestly to the central government authorities and let them judge."

Ali could detect the seriousness of my tone and he was not about to have a confrontation with us for reasons best known to him. After moments of reflection, he declared: "Alright; in order not to embarrass you with the audience, I shall have Osman released to attend the assembly, but he must then return to jail after the meeting."

He had only added fuel to the simmering fire in us: "Do you really think that we can agree with you to fool our people during the meeting only to be exposed shortly afterwards? There is no way we can face our people unless Osman is free in the full sense of the word."

My words were final and of course I was speaking for both of us, Bol and me. Ali understood that. He reflected for a moment and then tried to impress upon us the seriousness of Osman's wrong: "What Osman has done poses a threat not only to the security of Abyei, but also to the security of the entire country."

"What has he done?" I asked.

"What did he say in the public meeting?" Ali asked, rather cunningly.

I said I could not recall anything that was wrongful or could justify any criminal charges. I then proceeded to recall Osman's warning to the people not to speak their minds on the security situation in fear of the consequences against them.

Ali punctuated, "Yes, what else?"

I proceeded to report, "And he said that he would pursue the case of his Uncle Anyiel when the road opened!"

"Yes!" commented Ali in anticipation of more.

"And that he hoped we would help them."

This gave Ali his justification: "You see; now you know!"

I did not understand what he had in mind. "What do you mean 'now you know'?"

"Well," Ali explained, "he said, 'help us' didn't he?"

"And what do you understand by that, help with guns?"

I intended to refute his logic with an absurdity. To my surprise, Ali reacted: "You clever devil! Of course, you know."

Then he proceeded to tell us that according to his informants, Osman had said, "When you go back to America, help us with arms to come and fight the Arabs."

When I heard him, I laughed out loudly with a sigh of scorn and relief: "Let's go and take him out of prison and forget the whole affair" I said. "There is certainly no case against Osman. The report of your informants is utter nonsense."

We were talking with conviction and confidence. But Ali was not going to be easily defeated. "I had four informants at the meeting and all of them, reporting separately, said exactly the same thing. They could not all be wrong."

When I insisted that they were indeed wrong, Ali said that if they were, he would be forced to punish them, and that would discredit their system of information. He could not do that. He had to presume that his informants were right.

Ali then proceeded to tell us what Babo Ali Beshir had also said at the meeting. He wanted to prove that he had indeed been fully briefed on all that had transpired. But, perhaps, he simply wanted to give himself an excuse for displaying anger against Babo. We were to learn later that Babo had been interrogated by the police for his statements at the meeting.

On the case of Osman, we stressed to Ali that it was our word against the word of his informants and that we did not care whether they were four or a hundred, they were all liars. I asked Ali how anyone could assume Osman to be so stupid as to make such a dangerous statement in public when he was warning his people not to speak their minds. What was more, was he, Ali, not really insinuating that there was a possibility of our responding to Osman's request by sending arms from the United States into Sudan? How else would Osman's statement be dangerous to the security of Abyei and the entire Sudan!?

There was another angle to the whole issue. How could he, Ali, have the meeting infiltrated by secret agents when he had told us, and we had told the people, that they were to feel free and uninhibited, and that no one would be exposed to any danger of punishment on account of what one had said during the meeting that was open to members of the public?

Ali had no answers for our questions. He was obviously weakening. He argued that the case was no longer in his hands and that it would be for the judge to decide whether Osman was guilty or not. In the meantime, he was prepared to arrange his temporary release until the trial commenced. In any case, he suggested that we should go to the station to discuss the matter with the police authorities.

On our way to the police station, I reminded him again that according to the law, no one could be detained unless there was a prima facie case against him and that after listening to his allegations, there was no such case against Osman. Eventually and as we were arriving at the police station, Ali announced: "I will let him go free in deference to you. But Osman is very ill-mannered and should have faced imprisonment for his impudence." Osman was released and we went to the meeting together.

We talked at great length, presenting to the public the full report of our work during the entire month we had spent at Abyei, the consultations we had conducted, the main issues that had emerged, the conclusions we had reached on those issues, and the line of action we had agreed upon with the security authorities. It was a long and constructive talk, which would have reassured everyone, had Ali not decided to make some tough and threatening remarks, which ended the meeting on a confrontational note. It was in essence more of a childish display than an act of calculated antagonistic leadership.

Yet, that was the worst part of the Abyei situation; it was in the hands of a youngster who was as scared as he was determined to demonstrate toughness and soldiery. People left the assembly quite confused, not knowing whether to feel reassured of peace and security or threatened with renewed terror and intimidation. We had resolved all the differences and had presented a comprehensive plan that guaranteed full cooperation between the people, their leaders, and hoped the security forces. But the final words of Ali had not reflected the new spirit which we had just advocated. It suddenly seemed as though our month in Abyei had been wasted.

It soon began to rain. We were at home in what had been Father's courtroom, but with walls half-broken down and the thatch beginning to fall apart. Yet, it still provided shelter not only from the sun, but also from the rain. Many people clustered inside like a flock of sheep frightened by a lion roaring outside a disintegrating byre. Achuil Bulabek was there. They were all recalling with deep sorrow the destruction of the social order and tribal dignity which the officer's conduct during the meeting had demonstrated. They recalled that in the entire history of the Ngok Dinka, no Arab, whatever his authority, had ever spoken once the chief had said his last word to his people. Ali had not only spoken after we had said our final word, he had threatened and intimidated a people with whom he had just been reconciled. And then, he rose and left, thereby ending the meeting on the tone of disharmony, indeed animosity. Could that ever have happened during the time of Deng Majok? People raised the question rhetorically. "Never!" They unanimously agreed.

Yet, they saw some security in our presence. Soon, initiated by one young man, all were urging us to postpone our departure and continue our watch and protection over them just a little longer. They argued that it was with our appearance that death had been halted and that it was certain to be resumed once we left. Interestingly enough, our mothers and sisters were urging us to leave, as they feared that we ourselves might fall victims of the security forces. The insinuation of our involvement implied in the allegations against Osman was for them indication of Ali's intention to find some justification for doing away with us sooner or later.

But we had to leave because we had long exceeded our official holidays and, in any case, felt that we might help more by informing the central authorities of what was happening in Abyei. Fear had long left us; life and death seemed to be two interconnected aspects of existence. To be precise, we were not mindless of the dangers to which we were exposed and we even felt anxious occasionally, but we had decided to sacrifice ourselves to the service of our people, come what may.

The day before we left, Ali told us that he wanted to put us in the picture about arrests within our family which he was planning to make the very morning of our departure. According to him, all hostile elements in Abyei had either been weeded out and put in jail or had been sufficiently pacified. The only pocket of hostile activities that remained were in our family and confined to only a handful of cousins. After that, there would be nothing else to worry about. He urged us not to be concerned about the arrests. The people would be perfectly safe. He simply wanted to teach the concerned members of our family a light lesson and to impress upon the tribe that even members of the chief's family were not immune from the power of the law.

It seemed futile to enter into another argument with Ali. The problem was too profound and pervasive and the points of confrontation and potential conflict seemed endless. We became even more convinced that shifting the focus of our work to Khartoum would probably be far wiser than continuing the struggle in Abyei.

In the morning, as the military convoy that would escort us was getting ready for our departure and the crowds of people who wanted to see us stood in scattered groups, someone came running to tell us that our cousins had just been arrested and taken to the police station. All we could do was try to assure them that we were well aware of their arrest and that they would be safe. We urged them to calm the people down and permit no foolish reaction that would result in greater harm.

Then came the moment of departure, the convoy moving slowly and stopping from place to place as though halted by the gripping hands of the crowds of relatives and strangers that clustered around us, some of them voicing concern over the situation we were leaving behind, others discussing family problems, yet others wanting last small acts of kindness from us, and others simply bidding farewell.

We tried to meet all aspirations, delegating tasks that had been overlooked in the rush of things and for which there was no more time for action by us. It was a departure not dissimilar to our father's, yet with a profound difference. Our father had always left in glory, but we were leaving in partial defeat, reasoning and glossing over the arrest of relatives, whose fate we could not control and were apprehensive about.

We moved on to spend the night only a few miles away from Noong, our childhood home. Despite the power of those Mercedes-Benz trucks, they could only overcome the muddy conditions of the rainy season at the formidable price of slow speed, getting stuck every now and then, and proceeding only with the grace of the military manpower that was precariously abundant around us.

As we slept, the soldiers scattered around the camp to guard against any dangers, the most awesome of which were the Anya Nya rebels, whose whereabouts could not be predicted. Yet, we were to hear later from our people, the Dinka, who claimed to have learned from sympathetic military sources or Dinka informants, that there was a plan to stage a fictitious attack by the Anya Nya, have us killed in the process, and then have the announcement claim that we had been killed by the rebels, a familiar theme of the civil war. The plan was abandoned, thanks to mysterious reasons still unknown to us.

The rest of the journey between Abyei and Muglad was uneventful, though quite heroic as our military convoy forced its way through the heavy, muddy, flooded woodlands, meandering between thorny trees, with the trucks driven as much by the human push as by the engines. We all matched our surroundings with bare feet, and wet muddy clothes, caring about nothing but forging ahead.

We stopped briefly at Muglad where many Arabs came to express their condolences, others to renew their dedication to the friendship with our family, some of them offering a detailed historical account of the relationship, appreciating that we were rather disadvantaged on our knowledge of tradition because of alienating modern education.

Our first report was to the authorities at Fulah, the district headquarters, where we soon came to understand that our words were received with skepticism. We proceeded to El Obeid, where the authorities decided to convene the security committee for our briefing. The crucial elements of the security authority in El Obeid were the commissioner, known as Governor under British colonial rule of the province, the commander of the military force, the commander of the police, the attorney general's representative, and the province judge. The representative of the attorney general was a graduate of Khartoum University, three years my junior. The judge was incidentally the same man under whom I had trained in Nahud.

We were given full opportunity to brief the committee, but there was no doubt that we were viewed more as witnesses than as responsible personalities. At one point, the chairman, the commissioner, thanked us for the information we had furnished and said that as sons of the late Chief Deng Majok, what we had said would be given serious consideration. However, we should admit that there were other points of view.

I was offended. I thought of the representative of the attorney general and how senior to him I would have been had I joined the government service. Yet, there he was among those who saw me as simply the son of Chief Deng Majok. I gave them my thoughts, stressing that even more than being the sons of the late Chief Deng Majok, we were responsible sons of Sudan. Had we been in the government service, we would be occupying responsible positions. Even abroad, I said, we held significant positions. I told them all that, not to brag, but to argue that they should give our words more credence than simply those of eyewitnesses who were sons of the chief.

The argument was received politely but with little impact. It was even hinted to us that the mandate we had been given was to allow the Dinka to follow their rituals and celebrations of burial and not to select or elect a chief. By installing Abdalla as chief, we had exceeded the mandate. The members of the security committee were clearly prejudiced against Abdalla and would have preferred Adam instead. It may well be that the security people in Abyei had indeed given Adam more than a hint that he was favoured by the province authorities and that Abdalla was regarded as an undesirable element; which is probably why Adam was persisting in competing.

Since El Obeid seemed a clear disappointment as far as the Abyei situation was concerned, we headed for Khartoum more determined than ever to plead the case in even stronger terms than we had initially envisaged. Before we left El Obeid, I prepared a well-reasoned report, a copy of which we intended to leave with the province authorities, but the main objective of which was to present the case to the central authorities in Khartoum.

Initially, I tried to balance our case with understanding the structural problems of the young, probably frightened, commander, who thought that he was doing his job. I wanted to look for remedies without being vindictive. Bol thought I was too conciliatory and that our message should be clear cut against Ali and his men. I finalised the report more or less in the spirit Bol had suggested, as I did not want to be seen as compromising with a murderous enemy who was making the lives of our people miserable. But the report was, I believe, still sensible and objectively reasoned. We had it typed by our cousin, Hassan Arop, Deng Makuei's son, then working at the province headquarters. In our written and verbal reporting, the rational and objective substance and tone of the report eventually made us quite effective in Khartoum.

We first reported to Abel Alier, then minister for Supply, who, being a Southerner and in the absence of Joseph Garang, the minister for Southern Affairs, was a logical person to approach. Abel was so impressed by the written report and so moved by all he had read and heard about the situation in Abyei that he arranged for us to meet the minister for the Interior, Major Farouk Osman Hamdalla, a man who was highly respected and known for his seriousness, objectivity and humanity.

We found Farouk Hamdalla very different in his attitude from any responsible Northerner with whom we had ever discussed the situation in the South. He listened to us patiently and sympathetically. Once our reporting was completed, he telephoned his colleague, the minister in charge of national security in our presence, and I could tell from what he said and his general attitude that we had won him over to our side almost absolutely.

In particular, and in sharp contrast to the Kordofan provincial authorities, the minister stressed the fact that the report had been made by persons of important standing, both nationally and internationally. What would the world think of Sudan when I, a Human Rights official in the United Nations, reported to the world about the situation in Abyei and the failure of the authorities to act.

Our report had made a number of recommendations, among them conferring administrative and judicial powers on the chief elect, Abdalla, the withdrawal of the officer and all his men, his replacement with an older, more experienced and wiser person, with knowledge of the tribal situation, and finally the investigation of some of the tortures and killings that had been carried out in the area, in particular the death of Anyiel. Before leaving Sudan, we were assured that steps would be taken to implement the measures we had recommended. Abdalla was soon confirmed as chief and given administrative and judicial powers. Ali and his men were withdrawn and a new force took over under the command of Mohammed el Basha, from the Missiriya Arabs, unlike Ali Sid Ahmed who was from the far North.

The new officer was older and non-commissioned, having risen from the ranks. Lacking in education and being from a neighbouring and opposing tribe, his choice was most unfortunate, as would eventually become evident. As the choice was made in Kordofan, though under national directive, it was perhaps an ingenious way of keeping the situation in Abyei under the provincial thumb. The central government also established a commission of inquiry to investigate the allegations against the security forces in Abyei. The end of our efforts had been remarkably successful and there was jubilation among the people of Abyei.

Bol and I returned together to the United States. He had absented himself from his job so long that he was sure they had replaced him. He would have to look for a new job and we thought he might as well do it in the United States, where we needed to recover from the trauma of our experiences and the pathetic situation in which we had left our people. Naturally, our time was a complex mixture of sentiments. We were very happy to be together, and even in our deep sorrow about the tragedies that afflicted our people was a degree of communion between ourselves and our people that gave us a profound sense of awareness of our identity. We sat for hours reminiscing about our earlier days of childhood and adolescence and brooding over the catastrophe that had befallen our people. But sadly, within a year, our ruthless and unscrupulous enemies would transform our success into a tool for an even more deadly assault on our people.

That tragedy would fall on our people later. Meanwhile Bol took leave from his job in London and joined me on my way back to my duty station in New York. We left Sudan with mournful reflections on the plight of our people, which we had intimately experienced, tried to alleviate, but only relative and precarious success that was by no means assured. Our childhood appeared to be a golden age in which peace and security had been taken for granted, the dignity of the individual and of his community had flavoured the air we had breathed and added to the beauty of the environment that had been both natural and cultural. We thought of our father alive and full of vitality, the epitome of dignity and authority. We thought of the men who had been close to him as friends or court members and who had shared his dignity and authority. There was Achuil Bulabek; there was Chan Dau; there was Malai Kat; there was Ayuel Mawan; there was and there was and there was – all men whose memory brought back to us the picture of noblemen in spotlessly clean robes, turbans and riding stately Arabian horses, showing off the spirit of heroism and nobility. We contrasted all that with the tragedy we had just witnessed in Abyei: children who had not seemed to understand the meaning of games, faces full of anguish and despair, people subjugated and subdued into indignities we had never imagined possible for a Dinka to accept.

In New York, as we listened to the Dinka songs I had recorded, we could still hear the dignity of the past in the voices, in the melody, and in the rhythm, but our minds and souls wandered into the devastations of change. Some songs expressed our grief and brought back memories of the life and the untimely death of that great and greatly needed man - our father, Chief Deng Majok. It was uniquely moving to hear the voices of these educated men and women expressing their tragedy so simply, intelligently, humanly - even seeing its international dimensions:

> *How does the destruction of the world come about?*
> *Our land is closed in a prison cell*
> *The Arabs have destroyed our land*
> *Destroyed our land with bearded guns*
> *Guns which thunder and then even sound musical*
> *Like the ancient drums with which buffaloes were charmed*
> *Until their horns were caught.*
> *Is the black colour of skin such a bad thing?*
> *That the Government should draw its guns?*
> *The police pacing up and down,*
> *Gunners causing dust to rise*
> *Cowards surrendering to the force of the arm?*
> *A country we took back from foreigners*
> *A country for which we fought together*
> *And the English left our country.*
> *Only to be attacked with Bren guns*
> *What a treatment!*
> *Oh what a treatment!*
> *Southerners, people of Deng, son of Kuol*
> *What the Government is doing*
> *Is not a good thing;*
> *Waving their Bren guns*
> *Like frying sesame seeds,*
> *Counting their shells*

Then saying, "One million shots have not subdued the Ngok."
Our case is in Court
Our case is in Court with the people above
Achai, the sacrificed daughter of Pajok
And Ring of our flesh
Have a cause.
They seated the Court
And called upon God:
"God, why are you doing this?
Don't you see what has become of the black skin?"
The Court adjourned,
Our maternal aunt came
With the divinities from above
And the Spirit Ring,
They sat on the ground of the sons of Biong.
A storm of dust rose in Abyei
Cyclones reached the sky:
Family of Arop de Biong, nothing can be done
Who knows what the Government is pregnant with?
Even if they flatten us with bearded guns
Whom can we wish for?
This we shall always consider...

And so, there in New York, far away in the United States of America, we pondered; we lamented and wondered and speculated. As Dinka history had been a heritage of heroic survival against the ravages of unscrupulous invaders and human hunters, there was reason to hope and believe that our people would again overcome and survive. But the history of humanity had witnessed the survival of peoples only after devastating losses of lives or dehumanising mutilation of personality and culture. In what form would our people eventually survive? And what could we do, where, when and how in order to facilitate their decent survival?

Lines from a song by Chan Dau, which I had recorded during Father's last days in Khartoum, were most effective in summarising the challenges facing us and our incapacity to deliver. And for years to come, I would recite these lines to myself and others to remind us of what leadership is called upon to do:

A land that is destroyed, who holds it?
Yes, who holds a land that is destroyed?
It is the Chief who lands it;
He holds it and makes the cattle stand secure.

But where is the Chief to hold the land? That was Father who was no more. With these reflections in mind, Father's death had made our journey between cultures even more turbulent. We would strive from thence on to fulfill the obligations of a destiny which was only partially within our control. The course of our lives had been set not only in our childhood, but even before our conception, as part of a long chain in a genealogy whose roots went deep, far back to Jok, the legendary ancestor believed to have broken through the Byre of Creation and let his people go free. His people had gone, but not as freely as Jok had envisaged.

Successive generations of Jok's descendants had assumed his divine authority and led his people through unforgettable devastations, tragedies, and challenges. As we sat in the skyscrapers of New York with a vision stretching far back to our childhood and to our tiny villages of Noong and Abyei, we felt well aware of the limitations on our capacity to save our people, but we also realised the sacred responsibility we had inherited to continue the noble family tradition of service to our people.

The Author with his brother Dr Zachariah Bol and family members in Nairobi, September, 2020.

A NOTE TO THE READER ON DINKA PERSONAL NAMES

MANY PERSONAL NAMES OF DINKA SUBJECTS OR ACTORS APPEARING in this book may present some problems to readers who are not familiar with the Dinka language in general and some of the names in particular. Dinka culture may have what might be an equivalent to a Western family name, but strictly speaking the two systems are different. Among the Dinka, there is no one standard family name that applies to all the members over successive generations. First names are linked to those of fathers signifying son or daughter of a named father. As an example, the Author is officially known as Francis Mading Deng. His father, the Ngok Dinka chief, is Deng Kuol, while Kuol, Deng's father, is Kuol Arop. In turn, Kuol's father is Arop Biong. And Biong's father is Alor. As can be seen, one's own name is connected with that of the father. In some Dinka tribes, the connection is made by the prefix de or e to signify son or daughter of the father. There is therefore no single name that could be taken as a family name. If the Western naming system were to be applied, the Author's family- both male and female family members- would have Arop, Biong, Alor, Monydhang, Kuoldit, Dongbek, Bulabek, Jok- or whatever they would consider as a patronymic surname- derived from the last possible ancestor historically known or from legends or myths of clan origin.

Since Dinka society is polygynous, step siblings can share the equivalent of a first name. In Francis Mading's family, for instance, his father, Deng had a step brother, also called Deng. To differentiate the two, Mading's father was nicknamed Deng Majo- or Deng the Doggish, after his favourite dog, while the other Deng was given Makuei as a sobriquet. Sometimes, to differentiate siblings, they are given other distinguishing epithets such as "Macham", "the Left-handed One", or "-Baar" (hyphen after the name) "the Tall One." This differentiation applies mostly to females as well as males. Another way to give siblings sharing a first name is to resort to hierarchy by which the senior gets the descriptor "-dit" (senior) to their name, while the junior is identified with "-thi", which literally means younger one.

Dinka people consist of many subtribes, speaking many families and subgroups of dialects, which influence how personal names are created and pronounced. The Padaang subfamily of dialects, of which Ngok of Abyei are members, begin prefixes of names, mostly those derived from male bovine. Incidentally, there are exceptions. Mading or Makuei, for example, are the exception as their prefixes are "Ma-" and not "Mi-".

While most Dinka speakers would have Majok, Mayen, Majak- just to cite a few examples – derived from bovine male bovina and just a few, the Padaang speakers (and until recent times, some sub-tribes and clans within the population the area now known as Twich East County of greater Upper used the prefix "Mi" instead of "Ma-" just like their Padaang cousins.

The Author's father, Deng Kuol Arop, as shown earlier, was also known by his nickname of Deng Majo, which was later corrupted to Majok by the Twich-Rek Dinka speakers- of Bahr el Ghazal, a name that the Ngok Dinka might have turned to Mijok, but in this instance that was left to remain in its borrowed form. Surprisingly, Deng Kuol's personality ox was Marial, while that of his half-brother, Deng Makuei, was Majok. But the ox's name was never used as an optional one for the chief. Many Dinka used and continue to think that the chief of the Ngok Dinka was Deng son of Majok instead being Deng Kuol. I don't they think he is the son of Majok. They simply think he has the praise bull name of Majok. They certainly

A NOTE TO THE READER
on Dinka Personal Names

know that he was the son of Chief Kuol Arop. It was, however, the late Nyankol Mathiang Dut, the famed singer all over the two Sudans from Abyei, who in one of her songs has put the records straight: in one of her songs she refers to her native area as "Abyei of Deng Kuol." I believed she just stated what was well known among the Dinka.

Dinka culture reserves particular names for multiple births (twins in many cases). The first twin is Ŋɔ̈ɔ̈r (Ngor) for male and Aɲëër (Anger) for female; the second is Cän (Chan) for male and a female is named Acän (Achan). This literally means last. Ngor and Anger all mean the first or leading. The child that is born after the twin is Nyanbol or Nyibol for a female and Bol for male. Kɔ̈ɔ̈t (Kot), which is unisex, is the last name related to the phenomenon of multiple birth- being the third in line.

As the names spelled in Dinka indicate, Ngor, Anger and Kot, contain long vowels, namely /ɔ̈ɔ̈/, and /ëë/, which reflect the manner the name is pronounced. The current Dinka orthography was first devised and launched by linguists- all British academics hired by the Anglo- Egyptian administration of Sudan, following the Rejaf Conference of 1928. In addition to those language experts, Father Nebel of the Verona Fathers, who was the first to develop written Rek Dinka, was later to make a valuable contribution to the development of texts in Dinka. Father Nebel's Dinka-English dictionary remains a very useful tool for learners of the language, including a sizeable number of students whose first language is Dinka. The resolution of the conference selected several indigenous vernaculars to be used for teaching in primary schools in Southern Sudan. Dinka was among those African languages selected for educational purposes. Although that orthography has served well over the years, the system is in need of improvement: application of long vowels in many place and personal names. For our purpose here, the personal names cited above serve as examples. Other names using the Rejaf orthography and used in this book include Ngok, [Deng] Abot and Achuil, which should be written as Ŋɔɔk/Ngook, Aboot/ and Acuiil/Achuiil, respectively.

ABOUT THE AUTHOR

Francis Mading Deng is currently Deputy Rapporteur of South Sudan National Dialogue and Roving Ambassador. He formerly held the positions of Sudan's Ambassador to the Nordic countries, Canada and the United States; Sudan's Minister of State for Foreign Affairs; the first Permanent Representative of South Sudan to the United Nations; Special Representative of the UN Secretary General on Internally Displaced Persons; and Special Advisor of the Secretary General for the Prevention of Genocide. He holds an LL. B (Honours) from Khartoum University and an LL. M and J.S.D (Doctor of Juridical Science) from Yale University. He has authored or edited over forty scholarly books on a wide variety of subjects and two novels on the crisis of identity in the Sudan, and has held positions in leading American universities and think tanks.

INDEX

A

Ababa 180, 436
Abbo 86
Abboud 240-242, 288-9, 304, 325, 355-6, 358, 360-1, 374, 434
Abdalla 181, 234, 241-2, 309-310, 325, 400-404, 412, 420, 424-9, 434, 436-7, 444-5, 449, 460-61
Abdeen 247
Abdel 128, 138, 163, 172, 176, 181, 188, 222-3, 229-230, 236-7, 247, 290, 339, 407, 411
Abdrahman 235, 263
Abdullahi 150, 188
Abel 239, , 317, 406, 414, 434, 460
Abid 248
Abiem 38, 338
Abiong 32, 197
Abior 21, 28, 30, 36, 41-5, 87
Abot 20, 469
Abul 55
Abun 94
Abyei 12, 40-2, 45-6, 49, 55, 73, 85-7, 95, 106-, 111, 124, 129, 131, 141, 143, 146, 150, 155, 158-160, 162, 168-9, 176, 183-4, 188, 196, 198-9, 202, 206-7, 220, 224, 228, 232-3, 239, 248, 250-1, 255, 302-3, 306, 311, 333, 353, 405, 417-424, 433-6, 439-444, 444, 444, 448, 450-51, 453, 455-7, 460-464, 464-5, 468-9
Abyor 38
Achai 428, 464
Achok 19, 21-2, 60, 86, 252
Achok Mijok 19, 80, 82
Achol 23
Achueng 88
Achuil 35, 38-45, 48, 67, 257, 443, 449, 456, 462, 469
Ackie 318
Acknowledgements 11
Adam 103, 280, 309-310, 313, 325, 346, 400-9, 412, 424, 427-9, 434, 460
Adau 428
Addis 180, 393, 434

Adhaw 264
Admittedly 127
Adol 434
Adwok 241
Afraid 290
Africa 11, 141, 233, 243, 255, 265, 330-1, 334, 370-9, 376-7 380
African 9, 11, 13, 15, 17, 19, 21, 23, 25, 27, 31, 33, 35, 37, 39, 41, 43, 45, 47, 49, 51, 53, 55, 57, 59, 61, 63, 65, 67, 69, 71, 73, 75, 77, 85, 87, 89, 91, 93, 95, 97, 99, 101, 103, 105, 107, 109, 111, 113, 115, 117, 119, 121, 123, 125, 127, 129-130, 133, 135, 137, 139, 141, 143, 145, 147, 149-150, 153, 155, 157, 159, 161, 163, 165, 167-9, 171, 173, 175, 177, 179, 181, 183, 185, 187, 189, 191, 193, 197, 199, 201, 203, 205-7, 209, 211, 213, 215, 217, 219, 221, 223, 225-6, 229, 231, 235, 237, 239, 241, 243, 245, 247, 249, 251, 253, 255, 257, 259, 261, 263, 265, 267, 269, 271, 273, 275, 277, 279, 281, 283, 285, 287, 289, 291, 293, 295-9, 301, 303, 305, 307, 309, 311, 313, 315-7, 319, 321, 323, 325-7, 329-335, 337, 339, 341, 343-5, 347-8, 351, 353, 355-7, 359, 361, 363, 367, 369-70, 373, 375, 377, 379-80, 383, 385, 387-9, 391, 393-5, 399, 401, 403, 405, 407, 409, 411-412, 415, 417, 419, 421, 423, 425, 427, 429, 431, 433, 435, 437, 439, 441, 443, 445, 447, 449, 451, 453, 455, 457, 459, 461-462, 467, 469
Africans 295, 331-2, 372, 375
Agorjok 96
Agorot 21, 32
Agoth 125-126
Aguar 92
Aguek 124, 153, 374
Aguer 16, 88, 109, 130, 144, 228, 394, 434, 439, 445-7
Ahang 382
Ahmed 9, 150, 155-6, 171, 173, 186, 199-205, 219-220, 235, 237, 253, 258, 289, 337, 374, 435, 437, 461
Ajak 83
Ajang 23, 25, 67, 107, 150

- 473 -

INDEX

Ajbar 38
Ajing 79
Ajith 23, 163
Ajongo 122-123
Ajuong 38
Ajuot 125
Aker 52, 55
Akkrad 259
Akol 188
Akolawin 240, 292, 299, 313
Akot 121-122
Alak 181-182
Alan 368, 380
Aldrich 316
Alei 38
Alfred 112-113, 117, 124
Algerian 180, 223-4
Ali 37, 128, 168, 172, 174, 176, 184, 188, 197, 240, 258, 265, 267, 271, 325, 428, 437, 439, 441, 444-9, 451-457, 460-2
Alier 239, 317, 406, 414, 434, 460
Alitalia 363
Alladin 375
Allor 20
Allott 316, 339, 350, 372
Alongside 374
Alor 39, 43, 72, 181-2, 411, 436, 467
Aluel 75
Aluong 77, 79
Ambrose 137, 382
Amel 53, 55, 432
America 16, 226, 306, 373-4, 410, 454, 464
American 51, 237, 244, 305, 348, 367-8, 376, 382, 389, 471
Americans 51, 270, 362, 368, 375, 385
Amidst 26
Amin 337-338, 375
Amou 55, 144, 432
Amuor 52, 55-6, 66, 161, 198, 309
Andrew 253-254, 314
Andy 369
Angeer 79
Angelo 140
Anglophone 371
Anne 84
Ansar 235
Anthony 316, 343

Anthropology 326, 343
Anya 188, 251, 439, 445, 447, 458
Anyiel 38, 435, 438-9, 442, 454, 461
Apiny 208, 215
Arab 10, 13, 23, 36, 53, 64, 73-4, 128-130, 133, 138, 157, 167-8, 170, 177, 183-5, 187-8, 190-3, 200, 223, 233, 258-9, 263-4, 296, 302, 320, 322, 370, 405, 409, 434, 440-41, 444, 450, 456
Arabia 130, 320
Arabian 67, 462
Arabic 23, 47, 53, 74, 87, 105, 127, 130, 133-4, 156, 169, 171, 175-6, 178-180, 192, 229-230, 235, 238-9, 243, 395, 424, 444
Arabisation 170, 206
Arabised 53, 129, 170, 185, 414
Arabism 130, 265
Arabs 23, 34-7, 65, 73-4, 97, 107, 130, 138, 157, 166, 168-171, 177, 184, 188-9, 192-3, 200, 226, 258-9, 265, 370, 400, 441, 454, 459, 461-462
Arbab 300-302
Arie 381
Ariik 123, 374
Arob 11, 37
Arol 15
Arol Kachuol 15
Arop 20-22, 32, 35, 39, 42, 44-5, 47, 52, 55-8, 64, 155-6, 171, 199, 203-4, 307, 409, 411-412, 417-8, 426-7, 430-31, 433, 460, 464, 467
Arop Biong 21-22, 444, 467
Arthur 91
Arts 238
Asante 379
Ashamu 83
Asians 372
Astor 322-324, 344
Astors 322-323
Aswan 264, 297
Atar 134
Atem 11, 109, 111, 113, 159-160
Athecekou 57
Atlantic 381
Atong 83
Attiman 73
Aturjok 57

INDEX

Augustus 82
Aunt 202-204, 215, 228, 430, 435
Austrian 91, 270
Authority 37, 48
Awad 229-230, 248
Awan 211
Aweil 132, 188
Awel 57
Awet 57
Awich 208-209, 211-6
Awor 88, 202-4, 215, 228, 430
Awuor 435
Awut 76, 79
Ayak 25, 27-8, 188
Ayan 75, 78-9, 86, 92, 305
Ayii 188
Ayok 88
Ayom 38, 67, 249
Ayong 88, 94, 108-9, 153-4, 374
Ayuel 208-209, 211-5, 462
Ayyam 352
Azim 222

B
Babikir 236
Babo 36-37, 47, 184-5, 193, 258-9, 441, 454-4
Baez 372-373
Bagat 38
Baggara 23, 73-4, 129-130
Bagi 188
Bahr 109-111, 129, 132, 150, 326, 353, 419, 468
Bakr 150
Balanites 74
Baldo 325
Bar 228, 230
Baroni 29, 243, 259
Bartholomew 390
Basel 267, 271, 274
Basha 461
Bashir 433
Bashom 249
Belafonte 373, 375
Belfast 347
Belgian 294
Beneath 196-197, 199, 201, 203, 205, 207, 209, 211, 213, 215, 217, 219, 221, 223, 225-6, 229, 231, 233
Benjamin 122
Beny 382
Berlin 277-289, 316-7, 319
Berliners 278, 283
Bernadette 274
Beshir 188, 197, 246, 352, 414, 441, 454
Biong 18, 20, 34, 38, 44-5, 72, 75, 81, 96, 161, 203-4, 226, 228, 250, 307, 430, 434, 436, 439, 445-6, 464, 467
Bismarck 279
Blue 132-133, 135, 137, 139, 141, 143, 145, 231, 259
Bob 375
Bohler 273-274
Bohlers 274
Bol 12, 16, 44-5, 56-7, 61, 63, 66, 71, 82, 85-8, 94, 105, 109, 111, 113, 117, 123, 125-6, 133, 135-9, 141-2, 145, 149-150, 152-3, 155-6, 158-166, 168, 171, 173-8, 184-6, 193-7, 199-200, 202, 204, 206-7, 215-6, 220, 222-4, 226, 229, 231-3, 236-9, 244, 250, 252-8, 261, 264, 293-4, 296, 298, 300, 309-311, 322, 325, 332-3, 353, 361, 398-7, 401-405, 407-8, 411-412, 414-6, 421-424, 425, 429-434, 434-5, 437-9, 441, 447, 451, 453, 460, 462, 465, 469
Bona 124, 157, 195, 228, 231, 254-5, 264, 296, 299, 406, 408, 410, 417, 425, 433-5
Bonn 283
Books 11
Boston 81
Botswana 323
Brandt 277
Bren 462
Brewster 374
Bridget 322-323
British 35-37, 39, 48, 74, 91, 96, 109, 123, 137-8, 141-2, 158, 185, 194, 200, 233, 237, 252-3, 289, 316-7, 324, 335, 337, 343-4, 346, 353, 373, 405-6, 423, 459, 469
Bruce 392
Bucklund 333
Bulabek 20, 34-5, 38-9, 41-4, 48, 67, 124, 126, 135, 137, 157, 195, 228, 231-3, 236, 238-9, 254-5, 293-4, 296-302, 311, 425, 443, 456, 467

INDEX

Bushra 172, 223, 339
Byre 20, 52, 465

C

Cairo 87, 264-5, 280-1, 297, 299, 315, 343, 399, 403, 412, 414, 417, 436
Caldwell 380
Cambridge 173, 176, 223, 326
Canada 471
Caribbean 373
Carroll 374
Catherine 82
Catholicism 91, 295
Cemetery 312
Chan 56-57, 67, 85-6, 109, 111, 113, 144, 150, 164, 211, 409, 462, 464
Charles 375, 381
Charlottesville 83
Charpentier 382
Chaurman 397
Chicago 381
Chiefdom 38
Chieftainship 28, 43, 47
Children 421
China 358
Chol 23, 39-40, 45-6, 201
Christ 87, 148
Christian 93-94, 147-8, 173, 184-5, 206-7, 235, 243, 289, 306, 370, 385
Christianity 87, 185, 206
Christians 93, 179, 184-6, 243, 429
Christmas 94, 243, 353-4, 393
Chuen 188
Clarita 313
Classrooms 168
Coca 278
Cola 278
Colin 344
Comboni 243, 259
Congo 251
Congolese 338
Connecticut 375
Corps 375
Crawford 175
Creation 20, 465
Creighton 141, 156-7, 168
Cullison 368, 374

Cuor 87
Czechoslovakia 298, 311

D

Dam 325-326, 361
Daniel 75-76, 81, 83, 281
Daniels 112-113, 117, 119, 121, 123, 125-6, 133, 176
Darfur 345
Dau 21, 67, 409, 464
David 75, 77, 80-1, 83, 306, 322-3, 344, 381
Dean 9, 237, 393
Demach 83
Democrats 178-179
Deng 9, 11, 16, 19-20, 25, 28, 31-47, 50, 52, 56, 58, 61, 63, 67, 75-6, 81-2, 87-8, 102, 108-9, 130, 144, 148-150, 155-160, 181-2, 189, 195, 197, 202, 206, 209-211, 228, 230, 249, 254, 259, 296, 300-2, 309, 311, 324, 337-8, 370, 374, 394-5, 399, 408, 411, 420-1, 424, 426, 433-5, 439, 445-7, 459-60, 462, 467-9, 471
Deng Abot 22, 39, 145
Deng Majok 11, 15-6, 19-22, 28-9, 31-6, 39-47, 86, 102, 108, 145, 171, 185, 200, 210, 214, 216-7, 264, 289, 307, 360, 395, 416, 418-9, 422, 424, 434, 438-40, 443, 449, 456, 459, 462
Dengdit 94
Dengs 158
Denmark 334
Dennis 75, 81
Desolation 435
Dhaw 288
Dhienagou 20
Dhol 150
Dictoral 397
Dimo 140
Dinar 168
Dingweng 57
Dinka 10, 13, 15-27, 30-2, 35-7, 39, 41, 44, 48, 51-7, 59-65, 67-9, 71-4, 87-9, 91, 93-4, 96-7, 104-6, 109, 111-2, 116-7, 120-1, 123-8, 130-1, 133, 136-7, 139-140, 143-4, 146, 148-150, 160-5, 170, 173, 178, 182-3, 186-190, 192, 200-1, 206, 209-210, 215, 217-8, 226, 232, 243, 250-2, 254-5, 281, 297, 300, 303-5, 308,

INDEX

310-1, 318, 320, 322, 324-7, 361, 376, 381-382, 388, 394-5, 402, 405-10, 414, 416-20, 422-6, 430, 436-7, 439-445, 444, 450, 458, 460, 462, 464, 467-9
Dinkaland 91, 110, 160-1, 212
Dinkanised 140
Doctoral 397
Doggish 468
Donald 75, 81
Donato 239-240, 255
Dongbek 20, 467
Dorothy 11, 75, 84, 287, 305
Douglas 11
Dropout 372
Dugal 188
Duor 24
Dut 39, 469
Dutch 335
Dwight 397
Dylan 375

E

Early 133, 157
East 50, 178, 239, 253-5, 258, 261, 271, 276-8, 282-6, 317, 319, 334, 356, 380, 422, 468
Economics 238, 347-8, 397
Edna 382, 384
Edward 338
Edwin 318
Egypt 137-138, 173, 181, 265, 297, 370, 412
Egyptian 87, 138, 175, 181, 235, 264-5, 334, 469
Egyptians 180, 264, 297, 414
Eli 139
Elizabeth 80, 83, 317
Elliott 335
Emil 290
Engels 179
England 51, 141, 292-3, 298, 302, 312, 315-6, 318, 325, 330, 332, 334, 340, 351-3, 356, 360, 363, 370-373, 377-8
English 10, 87, 91, 96, 114, 125, 133, 135-7, 143, 156, 173-6, 180, 222, 243, 266, 272, 274, 277, 290, 317-8, 327, 332, 363, 371-372, 389, 395, 462
Englishman 173, 175, 222, 233, 344, 348

Enharo 343
Equatoria 179
Eric 112, 133, 149, 155
Europe 10, 239, 261, 265, 280, 293, 297-9, 301-2, 312-3, 334, 340, 353, 360, 377
European 48, 60, 105, 141, 147, 235, 259-260, 297, 306, 315, 353
Europeanised 147
Europeanlooking 168
Europeans 141-142, 295, 331
Euston 344
Everybody 420

F

Faculty 234, 237-9, 247, 250, 255, 292, 298, 339, 347, 351, 362, 390, 393, 412
Fahmi 147-150, 152, 154-5
Fakhreddine 392
Falkenstein 266-267
Fareed 339, 358-361
Faris 173
Farouk 460-461
Farran 237, 248, 395
Fateh 292, 299, 330, 338, 351
Fatherland 279
Faust 324
Fessmann 267-268, 272-4
Fessmanns 267-269, 271
Fessmans 271, 335
Finchley 317, 319
Finnish 334
Flora 318
Fodul 129
Folkways 426
Foremost 104, 262
France 223, 353-4
Frances 314, 331-2
Francis 9-10, 94, 158, 173, 175, 331, 350, 370, 373, 376, 395, 467-8, 471
Frankfurt 265-266, 276, 281
Fraulein 273-274
Frederick 94
Fredrich 279
Freiburg 267, 294, 296, 335, 338
French 318, 338
Freudian 94
Freund 269

- 477 -

INDEX

Fulah 162, 165, 215, 250, 252-3, 459
Fyodor 324

G

Gadir 290
Galilei 293
Galileo 293
Gamal 138, 181
Garang 290, 398, 412, 417, 434, 460
Genocide 471
George 318
German 255, 259-263, 265-6, 268-271, 273-282, 284-7, 293, 304-5, 334, 354, 403
Germans 253, 261, 263, 265-6, 271, 276-7, 279-280, 283-4, 286-8, 292, 403
Germany 29, 239, 253-6, 258-261, 263-7, 269-271, 274-281, 283-4, 286-8, 290-1, 293, 296, 298, 303-4, 312, 319, 333-4, 346, 353, 360, 395
Gezira 177, 236, 238
Ghana 343
Ghandour 341, 352, 358
Ghazal 109-111, 129, 132, 326, 353, 419, 468
Giir 125
Ginns 376
Glassmam 314
Glassman 369, 375-4, 379, 393
Glassmans 314, 369-70, 373, 375, 380
God 15-16, 21-2, 27, 34-5, 51-2, 66, 87, 92-3, 100-1, 106-7, 138, 146, 161, 163, 204, 210, 300, 376, 385-6, 400, 408, 449
Godfrey 10, 313, 326-7, 343, 376, 381, 390
Goethe 274-275, 324
Gogrial 128, 132, 150
Gordon 248
Goteborg 334
Gothic 275
Gouri 390, 392
Graveson 316
Gray 176, 243, 353
Greek 73, 261
Grief 31
Groundnuts 116
Grunewald 267
Grunwalt 274
Gulf 169, 171, 173, 175, 177, 179, 181, 183, 185, 187, 189, 191, 193, 195
Gum 113
Gumaa 225-226, 235
Gumma 235
Gyando 379

H

Hadi 236
Haifa 264
Haile 393
Hakim 139
Halaib 173, 181
Haleem 172, 176
Halfa 236
Hamburg 286, 335
Hamdalla 460-461
Hamden 369
Hamdi 53
Hamza 375
Hantoub 150, 156, 202, 231, 236
Harold 287, 376, 380, 393, 397, 440
Harry 373, 375
Harvard 369
Haselmere 344
Hassan 155, 234-5, 237, 264, 288, 290, 351, 375, 390, 392, 409, 460
Hassanein 240
Hearing 18, 90, 385
Heim 281
Heinz 267
Henderson 345-347
Hereika 436
Herr 273-274
Herskovits 394
Hilary 373-374
Hitler 269-270, 279-280, 346
Hitlerite 279
Holland 354
Homosexuality 123
Horgas 184
Housesitting 382
Howard 375, 390
Hudsons 317-318
Hurrah 120
Hussein 188
Hyde 315

INDEX

I

Ibadan 376-377, 381
Ibrahim 184, 240-1, 288, 290, 358, 361, 389, 434
Idris 128, 133, 175
Ife 377
Indian 352, 390, 412
Ingledew 243
Instantly 25
Intertribal 35
Iran 414
Ireneo 140, 250
Isaac 139
Isaiah 124, 153, 240, 296, 299
Islam 53, 171-2, 177-8, 185, 206, 295
Islamisation 206
Israel 409
Israeli 381
Italian 255, 303, 382, 385-6
Italians 298
Italy 238, 254-5, 264, 293, 296, 298-9, 311, 353
Izzeldine 375, 390, 409-410, 412, 436

J

Jaafar 173-174, 398, 404, 417, 434
Jallabiya 29
Jallabiyas 195
James 139, 314, 316, 347
Jane 314, 369-70, 375-6, 379, 381, 393
Janub 229
Japanese 370
Jaya 390
Jayakumar 390
Jeita 81
Jesus 87, 148
Jewish 370
Jews 376, 385
Jim 369, 375
Jipur 39, 43-4, 47, 201
Joan 372-373
Joe 368
John 368, 382
Johnson 11
Johnston 397
Johnstone 348, 350, 372, 376-9, 389, 393, 397

Jok 20, 75-6, 81, 83, 104, 465
Jones 173, 175-6, 222, 224-5
Joseph 124, 140, 153, 290, 296, 302, 374, 398, 412, 417, 434, 460
Juba 374
Julla 184
Jur 121-122
Juridical 471
Jurisprudence 316, 371, 380
Justin 157-158, 228, 232-3, 394, 434-3, 439, 445-6, 450
Justo 238, 296, 298
Juuk 94, 116

K

Kadugli 183, 417
Karamazov 324
Karib 237-238, 289, 312, 342
Kat 67
Kaya 81
Kennedy 306, 368
Kenya 83
Kenyi 140
Keryou 57
Khalid 172-173, 175, 433
Khalifa 175, 374
Khalil 181, 241-2, 290, 389
Khama 323-324
Khamas 323
Khartoum 9-10, 29, 87, 98, 143, 173, 201, 223, 228, 231-4, 236-9, 242-4, 248, 251-8, 260, 267, 274, 294, 296, 299, 302-3, 305, 311-3, 316-7, 338-9, 342, 351, 353-4, 356, 361-2, 375, 389-90, 394-5, 398, 402-1, 406, 410, 414, 417-6, 420, 422, 425, 434, 436, 442, 445-6, 457, 459-60, 464, 471
Khatim 374
Kheir 289
Khor 156-157, 167-170, 172, 175-8, 180-2, 185, 195, 205, 208, 220, 222, 231, 233, 236, 238-9, 253-4, 289, 333, 339
Kiir 144, 201, 209-210
Kolkech 444
Kooc 434
Kooch 16, 130, 216, 435, 439, 445-5
Kordofan 127-128, 132, 134, 148, 154, 162, 220, 325, 342, 345, 418, 461

- 479 -

INDEX

Koryom 19-20, 24
Kosti 141, 156, 177
Kot 281, 469
Kotjak 112-114, 117, 121, 124, 128
Kremlin 179
Kuach 121, 406
Kuaja 109
Kuei 52, 55-6, 109
Kuhn 266-267
Kuhns 266
Kulang 124, 153
Kuol 11, 19-21, 31-2, 35, 37, 40-1, 43-4, 56-7, 61, 66, 71-2, 75, 81, 83, 85, 87, 90, 92, 105, 108-9, 124, 159-160, 193-6, 198-9, 202, 204, 256-7, 307, 309, 400, 427, 430, 434-5, 438, 462, 467-9
Kuol Arop 19, 21, 24, 28, 31-2, 35-6, 39-40, 47-8, 56, 90, 124, 145, 345, 426, 467-9
Kuoldit 20, 467
Kwajok 109-111
Kwol 433

L

Lady 317-319, 324, 332, 344, 355, 363, 373, 377-8
Lang 94, 116
Langford 345
Lapps 334
Lasswell 376, 380-1, 393, 397, 440
Latin 243
Law 9-10, 233-4, 239, 245, 247-8, 250, 255, 292, 304, 316, 339, 347-8, 351, 362-3, 368, 371, 373-4, 380-382, 388-90, 393, 397, 412
Lawrence 82, 296, 313, 338, 356-7, 363, 373, 376, 380
Legum 344
Leipzig 239
Lenin 179
Leu 95-97
Liberation 313
Lienhardt 10, 313, 326, 354, 376, 381
Lino 87, 93, 99, 102, 106, 108, 153, 155, 251, 374
Lions 24, 68
Litigation 348
Logali 373-374

Lok 124, 153, 374
London 9-10, 171-2, 246, 292, 299, 313-7, 319, 330, 335-8, 341-2, 347-8, 351, 353, 358, 361-2, 367-8, 371-373, 380, 389, 394-7, 399, 404, 410, 412, 462
Lorach 267, 271
Lorries 128
Lossow 283-285
Lossows 283, 285, 293
Loth 78-79
Lowern 267, 269-270
Lual 11
Luckily 113, 209, 216
Ludwig 82, 84
Lufthansa 265
Luigi 241
Luis 87, 107-8, 155
Lund 334
Lynchmere 344

M

Maadia 414
Mabior 239-240, 255
Mabor 124, 153
Mading 16-17, 21-2, 27-8, 86, 143-5, 158, 194, 257, 307, 310, 403-4, 443, 467-8, 471
Maduot 298
Madut 96-97, 406, 434
Mahdi 45, 47-8, 235
Mahgoub 374
Mahmoud 184, 225-6, 240
Maine 380
Majakjust 468
Majid 163
Majo 41, 468
Majok 19, 32-3, 35, 37, 39, 50, 102, 240, 296, 299, 433, 443, 459, 468
Makuei 31-32, 34-7, 40-4, 46-7, 50, 56, 67, 87, 108, 189, 197, 249, 324, 399, 408, 420, 424, 468
Malai 67, 109, 111, 113, 462
Malakal 142-143
Malawi 381
Maleng 116
Maluach 113
Maluk 21
Malwal 45, 53, 406, 410, 433-4

INDEX

Mamoun 392
Manau 250-251
Mangar 57
Mannyuar 30, 38, 47
Mansour 433
Manyiel 123
Maper 25
Marc 392
Mareng 25
Margaret 392
Margaretta 333
Margo 368
Marial 32, 57, 468
Mariau 71
Marlene 272
Marx 179
Mary 313, 317, 343-4, 361, 380, 382
Mater 38
Matet 67, 249
Mathematics 175
Mathiang 469
Mawien 123, 374
Mawiir 149, 155
Mayen 94, 468
Mayom 108
Meimoun 169
Mekki 144, 184, 206-7, 374
Men 69
Merida 188
Michael 158, 162, 185, 338, 344-5
Michar 181-182
Mijak 38, 45, 451
Mijangdit 45
Mijok 19-22, 24, 31-2, 62, 76, 79, 89, 468
Mijok Duor 19, 28
Military 414
Milton 363
Minyiel 159-160
Mior 57
Miriam 375
Missiriya 36-38, 162, 165, 184, 193, 252, 258, 434, 436, 461
Mitrok 40-41
Miyan 39, 44
Miyar 63, 144-5, 159, 206
Mogran 259
Mohamed 246, 264, 289, 299, 434

Mohammed 73, 138, 288, 290, 292, 330, 338, 351-2, 374, 389, 392, 398, 434, 461
Monday 121, 126
Mongour 414
Monydhang 20, 467
Monyluak 165
Monyyak 400, 412
Monyyom 88, 109, 153
Morning 187
Morrison 343
Moyak 434
Muglad 129-130, 158-9, 165-6, 168, 183-4, 219, 224, 252, 258, 302, 458-9
Muludiang 238, 296, 298
Mundri 142
Musa 172-173, 175
Muslim 73, 92, 144, 173, 178-180, 184-6, 188, 206, 233, 235-6, 238, 240, 306, 337, 370, 414
Muslims 73, 157, 166, 168-9, 184-6, 206-7, 377, 429
Mussab 236, 238
Mustafa 9, 247
Mutawakil 375
Mutharika 381
Muzamil 341, 352, 358-9
Myers 397

N

Nadi 253
Nahud 36, 46, 154, 162-3, 205, 219, 253, 322, 417, 459
Nainai 42, 55, 100
Nairobi 83, 465
Nancy 314, 369
Nasser 138, 181
Natale 240, 292, 299, 313, 330, 337-8, 340-1, 344, 356-7
Nazi 266, 270, 279, 287
Nazir 37, 39
Nazis 269-270, 284
Nebel 91-92, 469
Neguib 138
Nelson 315
Newport 375
Nganluak 78
Ngarbeek 57

INDEX

Ngok 32, 35, 48, 67, 91, 94, 121, 128, 133, 163, 251, 326, 450, 464, 468-9
Ngok Dinka 12-13, 16, 20, 29, 35, 37, 53, 107-9, 127, 132-3, 136, 210, 233, 239, 253, 304, 324, 395, 418, 421, 434, 440, 445, 456, 467-8
Ngokland 95, 127, 420
Ngor 18-22, 25-8, 31, 76, 79, 125-6, 226, 228, 232, 305-8, 447-8, 469
Nhial 337
Nigeria 141, 343, 376-7
Nigerian 86, 377
Nile 132, 134, 231, 253, 299, 333-4
Niles 259
Nilotic 313, 331, 395
Nilotics 327
Nimbles 140
Nimeiri 398, 404, 417, 434
Nimir 36-37, 184-5, 193, 258
Nobody 404
Nonetheless 73, 126, 343, 371
Noong 22, 50-2, 55, 58, 65, 68, 72-3, 85-6, 99, 106, 129, 158-9, 165, 196-9, 202, 226, 232, 307, 309, 458, 465
Nordic 471
Northerner 9, 170, 230, 245, 248, 337, 342, 461
Northerners 130, 137-8, 143, 166, 168, 178-180, 226, 229, 237, 239, 241, 243, 248, 253, 336-8, 340-2, 351-2
Norway 334
Nosseir 290
Nuba 173, 181, 419
Nubian 297, 334
Nuer 143, 229-230, 281
Nugdalla 253
Nuri 237
Nya 188, 251, 439, 445, 447, 458
Nyal 150, 211
Nyamnyam 111
Nyamora 24, 50
Nyanaghar 32, 47, 418, 430
Nyanajith 23
Nyanawai 53, 55, 432
Nyanbol 52, 55, 63, 66, 144, 161, 198, 206, 309, 469
Nyanboldit 52, 55-6, 60, 63, 86, 92-3, 95, 163-4, 252

Nyandeeng 80
Nyangei 63
Nyankol 469
Nyanluak 75, 79
Nyanthon 77
Nyanwut 78-79
Nyibol 469
Nyok 46-47, 80, 87-8, 90-1, 95, 97, 107-8, 155
Nyuat 71-72

O

Obeid 141, 156, 166-7, 171, 176, 181-3, 411, 417-8, 459-60
Oduho 296, 302
Oh 51, 159, 462
Oliver 237, 248, 395
Olwak 240, 292, 299, 313, 330, 337-8, 340, 344, 356-7
Omda 38, 449
Omdas 101
Omdurman 180, 229, 231, 406
Omer 140, 237-8, 246, 289, 312, 342, 351
Omumi 39
Onek 368
Onken 11, 312
Opel 406
Ophthalmology 291
Osman 73, 150, 215, 265, 267, 271, 337, 428, 434-3, 439, 441-444, 445-4, 450-455, 457, 460
Othman 73
Ovaltine 319
Owen 132, 353-4
Owing 158
Oxford 10, 51, 255, 326-7, 331, 343, 345, 351-4, 376

P

Padaang 468
Padova 238, 254, 293-4, 296-8, 386
Pajok 20-21, 72, 464
Paris 335
Passens 272-274
Paul 324
Pax 294, 335
Penelope 260
Perceval 333

INDEX

Percy 333-335
Peter 11, 181-2, 314, 343, 369, 381
Philips 371
Phillips 81
Pieng 76
Piok 40, 45-6
Piyin 159
Poelchaus 287, 293, 317
Prague 298-299, 301-2
Prevention 471
Pritchard 376
Protestant 117, 147, 295
Protestants 385
Providence 399

Q
Qintin 397
Quinton 348, 376, 380, 388-9, 393, 397
Quran 148, 178, 180, 186

R
Rahma 47, 175
Rahman 128, 172, 223, 236, 339
Ramadan 92, 186, 236
Ramses 175
Ramshaw 109-111
Rannat 346
Rapporteur 471
Ray 375
Razig 229-230
Reech 11
Reinhard 266, 283-5, 312
Rejaf 469
Rek 32, 53, 91, 121, 125, 469
Reuter 281
Rhode 375
Rian 149
Richard 132, 243, 353-4
Rigil 162, 215
Riiny 137
Robert 348, 380, 393, 397
Robertson 347
Rockefeller 306
Rodger 255
Roman 248, 297, 316
Romana 294, 335
Rome 280, 293, 296-7, 399, 401

Rothenberg 274-275
Rou 160-162, 165
Rual 182
Rukun 229
Rumbek 126, 133-5, 137-142, 147, 154-8, 168, 172, 223, 228, 231, 233, 281, 367, 373
Russian 376
Ruweng 48, 53, 144

S
Sadat 414
Salaam 253
Salah 342
Saleh 248, 352
Salisbury 345
Sallie 314
Salvatore 123, 374
Sam 379
Samieha 235-236, 245, 259, 263, 266, 305
Samuel 289
Santina 82
Santino 254, 259, 300-1, 311
Sanu 296
Satti 175
Saud 320
Saudi 320
Savannah 419
Sayed 352
Scandinavia 289, 335
Schnapps 269
Schoolboys 112
Schreiber 392
Scotland 355-358
Scottish 201
Secretariat 390-391
Secretly 173
Seidna 231
Selassie 393
Semieh 237
Senn 363, 371
Sennar 251-252
Senns 363
Seretse 323
Serrer 38
Shah 414
Shaigiyya 175

INDEX

Shambe 152, 156-7
Sharafeldin 148-149, 153
Sharia 244, 248
Sheep 22
Sheikh 38, 128, 133, 163, 184
Sheikhun 174
Shemelle 184
Shengeitti 352
Shibeika 173-174
Shoke 73
Siamma 76
Sid 253, 337, 437, 461
Siddiq 235
Sie 278
Siemens 281-282, 288
Simbel 297
Singapore 390, 392
Singaporean 390
Sinn 168
Sir 318, 347
Sirr 374
Sitting 75, 392
Socialism 287
Soho 363
Solz 279, 313, 346
Southerner 129, 235, 237-8, 240, 245, 254, 263, 266, 281, 289, 296, 323, 337-8, 398, 414, 460
Southerners 13, 112, 130, 156, 180, 229-230, 237-240, 243, 247-8, 251, 263, 281, 302, 311, 336-8, 340, 343-4, 356, 358, 374, 395, 406-7, 462
Soviet 287
Spilker 266, 283, 312
Stalin 179
Sterling 382
Stevens 139, 348, 380, 393, 397
Stockholm 334
Sudan 9-13, 95, 108, 112, 138, 141, 152, 168, 172, 177-9, 181, 187-9, 207, 209, 228, 233, 236, 241, 248, 254, 256, 261-3, 265, 271, 273, 280, 284, 289-290, 296, 298-300, 302, 304, 308, 310-3, 319, 324, 326, 328, 334, 336, 339-347, 353, 356-362, 367, 370-372, 374, 376, 382, 389, 391-392, 394-6, 398, 403-2, 406, 410, 417-6, 427, 434, 455, 459, 461-463, 469, 471

Sudanese 11, 53, 86, 112, 130, 137-8, 142, 147-8, 168, 172-3, 175-6, 179-181, 194-5, 200, 206-7, 229, 235-6, 238, 240, 247, 252-3, 259, 261-3, 265, 273, 275-6, 283-5, 288, 290, 292-3, 295-6, 301-2, 306, 308, 317-8, 320, 324-5, 337, 346, 351-2, 354-5, 358, 360, 363, 375, 380, 382, 434
Sudanisation 179
Sudans 469
Suleiman 147, 259
Sun 373
Sunday 121, 240, 344
Supervision 116
Surrey 344
Sweden 333-334, 336, 353-4, 377
Swedish 333-334
Switzerland 267, 271, 294, 338

T

Taggat 175-176
Taha 128, 172, 176
Talat 339, 358-361
Tamarind 188
Taqqat 156-157, 167-170, 172, 176-8, 180-2, 185, 195, 205, 208, 220, 222, 231, 233, 236, 238-9, 253-4, 289, 333, 339
Tauber 274
Taunus 266
Tayeb 173-174
Tea 187
Teng 254, 259, 300, 311
Teter 82
Thanksgiving 51
Thiik 125, 137
Thokloi 45
Tibbs 158, 162, 185, 344-5
Tiel 31, 38, 52, 55, 159-160
Tiet 92
Tigani 237-238, 289, 296, 298, 312, 342
Toby 298
Tom 233
Tongliet 39-40, 109-110
Tonight 214
Tonj 111-114, 117, 120, 122-3, 126-8, 131-5, 147-9, 154-5, 172, 193, 228, 232-3, 374
Torit 179
Torts 246
Trafalgar 315-316

INDEX

Tragedy 398-399, 401, 403, 405, 407, 409, 411-412, 415, 417, 419, 421, 423, 425, 427, 429, 431, 433
Trevelyan 313, 317, 343-4, 361
Trott 11, 279-280, 312-3, 346
Tshekedi 323
Tswana 324
Turabi 234-235, 237
Twic 32, 48, 52-3, 57, 94, 116, 121, 125, 149, 208, 406, 408
Twich 468
Twicland 208
Twining 10-11, 246, 248, 260, 344, 347-8, 350-1, 380-1, 394
Twins 57

U

Uganda 112, 126
Ukel 434
Umma 181, 235, 241
Unguec 122
Unguel 122
Unity 100
Ustaz 174

V

Vanstone 135-136
Vatican 294-295, 297
Venice 293, 298
Verena 11, 279-280, 286-7, 292-3, 299, 303-4, 312-3, 322-4, 335, 346
Verona 91, 469
Vice 188
Violent 213
Volkswagen 298

W

Wada 123
Wadi 231, 236, 264
Wahab 247, 407, 411
Washington 375
Wathba 240
Wau 110-111, 132-3, 150, 152, 207, 374, 406
Welfare 239
West 178, 181, 187, 255, 261, 263, 276-8, 282-4, 286, 331, 334
Whitely 327

Wiesenthal 335
Wieu 253-254
Wife 63, 400
William 10-11, 246, 248, 260, 296, 302, 337-8, 347, 350-1, 380-2, 394
Williams 135-137, 139-141
Willis 343
Willy 277
Wiltshire 345
Wisal 235
Wives 55
Wol 296, 313, 338, 356-7, 363, 373, 376, 380
Women 109, 111, 113, 115, 117, 119, 121, 123, 125, 127, 129, 131, 391-392
Wor 99, 101-2
Wunrok 128
Wuor 87-88, 91, 93, 97, 106, 108, 155-6, 251

Y

Yaak 11
Yai 251, 426-7
Yale 10, 314, 347-8, 350, 362-3, 368, 371-375, 376-9, 389, 393-7, 471
Yamani 9
Yusuf 228-233

Z

Zachariah 16, 82, 94, 158-9, 185, 195, 232, 434, 465
Zackariah 12
Zaire 251
Zaki 9, 236, 238, 247
Zein 247
Zell 267-269, 272-5, 335
Ziada 300-302, 311
Zu 279, 346
Zubeir 175
Zulfu 222
Zurug 436

www.ingramcontent.com/pod-product-compliance
Lightning Source LLC
Chambersburg PA
CBHW051533010526
44107CB00064B/2713